The People of Providence

Tony Parker was born in Manchest[...] many books including *Lighthouse*, [...] *Hill*, *A Place Called Bird* and most [...] *Life: Interviews with Twelve Murderers*. He lives with his wife in Suffolk.

Tony Parker

The People of Providence

**A housing estate and
some of its inhabitants**

PICADOR
PUBLISHED BY PAN BOOKS

First published by Hutchinson and Co. Ltd 1983
Published in Penguin Books 1985
This Picador edition first published in 1992
by Pan Macmillan Limited
Cavaye Place, London SW10 9PG
9 8 7 6 5 4 3 2 1
Copyright © Tony Parker 1985

ISBN 0 330 316737

Printed in England by Clays Ltd, St Ives plc

For my son John Parker,
with much love

Providence has a wild, rough, incalculable road to its end, and it is of no use to try to whitewash its huge, mixed instrumentalities, or to dress up that terrific benefactor in a clean shirt and white neckcloth of a student in divinity.

Ralph Waldo Emerson

Contents

Introduction

The little blue mini-vans of the mobile caretakers trundled round and round all day through Providence Estate. Sometimes in one stationary at a kerbside its driver would be having a break, sitting smoking a cigarette.

– Going to what? Bloody hell, write a book, well good luck to you mate, that's all I can say. Written books before, have you? *Not* a fiction book, just a straightforward book about Providence? Well, I don't want to sound rude but I mean who the bloody hell's going to read that, what's there to write about round here?

No I don't live on the estate mate, no I certainly don't thank God. The rubbish of the local authority, that's who lives here if you want my honest opinion about it; and there's no one gets more experience of it than me, I can tell you. Cleaning up shit is all what my job is mostly nowadays: shit from the corridors, shit from the lifts, shit from the stairs. Look I'll tell you something, and this is without a word of a lie: you see that tower block over there, the one on the right, Bolton I think it is? Would you believe last week I had to go up to the seventeenth floor there to mend one of the fire doors that was jammed, and do you know what there was on the balcony round the back of the lift? A pile that big of shit! Someone'd gone up seventeen floors to go out on that balcony and have a crap – seventeen floors. I ask you, what sort of a person is that? So put that in your book about Providence then. If you dare.

Used to be a nice place: used to be, I'll say that. Oh yes, when I come to work here seven years ago it used to be quite a nice place. But now, nowadays . . . bloody hell! That's all I can say, bloody hell. . . .

But there's still nice parts though too you know, still some very nice parts. Well to my way of thinking they are, oh yes. Gorrivale Square, Jesmond Close . . . not bad, not bad at all. And some of those three-storey ones, look, those flats over there; they're not bad some of those, they're quite nice those really on the whole.

In one word? If you asked me to sum up the estate for you in one word what'd I say? Well, I don't think I know, not really, it's very hard isn't it, just one word? But what I'd say is 'mixed'. That's the word I'd use. I'd say if anyone was to spend a day or two days to start with, just walking about and looking at it – that's what their impression would be: 'mixed'.

No, don't mention it mate, nice talking to you; might see you around, I'll give you a toot, good luck mate, cheers.

As he switched on the engine he wound the driver's side window down.

– Eh, don't get me wrong though will you? I don't mind coloureds you know, so long as they're good coloureds – know what I mean?

A fair-haired young woman in a gaberdine mackintosh crossing the pedestrian shopping precinct in Robins Walk stopped with a polite smile.

– Sorry love but if it's insurance we've got more than enough thanks.

A book? About Providence Estate? Go on, you're joking! Really? Blimey, that'll be a job! I must read it, when's it coming out? Oh I'll not be here by then I shouldn't think. Mm? Well, if I could think of one word to tell someone what a place is like. . .

'Mixed'? Well yes, that's one word for it, I think that's about right that is, 'mixed'. 'Mixed' – how do I think he meant? Well you know . . . I mean, there's all sorts of people here all together, isn't there? I should think that's what he meant. You've got people who do what you might call hard physical sort of jobs, those that work in the docks or on the building sites – the what do you call them, 'manual workers' is it? Then you've got the people who work in offices and banks and shops and that. Then there's those who're the sort of posh ones, posh jobs like lawyers, there's quite a few of that sort lives around here, it's surprising. And teachers – and old people – and families – people living on their own – and kids, a big lot of kids. Happy people and sad people and odd people and peculiar people – a big sort of mixture, so that's absolutely the right word for it that is, yes . . . 'mixed'.

An elderly man with the collar of his overcoat turned up, coming out of the library, two books by Hammond Innes under his arm.

– It would be extraordinarily difficult for me to try and summarize a place such as Providence Estate in a hundred or a thousand words, so it would be totally impossible to do it in one.

Certainly if somebody has already said to you 'mixed' I would say that was an appropriate word, certainly. I couldn't say precisely what they might have meant, but I should have thought a moment's glance round would have made it clear because it is instantly visible, isn't it, how mixed it is?

You have the group of tower blocks over there, then those long six-storey things, I think they call them 'linear' blocks over there; then in that direction there are those small maisonette-type low buildings of flats. And if you go through that way you come to the old houses that have been refurbished; and beyond those, ones that aren't going to be done up and are scheduled for demolition, though heaven knows when they're going to get on with it. And the prefabs of course, scattered around here and there. . . . So I'd say yes, high-rise towers, long blocks, modern small flats, old places done up, others dilapidated . . . a large 'mixed' area very obviously, no one could quarrel with the word. And not at all unpleasing to the eye; all in all, not at all.

You're welcome sir, good afternoon.

Twelve perhaps thirteen years old, the small boy in a royal blue blazer and grey flannels with a too-small cap on his head and a satchel over his shoulder looked thoughtfully into the distance.

– 'Mixed'? What did they mean, 'mixed' how, what sort of way? Did they mean the people or the buildings or what? Funny word to use about the estate isn't it, really; could mean all sorts of things couldn't it, to different people? 'Mixed'. Mm, yeh. . . .

He went on staring into the distance. After a while he began slowly nodding his head.

– Yeh, well, if you come to think of it, that's quite a good word. I mean like where we are now, standing on the footpath in the middle of the grass . . . you see over there's the towers, back that way there's the flats, then there's the shops and Robins Walk. So you could say if you wanted to that over there where the buildings are, that's like town, and here where we are, with the grass and the trees, this is like country isn't it? I mean if you don't look that way you can't see buildings and if you don't listen too hard you can't hear traffic. So it's all like a mixture between town and country, right? Not built over everywhere, but not like out in a wood or something either. 'Mixed' is a very good word, I'd say that was about right yeh.

Part One

THE TOWERS

DARWEN

'When we first come to Providence'

Linda and Alan Norris

Small and neat in a grey wool roll-necked pullover and check-patterned slacks, she curled her feet up under her where she was sitting at the end of the sofa. Her husband sat on the floor on a cushion on the rug opposite, leaning back with his knees drawn up, supporting himself on an elbow on the seat of the armchair: a tall thin-faced man in an open-necked shirt and jeans. He was thirty-two, she was twenty-four. He nodded emphatically as she spoke.

– I don't mind saying it. It's true, isn't it Alan, when we first come to Providence just a year ago almost now, our marriage was more or less on the rocks. We'd been living for two years in two horrible rooms at the back of an old house in Wandsworth; it looked like we was going to be stuck there for ever. I went to the GLC, I said what chance was there of getting something, anything, anywhere? They said all they could do was put our names on the list, but we shouldn't get excited about it: because we was something like number 1395. The man said if we had a baby that'd put us up a good bit; but neither of us would have even contemplated it then, if we were thinking of anything what we were thinking of was parting. I was working, only a clerk in an insurance office but I was earning enough to keep myself if I went on my own.

Every night all we did was sit in front of the old black-and-white telly we had, then Alan'd usually go down the pub around nine o'clock for a drink. Sometimes I'd read or do jigsaw puzzles. God, I can't even believe it now, how dreary it was. It was terrible Alan, right?

– Jesus, well I don't know how either of us stuck it. It was a bit easier for me: yes, it was Linda, just a bit because I had a more interesting job than what you did. She was in this lousy office. I was an electrician with a firm of shop-fitting contractors, so I used to travel around. One week I'd be working up in north London, the next say in Chatham or one of the Medway towns; at least I had a bit of variety. Let's be honest, to both of us daytimes when we was out working were the times we enjoyed. At night like Linda says we were bored bored bored. Funny thinking back about it: you forget even though it was only a year. . . .

Well, let's have more coffee eh, and then work out when you're going to come and talk to us. Do you want it always we should be together, sometimes me on my own, sometimes Linda on her own, or what?

Alan: What I am now is a driving instructor with one of the nationally known firms. I started a few months back. I've always liked driving, only I never thought I'd be able to master the teaching part of it. I'd never reckoned myself to be a very patient sort of person: I thought the trouble'd be that I'd be effing and blinding all the time at people who weren't doing things right. But they send you on a training course, and that sorts you out about things like that. The other thing they teach you – you'd be surprised how hard it is to learn this actually – is they teach you how to control yourself the other way, not laugh at people who're making idiots of themselves. That's more difficult, it's more difficult not to laugh at people than not to get annoyed with them.

Changing my job, starting on something completely new once we'd got settled down here, that must have been, you know symptomatic. I told you didn't I I was an electrician? But it wasn't a good job; I've got one or two beginning certificates and things; but I was lazy, I wanted to earn a living and have money in my pocket. Only I wasn't prepared to go to night school and study to improve the prospects for myself. I wasn't ambitious, no way at all. I'm not saying I'm all that ambitious now; but at least I've got more sort of interest and pride in what I'm doing, I want to do it well. And I go to evening classes now, once a week: not anything to do with work or the thoughts of ever getting a job with it, but just as a hobby I do photography, I enjoy it.

Linda'll tell you, I don't think I'd ever enjoyed anything ever at all before we come here. I was a right miserable sod, a real loner. I always had been: I never talked to people, had nothing to do with anyone and I didn't want anyone to have anything to do with me.

When I went down the pub I'd stand in a corner on my own, not looking for anyone to come up to me and not giving them any encouragement if they did. That's a question I often ask myself, what did Linda see in me? I don't know the answer, you'll have to ask her. But I do know sometimes I used to come back from the pub and I'd look at her, and I could tell she'd been crying. It can only've been because she was so lonely. That was what her life was like then, with me.

Well, she's not now though, she's never like that: we've got baby Cindy, and we've got this nice flat, and as far as I can tell she seems to be happy all day long.

– I still don't really know, you know, to this day how we were so lucky as to get this flat. They'd told us we were way way down the waiting list, we never thought we'd a chance in hell. We decided well we'd lose nothing if we kept plugging away except the price of a phone call: so Monday mornings we took it in turns, one or the other of us rang up the GLC housing and said were they any nearer offering us anything. Not nasty, only a polite inquiry sort of thing; but regular as clockwork, Monday mornings around ten o'clock.

And then one day I suppose it was after oh about eight months, something like that – this woman said to me 'Oh Mr Norris' she said. 'Yes we do have something this morning if you're interested, we've got a flat come vacant in one of the tower blocks on Providence Estate.' I said 'Right we'll take it.' She said 'Well you haven't seen it yet, I'm saying would you like to go and have a look at it?' I said 'Yes we'd like to go and have a look at it. Only as well as us going to have a look at it, I don't want any misunderstanding, we'll take it, all right?' She said 'All right that's definite then; so let me know when you want to come and get the keys and go in and look at it.'

When I went home that night and told Linda she didn't say a word, she just sat down and burst into tears. I'm not very good at things like that; I said 'Right well I'm just going down the pub for a bit.' And I went off and left her sitting there crying. I remember when I came back – funny the sort of stupid little things you remember – I remember she'd laid the table all nice and neat with a clean cloth and everything. I thought oh celebration. I said 'What're we having?' and she said 'Wait and see, it'll be ready in a minute, go and get washed.' You know what it was? Sardines on toast.

She's not one for getting excited as a rule, Linda. She didn't say much at first except ask me to tell her as much as I could remember about the telephone call I'd had with the woman. Then after a bit she said 'What did you say it's called, Providence Estate? Where is

it, north of the river, south or what'? I said 'I haven't a clue.' I did
and it was absolutely true. She said 'Well don't you know the actual
address or anything?' I had to say I didn't. She just gave me one
look; you know, as much as to say 'You bloody idiot, I bet there's no
bloody flat for us at all really.'

– I might've known, I mean what Linda would do after that business
I was telling you about last night about me not knowing where the
flat was or anything. The next morning she was on the phone to the
housing people, and then she rang me up at dinner time to say she'd
found out the address, she was going to get off work early and if I
did the same we could go and have a look at it.

We met at Oxford Circus at four o'clock, we got a tube, then we
got a bus and we got off in the main road over by the park, then we
walked through and came out onto the estate. We asked someone
which one was the tower block called Darwen; then we asked someone we met coming out as we were going in which would be number
fifty-two. They told us that'd be the fourteenth floor. So up we came
in the lift, then we were stood out there on the landing outside the
front door. 'Right' I said, 'come on then, hurry up.' 'Hurry up what?'
she said. 'The key' I said, 'open the bloody door, hurry up let's get
in and have a look.' 'I haven't got a key' she said, 'all I want to do's
have a look in through the letter box.' I went stark raving mad. I
said 'Do you mean we've come all this bleeding way just to have a
look through an effing letter box?' She said 'Stop screaming and
ranting and using that sort of language, whatever sort of people'll the
neighbours think we are?'

Then we both suddenly burst out laughing, I suppose because she'd
used the word 'neighbours' you see. Somehow that seemed to put the
sort of seal on it; we both knew then that whatever it was like inside
we were going to live here. We were like a couple of kids: we got
down on our hands and knees and started trying to peer in. We
couldn't see anything at all except the hallway. But that was enough:
hallway, I ask you! It was massive, it looked like bloody Buckingham
Palace compared to what we were living in.

We were laughing and giggling, and we kept pushing each other
over when we were trying to look inside. We were making a right
racket, then we suddenly looked up and there was a woman from one
of the other flats on the landing. She'd opened her front door to see
what all the noise outside was about. She didn't know us from Adam,
but when we told her we'd been offered the flat only we hadn't got
a key and we were trying to see what it was like, straight off she said

well to come into hers and have a look at that, because they were all exactly the same and that'd give us a good idea.

– I think that's the thing that's struck me most of all about living on this estate, what I was saying last night about all the people being so nice and friendly. When we were living in rooms in Wandsworth you never knew a soul, nobody seemed to have the slightest interest in anyone else at all. You could live like we did in the same house as ten other people, and unless you passed them on the step coming in or going out you wouldn't even recognize them in the street if you saw them. But here everybody's 'Good morning', 'Good afternoon', 'How are you today?' and all that sort of thing all the time: they'll chat with you coming up in the lifts, give you a nod when you see them washing their cars round the back by the garages. It's just like you're all part of one big family and they all really enjoy living here.
I think most people do enjoy living here on Providence. I think the only ones who don't must be those who've been here too long and are always telling you it's gone down since whenever it was they first came. Those who are here now – well, I suppose most came from the same sort of situation we did, living in furnished rabbit hutches. If they're not happy with what they've got now in comparison, I can only say I feel very sorry for them. To me living here's fantastic, it's perfect and I can't imagine ever wanting to be anywhere else. I suppose it might be difficult a bit when Cindy starts growing up and going to school, and when we have another one; I suppose the fourteenth floor of a tower block's not an ideal place to bring up toddlers in. But that'll be a good few years yet before we have to start thinking of moving to somewhere else.
This is the first real home I've ever had. We go out on the balcony there, we've bought ourselves some binoculars for it: we stand out and look at the view all round, you can see all of south London. I breathe the fresh air – and it is nice and fresh out there – and it's peaceful and quiet. I sleep deep at nights and I'm content.
We don't go out much because of Cindy. I go to photography one night, Linda goes to cookery one night, and that's it. The rest of the evenings we sit at home, perhaps have a can of lager each or something if we're watching the telly. Now and again we look at each other, sometimes we perhaps hold hands for a few minutes. We neither of us needs to say anything; we both know what we're thinking. It could've been all very different.

Linda: The first week when we moved in I simply couldn't get used to the sheer size of it, it just seemed absolutely huge. We'd hardly any furniture, and I used to walk about from one room to another and stand in the middle of the floor looking at how big they were. I'd had a week off from work which was due as part of my holidays, and at the end of it I said to Alan I was going to give my notice in as soon as I went back and from then on stop at home. I said I was going to buy lots of emulsion paint from Woolworths and I was going to decorate the place from one end to the other. Alan gave me the biggest grin I'd ever seen him give in his life: he said he'd been thinking exactly the same thing, he was going to take a week off too and we'd do it together.

That week we were at home I decided I was never going to work again, not unless we were ever really really desperate. I wanted to stay at home. have a baby and make a real home. And that's what we did. It was so important to me that Alan and I should be happy. I was getting to the state I didn't know which way to turn, I couldn't see any way out of it except for us to separate. I felt such a failure: Alan'd had a really rotten life, his mum'd died when he was little and he didn't get on with his dad or his dad's new wife. He lived with his gran, then with his auntie, then with another auntie – and I used to think 'And now me, I've gone and made things worse than ever.' Well anyway that's all water under the bridge now: he's changed so much, he's a new different person all together. And if you asked him I hope he'd say I was different and nicer and easier to live with too.

– What we've got is first this big sitting room with the floor-to-ceiling windows opening out onto the balcony: then through that door there's the big kitchen, then that door there leads out to the hall. Off one side of that there's the large bedroom which is ours; then opposite that there's the smaller bedroom which is Cindy's; then along towards the front door there's the bathroom and separate toilet on one side, and a little sort of walk-in cupboard opposite that. The hall's wide, that's one of the best things in the flat; it gives you the feeling of airiness and space as soon as you come in. The other thing I like is the high ceilings that all the rooms have; and the central heating; and the balcony which runs from outside here along as far as our bedroom; and the easiness of keeping it clean; and the friendly neighbours; and the built-in cupboards round the kitchen walls . . . well, I could go on for hours about all the good things, so you'd better tell me to stop.

There are disadvantages too, yes naturally there are. Only let me think a minute first, beeause I don't ever think about them very much. . . . Well funnily enough the one I thought before we came would worry me hasn't, and that's being so high up. I don't like heights, or at least I always thought I didn't; so I did once or twice wonder if it'd worry me, being up so high. But so far it hasn't done at all: the only time I've even thought of it was once when there was an electric power cut when I was pregnant and I'd been out shopping, and I had to walk all the way back up the stairs to the fourteenth floor. It took me about twenty minutes at least, I thought I'd never make it; but anyway I did in the end.

Now as far as I'm concerned I don't seem hardly to ever think about the height. Sometimes I look out over the balcony and you can see all the people and the cars and things down below, and it's nice, I like it. Sometimes it gets a bit windy, I mean noisy with the wind; but I don't mind that, I imagine it's something like being in an aeroplane.

Honestly nothing else really, nothing I could complain about. It's all plusses. I like the shops down in the precinct in Robins Walk, I like being near the park so when it's a nice day I can take Cindy out for a walk in her pram. I even like housework here, which is something I could never have imagined myself doing if you'd asked me a couple of years ago.

We haven't got as much money as we had when there was the two of us and I was working, but I don't mind about that. I don't ever want to go to work again; I want to have another baby before long. That's about the limit of all I want out of life as far as I'm concerned. I think when you've been unhappy and thought you've made a complete mess of your life, then suddenly somehow you get a second chance – well it's fantastic, like a miracle. All your gloomy thoughts go out of your head, you start living and enjoying life again and being thankful for what you've got. I'm not just thankful; I do enjoy being here, really enjoy it. I'm not a very religious person, so I say being up here is I'm sure it's the nearest to heaven I'll ever get.

DARWEN

'Home to Corofuckination Street'

Frank Potter

— That's right lad, sit yourself down, choose your own packing case: they're all the bloody same, so pick whichever one you like. Well, like I said to you on the phone, Friday I'll be gone for good so you've only just caught me: but I'll gladly sit and have a chat with you every day this week until then, very willingly. Then Friday morning I'm off: shake the dust of Providence Estate off my feet for ever. Home for good, back to civilization thank God. I've not packed up the kettle and that, should I make us a cup of tea before we start? Sorry the place is stripped bare but there you are, I'd nothing else to do but pack. I wasn't expecting visitors so I'm a bit in front of myself like.

A stockily built grey-haired green-eyed man in his sixties with his shirt sleeves rolled up. He brought in two huge mugs of tea, teaspoons, a sugar packet; he put them on a standing-on-end suitcase and sat down cross-legged on the bare boards of the floor.

— I'm sixty-one, and I've lived here in this eleventh-floor flat almost from the day it was built, that's close on twenty-three years. I'm a widower, my wife died last year. She was a London lass by birth and she liked living here very much, which is more than I ever bloody did. I'm a Lancastrian, I come from Bootle, but I was mostly brought up and went to school in Crumpsall, Manchester. The first twenty years of our marriage we lived near Oldham: so twenty years up there, then about twenty down here, I suppose that was about fair on both of us wasn't it? Only she liked the north more than I liked the south, she was much more adaptable you might say. Me, I've always been one of the awkward buggers, I not only kept my Lancashire accent when I came to live down here, I put it on much stronger than it really ever was, till that got to be my only way of speaking. It used to make Elsie laugh when she heard me in shops and places, she knew it was nothing like as broad as I used to make it out.

I worked in Manchester for an advertising printing firm, we did calendars and yearbooks and things of that sort. I was on the selling side, selling advertising space to people. Then one day we got bought out or taken over or whatever you like to call it by a company in London: they said they'd either give me redundancy payment, or if I wanted I could move down to London and work for them here.

Funny, when I was a young man the idea of living and working in London was the be all and end all. But moving when you're getting on for forty is a different matter; perhaps by then I was too old and set in my ways. I knew Elsie'd like it though, she had one married sister living near Harrow and another one down this way. So there was nothing much to discuss about it; I said to the firm 'Right' and that was it, we were off. We hadn't the faintest idea where we were going to live or anything, but that didn't greatly matter; there was only the two of us, we'd no children.

First of all we stayed with Elsie's sister at Harrow for a week or two, then we moved on to the other one. I used to go to work on the bus in those days and every morning the bus went down along the main road there; I used to ride on the top and I could see this estate as it was being built. I thought one day I'd inquire from the council and see if they were all taken, and if they weren't did you already have to be a GLC tenant to get one.

I rang them up, and well you wouldn't believe this these days, but they straightaway said they had quite a lot of the flats here in the tower blocks that weren't spoken for. I think people can't have been too keen on them, not like today when folk are thankful for anything. I told Elsie about it, so we decided we'd come and have a look and they had what they call a show flat in one of the other towers; I think it was Kendal or Chorley or in one of those over there. It looked very very nice: it was higher up than this one, say the fifteenth or sixteenth floor perhaps, but exactly the same size and layout and everything.

I believe I was a bit doubtful about it at the time, but Elsie wasn't; she was all for taking it there and then. She said it'd be just like home for me – you know with the tower blocks all being called names of

25

Lancashire towns. I said well one of them wasn't, Kendal wasn't in Lancashire for a start. I never did find out what the idea was of giving them all those names. Ridiculous isn't it, you live somewhere all that number of years and never take the trouble to go into it.

Anyway stop me if I'm rambling on, when you get to my age you do tend to reminisce a lot about the past. I suppose dismantling it all's got a lot to do with it; being here twenty-three years and all the memories, it's a long time.

So the long and short of it was we said yes we'd like to have it and they gave it us. It was a real showplace estate in those days; we used to get all sorts of people coming to have a look at it from all over the world: Russia, Africa, Palestine, I think we once had even people from India to look round. Some of them would come and knock on your doors, they couldn't speak English most of them, but they had an interpreter: he'd say who they were and where they were from, and please could they come in and have a look what it was like inside.

They were right posh these towers; no question of it, in those days they were right posh, that's what they were. All nicely spaced out with grass and trees and a bit of landscaping, little hillocks and things. A very desirable development, as they used to say. The lifts always all worked, a resident caretaker for each building, toilets on the ground floor: it was all very very smart, somewhere really good, somewhere you were proud to live. Do you remember those what they used to call 'garden cities' before the war, Letchworth and Welwyn and those places? Well that's the nearest to it in atmosphere I mean, it was like them. All very well kept and peaceful, with a sort of rural air about it, hardly like being in a city at all.

And not like it's got to be in the last eight or nine years either I can tell you, not one bit. You wouldn't recognize it now, compared with what it used to be like you wouldn't. No by Christ, not at all.

– Yesterday I was telling you what it used to be like wasn't I, compared with what it's like now. You won't need me to tell you though, you'll have seen a lot of it already for yourself. People pissing in the lifts, kids writing on the wall, those big blocks just over the road – Vernon, Cramner and the other one, what is it, Foxman is it? My God, what places to put people to live. And they put anyone in them you know; some of them only stay a fortnight. They don't pay their rent, they get notice to quit and that's it, out they go and another lot comes in. You can't expect people to take any pride in where they're living under those sort of circumstances, can you? Every one of them are all problem families, you know; and all blacks or nearly all of them. It's dreadful, we'd have moved anyway even if Elsie'd been

26

alive now, most certainly we would. It got so she hated it. I'm not exaggerating when I say she was frightened to go out sometimes in the winter in the late afternoons to the shops or something, she didn't like to have to walk back past them in the dark. Old Enoch was right, you know, when he said we should send them all back home. The thing is that their ways aren't our ways: they never will be, we're two completely different sorts of people. We'd stick out just as much if we lived in their countries. I think it's all wrong, it should never have been allowed to get to this stage ever. Still, it's too late now: at least I'll be out of it though when I get back up north.

Where I'm going is a little place outside Warrington. It's a village, I suppose you might call it almost a small town really. It's got the one main street with houses all along it each side and I've bought one of those. A terrace, two up and two down, that's all someone like me on his own needs. I shall really enjoy living right in the middle of somewhere again, instead of like this stuck up in the sky with nobody ever passing by your window. The thing now you see is that without Elsie I get very lonely on my own. It's no sort of life for an old man at all. I've never been the sort of person who lets things get him down, but I've been getting a bit that way a bit since she went. The doctor said he could give me pills and such like, but he was perfectly straight about it; he said they weren't the answer. He didn't think it was at all a good idea for me to go on as I was, living here on my own and only going to work in the morning and then coming straight back at night.

I've never been a great one for going out and mixing with people, I've not made any friends down south much. Then one day not all that long ago it suddenly came to me. I thought what the bloody hell was I doing, what was I going on working for? Why didn't I cut out of it straightaway and please myself what I did for the rest of my life? I could afford it, with being careful with money, I'm not short of a few bob. And I do know one or two people up north. One bloke particularly who I've known ever since we lived there, him and his wife we've sometimes been on holiday with them, or they've been down here a couple of times to stay with us for a few days. So I rang him up on the spur of the moment right out of the blue: I told him I was thinking of packing up my job and coming back north to live, what did he think the chances were of me finding a little place. I said I didn't mind where it was so long as it wasn't stuck out isolated in the country. Most of all I'd like it if it was somewhere in a terrace say, somewhere where there were people round and about all the time.

You'd scarcely credit it but he was back on the phone to me in

27

about only three days. He'd seen an advert in the paper for this house for sale, and he read the particulars out for me. I was over to Euston Station and on the train for Manchester before you could say Jack Lightning. He met me in his car and drove me over to look at it: and there was going to be no messing about as soon as I saw it. As far as I was concerned, it was just what I wanted. It's lovely it is, just the job. So that's where I'll be going on Friday, eh: day after tomorrow, home to Corofuckination Street.

– I said I'd have a think for you after you'd gone didn't I yesterday? So as far as I can I have.

I'd say the basic thing really is that I'm a northerner; I always have been, always will be. In all the years I've lived in London I've not made a single friend, not what you'd call one real friend. Whether it's me or whether it's them I couldn't say, but that's the fact: not one single one. I don't like southerners, there's something that to me's just not well what shall I say, not really genuine about them. They're alright to your face, but there's something sort of distant about them if you know what I mean. Not every single one, I mean I wouldn't say that. I couldn't could I, not having been married to one. But what I mean is they've got a roundabout way of doing things and saying things. I'd say they're standoffish, most of them, nearly every one. If you're a northerner you say what you mean; even if it sounds rude you say it because that's what you think. But down here you must never do that, you must never say what you really think at all. I can't put it any better than that.

The other thing you asked me to think about, that was the estate itself wasn't it; how it'd changed over the years since it was first built. All I can say is what I've already said about that; when it was first built it had got lots of character, and a good character. Like I told you, the GLC were so proud of it they used to invite people to come and see it.

They certainly bloody well wouldn't do that now though, would they? They'd be too downright bloody ashamed of themselves for building those fucking great blocks over the road there, Vernon, Cramner and the other one, wouldn't they? All they are is tower blocks laid on their sides. A disaster they are, all you need do to see it is walk past them, you don't even need to go inside. Stairwell windows smashed all the way up, the garages underneath them with their doors broken in and the inside filled up with old mattresses and junk, obscene writing sprayed with aerosol paint everywhere on the walls, doors kicked in. Three whacking great bloody eyesores, each one of them; and built there barely a hundred yards from what was once the model little group of these tower blocks. Obviously the GLC didn't build them like that in the first place, I mean I suppose they intended them as nice places for people to live in like these. What went wrong I don't know but something did, something went very very wrong indeed. Whether it was the people they put in them or what, but good God. . . . And I get bloody furious about it when kids from over there start coming over here into these towers and wrecking our places too. The hallways, the landings, the stairways outside the fire doors – you see kids rushing about and shouting, riding up and down in the lifts, writing things. I once saw a little kid actually pissing up against the wall once, right out there on our landing by the lift. As soon as he saw me coming the little bugger ran off like greased lightning down the stairs didn't he? Black boy he was.

Being calm and sensible about it, you see when these towers were first built we had a resident caretaker in each one, he had his own flat down there off the hallway on the ground floor. Everybody knew him, and likewise he knew everybody who lived here. If anyone came in, a kid who wasn't from here, he knew straightaway and told them to buzz off and go on and get out of it. And not only that – because there weren't all that many people around those days, he'd very often know when he saw someone what their name was and where they lived. I think that was a great deterrent to kids, that the caretakers of the buildings knew who they were: they knew they'd go and tell their parents about them if they did anything they shouldn't. Mind you some parents these days, if you went and told them their kids'd been misbehaving they'd stand there and swear at you, tell you to fuck off and mind your own fucking business that's all, wouldn't they?

– I thought since I was off tomorrow I'd get us in a little bottle of wine to drink while we had our last talk, sort of a farewell celebration like. Sorry it's got to be out of mugs, anyway good luck, all the best, cheers. Not brilliant but not too bad; I suppose that's about as much as you can say. Some of the cheap wine they sell these days, if you put some in a bottle and took it to the vet he'd say he was very sorry but your dog'd have to be destroyed. Cheers again, yes, cheers.

I think about all I've done is given you a long moan about southerners and blacks and everything. You must have thought I was a right miserable bugger. Providence Estate could only take a turn for the better once I'd gone. But I suppose I'm not a really typical inhabitant at all. All these years I lived here with Elsie, well we've lived here but we've never took much part in the actual life of the estate itself. The last few years before she died she was never a well person, she was ailing: we didn't go out and we didn't know anyone, and always during the daytime I was up in the City working. The only time I was ever on the estate would be Saturday mornings, when I went down there to Robins Walk to the shops. I never got to know anyone though, not even the shopkeepers: somehow I never fitted in.

An example? Oh well yes, easy, straight off. Saturday mornings, every Saturday for years I'd go in the newsagent's to get my *Daily Telegraph* which he'd have there keeping it for me. And every time, he'd get it out from under the counter. I asked him once, he said mine was the only one he had. There was never any copies on the counter, all he had were piles of the *Sun* and the *Mirror* and the *Sketch*. Not a *Daily Telegraph* in sight, never another one there in all the years.

Does that make me a snob? I always think I'm as much a working-class person as anyone else, never someone who put on airs and graces. Oh well, too late to change now, eh? Cheers, cheers. You know, in a bit I might have a drink problem, living on my own.

BOLTON

'The truly very good things of life'

Lloyd Malcolm

Soft-voiced and gentle-mannered, he sat almost formally upright on the edge of a large black leather-covered armchair, with his hands clasped between his knees. Slight in stature, polite, middle-aged, neatly trimmed short black hair, a dark lounge suit with a white shirt and a maroon silk tie.

– I am sorry but I have to say first that I am not exactly sure how old I am; I think it is perhaps thirty-seven or thirty-eight. I was born in the Leeward Islands in the British West Indies, on the island of Antigua actually, in the capital of it, St John's. I came here when I was a boy just over twenty years ago, to join my parents who were already living here, my father working then as a bus conductor in Birmingham. I had a brother and a sister older than me who were already in this country. They worked in the same factory together with my mother, something connected with the garment trade I think, it was owned by an Indian man who paid them very low wages.

My parents were very good to me. At home in Antigua I had always been thought of as the clever one at school; when I came here my father said I must not work but should go to college and study to become an engineer, which I did. I thank my parents for it now that they made it possible, but at the time I didn't appreciate it. I wanted to be earning money like my brother and sister, to have money to spend and be able to go out and enjoy myself, not sit at a desk all day and then have to study at home all the evenings.

When you're young you don't have foresight, you don't see things like that, and so I was very resentful. In Antigua everyone wanted the chance to come to England, everyone knew there was work here and money: it was thought of as a place where the land was paved with gold. I smile now, but it was a great shock to see how things were when I first came. Don't misunderstand me: of course compared to Antigua it was very different and there was very much more wealth. But soon you saw what big differences there were in how much money there was between people, what they had, how many things you needed to buy, expenses like rent and travel to work and electricity and so on. No matter how much was earned it never seemed to be enough.

My parents were making sacrifices especially for me so I could go to college, but I didn't appreciate it. I did very often feel resentful towards them. I have tried with my own son Clive who is now fourteen to explain how I couldn't see those things in the correct light concerning education at the time. I think he understands it, or understands it better than I did at least.

However, it was about four years altogether that I studied; I took my City and Guilds certificates, then I went on to take the necessary specialized exams. So now I am a fully qualified engineer with some letters after my name you know? It's silly to think these things mean much, but all the same they do: you can see on people's faces when you go for a job, they have to have two looks at you to make quite certain you are really the person who has such good qualifications.

I work now as an inspector in a factory. We make machine tools and such things; all the work is contracted for by the British Government, there is nothing which is commercial. This means it is a very secure job and a very well paid one. My wife and I have talked it over: we have decided we have now saved up sufficient money for us to be able to buy a house on a mortgage so we shall soon do that. She works also for the government, in a departmental accounts office in one of the ministries. You see we are very respectable people now aren't we? We laugh often about it together; but even though we make a joke about it, it is a very nice feeling all the same.

She was my childhood sweetheart. As soon as I'd finished my examinations I sent for her to come to England to join me, and we immediately got married and came to live in London. My first job already was in a government factory also, and I think this is how we came to get the flat in this tower block. They had not been built very long; this one was brand new and there had been no one living in it before us. Because I was working for the government that gave me some kind of priority on the housing list I think.

We have lived here now in this seventeenth-floor flat for fifteen years, now almost sixteen. We like it very much; we have always liked it; but our dream is always to be able to own our own home, which is the reason we are soon now going to move away. We're not quite sure yet where we will live – we would like it to be a nice area, perhaps a little more further out from the actual area of London itself. There is no hurry to go though, and we shall take our time before we decide.

I hope you will forgive me but I have an appointment this evening, a meeting I must go to shortly. But I shall be most happy to talk with you again tomorrow evening if that will be convenient for you, when I shall not have to go out.

– These are some photographs of where we lived in Antigua. We took them last year when we went back there for a holiday. As you can see it is very different from England, both in the housing conditions for people and very obviously too in the weather. That is really something I think I have never quite got used to you know? And the extreme coldness so very often, and how it rains and rains and rains. I very much miss the sunshine.

But I would never want to go back there to live. No. Here the living standard is much higher as you can see, if you are willing to work. Whereas there no matter how hard you work you will never better yourself. Here you study and work, and you know in time it will bring benefit and rewards. This is what I constantly tell my son: that all the things anyone could want in life are here, you can attain them if you wish, it is entirely up to you. No one will give them to you, they have to be earned. But they can be earned, that is the important thing. In Antigua all you can do unless you are a wealthy person, which scarcely any of the indigenous people are, is work all your life in the sug..r plantations or the cotton fields and you will never get anywhere at the end of it. I think he began to see this for the first time when we took him with us last year to Antigua: he had had no real understanding of what it meant to someone to be born and brought up as he was in England.

I do not mean just material things. Those are important, but there is something more important here than money which you can earn. It is respect from other people, for yourself as a person. I do not agree at all with black people who talk of England having so much colour prejudice against black people. In my experience it is absolutely not true. In my job I have a section in my charge, ten people who work under me: everyone of them is white, and I can truly say that never once has any one of them been rude in any way to me on account of my colour. Sometimes people will swear of course – all people in factories swear – they call me 'a silly bastard' or 'an awkward sod' or some expression such as that. But no one has ever to my face said 'You silly black bastard' or 'You black sod'. Emphatically no. Never. I see on television such things as marches and demonstrations by the National Front, and I sit and wonder who those people are, where they live and where they work. Because I have never come across them; and I am talking now not just of my work, but in pubs and shops and restaurants and places. I have never once experienced racialism against me.

My son says to me at school he does sometimes get things said to him by some of the other pupils; I think that is only because they are children, they are just saying things, repeating things they have heard because they think it is funny or clever perhaps. I am a pacifist. I tell him very strongly that if any of his school friends speak to him in such a way he must forgive them because they don't really know, they are not old enough to know what they are saying. I think Martin Luther King was the greatest leader the black people have produced and I was very sad when he was murdered. But a man like Malcolm X, I had no time for him at all. I think he preached racial hatred, he wanted the blacks to retaliate against the whites for all the oppression they have given them over the years. Well yes it is true that they have, but I think those things must be forgotten and forgiven, we must all be determined to live together in peace.

I do not know if you have come across any of the black people who are known as Rastafarians yet, but I am strongly opposed to them. I think they do great harm to black people as a whole. Their movement – they call it their religion, so I suppose that is what it is – is one which to me has too much hatred in it. I think it is very frightening. One of the tenets of their belief is that black people are superior to white and they should not mix. This seems to me a very bad thing, I think it can cause only trouble. And besides, black people who live in England I think should follow the ways of England; they should not try to keep themselves apart from others and look down on them and hate them. Being 'superior' to white people – I think that is an awful philosophy to teach. There is no difference at all between black and white; if you are Christian and believe in God there can surely be no argument about it: He made people of all races and all kinds. It says in the Bible that He created man in His own image. Not a white man or a black man or a yellow one, just Man He created: and therefore every man is in some way a part of God.

I'm sorry you must forgive me if I sound as though I am preaching or a politician. My wife says sometimes that that is what I ought to have been, because I feel so strongly about this subject. She says I should talk as I do to as many black people as there are who will listen, because it is so vitally important for the future.

It may sound strange to say this but it is true: I have many more friends who are white people than I have who are black people. All our neighbours here are white: the people on this floor of Bolton, those below us, all of them are white. I know one or two in the other towers who *are* black, but most of them – at least most of them in the tenants' association which I belong to – they are nearly all white without exception. Perhaps it is that the black people who come to England are reticent, perhaps they feel they will not be welcome; or perhaps already many black people begin to feel they prefer to keep themselves to themselves, because of the things they see on television or what they read in the newspapers about Mr Powell and his friends. It would be very sad if they should feel so, if that drift into keeping themselves separate were to continue and grow.

I would say this to anyone who would listen, and I am speaking absolutely from my experience and not just theorizing about it. Ever since I have been here, which is now getting on for twenty years now, from my neighbours I have never received anything but courtesy and friendliness. They do not invite me into their homes; but I think that is the English way; I have long since realized it has nothing to do with my colour. They respect me as I do them.

Over the years I have held various positions of importance in the tenants' association. I was the secretary for two years. I have been at different times the Chairman and the Vice-Chairman, and at present I am the Treasurer. We meet once a month in the community hall. It was a meeting of the association I had to break off our talk for and go to last night. I would not miss any of the meetings for anything, because it seems to me if black people want to be accepted into the community then they must be prepared to work for it, to be very conscientious and very reliable. Perhaps even a little more conscientious and reliable than white people, because they have something to prove – that they will be responsible, that they are respectable, that they do deserve to be treated as everyone else is.

It may be because I come from a poor family, and because I am aware of the difference between what my life would have been if my family had stayed in Antigua and what it has become now. This is not something I shall ever forget, or that my wife and I would like our son to forget. To tell you the truth about this my father died ten years ago now, and my mother soon afterwards. They were both then still poor, and uncertain whether they had done the right thing or not for their children in bringing them to England. If they had only lived a little while longer they would have seen what they did was right.

My brother has become a teacher, my sister was first a nurse and then a nursing sister until she got married and had children and I am an engineer with a very good job. So I think there can be no question the sacrifices they made for us were ones we should always remember and be grateful for.

But – and it is very important this 'but' – there would have been no point in them doing that in some country where the opportunity did not exist for us to take advantage of what they did. There would have been no point in them scraping and starving for us back home in the West Indies, there would have been no future for us there. I constantly remind my son of this, as I have said; I try to encourage him to be aware of the opportunities that are open to him, and to study and work hard as I did, so he can take advantage of them.

But he is young you see. He has had an easy and comfortable time, a good home, sufficient money for food and clothes and all the things he needs, so he does not understand the necessity to work hard at school. He is after all only fourteen, but he will grow up, he will mature. He is a good boy; he has never been in trouble of any kind; so if it pleases God he'll turn out OK. Sometimes my wife says perhaps we expect too much of him too soon: if we do, it is because we are a little too anxious for him to do well.

I think an important factor to us, and one which quite rightly cannot be disregarded, is that not only have I been fortunate in the opportunities I had given to me by my parents, and not only have I worked and studied hard and taken advantage of them and done well – but you see I have not only done well as a black person, but I have done better than many many white people have. This makes it quite natural then for some to be jealous about it.

If they do not know me, do not know my background, they think in some way I have special privileges; they want to jump to that conclusion immediately rather than ask me. What puts this into my mind is something my son said not very long ago. He came home from school and said one of the white boys there had told him he knew that I, his father, lived on the National Assistance and didn't do any work; all black people were lazy and good-for-nothing idlers who ought to be sent back home. Of course it upset him very much; it upset his mother and me too when he told me of it. I didn't want him to boast about me, but I wanted him to be able to hold his head up and to tell his school friends that all I had I had worked for, worked and studied for very hard for many years indeed. He said it would sound like boasting. He thought too that this particular boy who had said this, his own father had recently lost his job, and he did not want to say anything to him that would make things worse.

You know, I felt probably my son was right: it was probably better he should keep quiet. If the boy felt that, he felt that, and if his own father had lost his job, he was going to feel all sorts of things about other boys' fathers, not just the black ones. My son's colour, this was a very easy target for him to aim at. But it was a situation which I thought was sad.

What I eventually decided to suggest to my son was that he should ask some of his friends about it, ask them to tell him what he should do. He did this, and he told me most of them said he should try his hardest to ignore it, try to forget about it. I felt that was a step forward for him, a lesson in life: it was not only black boys in his class who he asked and who said that, several friends of his who were white too. I felt the step forward was he'd been able to discuss it with them, he had been able to talk with black boys and white boys about a problem which had occurred because he was black. It had taken great courage for him to do that, I was proud about it. I was proud too at the response he had got, because it showed very much more clearly than anything I could say to him that there were plenty of young white people who were ready to listen to him and to understand. I told him he should not forget it.

– To sum up what we have been talking about in these evenings, I would repeat to you that I regard myself as a very fortunate and contented man. In every way. In having good parents who gave me and my brother and sister such opportunity to have so much better a life than we would ever have had in the West Indies, in being able to come to England and have the openings put before me to benefit from. These are things I shall always remember and be grateful for.

It is true I haven't said anything critical at all about life in England, but I assure you that is because I feel genuinely there is nothing serious for me to criticize. We have the same trivial everyday worries and troubles as other people do, black and white, but none of them, at least so I feel, is to do merely with being black. It seems to me – especially as we are now within sight of owning our own house – that everything is going along well, all is very good. To complain or criticize small details would seem as though I was being very unthankful for all the truly very good things of life which I have.

KENDAL

'Here there is terrible stiffness yes?'

Mr and Mrs Banks

The silver-framed photo on the sitting-room sideboard showed that thirty years or more earlier he had been a strappingly handsome sergeant in the British Army; the bride on his arm, a tall thin pale German girl in a drab two-piece suit, was clinging to him with a shy smile in the middle of a small group of soldiers and their girls or wives.

In the kitchen the table was laid: yellow gingham-checked cloth, rose-patterned and gilt-rimmed cups and saucers and afternoon tea-plates with forks. The matching teapot and milk jug and sugar bowl on a tray on a nearby worktop. There was no room for them on the table because the middle of it was occupied by a large chocolate cake with coffee icing and with two layers of coffee cream.

He seemed small, and was bald except for a narrow dark-grey circlet of hair round his head just above his ears. In a voluminous floral housecoat, she was large and plump; between them an avalanche of hospitality and talk.

– Please eat as much of the cake as you can my darling, I made it specially for you coming. Here, I cut you a small slice to begin with so you can see if you like it.

– Bloody hell woman, is that what you call a small slice, he's probably not long since had his dinner.

– You shut your face my darling, he will say himself if he can eat it or not.

– She's got no idea you know, she never has had. Over there in Germany where she comes from, they eat cake cake cake all day

long. Cake for breakfast, cake for dinner, cake for tea . . . don't you
eh, I said over there in Germany where you come from –

– I heard what you said my darling, and it is so stupid I just bloody
ignore it. This man knows it is stupid too, so he will ignore it as well.

– That's why she's so fat you know, she makes these cakes all the
time and then she eats them all herself.

– Then why do you not eat some also? Look at you, what you are
is skin and bones. He eats nothing you know, nothing; I cook for
him every day and he just leaves it.

– That's because I've got to be careful because of my stomach, isn't
it? I eat fish don't I, I eat fish all day long. I've got fish coming out
of my ears, I eat so much bloody fish.

– There is no nourishment in fish, not like there is nourishment in
my cakes. There is egg and butter and sugar and cream, everything
lovely and fresh and with nourishment. Your doctor is a fool.

– It's because I've eaten nothing but bloody cake for years and
years that I've got this bloody ulcer, isn't it? That's what he said.

– He said no such thing. What is this man going to think when he
hears you say things like that, that I poison you?

– I don't know what he's going to think. Only he's come here to
talk to us about living on the estate hasn't he, so what's he going to
think if he hears us arguing about cake all the time?

– Living on the estate, phewf I could tell him about living on the
estate, I could tell him a few things.

– That's exactly why he's come you silly woman. So go on then tell
him things.

– What sort of things, what sort of things should I tell him? How
unhappy I am, do you think he wants to hear things like that?

– Yes if you like, tell him whatever you like. Anyway you're not
unhappy so there's no point in telling him things like that.

– I am not unhappy? I am not unhappy? How can you say things
like that when every day I tell you how unhappy I am?

– You don't, you weren't unhappy yesterday, you were singing.

– You think if I am singing that means I am not unhappy? You see
what an understanding man I have for a husband heh? Phewf. I could
tell you some things.

– Well *tell* him some things, I'm not stopping you from telling him
things, am I?

– You are arguing with me whether I am unhappy or not.

– I'm not arguing with you, I'm merely trying to point out that
you've got to take all sorts of things into consideration and give a
balanced view that's all.

– Oh you think my view is not balanced, yes? Maybe you think *I* am not balanced, yes?

– Well you don't talk as if you are sometimes. But look anyway never mind all that, he's sitting here waiting to talk to us, he's got his tape recorder running all the time and all we're doing is wasting his tape going on arguing about bloody cake for God's sake.

– The tape recorder is switched on, it has been switched on all this time?

– He told you it was.

– Oh my God, we must stop arguing and we must talk sensibly with him.

– That's exactly what I've been saying for the last ten minutes, isn't it?

– You must excuse us please, we don't usually argue like this all the time.

– Yes we do, pretty near.

– We do not.

– We *do*. Look, are we going to have an argument now about whether we argue or not?

– No no. Come along let us be sensible then. Only you must not contradict me otherwise I shall start arguing. You would like another piece of cake first young man?

– He hasn't finished that one yet.

– He can speak for himself, be quiet, do not be so rude. I apologize to you for my husband, he is a typical Englishman, he has no manners at all. Please: finish up your cake, and then you can have some more; we will take it into the sitting room with us where we shall be in comfort.

– The missus was going past one day, oh twenty years ago nearly, and she saw them building another new one of these towers, so we put in for one. We'd been living in a four-bedroomed flat, a council one at Hackney. But with our son and daughter both growing up and going to college or university it was much too big for us. We had to wait I suppose about, what would it be love, six months?

– Yes about six months.

– We could look it up for you if you like, she's still got the rent books in that bureau there from the day we came.

– What? Nonsense.

– They're in that bottom drawer.

– No they are not, I threw them away many years ago.

– You threw them away? You never even threw a bus ticket away.

– I tell you they are not in that drawer, if you don't believe me go and see for yourself.

– Look it's not all that important now, is it? All the same I'll have a bloody good look when he's gone, I'll tell you.

– Look to your heart's content sweetheart, but they're not there; it was at least three years ago I threw them away.

– Anyhow, we wanted a smaller place to live, so that was it, we came here.

– It was a pity, we have never liked it.

– What are you talking about, we liked it all right at first.

– You did perhaps, but not me, no never.

– Oh well, have it your own way. But why didn't you take the chance to move then, that time six years ago, when Kathleen and her husband told us about that nice little house going near them?

– And live in Basingstoke? Whoever would want to live in Basingstoke?

– All right, well what about when Henry and Penny said why didn't we look for somewhere round where they are?

– You think I want to live in Margate on the doorstep of my children?

– Bloody hell, you are, you're downright bloody impossible you are, do you know that? Anyway, where were we? This can't be any help to him at all, all this business can it? We came here, and we've been here fifteen years, and despite what she says –

– I will say what I say, you do not speak for me thank you. And if I say I am unhappy and do not like it –

– Will you just let me finish? Please? What I was going to say was that it's always been more hard for her living here than it has for me.

– Because I am a German and English people do not like Germans not at all.

– God, you're as bad as the bloody blacks you are! That's what she always says. Look I've told you it's nothing to do with you being a bloody German, half the people in the shops and round about don't know whether you're a German or French or Spanish or what the hell you are. A lot of English people don't like foreigners; not foreigners of any kind, full stop. Not just Germans. Anyhow, it's been worse for her not only because she's a foreigner, but because most of the time, in the last few years anyway, she's been at home, she's not been working any more because her health wasn't up to it. Until last year when I retired I had a job as a van driver for a firm in the West End, so I wasn't here during the daytime all that much. But for her, coming from a little place like Oldenburg she never got used to –

41

– Excuse me darling, I do not come from Oldenburg.

– Yes you do, originally.

– Excuse me please, but I should know where I come from: I come from Essen.

– Not originally you don't. 'Originally' means where you were born – and you were born in Oldenburg, right? And Oldenburg was a little place.

– Not like Nottingham where you come from you mean?

– Nottingham's ten times the bloody size of Oldenburg, and I know that because I was looking it up in a book the other day, so don't let's go on about it. I'm trying to put him in the picture about you, that's all. You were never brought up living in a big city, and even though we've lived all these years now in London, you can't help it, you don't care for it and you'll never be used to it. All right?

– I have done very well to become used to it.

– You've done marvellous to become used to it, I'd be the last person to let anyone say any different. Only it's true, isn't it: it's not just the place, it's you? In the last few years you've not been very happy living in London at all, we'd both like to go and live somewhere else, somewhere smaller.

– But not Margate.

– Granted, right, not Margate. God, you don't half make things bloody difficult, you know.

– She's not very well today the missus, she's lying down: she says to give you her love, she'll see you and talk to you next time.

I often think that for her, she must have more bloody idea of what the coloured people have to go through than any of us whites you know. Because she's foreign, because she's not English, because she's got an accent, as soon as she opens her mouth people know she's not English and they do, they talk to her differently. I don't mean they're rude or things like that, but they sort of lift their voices if you know what I mean, start to talk louder and more slowly to her, as though she was some kind of halfwit. It makes her very conscious that they can tell she's different from them and they're not going to talk to her as though she was the same as they are, they're as you might say emphasizing the difference between them and her.

We've never joined in much on community things on the estate. For instance there's a social club down in the precinct, we've been perhaps only three times in all when we first came here, but she very quickly got the feeling she wasn't wanted. I don't know whether she was right or wrong, but that was what she felt. It must be very hard for us to imagine what it's like to be a German or a coloured person or any sort of non-English person at all. What it is down there at the social club is mostly bingo; that doesn't greatly appeal to either of us.

There's a bit of snobbery there too. I don't think I've ever said this to her as a matter of fact; but I think Londoners tend to be a bit snobby about people who can't trace their ancestors back to the Lambeth Walk, if you know what I mean. She's a German, I'm a northerner, or at least what they call a northerner; so neither of us ever really will fit in. It might well be the same if I was a southerner living in the north I suppose. But it is a fact, there are these differences between people and anyone who says everyone's the same is just talking out of the back of their heads.

Sophie's never had any real family, I mean German family. Most of them got killed in the bombing or were refugees and disappeared from sight altogether in the different zones. When I met her when I was in the British Army it was in Berlin; God knows how she'd got there, she was only a young girl. It's not something she ever talks about, it was a time in her life she wants to forget about. We've never been back there, she's never expressed the slightest wish to: she must've been very lonely though, very often in her life since. I'm not a big family man myself, my parents died when I was very young; in a way perhaps that's why we were brought together. We'd both not had much in life really in the way of home things until we met.

Life to us is each other and the children. I don't suppose it'd matter all that much where we were. There's a bit of a feeling when your kids have got married and started their own lives and families that that's the end of it, that's the finish. But we've been lucky in that respect, we usually go and see one one weekend and the other the other. The boy and his wife are talking about maybe emigrating to Canada next year; if they do, well who knows, we might think about following on after them. That's a dream though, isn't it, you can never tell in life about things like that. We've had a good life, most of the things we want out of it, marriage and a home and kids; I don't think either of us could really complain.

About all I'd ever say I was short of now was a little bit of a garden, I think it'd be nice if for the older people they had allotments or something round the back here. There's not a lot to do when you're retired during the day. Another advantage of that would be it would give people more of a sense of pride in living here. If they felt some part of it was their responsibility and it was up to them to look after it. These big towers, they're very impersonal; you pay your rent every week, send it in, and that's about all there is to it. You ride up and down in the lift when you're coming in or going out, but

43

most times you hardly ever see anyone else. If you do you don't know whether they live here or are just visiting or what. We only live on the sixth floor – what it must be like at the top, you must feel more isolated and cut off than ever up there.

What they call a high-rise block like this is no sort of a place for retired people. In the olden days when there was the caretaker who lived on the ground floor, that was much better: he knew your name and you knew his, so there was always one person who was the same one you'd see every day. A little thing like that even, it gave you a sense of belonging. All that's gone now: not just from here from everywhere, it's everywhere in life. I blame the government myself; look out for number one and don't give a bugger for anyone else, that's the Tory philosophy and it permeates every aspect of everyday life. This is getting to be increasingly not a very nice country any more; I think if our boy and his wife do go to Canada, we'd make every effort we could to go there after them.

– My husband, he is a very British person. I think it would be very hard for him to leave England you know. He said to me he'd been talking to you about going to Canada – I don't think he ever would really want to even if he could.

It would make not much difference to me one way or the other. I was very young when I left Germany, just a girl without much knowledge of anything. I have never felt I was particularly belonging to Germany or this country or anywhere. Here there is terrible stiffness yes? If you are not English you are not English and that is hard luck for you, but you will never become one of us. Perhaps all countries are the same, I don't know, but it is something I have never been able really to overcome in my mind you know?

Even when I was working – and I did work, I worked very hard in the canteen of an office equipment firm, I was the manageress of it for nearly ten years – even then, I always thought no one wanted to be friendly or let you get too close to them. Perhaps it is me, who can tell? Perhaps if I had stayed in Germany I would have been the same because it is something about my character, it is very difficult to say.

I've had a good life, I have been very lucky. I have a good husband who has always been very good to me, we have our two nice children who we have brought up to be good people and to behave themselves and we have two grandchildren, one of them with each. We spend a lot of our time squabbling you must think. But of course this is difficult now my husband is retired and at home all day. We have no one else to talk to but each other, so it is only natural we get a bit fed up with ourselves sometimes. Also my health is not good, and this makes me bad-tempered. But we have been married a long time to each other, we have had very happy times, we understand each other very well.

I think if I had a family of my own, relatives in Germany, it would be good. But I know no one there, I do not ever really feel now it is where I belong. I am a stateless person you know? Always the English, that is the first thing they say to you 'Where do you come from?' they say. I say 'I come from Providence Estate in south London' – and they give me a funny look, they are not sure whether it is a joke or not.

It has been good to talk to you also. Any time if you come back, I promise you there will always be cake. I will make a special one, for you.

CHORLEY

'Making it upwards'

Trevor Berry

— It's all what they call a challenge right? Life and things: you start off at the bottom and you keep your mind on making it upwards. It's all down to me now, see what I mean?

A well-built open-faced young man with brown curly hair. He put his bedroom-slippered feet on the plate-glass topped coffee table and looked round the room as though he was weighing it up for the first time.

— So far I suppose you could say I haven't done too bad. The only thing here that's not paid for is the three-piece suite which is on the HP from the Co-op; otherwise every thing in it including the carpet is all our own. Mind you we've not bought most of it, it was given us last year when we got married. The wife's her parents' only child, so they were very generous to us, very generous indeed, I've got to say that. And myself I've only got one brother, he's only sixteen, so my parents gave us a lot of things as well. We had a good start, only that was it, from then on we think of ourselves as being entirely on our own. Course we're not really; if we ever got in difficulty there'd always be her people or mine to help us out. But I wouldn't like that to happen and neither would Sylvia. We'd both feel we were letting ourselves down if we had to start turning back to them. It's got to be upwards now; and so long as we're sensible, which I think we are, I don't see why it shouldn't be.

– I'm twenty-one, my name's Trevor but I never get called that, it's always 'Trev' and Sylvia's always called 'Sylvie'. She's nineteen. She's just come back home from hospital with our first baby, a little boy three weeks old. We've called him Paul Alfred after my dad. We said if it was a boy I'd decide on his name, if it was a girl she would; so next time we hope it'll be her who's the one to choose.

I'm not at all an educated sort of person. I left school when I was fifteen, then in three years I must have had something like twenty different jobs. I worked in a supermarket stacking shelves, in a greengrocer's, for a couple of weeks in a garage on the pumps, then in an ironmongery wholesale stores, did a bit of window cleaning. I was in and out of work like I don't know what. The only thing I never did was draw the dole money, the unemployment. My dad wouldn't let me, he didn't agree with it. He said everyone should work for their living, not live off of handouts from the state or anyone else. He was a docker, well he still is. So far as I know he's never had a day off work in his life. He'd always give me pocket money to keep me going if I was short, but as soon as I was in work again I'd got to pay it back. He kept me up to it too – he used to write it down in a little notebook, then I had to give him so much a week out of my wages each time till it was paid off. I think he was right to do that; I don't like to see all this scrounging that goes on these days, people not working because they can get more by being on the social security, I think that's all wrong.

For the few weeks we were waiting to move into this flat here we were living with the wife's parents over the road there in Cavendish. I said to her father we were going to pay rent because that was the way I'd been brought up: he didn't want to take it did he, but the point was it made me feel better about it and Sylvie saw it the same way.

When we came in here first we had a flat on the ground floor. It was all right, nothing wrong with it, they're all the same size and layout and the rest of it. But Sylvie went to the GLC office and said she'd like to be higher up where there was more of a view out of the windows. She must have been about six months pregnant then, but she said she didn't mind even though it meant she'd have to climb stairs if the lifts broke down. There was this one that'd just happened to come empty on the fifth floor and they said we could do a swap if we liked. I've no complaints about the GLC, I'm well pleased how they've treated us. Some people were surprised they'd let us do it but they never argued about it, gave us the keys to come and have a look one week and the next one we were in here.

I don't know why but I think this one, Chorley, is the nicest of the tower blocks. Whether it's the type of people you've got living here or what, but sometimes I go in the entrance halls downstairs in some of the others, when I come back here this one always seems the best kept.

I'll tell you something so long as you don't quote details about it, right? When we were going to move up here from the ground floor, a bloke come round one night, and he said he'd give me seventy-five quid if I'd lend him the keys of the downstairs flat for one day. What he wanted to borrow them for was so he could get duplicate ones cut, see. The day we moved out him and his wife and kids would move in and then the GLC would be stuck with a squat, yet one more. There's a lot of it. There must be half a dozen families who are squatters in every tower I should think. Most of them are darkies. This bloke wasn't though, he was a white person same as you or me. He was a bloke where I work, to be honest. He was getting desperate you see, him and his family had been on the list for rehousing for years; I was, I was very tempted to let him have them, I can tell you. I wouldn't have done it for a coloured person, but when it's one of your mates at work that's different right?

Anyway in the end I didn't: Sylvie said the GLC might find out how he'd got hold of the keys, he might tell them himself if it came to court or something. She said it wasn't as though we were short of seventy-five quid, which was true: only it wasn't the money to me, it was the principle. This was a genuine case, someone who needed help, and I was in the position to help him. I don't agree with squatters though – the GLC won't take rent off of them, and so what they're doing is living rent free when other people are having a hard time making ends meet. That's why I think they should crack down on these darkies who're squatting really hard, bring the police in right away and turf them out, women kids the lot: put them out there on the street. Mind you they're very crafty some of them, they'd soon find their way back again a lot of them would no matter what you did to try and keep them out.

Another thing I think is very wrong is people who don't pay their rent. I read in the local paper the other day that someone in one of these tower blocks had been taken to court and he owed something like four hundred quid. Four hundred quid, and all he got was a warning; something like he'd have to pay it off at so much a week. I think that's ridiculous. There's people like us paying our rent every fortnight on the nail, never been a day late with it since we came here; and then there's other people who get away with murder. You can't say that's not wrong and shouldn't be put a stop to. If I had my way the mobile caretakers would go round with bolts and put them on the doors of people who didn't pay. Lock them in or lock them out, depending on where they were at the time: that'd stop all the nonsense right away.

It's all to do with the way people are brought up, well I think it is myself. But those that were brought up right and know how to behave get treated no different from those who weren't. It gets you very discouraged sometimes to think you're going to bring your own child up properly, but you don't know whether that's not going to turn out in the end to be a handicap to him, see what I mean?

– The wife's gone over to her mam's this afternoon with the baby. She goes twice a week on a Tuesday and Thursday, she's very good about things like that: then on Sundays we go one week to my parents and one week to hers. They all live round about here, all within walking distance so it's not a great long way to go. Hers live in the flats at Cavendish, mine live at the back of Gorrivale Square. We both of us feel family ties are important – you never know when you're going to need your family or when they're going to need you. Neither of us would ever want to move very far away to live. I think it'd hurt them, they'd miss us and we'd miss them.

Sylvie and me first started going together about four years ago. She was fifteen, I'd met her at some job I was in at the time, but I forget which one now. I think it was a shoe shop – that's right, she came in to work on a Saturday to earn herself a bit of pocket money. Her parents were over the square but we didn't know each other. I won't say she was the only girl I'd ever been out with, but she was definitely the only one I fancied marrying – the others had all been sort of very casual. But with her well, it was just one of those things. She felt the same way towards me, even though she was what some people thought was a bit young.

We went steady about two years, then we had a talk with her parents and mine and told them we wanted to get married. They said, well, that was obvious for a long time, what were we waiting for; and that was it. We did discuss at one time whether because we were so young we should live together for a bit to see if we were suited to each other. But it was never a very serious idea; it'd have hurt our parents if we had done that, especially as we were both from well-known families in the area.

My dad was strict though: he said to me if I was going to be married I'd have to settle down, and get a proper job and stand on my own feet. He said he and my mum would help set us up in our own place, but from then on we was on our own. I was lucky, only the very next day or something I saw this card in the window of a firm of minicabs, saying they wanted an office manager. I'm a bit of a cheeky sod at times if it's necessary. I walked straight in and persuaded them to take the card out of the window there and then, because I was the person they wanted. Maybe they were trying to call my bluff but anyway they gave me the job. Well, I know they've not regretted it. I've been there ever since, over a year now, coming up for eighteen months.

I was lucky in another way too. The bloke who owns the firm had some capital left to him by his father who died or something. Not long after I joined he bought out another firm, and then another one not long after that. That makes him quite a big business now, in a small sort of way – we've got something like about twenty motors altogether now. My job's to take all the phone calls as they come in and give the work out. I do all the timings and pricings for the runs. We do a twenty-four-hour service and run on three shifts; me, another bloke we've taken on, and the manager himself all are on the central switchboard in turn. The manager's a young bloke, only a few years older than me. His mother runs the office and the accounts. We've got some good contract work, so so far it looks as though it's all going nicely.

What was I saying before though? Oh yes about my dad when we first got married, him telling me to get a job and stick in it. I think I've proved it for him now. I get a good wage – it's not all that short of what he brings home himself. The other thing we had to do was find somewhere to live, but that wasn't difficult. With both our families being local and both GLC tenants, the housing people like to keep you together in the same area if you ask for it, so we got priority on that. If we'd asked for some other estate it wouldn't have been quite so easy. But they told us straight off we'd be offered somewhere within a couple or three months of getting married. In the event it turned out it was just under eight weeks that's all.

We shan't stop here indefinitely – two years will be about the limit, then we'll want to start thinking of a house. I'd like it if it was in Gorrivale Square or somewhere round there. There's some old houses along one side that they're doing up, converting into places for two families. We wouldn't want to be too far away from here: this is where we belong, when my son grows up I'd like him to be the same, go to school in the area and all the rest of it.

I want him to do a lot better at school than I did though. I never learned anything. I didn't like it, I was hopping the wag whenever I got the faintest chance. 'Hopping the wag', well it means playing truant doesn't it? Everyone uses it, every kid at school anyway; it's the name it's always been known by so far as I know. I've got no idea at all where it comes from; all I know is everyone used it at school, and I'm sure still does now.

Anyway like I was saying, I'd want my boy to do better than I did. I'd want him to work hard, pass all his exams and things. I don't want him to be brilliantly clever, but I'd like to feel he had more choice of the decent jobs when he grew up. Because what worries me you see is that the way the country's going at the moment, with all these blacks coming in all the time, well it stands to reason doesn't it that by the time he's grown up there's going to be less houses for white people, less jobs for white people, less everything for us. If he hasn't got a bit of an education, then he's not going to stand no chance: I mean he could even find himself ending up working for a black man, if he's not that little bit more clever.

That would be the one thing that would make us move away from here definitely, if the blacks took over. If that happened we'd want to move somewhere right out in the country, right away, even emigrate say. It's a subject I give a lot of thought to and the way I see it, if they stopped any more blacks coming in at all, there's still sufficient of them here now for them to outnumber us if they start having large families. By the time my boy's eighteen or nineteen, or perhaps younger, sixteen or seventeen – when he's in his last year at school he could easy find him and his mates are in the minority, about the only pure whites left in the school. All the rest would be black or brown, or half and half, know what I mean? So that's why I say I want to make sure he pays attention to his books and works hard.

If he ever came home with a coloured girl and said she was his girlfriend, I wouldn't let him in the house. I'd not stand for anything like that. And if it ever got to the point when he married a black, that would be completely the end of it. I'm not racially prejudiced, but to me it's downright unnatural for races to mix themselves up, the whole idea's unnatural. Know what I mean?

– In the last couple of weeks when you've come round and we've been talking, I expect I might have given you the impression I was a bit anti-black. But I don't hold with the National Front. Last week I saw a kid writing on the wall downstairs by the side of the lift with a felt pen, writing 'Blacks go home'. I knew who he was, he doesn't live in this tower, and I said to him to go home and get a cloth and come back and rub it out, otherwise I'd go round and see his dad. I told him we had some black people living in Chorley and what would they think if they saw that sort of thing written up by the lift? I said they'd think it very offensive, wouldn't they?

I don't mind blacks living here so long as they behave themselves.

I keep separate from them, and I like them to keep separate from me. I don't go for all that business they have in South Africa, separate toilets for blacks and whites, separate seats in buses and entrances to buildings and the rest of it. But I think they're right basically in having two sets of different schools, because once the kids are educated to know they're different, then I think that stops a lot of the trouble later on.

Another thing I might have given you a wrong impression about, because I'm not very good at talking, is I'm a very goody-goody person, who turns his nose up at anyone who steps out of line. I'm not. I mean for instance I haven't so far voted in an election, but if I did I'd vote Labour. But I don't hold with thieving.

I wouldn't ever thieve myself because I've been brought up not to take things that aren't yours. There's a terrific lot of it goes on in the docks where my dad works, but there's never so far as I know been a single thing in our house ever that was nicked. You hear about people whose larders are full of tins of ham and things, but I've never known it in my own home. On the other hand though I'd never shop someone to the law if I knew they'd done something. It's not that I've got anything against the police, I think they do a good job – but I don't like them much, I don't think most people do. You hear too many stories about them, how they fit people up for things. My attitude is keep well clear of them altogether. Once you've got a record about something, that's going to be on a computer somewhere for ever; it could ruin your whole life.

I'd say I'm a reasonably happy person, not the sort who ever gets very miserable. I've a nice wife and a lovely little baby, we've got a good home, parents who've always been good to us, so there's nothing that's missing. I'm someone who likes everything to be right and proper, and life to go on slow and steady. I think you've only got one life, so it's up to you what you make of it. It ought to be improving all the time, sort of thing; and it's down to you, you're the one who'll make it.

PRESTON

'An end sixteen floors below'

Audrey Gold

– I suppose people would say a brassy-looking blond, they'd have to
wouldn't they? Short hair, chopped off jagged all round, dye growing
out. Thirty-five, two kids, smokes too much, lives on the sixteenth
floor of Preston House, doesn't go out much, takes pills. I don't know
what else to say. And what sort of a person, I don't know: not much
of any kind of a sort of a person really.

*She stood frowning at herself in the chain-hanging mirror over the
sideboard, took another cigarette out, fumbling in the packet without
looking, and let it dangle in the corner of her mouth before lighting it.
She went on idly poking at the spikes of her hair: a sharp-featured
face, thin and lined. An old navy-blue jumper and jeans, worn bedroom slippers with faded pink pompoms.*

– We've been here ten years. I've a daughter Gail thirteen and a boy
Simon eleven. They're both at school. My husband is away at present,
he works for a construction firm – prefabricated factory buildings.
He's a site foreman, they work different places round the country so
sometimes he'll be away several weeks on the trot.

I work as a night cleaner with one of the contract firms that does
offices around Victoria. I get there for ten o'clock, then we work
through till six in the morning. I get an early bus back and I'm here
for seven in time to get the kids up and give them their breakfast.
Most days I do the housework or the washing and ironing or shopping
or whatever, then I go to bed about half past ten and sleep till say

four when Gail and Simon are home for their tea. It's something you can get used to, living the other way round you might say – I've never been a person who needed a lot of sleep. The wages are pretty poor – most weeks for five nights' work I'll bring home something about twenty-five, twenty-six pounds and then there's the fares to come off that.

There isn't a night-time canteen open for the cleaners. We clean the canteen kitchen though, so we're allowed to boil ourselves a kettle and make tea there when we have our break halfway through the night for our sandwiches. I think the hardest thing I find is you can't smoke.

That's all I can tell you really about myself and what it's like living here.

– I have up weeks and down weeks. I'm afraid I wasn't much help last time because it was a bad down week. After you'd gone I thought you must have thought I was real rude, not offering you a cup of tea or anything, not even sitting down myself most of the time. When I'm like that I can't bear to stay still, I have to be moving about. I feel better though this week. What would you like, tea or coffee?

I can only give you my own idea of what it's like living on an estate, other people might tell you different, I'm sure they would. To me living here on the sixteenth floor on my own, apart from the kids who're at school all day, is as near I could imagine as to what it must be like living in hell. When I was a kid I used to read in books hell was down under the earth somewhere; but it's not, it's up here in the sky.

When we first came to the estate we'd been rehoused from Kentish Town. We were in a furnished room with our daughter who was a toddler. Then I had Simon, and that put us up the housing list with a jump. The first place they gave us was one of those prefabs round the back of Burley Street. It wasn't ideal, but where we'd been was so awful, damp running down the walls and mice and no hot water and only an outside toilet, that anywhere had to be better than that. The GLC told us we'd only be in the prefab as a temporary measure; and it was true, it was only a few months before they offered us here. I'd been hoping for one of those nice flats in the smaller two-storey blocks, Moxley or Rivers: but this was what they came up with. We looked at it, and compared with what we'd been used to it was great. We didn't have to take it, we could have hung on and waited, but we didn't know how long that would be so we said yes. We asked could we stay on the list for something else later on if anything came up: that was after we'd moved in here. They said well they'd put our name down but it'd be a long, long time. As far as they were concerned when we took this we were rehoused. That was quite right, we were, so I suppose we can't complain.

I don't know which was first, me going wrong and not being able to get on with the place, or whether the place that started me going wrong, I mean depressed. It did, it got me down and down. I went to see the doctor – he said I was a young woman and he didn't want to put me on pills, I should get out more, build myself up a social life. That's not all that easy for a woman with two small kids, especially if she's living somewhere like here. It's not like a street where there are other people, and even if you only go out of the front door there'll always be someone to talk to. No more than 'Good morning' and 'Nice day' and so on, but that's something. Whereas here – well, apart from this one there's three other flats on this floor, each with our doors at the four different corners of the landing when you come out of the lift. In the one opposite ours there's an old couple who never seem to go out, ever – I think I've only seen her once all the time we've been here, when we both happened to be getting our milk in. At one of the other corners, the flat there there've been so many different families one after another I've never known any of them; and the third one, well, I haven't a clue who lives there. So that's my neighbours, or the immediate ones.

I used to go out it's true a lot more than I do these days. I'm talking about when the kids were younger. Sometimes I'd take them over in the park in the summer if the weather was nice. But I had a couple of experiences over there so I stopped going a long time ago. One was a tramp who was drunk, exposing himself; another was a gang of boys fighting all over the path. They were knocking down passers-by who got caught in the middle of it; stones and bottles were being thrown, it was very frightening.

The other thing that's put me off going out except when there's no choice and I have to, like going to work at night and coming back in the morning, is the lifts. We've had very bad experiences with them too. I suppose it was five or six years ago now. One night Alec my husband had gone out to see some friends. And he just didn't come back. Thinking back I ought to have done different about it than I did; but my nerves were bad, so I didn't do anything. I wasn't working myself at that time. I just sat up all night in this armchair like I am here, drinking coffee and smoking my way through a packet of cigarettes and I kept bursting into tears, and having to try and stop myself in case the kids heard me and woke up.

The thing was you see I thought he was spending the night with another woman and that's why he hadn't come home. We didn't have

55

a telephone so I couldn't phone the police, but I wouldn't have anyway even if we had, it's not the sort of thing you feel you want to tell people about. Then just after seven o'clock in the morning he came walking in through that door, looking a bit rough but quite calm and collected. He said he'd got home at half past eleven the night before, started coming up in the lift and it'd stopped halfway between two floors. There's a bell in it for you to ring in an emergency, but you can't hear whether it's ringing or not if you're between floors, so you don't know if anyone's hearing it or not. But even if they do, it's up to them whether they do anything about it: they might phone for someone to come from the caretakers or they might not.

Well he rang for a bit but nothing happened, nobody came to his rescue. So he took off his coat and made it into a pillow and lay down and went to sleep on the lift floor. Next morning somebody going out early to go to work reported the lift out of order and the first thing he knew was the lift started, the doors opened at a floor lower down and he could get out.

Ever since then that's always been my big fear, that that might happen to me. Every night and morning my heart's in my mouth when I'm in that lift. If I'm on my own and a man ever gets in, I won't stop in it, I get out at the next floor and wait till it comes back empty again. The idea of being caught in it on my own, ringing the bell and no one hearing; or them not being able to mend it, me being there for hours . . . I don't even like talking about it.

I don't know which is worse but another thing was during the power cuts when none of the lifts was working. Simon was four, I'd been out with him and we'd got a lot of shopping. When we got back we found the lifts were out. There was a notice on them saying it was going to be three hours before the power came back on again. I decided the only thing for it was we'd have to walk up. So there I was with a four-year-old toddler and I had one of those shopping trolleys with wheels that all the things in it kept falling out of because it had a tear in it down one side. I had to keep yanking that up each flight of stairs. Simon was crying, I was crying, it was terrible. I know I shouldn't have, because it wasn't his fault, but I kept on smacking him. It was winter, in the afternoon, dark because there was no lights on; I had one of those little flashlamps on a key-ring thing. That was an experience I wouldn't like to go through again ever. If it ever did happen again I wouldn't even start to try it, I'd go off and go to the pictures or something.

It was round about soon after then I went to the doctor again. I told him I couldn't cope at all, so he put me on some pills which I've been on them regularly ever since.

– I was glad you came today, I think if you hadn't been coming, I don't know, I was so down I don't know what. I don't go out on that balcony these days; I daren't because I think I might one time do something silly.

I suppose you'll have guessed by now, so there's no point pretending about it. My husband's not away on contract work, he's left me and gone off living with somebody else. I mean that much was true about his job, but he's been living with this woman two years now. Once in a while he comes to see me, well the kids; and he's quite good about sending money. I've not met her but I suppose she's younger than me, prettier and more attractive. I've got to say that wouldn't be all that difficult though, would it?

I get this feeling a lot you know, that if we hadn't come here to Preston, if we'd been able to get one of those flats in Moxley or Rivers it would have been different. I don't know why but I've got the idea people who live there are happier; there's more of a community spirit, helping one another, that sort of thing. I think definitely here in these towers people don't want to know you.

There's a social club in the shopping precinct but I don't know if they have women there on their own. The impression I have is it's a social club for the older families on the estate; they all seem to stick together, they've all known one another for years.

They play bingo, things like that, which is all right if that's what your idea of a good time is. But it's not mine, not yet anyway, I'm not quite that old. I met someone once who was something to do with it, she said to go along any time. Saturday was the big night she said, bring my husband and kids. I didn't know what to say to her, perhaps I wasn't being fair to her but I got the impression it was only for respectable people. They all seem to know one another, those who go there: it's what they call a click, people from Gorrivale Square and Jesmond Close. If you're not one of them they don't really want to know you.

A woman who lived in Kendal, one of the other towers, she was in the same position as me, her husband had left her. She said she went once to the social club but she wasn't going again, everyone was too standoffish. She said the men were all right, but any time she started talking to one of them his wife'd come up as though she was frightened she was going to try and run off with him. I'm not saying people would be different anywhere else about it though, so perhaps it's not fair to say it's only those on this estate.

The loneliness is something you'd get anywhere, but I do feel it that being up here makes you more conscious of it, it makes it much worse. I hate looking out of the windows: you don't see people, all

57

you see is sky and buildings a long way away. I don't hardly meet anyone ever to talk to from one week to another. I've no family of my own, both my mother and father died when I was very young. I do have a brother, but I haven't seen him since we were young and the last I heard of him he was in the Army somewhere.

I suppose the best thing would be to get another job. The office cleaning one I do at nights brings in a bit of extra money on top of the allowance I get sent me by my husband when he remembers, but it's not the sort of job where you meet many people. We work in teams under a supervisor. She ticks your name off when you get there and makes you up into groups of six to do different sections, so you're hardly ever working twice with the same person two nights running. Then when you've finished, all everyone wants to do is get back to their home, so there's no standing about and chatting.

It's hard to know where to start though, about trying to do something else. The year before last I worked for a few months as a packer at one of the mail-order warehouses. It was good as far as hours were concerned, nearly everyone was part-time; you could do whatever hours suited you best, made your own time. But the pay wasn't good, you had to work almost full-time hours to get anything like a wage. In slack periods they'd tell you there wasn't enough work to go round and you could only do two hours or whatever it was on that particular day.

For a person like me, life's not much more at present than clinging on. More than once I've thought there isn't any point to it at all, except for the children. But they're growing up, it won't be long now before they're able to stand on their own feet. It's not something I get in a worked-up state about; it's just fact. I think about it quite often. I think one day if I decide to finish with it, all I need do is go out on the balcony and it's there, an end sixteen floors below.

– After we talked last time I did go to see the doctor again. I said I didn't feel the pills were doing me much good, I was down much more than I was up these days. He gave me some different ones to try, they seem to have made some difference, well a bit. Least I've promised Gail from now on I'll try and go out with her once a week on a Saturday afternoon, take her out looking round the shops and perhaps go in a Wimpey Bar.

I asked the doctor about housing too. He said definitely he didn't think it was a good idea for me to go on living here and he'd give me a letter for the housing people, so I can send in for an application form to be moved on health grounds. We'll see if it makes any difference, but I'm not banking on it. Perhaps I will hang on till things get better, though I couldn't tell you why. I've quite enjoyed talking, even if it's not been much else but saying how sorry for myself I felt. It's something to find out I still can talk. I've been a very silent person for a long time, which is not very good if you think about it is it?

LANCASTER

'Come up to the Starlight Roof'

Desmond Blair

*Fifty-five, he looked nearly ten years younger: his fair hair was thick
and curly, his smiling blue eyes were bright, his face was lean and
tanned. Warm summer evenings on the balcony of his twentieth-floor
penthouse, sipping chilled white wine and looking at the lights of the
city shimmering in the still distance.*

– Always delightful isn't it? When I invite my friends I say 'Come up
to the Starlight Roof.' I don't remember how I started referring to it
like that; the name of a show once wasn't it, in Town? Or maybe a
nightclub in America. But I've never been there, nor did I ever see
the show, so I can't make it sound realistic as a choice can I?

Um, what shall I say about myself? A little more wine first to give
me time to think about it. I'm fifty-five but I've told you that already;
a bachelor, you know that already too. I work for one of the West
End stores, a window-display manager. I thoroughly enjoy it, and
I've been with them, goodness, twenty years. I've lots of friends, my
hobbies are reading and listening to music – and especially like we
are now, the sitting-room sliding door at the end of the balcony open,
Beethoven's Second Piano Concerto on the record player. Or is it
the Third, I'm always getting the numbers mixed up? Oh and potted
plants too, they're another hobby.

And without hesitation I'd say I'm a truly happy man living here,
absolutely completely happy. I wouldn't want to live anywhere else
in the world. Music, wine, sitting on the balcony – what more could
one ever want? Shall we listen to the end of this movement then go
on talking again?

– I came here seven years ago. I'd been on the housing list for yonks, living in bedsits and unfurnished rooms. The last place I had was in Notting Hill Gate. I liked it but it was so frightfully expensive. I'd heard about these penthouses on the tops of the tower blocks, so I thought I'd go along to the GLC and see what I could find out about them. Not having ever been a GLC tenant I didn't think I'd stand much chance of getting one. They said these places were four on the top of each tower: they were very tiny, and only let exclusively to single people; but if I wanted to, I could go and have a look at one though they couldn't give me even the remotest idea when one would ever be available.

I came along out of curiosity mainly, and I got no idea at all what they were like. The one I saw was over there on the top of Darwen: it was a Saturday morning, it was raining and the sky was very dark and overcast. The old lady who was living there was very nice, but what really surprised me was she had a frightful sort of upper-class bray: all the business about *frightfully* sorry the place was so untidy, she'd got the most *fearful* headache, she hoped I wouldn't think her *terribly* rude if she lay on the sofa and let me look round on my own. I was in and out in about five minutes, not getting any idea at all really. The general layout seemed pleasant, it was small and looked as though it wouldn't involve a lot of housework, and that was about it.

I went back to the GLC and said I'd be glad if they'd please put me on the list for whenever my turn came round. I didn't expect to hear anything for ever more, but whenever I changed my address, which was I suppose four or five times in the intervening period, I let them know. Whoever keeps the housing lists at County Hall, they certainly do a meticulously careful job: because seventeen years later would you believe, there was a letter from the Housing Department to say my turn had come round and if I'd like one of their penthouses would I please let them know within fourteen days. They must take the names strictly in order, because a friend of mine had gone on the list a few weeks after I had, and he got his offer of one about a couple of months or so later.

As you can imagine, I was over the moon. When moving day arrived I took a couple of days off work. I think it was a Friday, and I remember it was an absolutely gorgeous sunny spring morning. I came in the van with the removal men from Notting Hill, and I was thrilled to bits watching them bring all my packing cases of books and bits and pieces in and piling them all over the floor. I'd bought a bottle of wine, so when they'd finished then we all came out on the balcony and had a drink. One of the removal men kept looking out over there right across to where we'd come from, and he kept saying 'Cor! Bloody hell! Cor!'

The only furniture I'd brought with me was a divan bed, a fireside chair, and a kind of clothes-hanging rail with castors on its feet that I'd borrowed from a friend. I'd been when the place was empty the weekend before to have a proper look at it and measure up, and it was so small I realized every bit of furniture I'd got either wouldn't go in or would look quite ridiculously big in proportion. I'm good with my hands and I enjoy making things, so I decided to design and make a whole new set of furniture and fixings, with them all scaled down to be in proportion. For the first eighteen months or even two years that I was here, that's all I did, make furniture. The white little dining table and chairs, the low fitted bookshelves round all the walls everywhere, a white low sofa that I fold down at night into a bed – I made them all. I cheated on one of the two easy chairs that's all, I didn't make it – I bought it and cut six inches off its legs. But everything else I actually made, apart from the kitchen equipment. In there I planned out everything very carefully. For instance the little fridge has got a tiny oven on top of it, which is perfectly adequate for one person and the odd small dinner party now and again. The work surfaces fold up against the wall if I want them out of the way, the cupboards round the walls at head height are narrow but what they lack in depth I made up for in length. One of my friends says it's all too '*bijou*'. I think that means 'jewel' actually, and I think it means 'my pet' too or something; so I don't mind, that's how I feel about it exactly, I love it.

Look come on, we've never done it properly have we yet, the conducted tour? It'll take all of two and a half minutes at the very least.

Right this is the front door, we'll start here. As you come in you step straight into not a room but a little open-air paved patio sheltered on all sides by the walls of the flat which is built round it. The walls are almost all glass from floor to ceiling, and most of them slide back so you can step straight in or out. This patio is really marvellous: very tiny, only four steps across, but because of that it's completely sheltered from the rain unless it's absolutely bucketing down. I hang my washing out, it's bone dry overnight, I never have to worry about it blowing away or anything. And I grow all these climbing plants in big white troughs. They grow wonderfully, some of them are flowering and at different times of the year I have different colours: that's a crimson hibiscus, that's a magenta bougainvillea, that blue one's a clematis, 'Nelly Moses' I think it's called. And a little bay tree.

Then straight ahead of us through this glass door is not exactly a little hallway but more a short carpeted corridor. At one end of it is the combined bathroom and loo, then here's the kitchen next to us, then along this end is the bedsitting room or studio room or whatever one likes to call it. Windows round one side wall leading on to the balcony; windows along the full length of the other wall out to the patio. They're all from floor to ceiling so it's beautifully light and airy: double-glazed so it's cool in summer but lovely and warm in winter with the central heating. The balcony goes all the way round three sides on the outside.

And you know when it's like now, the table lamp on through there in the sitting room, this little lantern in the patio – I think it looks magical, it gives me a thrill just to stand and look at it. I can't imagine I'd ever want to leave and live somewhere else, never for the rest of my life.

– I know the other three people who have penthouses up here, those who might be called my immediate neighbours. Jocelyn who lives opposite is a solicitor. Mr Marcheson over that side, he's a widower, and I think he's with Regent's Park Zoo. Then there's Lady Margaret round that way, a hundred and forty if she's a day. Honestly I don't know for certain if she is a Lady or an 'Hon.' or something, but I've always understood she is. I think GLC policy when they built these towers was not only to provide a small amount of accommodation for single people on their own but also to have some kind of social mix as well. Lady Em would definitely be aristocracy; I suppose Jocelyn would call himself upper middle class, since he went to school at Harrow; I'm sort of working or upper working class in background, my father was a ship's captain. Mr Marcheson, I don't know very well but I think one could call him straight middle class.

We don't mix all that much as a general rule, I mean we only have a drink together at Christmas. But we do see each other regularly several days a week when we're waiting outside in the lobby for the lifts, and we exchange pleasantries about the weather and so on. We tend to have the same sort of daily problems too: if the milkman hasn't delivered it's a safe bet he hasn't been to any of the others up here, if the electricity's off we're all on the same circuit so the others'll be in the dark too. That does give us a kind of feeling of all living together in the same street to a degree. A year or two back in the power cuts, Jocelyn and I took it in turns to call on Lady Em and see if she wanted things taken to the launderette or from the shops. None of us got caught with the lifts being out of order: there was a notice in the hallway downstairs at the bottom of the tower giving us advance warning of the times the power would go off. We all copied it down so we had no terrible traumas so far as I can recall.

I'm not really a member of the community of Providence Estate. I'm not a great one for taking part in any social activities, so I don't really come much into contact with people who live here. I do some of my shopping now and again in Robins Walk precinct, and I use the library there and I'm registered with the local GP but don't see much of him because I'm hardly ever ill. But most of my shopping gets done where I work. Food for instance, we've got a very good food department: as a member of staff I get discount, so I get the bulk of what I want there.

I'm not a great one for pub social life either, I prefer entertaining at home. Once a week I usually have a lunch or dinner party here at weekends with friends, or go to their place say in Notting Hill Gate where I used to live. Two girls I'm very friendly with are teachers over in Ladbroke Grove and I often go to their flat there. So my social life's not greatly connected with the estate: I happen to live here, and I think of myself as in it but not of it. Well I suppose I ought to qualify that because it's not entirely true. Seven years is a long time to be somewhere. I've never lived in any place longer than that, this is where I've settled and want to go on living for good now. So in that way I do feel myself as belonging here on Providence. If anyone asks me where I live, I always tell them on a big GLC housing estate in south London. I see that look come into their eyes which always does come into their eyes and I say I absolutely love it on top of a tower block and wouldn't want to live anywhere else at all.

They ask me things like don't I feel lonely living up so far away from things, and I say no never, because I don't.

I explain to them that everything about it as far as I'm concerned is simply marvellous. That it's so utterly quiet and peaceful for a start: you don't get street and traffic noise, no cars or motorbikes roaring up and down day and night, no one shouting, no fire engines or police cars with sirens, nothing at all to disturb you in any way at all. No noisy neighbours, and you don't have to worry about making a noise that'll upset the neighbours either. Now and again I've had quite big parties up here, twenty or thirty people until one or two in the morning; drinks, dancing, the record player on full blast and all the rest of it. One time I said to Lady Em, after my birthday one year it was, I said I did hope we hadn't kept her awake. She wasn't just being polite, she said she hadn't heard a thing. Because another time when Jocelyn had some people in, he did the same thing with me and apologized to me next day for the noise: but I'd not even known he'd had people there. Any noise there is goes right off up into the sky without troubling anyone. And as for people underneath, since we're actually on top of the roof rather than with just a floor and ceiling between us there's not a sound can either come up or go down to them.

Yet I don't think of my penthouse as utterly detached and separated from the estate. When I come into the downstairs entrance on the ground floor at the bottom, that's where home starts for me. I've got to know one or two people in the actual tower itself, chatting while we're waiting together to come up in the lift for instance. They nearly always get intrigued if you tell them you live in a penthouse on the roof; and they jump at it when you ask if they'd like to come up one evening for a drink and have a look. So I've made a few friends in that way: there's a young man and his wife from the eleventh floor, we take it in turns, I go down to them for a drink or a meal once a month then next time they come up here to me. The wife's a very nice girl; she can't keep out of the kitchen when I'm cooking, she thinks she says it's all so – well actually the word she uses is 'dinky'. I'm quite a good cook and I like experimenting with Indian and Chinese dishes and that sort of thing. All she knew about Chinese food was it was something you got at takeaways. She's got quite keen on learning about it now. Another couple I'm friendly with are two elderly ladies on the seventeenth. Listen at me, I don't suppose either of them's all that much older than me actually. They're very keen on chess, and one or other comes up for a game about once a week. They both think I need looking after; they say I don't get enough to eat and don't look after myself, they're really very sweet. I tell myself one day I'll have them up for a meal and do a terrific banquet for them, but that might look like showing off. Another thing they're always telling me is I should find myself a nice young lady and get married. I say to them if I did I'd have to move out of this lovely home, which is true because the GLC won't allow more than one person to live in each penthouse. They say as well they're sure I must get lonely up here on my own. If they only knew what a very full life I have! I seem to have friends dropping in all the time, especially in the evenings in the summer. They come for a drink on their way home from work and a breath of fresh air on the balcony; or just to relax at weekends because they all say they find it an easy place to relax in. I can understand it, I certainly find it like that myself.

– In the seven years since I came, I've never yet been away for a summer holiday. I could easily afford to go anywhere I wanted, but there's nowhere I want to go that could compare with doing what I do on holiday which is stay right here. If the weather's nice – and it might sound silly but I long ago persuaded myself it really is nicer up here than down on the ground – I sit out all day on the balcony. I make myself little salad meals, have a gin and tonic or two in the evening around six, then a quiet meal on my own or with a couple of friends, and play the record player and drink a bottle of wine. Each time it's a really warm night I put a sun lounger out on the patio and sleep out there. And doing that for a couple of weeks at a stretch is a wonderful holiday. It's not because I'm mean about money, simply because I don't know anything to beat it. You can keep holiday flats in Malta or Ibiza; nothing suits me better than pottering around here in a pair of shorts and a sunhat. I don't often feel lonely as a rule, but if I do all I need do is pick up the phone and invite friends round in the evening, or invite myself to their place.

In my holiday weeks I treat myself to a couple of theatre tickets, go and watch cricket at Lords or the Oval, and that's the perfect holiday to me. No travel, no packing, no waiting in airport lounges, no rip-offs about prices of food. What else more could anyone want? I think the general public's whole idea of council estates should be altered – they're not all one great amorphous mass of exactly similar people. The people on an estate aren't all the same, the places they live in aren't all the same: you only need to walk round this estate to see that. Tower blocks, those long things over there, what do they call them, 'linear' blocks is it? Then if you go round Gorrivale Square there's a mixture of Georgian houses, Victorian houses, nice little blocks of flats like Moxley and Farnham: a tremendous variety of architectural styles which is as it should be, I hate everything looking the same. You get all kinds of people too, and that's another thing which is good: in the shopping precinct on a Saturday morning there's every colour of skin under the sun, which is marvellous. It gives me a real sense of, what is it they say, 'one world and only one mankind'. Lively and colourful, I love it, it's great. I know I'm specially lucky, but to be any sort of council tenant is the best value for money anyone can get. And even if it is a horrible cliché, for me happiness is living on Providence Estate.

Part Two

THE FLATS

MOXLEY

'Not a word against the Queen'

Joan Kirkby

– I live in the best flat in the best block of flats on the best council estate in the whole of London. I'm – blimey – forty-eight, I've got two children grown up and married, that's Johnny twenty-four and Mandy twenty-one; and young Mark is still with us, he's twelve. I've been married twenty-eight years; my husband's Leonard. He's a carpenter and joiner, and he's the best husband anyone could ever wish to have. We've lived here sixteen year and we wouldn't ever want to live nowhere else. I don't mean nowhere else but this estate neither: I mean we wouldn't want to live anywhere in the world but on this estate, because here where we are is the nicest part.

I wouldn't give you a thank you for one of the snobby parts like Jesmond Close, and I definitely wouldn't want to live in one of those tower blocks the other side of Robins Walk. I feel very sorry for anyone who has to live there, it must be awful: so lonely, you never see anyone it'd drive me mad. My mum used to live in that one called Chorley. She hated it so much, we went to the council about it. In the end we got her into one of the flats on the ground in Farnham, the next block to this one. She's dead now, she died last year; and it's nice to feel I had her here near me the last ten years. I'm sure she felt the same way.

These blocks of flats have got three floors counting the ground level which is nearly all flatlets for old people. They've got a first floor and a second floor with a balcony running along outside. There's three families to each floor, and then I think it's four old people on the bottom. So you'll get between twenty and thirty people all told in one block. That's a nice number, and it gives everyone chance to know everyone. Some of those big long blocks like Vernon and

Foxman they've built near the towers, they must be terrible: five hundred people in each one of them, someone told me once. What chance have any of them got living there of getting to know one another?

In these small blocks it's far better, it's far different from that. To start with we're nearly all local people, all got moved in here together from the same streets, when our houses there were pulled down. So that gives us a good community spirit. If it's somebody's birthday on your landing, we always have a bit of a singsong along the balcony. If it's a wedding or a funeral, everyone turns to and cleans the landings and the stairs because there'll be visitors coming. And if ever anyone's in trouble, say with someone sick or something, they'll come and knock on your door if they need help and they'll ask for it. And that's how living should be – I can't stand unfriendly people. And all that's why I say I wouldn't want to live nowhere else, this is the best place there is anywhere.

'Scuse me a minute love, I think that'll be Mr Cross at the door, he said he might call if he was passing through. I'll just go and tell him I've got company and I can't see him till next time.

Joan Kirkby was small and plump with dark hair and brown eyes, and a bright floral-print dress of yellows and greens. She smoked heavily and laughed often. Two budgerigars twittered quietly and constantly in an ornate cage on a stand. The room was papered in a pattern of large blue flowers climbing up Grecian columns, and comfortably furnished with a leather-upholstered three-piece suite and a shaggy-pile grey carpet. A cocktail cabinet, a sunray clock on the wall, mounted display shelves in each corner with porcelain flower bowls and cart-horses and lions and dogs and a wooden elephant and photos in silver frames.

– My favourite place is this room, I call it my living room, not sitting room, that'd sound too grand. And it is a living room, it's got a lived-in feel to it, everything there is in it has got some connection with our lives, everything is a reminder of something. That china bowl of flowers was given me by my Len when my mum died, the lion we bought on our holidays at Margate, the wood elephant Mark gave me for our silver wedding. Everything's all got a special meaning: even the budgies' cage was a present to them for their first birthday.

It's funny now to think when we first came I was right miserable about it, I wept buckets. I'm a person who doesn't like change you see. The street where we'd been living was a right slum, but it'd been our home for such a long time you see hadn't it. It took me weeks to get used to here, I was the miserablest person in the whole block. I didn't settle down properly at all not for the first four years, not until I had Mark. Then everybody was so neighbourly; they helped me with shopping for me the last few weeks, and they had a big party on the landing when I came back from the hospital with him. It taught me a real lesson, I realized what a right miserable sort I must have seemed to everyone up till then. So after that I pulled myself together. I've been happy ever since, much happier here than I ever was in the old street.

I know it might sound stupid but I am, I'm still a person who doesn't like change. When it comes holidays and we go away to our caravan at Margate, I really hate it I do. I can't wait till the holidays are over and we can get back home. Len won't let me do any cooking while we're there; there's a self-service restaurant on the caravan site and we eat all our meals there, even breakfast. He says for those two weeks I've not got to lift a finger. I must be right spoiled because I don't, I really don't appreciate it one bit. I'm always grumbling about everything the whole time, I don't know how him and Mark put up with me. It's all because I want to be back here. Then, as soon as we get back, I clean the whole place through from top to bottom. Len laughs at me because I've cleaned it all for days before we've left haven't I, and there's been no one in it while we was away. But it just gives me that feel of being back home, getting everything back under my hands again. That's why I like doing housework: all the time, any time, I never ever don't like doing it. I can't understand women who say it's a chore, to me it's my pleasure. Have another cup of tea and some more biscuits love. Go on, then I can have another biscuit too though I know I shouldn't.

We've had our worries and problems in our time, but who hasn't, and ours've been no worse than anyone else's. The main one, which is over altogether by now thank heaven, was when our eldest boy Johnny was younger. When he was at school, him and some of his mates were hopping the wag like all kids do, and one day they got into trouble for thieving. I don't remember what it was they'd had, I think it was some tyres they'd nicked from a scrapyard. When the police came round asking for him and told us what it was about, I cried for nights in all that time we were waiting for him to come up in court. Len and I were asking ourselves why it'd happened, what had we done wrong in the way he'd been brought up, because it wasn't as though he'd gone short for anything.

Then we had to go to court. All you can do is you have to sit there and listen. It makes you ashamed to know it's your son who's mixed up like that in something. I don't know who was the worst out of the three of us, him or Len or me, we were all feeling terrible. In the end all he got was a ticking off and a ten-pound fine, and he was bound over for twelve months.

When we got home we sat down and we had a real serious talk with him, about how lucky he'd been not to get something far worse for punishment than he did. We made it clear to him that from then on if there was the slightest thing, anything at all, he was down as having a record now and in all probability next time he'd get sent away. It worked – there's been nothing at all since, and as he's grown up and married now and they've started a family of their own, I should think things are going to be all right. You can't ever forget it though, something like that. Not long ago our youngest, Mark, he was looking as though he might be going the same way; he was knocking around with a gang of boys older than himself spending all their time round the garages at the bottom of Foxman and Vernon. Len and I had a talk, and we asked Johnny to come over and give Mark a real good talking to, which seemed to us the best way to handle it. Johnny did, he told him straight not to be a fool, and so far as we know Mark's seeing sense and is all right now.

– When I told my daughter the other day about our talks she was really surprised. She said she couldn't imagine me talking to someone about my life and my ideas about things. It's funny how your own children don't think about you as people who might now and again do things on their own. She's always taken me for granted as her old mum who used to feed her and do her washing when she was young. I suppose all kids do that with their parents; when I thought about it I thought well I expect I was just the same with my mum. Before she died I never had one conversation with my mum about anything deep with her, not in all our lives.

My Len, he's not like that though. I tell him what I can remember about what sort of questions you ask me and what sort of answers I give you, and he says he thinks it's a good thing for me to do it. Mind you, he'd think anything was a good thing for me to do that wasn't connected only with the home and housework. He's always saying I need my horizons broadening and I ought to think about outside things much more. I told him that all right then, today I was going to tell you about my favourite subject, which is the Queen.

I'm a real hundred per cent royal, I am. You hear people criticizing her, saying what does she want all those palaces and all that money for, why doesn't she work for her living and all the rest of it; and I do, I get downright mad about it. Not a word against the Queen will I listen to ever, not one. I think she's a wonderful person and she does a wonderful job. I wouldn't say I'm all that keen on her husband, but then he's never been brought up to it like she has. I think she's so unselfish, she devotes all her life and always has done, to the good of her people. I don't know about her giving others all these honours and awards, I think if ever anyone deserved to have the biggest one of the lot, I think she herself does.

When the Jubilee was on, I went to see her in different parts of London, altogether about six times. I went to the docks when she was there, I was in the Mall at five o'clock one morning waiting for her to come past at eleven, I stayed up till midnight one night outside Buckingham Palace, I was one of those cheering her in the rain outside St Paul's Cathedral. And there was somewhere else too, I forget now where it was, that I went to see her as well. On one of the walkabout tours she did, I was as close to her as we're sitting opposite each other now. That was the most exciting moment of my whole life.

I think the Queen is a really lovely person; I don't care how much money she's got, she earns every penny of it. But it never changes her, deep down she'll always be an ordinary everyday person with a house to run and a family to bring up. You can tell that from her face, when you see her among people; she's right close to them, and she really cares for her people and what happens to them. I'm sure in elections and things she votes Labour like all the rest of us ordinary people do.

Anyhow, that's it and I wanted to get it off my chest to you. There's too many people always knocking the royal family, it shouldn't be allowed, it's quite wrong. I know the Conservatives try to make out royalty all belongs to them; they're forever waving the Union Jack aren't they when they have their conferences. Well, it doesn't take me in, and it doesn't take the Queen in either, I wouldn't mind betting that. The only people who are Conservatives are business people, those who own banks and things, and want to conserve what they've got. But the Queen doesn't really own anything at all herself – it's all the state's and when she does it's got to be handed to the Prince of Wales, so she doesn't get much of it herself. I don't know why people don't give her a lot of credit for that.

All my family, they all always pull my leg about it. My daughter says she doesn't understand if I feel like that, how it is I vote Labour. I tell her she's got hold of the wrong end of the stick, one day she'll realize the truth. We have some terrible arguments – only in fun though, it's not something we carry on afterwards. I've never voted any other way: the Conservatives are the monied people, the Liberals are nothing but a lot of toffee-nosed stuck-up middle class, and it's only Labour who are for the working class. To tell you the honest truth, I don't know anyone who does vote for the Conservatives, not in our part of the world. I've never heard of anyone doing it.

– You wouldn't believe it what a horrible family I've got, they are, they're right horrible they are. They all always come round for dinner on Sundays; last Sunday there was Johnny and his wife and kids, and Mandy and her husband, and Mark. Len got me going telling them what I'd been saying to you about the Queen. I was all quiet and sensible about it and told them everything what I'd said that I could remember. Well you should have heard them! They started falling about laughing all over the place something really dreadful! I told them if they didn't stop it I was leaving home. I don't know what they think's so funny about it; I told them most people think like I do, they all ought to go and try living in Russia if they think it's so funny. And they wouldn't leave off, they're awful. My daughter Mandy, she is, she's the worst one of the whole lot.

That's her, this picture of her is outside the church at her wedding. That was two years ago, oh I did, I cried and cried. You do, don't you, much more when it's your daughter than if it's your son. She and me have always been very close, and I'm glad to say we still are – she rings up twice a week every week to see how things are going here. Her husband, our son-in-law David is a very nice young man, we all get on well: in their case it's true, when she got married it wasn't losing a daughter, it really was like gaining another son.

That's his parents with Len and me; and then this is all of the guests together. It was a big do, we had about a hundred all told. I've got dozens of photos. These special ones I keep out and look at them nearly every day. That's Mandy and David, and that's the bridesmaids and the vicar at the church here who married them. He's quite dishy isn't he, the vicar? I could quite fancy him, even though we don't ever go to church. But I'm not all that keen on that man there: he was the best man. He was David's best friend. Well, he was until his own marriage broke up because he went off with some-one. She was a married woman too.

I don't hold with that sort of thing. There's nothing wrong with a girl having a good time when she's younger, or a boy either for that matter. But once you're married that's it. You shouldn't mess about: you've made your choice so you should stick with it. You can usually tell long before it gets serious whether something could develop out of an acquaintanceship or not; least the woman always can, I wouldn't know about men. If there's any danger of it getting out of hand, I think you should stop seeing that person there and then before it goes any further. I may sound old-fashioned about it, but I do feel very strongly that people let their families break up much too easily these days. I've told both my children when they were engaged – before they got married I said if I ever heard so much as a whisper about them messing with someone else, they needn't expect any sympathy about it, I'd be down on them like a ton of bricks. What makes me feel so strong about it I think was perhaps my own dad and mum: neither of them was all they might have been in that way, and it didn't get them happiness from it. You've got to be able to rely on your partner not to play tricks on you. That's always how Len and I have been right since we were married, we've both known that whatever else happened we could always trust each other that way.

He goes out Fridays for his game of snooker, and he's always back here on the dot by ten o'clock. I tell him I don't mind if he stops till eleven but he never does, he says he'd sooner come home. I never go out in an evening myself, I never have not on my own, there's nowhere I'd want to go. Mandy says that's old-fashioned for women nowadays; but if it is it is, that's how I am and I'm too old now to be any different. I tell her I've seen the other side of things with my own parents. I wouldn't want my marriage to end up like theirs, with them both rowing and sick of the sight of each other. One man one woman is what I believe in. If I didn't have a husband as good to me as Len I might think different, but I haven't and I don't. So I can't say about that, I can only speak from my own experience.

If my children have the good life I've had, I'll be well content. You can only do your best for them and try to bring them up in the right way and hope they'll get the benefit from it. We've been lucky, our two eldest so far have got married to very nice people. Johnny's got two children and Mandy's due in the spring, so there's grandchildren coming along and that's a new lot of different things to look forward to. It's like having your own children all over again, but with not the same amount of worry. Len and I are well pleased about it all, we were saying about it only last night. It makes you feel life goes on doesn't it, realize what the point of it is. I'm not much of a church person, so I don't believe in any more life after when you die: it's just all here and now, and if there is any part of you that's going to carry on after you've gone, the only way it can do that is in your children and grandchildren. Well anyway, that's what I think.

MOXLEY

'Teacher Miss'

Clare Foster

The sitting room of her second-floor flat had a large picture window with a view of the distant group of towers. It had a light blue and white mottled carpet, buttercup yellow moquette armchairs, a shaggy off-white rug. Along the walls melamine shelving on varying-level fittings carried books, records, a run of the National Geographic, *a terracotta figurine, a sweet jar filled with polished pebbles, an arrangement of cornstalks and honesty in a M'dina glass vase.*

– I teach at a local girls' school, my subjects are history and economics up to 'O' level with the fifth form. I'm twenty-five and I've been there – and here – for three years. The flat comes with the job, not necessarily this one, but one somewhere on the estate would. Accommodation is automatically offered if you're a teacher at any local school. It's a two-bedroomed flat, and my flat mate is Deidre, another girl who teaches at a different school in the area.

There are two hundred girls at the school, in the age range from eleven to fifteen, and there's a junior school attached. By no means all the girls come from this estate, the catchment area is much wider. Similarly, a lot of girls on the estate go to schools further away. Our school has a good reputation, and there are a lot more girls wanting to come than there are places. I never quite understand what makes parents pick on a particular school as the one they want their child to go to; nor do I understand how a school's reputation becomes what it is. Word of mouth, which seems to be the usual thing at the bottom of it, is really very unreliable. But it never fails to surprise me how parents will put our school as their number-one choice when they've never been to see it, never talked to a teacher there, and don't ever come near it if their daughter does get in. And they then tell other people in their turn that it's a very good school. Weird.

This is my first job since leaving training college so my own experience has been limited, but I can see nothing special in our school that would make me feel I wanted a child of mine to go to it. It's a perfectly ordinary run-of-the-mill girls' school with nothing to recommend it. I wouldn't say there was anything specifically bad about it, but there's nothing either that makes it what I think a good school should be. The attitude that comes down from the Head, and affects both staff and pupils, is that education is something which has to be gone through as painlessly as possible. There's never any suggestion it could or should ever be something creative and enjoyable: work is the be-all and end-all, and without any clearly defined reason or objective in view.

I find this depressing. I might be wrong in saying it, but I think it's due to a very much working-class attitude, particularly concerning girls. What girls do is go to school, get the rudiments of an education, leave and take some kind of routine job, and then get married and have children. Women's liberation, where are you? The gender role-casting is a hundred-per-cent taken for granted: boys and men have one set of activities, girls and women another, and all line-crossing is prohibited.

To give an everyday example, one evening last week I'd been to see a friend on the other side of the estate and I was coming back at half past seven through the shopping precinct at Robins Walk. There must have been at least fifty or sixty boys on their skateboards there, whizzing about; but as far as I could see there wasn't a single girl, not one even watching them. Girls don't get given skateboards for a start. But what I thought was extraordinary in addition was they don't seem to be out in public at that time of night. Or if they are they must all go somewhere else, because they're taking it utterly for granted skateboarding is not an activity for girls.

They don't seem to be particularly unhappy or suppressed about their situation, girls seem to accept it absolutely without question. It's not strictly speaking in my province, but I did try once last term to get a discussion going in class about it with some of the fifth-form girls. It fell like lead – I don't think most of them even grasped there was any such subject for discussion as women's roles. There's a bookshop over the other side of London I go into occasionally when I'm staying with friends I have who live near there. It's a feminist one, run by a women's collective, and it's in a residential suburban area. Presumably it must be viable as it's been going now for a couple of years. I often wonder how long it would last if it was here – not more than a month I should think. There's a tremendous long way to go for feminists even in the middle class, but in the working class they haven't even begun.

I've a friend who's a teacher at a boys' school: there it's different, there's parental pride in boys, and a wanting for them to get on merely because they are boys. The working-class *milieu* is a totally male-orientated one: mothers don't want or expect anything for or from their daughters. Those daughters when they grow up imprint the same outlook and attitudes on their daughters, and so it goes on from generation to generation.

It must sound like the height of snobbery when I say I wouldn't want any child of mine to be brought up and educated in a working-class area. And it may be snobbery, but it's entirely because I find attitudes towards women so repressive and I can't see them changing, not in my lifetime.

– I wish now that when I was at college I'd done sociology and psychology as my main subjects; they seem to be much more relevant now to present-day society than the ones I did. I only realized it when I came to work here. If an opportunity presented itself in the future for me to go on and do further study at a university for example, that's the field in which I'd like to do it. I think that's very unlikely though, because of the necessity for me to earn my own living. I don't see any prospect of marrying and being content to raise a family; as an idea that doesn't greatly appeal to me either. I meet so many mums at school whose lives are scarcely their own at all: their children are put first, their children are their only interest, there's nothing else in life for them. They're content it should be like that, which is how they manage to go on with it; but I couldn't and wouldn't be myself.

With an outlook and attitudes like mine, I do feel somewhat isolated. I have no other friends on the estate besides Deidre. She and I get on well together, which of course is essential if you're going to share a flat. We met when we were at college, we had rooms next to each other for the first two years and then shared digs, so by then we knew we could get on and wouldn't have any problems between us.

I think it would be impossible for me to have friends, largely because of the class difference I was talking about: and it's made even more difficult by my occupation. When I go shopping I often bump into the mothers of the kids I teach, some of them not much older than I am, but they always give me a status much higher than I like. The doctor gets the same kind of thing, I imagine: nobody talks to you as a person, only as a symbolic figure. I'm 'Teacher Miss' to the girls at school, and I'm 'Teacher Miss' to their mothers too when they meet me on the street. I find it awkward and embarrassing because I've not been able to find any way of changing it. And mothers who are twice my age treat me with this inordinate respect, which means nothing but a complete block to communication between us. They won't question anything I say, and they wouldn't dream of arguing about anything in the way of an observation I might make in passing.

I'd describe myself politically as mildly left-wing: and sometimes I say things to them about the school and how we haven't got something I think we ought to have because the government or the local authority hasn't made proper provision for it. 'Yes Miss Foster' they say, 'No Miss Foster three bags full Miss Foster.' If I'm particularly annoyed about something, which I quite often am, I'll let fly with a remark that the only way we'll ever get the situation altered is to have a change of government. Off we go again 'Yes Miss Foster, quite right Miss Foster'. But they're not going to do anything about it, however strongly they might genuinely agree with me. The most important thing to them seems to be to placate me and go along with whatever I say.

I don't know if you've been in Absalom Road yet; there's that long terrace there of houses which are all due for demolition. A lot of the people who are still living there, pretty nearly all of them in fact, are squatters: and you may have seen a few of the black people down at this end who are Rastafarians. You can tell which ones are the Rastas because they usually have their hair in dreadlocks and wear knitted woolly hats in their colours of red and yellow and black and green. I thought it might be a good idea one day to ask one of them if he'd come to the school and tell us about their religion and its history. The Head was away ill; and the Deputy who is a much more enterprising person gave me permission to approach one of them. Nothing came of it in the end – the man I went to see said he'd talk to his friends about it to see if they agreed but I presume they can't have, since no one got in touch with me.

However, the point I'm making is that a lot of people, including quite a few of the girls at school, including a number of the black ones, are really very frightened of the Rastas and repeat all kinds of scare stories about them. I took it for granted, when I told the girls that a Rastafarian might be coming to talk to them that there would be some complaints at least from a few of the parents. The Deputy Head was convinced there'd be a flood, but was prepared to back me up when it came. But what happened was that there wasn't a murmur about it, not a single complaint seemed to be approaching from anyone. I found it astonishing, and naturally I began to wonder if the girls had got together and decided none of them was going to tell their parents.

The next Saturday morning when I was out shopping I saw one of the parents, and I decided to take the bull by the horns. I asked her straight out did she object to my inviting a Rastafarian to come to the school and talk to the class her daughter was in. Immediately it was 'No Miss Foster, oh no of course not Miss Foster'. Well I may be doing her and all the other parents a terrible injustice, but I simply don't believe this estate is the central tolerance point in the world. What I do believe, and what I conclude from that experience, is that it was more important to the parents not to upset Teacher than anything else. I've often wondered since then just how far one would have to go before the parents would be stirred into action.

I won't start on any other subject now, someone's coming to see me at half past five and I've a few things I must attend to first.

– I seem to remember last week I was talking to you about the attitudes of working-class people, particularly parents' towards their children's education. It struck me afterwards it was very presumptuous of me to generalize in that way, because I remembered my own childhood; and what I said in no way applies in my own case, although I come myself from a working-class background, even if it wasn't one exactly like this here.

I was born in Barnsley, my father was a coal miner and my mother worked in a factory. I was an only child, and I went to a girls' grammar school in north Yorkshire. It was a long struggle for my parents to keep me there, but I was their only child and I remember my father was always telling me a good education was the most valuable thing there was in life. That I was a girl, and he might ever have wished he had a son instead was never something I even ever thought of. It was never suggested – nor was it ever suggested either that being a girl was some kind of handicap, or in some way you were a second-class being. In the end I didn't turn out as educationally talented as my parents hoped I would: there was not much chance of my going to university. Teacher-training college was about right, it was my level. I did well there and enjoyed it, and I think my parents were pleased enough. My father died during my first year, but my mother's still alive and living with her sister in Leeds.

I came to live and work in London because the glamour of London attracted me like it does a lot of young people in the north. You look on London as the centre of everything worthwhile in the country:

music, theatre, art exhibitions, fashion, the lot. I wanted to work and live in a working-class area of it because that was the background I'd been brought up in, and so despite what I've been saying in the past weeks about attitudes I don't feel alienated from the environment here. I should hate to live in one of the plushier places like Kensington or Finchley or somewhere of that kind. I'm happy and settled here in this part of London. I don't see myself staying here though for good, I'm fairly sure I won't.

As I've said before, marriage is not something which greatly attracts me as an idea. I quite like men: but I've never met one yet who I've thought I'd like to settle down with. I like children but I wouldn't want to have too many, not more than two at the outside.

Perhaps this is the time to tell you, if you haven't already worked it out, that I do have a child – I've a little boy who's six months old now. A woman who lives in one of the flats further along on this floor looks after him for me during the day. She's two small children of her own, and she's exceptionally nice with him. Normally I call in and collect him as I come home from school, but up to now so far when it's been a day you were coming she's kept him an extra hour or so for me. I had him as a result of a brief affair with someone who's a good deal older than I am, and married. The whole thing had completely ended before Julian was born, and I don't think I've any particular hang-ups about it now. His father knows of his existence: he came to see him not so long ago, but it was a hideously embarrassing experience for both of us. If I'd ever been in love with him, which frankly I don't think I ever was, by that time I didn't feel a flicker for him. He was polite and did his best to make conversation, but I think the thing uppermost in his mind was whether I was going to ask him for money towards maintenance. During all the time I was pregnant I hadn't even ever tried to even contact him, so he needn't have worried. All the same, I think he did worry when I got in touch and asked him if he'd like to come and see his baby.

I could have had an abortion, or I could have tried to have the baby adopted. Neither of those alternatives seriously crossed my mind though: all along I wanted to have the baby, I've no regrets about it so far. I may have later as Julian grows up, I may feel it's not good for him not to have a father or at least a father figure: but I'll deal with that situation if and when it arises, or try to. This much I am sure of – it would be stupid to try and guess a long way ahead what the problems are going to be and take steps which I hope will avoid them. The problems you're expecting usually don't materialize, and the ones that do are those you never thought of.

In this respect, about having an illegitimate child I mean, I've had nothing but helpful understanding from everyone I've come in contact with round here. Some people have offered me very obvious sympathy, which is something I don't need, don't want, and feel is entirely inappropriate. But as far as I can tell most people's reaction seems to have been one of acceptance and a desire to be of help in absolutely practical ways. At school the Head and Deputy both know: when I said I would have to be taking maternity leave their only questions were about how long I would be away, and assurances that I could take as long off as I needed without worrying about whether my job would still be here when I came back.

Equally my flatmate Deidre has never been anything but tremendously helpful. She could have complained with good reason the first few weeks about Julian crying at night, but she never did; fortunately that soon wore off and he settled down. She also made a point of saying to me she thought I should go out for an evening at least once a fortnight, and if I would there'd be no problem about a babysitter. In that respect she's been wonderful. Sometimes my evening out is a visit to the theatre and I go with her; in that case I give the flat key to the woman further along, and she pops in two or three times while we're out to see that Julian's all right. If he's awake and crying she takes him back with her to her flat.

I think all the people who live in this block know now that I've got a baby because they see me with him in the pram. A lot of them make a point of coming to have a look at him when I'm going down the stairs going out. Some of them give the impression they think I'm married and have got a husband, but he's probably gone off and left me or died. But as I don't wear a ring I'm sure a lot of them have a fairly shrewd idea what the true situation is. Unless I'm being particularly obtuse about it, which I don't think I am, no one has ever so far as I can see given me a moment's embarrassment about it. I've never seen anyone looking sideways at me or trying to pretend they haven't seen me.

This has made an impression on me I'm sure I'll never forget. Your *Guardian* women trendies make a big thing about women's right to have children without necessarily tying themselves down to a husband and home. Well here, in this truly working-class part of the world, it's accepted fully and naturally without discussion. There's no patronizing, no condescension, no effort-making whatsoever. It's entirely genuine, and in that respect much more agreeable to be living among. In all fairness I'd like that to be put alongside my criticisms of working-class attitudes towards women; they might in some respects be rigid and unseeing, but in others they're far more tolerant than anyone in other classes and other groups.

MOXLEY

'Sylvia Deeds was a lady'

Mr Elliott

The handwriting was irregular and thin, each line falling away at the side of the notepaper.

> No. 5 Moxley Ho.   Weds.
> Dear Sir,
>   Thank you for letter recd, I will help you if I can. It would be best for me on Mondays at midday, as all other days is busy.
> Yrs truly,
>   Mr. J. Elliott.
> P.S. Please knock as bel out at present.

He lived in a ground-floor flatlet which had its front door opening into a large bedsitting room, off which there was a kitchen at one side and a combined bathroom and toilet at the other. A slight frail hollow-cheeked man with sparse white hair and pale-blue eyes, he sat stiffly upright in a dark suit and collarless shirt in a wooden fireside chair.

– I'm seventy-eight and I've lived here ten years. Before that I was in another GLC old person's flat but I didn't like it, it got to be too noisy with the people up above me who was West Indians. A social worker came to see me, she said she thought I would be better off in somewhere like this where I could get out of the door without having to keep going up and down stairs all the time, and a few weeks later they moved me to here. They asked me if I'd like to go into an old people's home but I said I didn't want to. They said would I go and look at an old people's home, I said no I didn't want to, I'd sooner

83

have my own place with my own few things that I've still got. The bed there I've had for thirty years, that wardrobe where I keep my clothes in belonged to my sister, and that sideboard with the cupboards is one I've had a very long time, I should say since before the war. I keep my collection of tapes there in that top right-hand drawer with my tape recorder which I use for playing them on. I don't use it now for recording things with; you have to press two buttons down at the same time with your fingers and I make a mess of it. I used to try and record music I liked from the radio, or some of the singing on a Sunday evening on the telly, but I gave that up a few years back.

I have had a very long life and if you were to ask me, I'd say it had been rather a poor one. I mean poor financially because I've never had much money at all, but poor in other ways too. My life has not been a very interesting one, not in my opinion it hasn't. I will tell you about it but you must ask me questions about what you want to know; if you don't, I shan't be able to think about things to say.

It is a busy life I have now because I find different things to do each day, and also at present I am always going to the hospital a lot. They are doing tests on me and they've told me they might have to have me in for another operation again. I have had four operations the last three years: one was for gallstones in the bladder, two were for the stomach and the first one was that I had a collapsed lung.

Mondays is best for you to come, because Tuesdays is my shopping day, I do the whole shopping on Tuesdays for the week. I go to the Co-op in Tullbrook Road because things are cheaper there; you have everything together where you can look round and pick out the things you want. They are good for people on their own like myself too: you can buy say one chop if you want one, or a small piece of meat only as big as that. They have cheese in small pieces that big, and you can buy two eggs at a time if you want them. Another thing they do is very small joints of meat: one that size will last me three days, roasted on Sunday cold on Monday and cut up in a stew with vegetables on a Tuesday. That way it comes out as good value. I find bacon is dear, if you're not careful it fries down to nothing. You think you're going to have a nice meal with bacon and say an egg, and then if you overcook it there's nothing left before you've started. The Co-op will also have a chicken leg or a chicken wing that you can buy on its own, which makes a change and a very nice meal.

I've forgotten now what I was talking about. Oh yes, the days of the week. On Wednesday I go to the old people's Day Club at near the church in Gorrivale Square. A bus comes round for you to see if you want to go at ten o'clock in the morning, and then again at one o'clock if you only want to go in the afternoon; then they bring you back again at about half-past four. Sometimes there are as many as a hundred people there at once and I find it a bit noisy. But they have quiet rooms where you can go and sit if you wanted to look at the newspaper or have a game of dominoes. I played a game of dominoes there with someone that lasted five hours one day.

Once a month they have an outing to somewhere, like the Tower of London or the fish market or down to the hop fields. You go in a coach, they give you sandwiches and an apple to take, it's all very well put on and makes a very enjoyable day. I don't go sometimes because I don't feel up to it though.

Thursday is cleaning and washing day. I hoover round and dust, polish the furniture, clean around generally and mop the floors in the bathroom and kitchen. Then in the afternoon I take my washing to the launderette in Tullbrook Road, then bring it back and iron everything. I like to have a clean shirt to put on every day, clean sheets every week, a clean tablecloth every other day. I think if you start letting things go you'd soon end up a disreputable-looking person in your personal appearance. There are one or two like that at the Day Club, you can see them beginning to go.

Fridays I usually go the club again and I might have a game of bingo: depending on how I feel, or perhaps I might sit and watch the big colour television they've got there. I wouldn't say I was a very social sort of person, I don't mix with people much, I've never been one for that at all really in my life.

There isn't much to say about Saturdays and Sundays. Mostly it depends on what the weather's like. There's a man I know at the Day Club, I might meet him in the pub for a drink: I drink one glass of lager but no more than that because of my stomach. Sunday afternoon I might watch a film on television, Sunday evening I sometimes go to the healing. That's spiritualism, there's a healing meeting every week over near where my sister lives. I don't go to seances very often because I don't get much from them, I like the healing better. At the seances there's a lady who's a medium, she's called Esme, she does clairvoyance. Each person has a guide in the spirit world, mine is called Red Feather, he was a Red Indian. They ask you if you want your guide to bring you someone you used to know to give you a message, but I've never had anything with Red Feather. I asked if my father was there, and another time my sister who'd died. They call it 'passed over'. But there weren't any messages I could make sense out of. Esme says it's probably because I'm not psychic enough. The healing is better, if you've got a pain the healer will put his hand on you and you can feel the warmth coming through.

I've never been married, I'm single. I look after myself and mostly keep myself to myself. My most enjoyable time is in the evening after my tea when I sit and play my collection of tapes. But I'm careful not to play them loud because of other people. Would you like to hear one of them before you go? Open that drawer and look through and pick out one you like.

Mario Lanza's Golden Hits Volume I. *Mario Lanza's Golden Hits* Volume 2. *Favourite Arias From the Operas sung by Mario Lanza. Twenty Great Songs by Mario Lanza. Mario Lanza's All-Time Favourites. Down Memory Lane with Mario Lanza. My Songs Are Your Songs, sung by Mario Lanza. Opera Time with Mario Lanza. The Voice of Mario Lanza. Mario Lanza's Golden Hits* Volume 3. *Immortal Moments with Mario Lanza. Nights at the Opera with Mario Lanza. More Nights at the Opera with Mario Lanza. More Nights at the Opera with Mario Lanza* Volume 2. *The Singer and the Song: Mario Lanza's Personal Choice. Specially For You: Memories with Mario Lanza. This is Mario Lanza's World.*

– As time goes on I find it much easier to talk than I thought I would. I think about what we've talked about and try to remember things for you, to talk about for next time.

I had a bad childhood, my mother died when she was forty and there was twelve of us children left for my father to look after. I think I was the youngest one, I went with two of my sisters into a home where I stopped till I was fourteen, then I was put to a job as a tea boy in a factory. That was the end of my education: and it was the end of our family too. Apart from the one sister I go to see, all the others I've not heard of in sixty or seventy years, I should think they're probably all dead by now.

I never had a trade. All my life I've had to get by without a trade, which means I've never had good jobs, only kitchen portering and being a packer or a labourer and things of that sort. I was in the First War towards the end of it. I joined up as soon as I could at sixteen and a half. It was better than no work. I never went anywhere, I stayed in England working in stores and camps, then when it was over I came back to the poorly paid jobs again. I think it's those sort of things have made me as I am, I have what's called an inferior complex. I don't know anything about anything and I don't find it easy to mix with people, I'm a very bad mixer. My sister is the domineering sort, she's two years older than me and that's how it's been all our life. I've always been frightened of her. She's been the one to tell me I should do this or do that, and most time's I have; or if it was something different I wanted to do, I had to do it in a way so she wouldn't find out.

Sometimes I have had the wish that I could undo things and start all over again. I would have liked to have had some sort of an education, at least so I could put a letter together for example. The one I wrote to you when you wrote to me asking me if you could come and see me for the book you were doing, I had to get the lady next door to come in and help me with writing the answer to it.

I about read a newspaper but not much else, but I don't take a lot of interest in things that are going on. I vote at elections, I always have done, but otherwise I don't take part in things. I have always voted the same way every time but I don't know much about it, I think I vote the way I do because of my father. I heard him talking about it once, saying what he voted, so I've taken the way I vote from him. Politics is a subject you don't talk about to my mind, because it's a secret ballot and you don't tell anyone. Did you say this is all confidential with no way anyone could tell who I was? All right then, I'll tell you: I vote Conservative. No one else in the world knows that.

If I could go back and start again and have an education, with my education that I had I'd like to have been a ballet dancer. I never told anyone about it when I was a boy because it's not the sort of thing you could tell anyone in those days. My sister's always had a sharp tongue, she'd have made my life merry hell if she'd ever found out; she would have laughed at me and said it in front of other people, and poked fun at me for it for all the rest of my days.

But once on a Sunday afternoon last year I saw a film on television, it was about a man who is a world-famous ballet dancer, he's got a name like Newrack. I believe there's a racehorse called by the same name too. It was wonderful to watch him, the way he danced was beautiful. Of course I never could háve done it the way he did, but that's what I would have liked to have done, I'd have liked to have been like him. There was a serial I used to watch on Sundays sometimes too, it was called something about ballet shoes.

I've never seen a ballet in a theatre, but whenever there's music from the ballet on the radio I make sure I listen to it. The one I like best is called Sylvia Deeds or some name like that. The music for that one is very beautiful. I don't know who wrote it or who the story is by – I believe Sylvia Deeds was a lady, perhaps even a princess. She must have been very beautiful for someone to write beautiful music like that about her. When I think about it I've got an idea that she was Polish, a Polish lady or something, but I can't be sure.

I asked them at the shop once where I get my tapes if they had a tape with that music on it but they didn't, the girl said she'd never heard of it. It was the Co-op, they have all the different tapes in a wire rack near one of the doors. She said I was welcome to have a look all through it. I did but I couldn't find anything that looked like it might be it.

I can afford to buy about one tape a month, one every four or five weeks say. The last one I got is called *The Magic of Mario Lanza*, a selection of his best songs: shall we have a listen to it before you go?

– They've sent for me to go into hospital again for another operation with my stomach on Friday, so it might be a few weeks before we can have any more talks after today. I won't be back here by next Monday, but if you come the week after that and I'm still not here, I expect they'll be able to tell you at the Day Club what is happening and how long it will be before I am back. Or you could ask at the lady next door's she might know. I can't tell you what her name is I've never asked her, but I shall be leaving the key with her in case of fire or so the gas man can read the meter and things like that. She said she'd have a look and see if there was post or anything; and if there was and she could manage it, she'd bring it to the hospital. But it would only be bills or football pools, so I can do without those for a week or two. I wouldn't expect her to come anyway: people say things like that but they usually don't really mean them, it's only because they feel sorry for you.

I've got my case packed there on the bed. I've done my packing because I like to be ready in good time. All I have to do now before I close it up is darn a hole in the elbow of that brown cardigan hanging over the chair there. I'm going to take that with me in case I need it for sitting up in bed. The doctor said to me that when I got over this operation I was going to be as right as rain: he didn't tell me what it was for and I didn't ask him because you don't like to bother them. He said it was essential for me to have the operation; they know what they're doing so I'm not worrying about it, I leave that sort of thing to them.

It's gone very quick the last two months you've been coming hasn't it? I was thinking about it the other day and how quick it had gone. Are you married?

I would have liked to have talked more about that subject and asked you questions about it: such as how long have you been married, do you have children and that sort of thing. I was married myself once.

It would be just after the War, the First World War as they called it, not long after I'd come out of the army. I was married for two years, then one day I came home and there was a note on the table to say she had left me and wasn't coming back. I've never heard a word from her or about her from that day to this. I should think she very likely went off with some other man, but I don't really know. She had taken her clothes and shoes. We neither of us owned very much because I wasn't earning good money, so what she had easily went into one suitcase.

My sister said it was good riddance, she didn't like her and she never had liked her and nor had her husband. I don't know about her husband because he'd never said; but my sister had often enough, and in front of her, so there was no love lost between them.

I never felt like marrying again after that – it seemed to drive me more back into myself than ever. It was a big shock, it was like getting a slap in the face. It's such a long time ago now, but I believe her name was either Cora or Connie, one of those. I hadn't thought about her for years and years, it all happened nearly sixty years ago now. I've not ever given it a great deal of thought in recent times. I'd go so far as to say that I've not had any feelings for women of any kind since then: I felt that I had had feelings and they'd been taken advantage of, so it was safer not to have them any more. Sometimes I've thought I would have liked to have had children in my life, but that's the only aspect of it I've missed. There are people at the Day Club you hear talking about their grown-up children sometimes, and not always very happily either. So you can't rely on it – perhaps I might not be missing all that much.

I will see you in two weeks' time shall I? No, don't waste your time coming to see me in there. I don't even know what the name of the ward is that I shall be in.

But it was not possible to see him in hospital: he died three days after his operation without regaining consciousness.

FARNHAM

'Some bloody do-gooding cow'

Mrs Williams

Her blue eyes blank with cataract, she sat in an old armchair with her two rubber ferruled sticks leaning against the arm of it and a pink ribbon in what remained of her wispy grey hair. When she heard the front door close she leaned forward slightly, listening.

– Has she gone dear, that young woman? There's just you and me here is there? I can about make out your shape if you're right in front of me, but I couldn't tell you what you look like. Are you a young man dear, you sound as though you are? Well that's young to me, I'm eighty-seven, so to me you're no age at all are you, goodness I've got grandchildren your age nearly.

Who was she, that young woman; do you know her very well, what is she, a social worker or something? I can't recall I've ever seen her before in my life. She sounded quite a nice young woman though didn't she, do you think she's all right? You can never tell these days can you, people come to your door and you don't know who they are, it's best not to let them in. She's from what do you say, Age Concern? I've never heard of that, what is it, what's it about? I don't remember anyone coming before from anything called that. When did you say it was, last week? If they did it's gone right out of my head.

And who are you dear, who are you from, what have you come to see me about? It's not that thing they call meals on wheels, is it? Because if it is, I don't want to sound rude dear but I don't want anything to do with it, you're wasting your time.

– I was left a widow when I was thirty, with five children to bring up: the eldest girl was twelve, then there were four boys, the youngest of them one year old. My husband worked on the railway, they came and knocked on my door one day and said he'd been run over by a train. I said I wanted to go and see him but they said they thought it would be better not. He'd only been on the railway about a month, too. He was a nice man my Wilfred: I still sometimes have a dream about him: I see him as real as anything, I wake up convinced he's here and I'm with him and we're sitting talking about how we're getting on and all that.

In those days there wasn't the social security and the other things what there is nowadays, so I just had to get on with it. I took people's washing in for them, I went and did cleaning in shops round about, I went on Sundays to help them if they wanted things carrying. I did everything that anybody would offer me, to bring money in. I would never tell anyone I couldn't manage, they'd have taken the children off of me if I had and put them in a home. I wasn't going to let that happen.

Being the eldest, my daughter had to stop at home and help me. She didn't get much schooling but that couldn't be helped: with me out at work till all hours there had to be somebody at home to fend for the boys. None of them got much of a schooling either, they had to leave as soon as they were old enough and get jobs. Things were very hard in those days.

Not being an educated person I couldn't get a regular job myself either: not until I was well past forty, then I was a cook at a road-haulage depot canteen in the docks. I got that job about the time when my youngest boy was old enough to leave school and earn his keep, which was when I didn't really need a steady job any more. But I took it and I stayed there more than twenty years. When I left they gave me a big party and a clock and there were speeches and they said 'Our dear Mrs Williams'.

After that I lived with my married daughter for a while. But her and me have never really what you might call got on. Her and her husband, they're very interested in one of these religious things, they go out knocking on people's doors and giving them leaflets and trying to convert them to their way of thinking. They say they're doing the Lord's work but I don't hold with it myself.

She told me one day she'd seen they were building these flats and she'd been and inquired off of the GLC if they had any old people's accommodation in them. The GLC told her yes they had, there were these ground-floor flatlets and if I'd like one they'd see what they could do. So that's how I got this place, and I've been here ever since

91

it was built twenty years ago. It was all brand new and very nice and smart when I first come; but the last six or seven years it's never had new wallpaper or a lick of paint or anything at all. I think they're supposed to do them out every three years, but they haven't done mine all that time. I expect it's this wicked Tory government we've got, they've never cared about old people have they? They never care about anybody but themselves they don't, leastways that's my opinion of them, I wouldn't give them houseroom.

I do get very tired dear, so I can't talk for long. Yes, that'd be nice, I hardly ever have visitors, you come and call on me whenever you like. Don't bother with the knocker, shout through the letter-box so's I'll know who you are: you might have to wait outside awhile for me to get to the door, but I'll recognize your voice and I'll come and let you in.

– What I live on is my state pension, but I don't like it because I don't like having to have charity. Now and again one of my sons will come over to see me and when he's gone there's a five-pound note left on the table: it makes me cross, but I think it'd make them cross if I gave it back to them so I use it for the electric because that's such a terrible expense now. This flat is all electric and it eats more money than I eat food. I used to have a gas stove for doing my cooking on, but as my eyesight started to go I couldn't tell when I wanted to turn the gas down if I hadn't turned it out. Sometimes it would be on and I hadn't lit it, and there was matches with a chance of a dangerous explosion, so they came and turned me into all electric. I think it was from the social, some bloody do-gooding cow interfering like they do: I can't stand these people knocking on your door saying they've got some form or another that's got to be filled in, how much is your rent, what do you do about your washing and all the rest of it. You're not from the social people are you dear? No I thought not, you don't sound like you are.

There's a lady comes in on a Tuesday and a Friday, she's one of the what they call home helps. Her name's Matty, she's been coming for seven years, and if it was left to me she might just as well not bother only the problem is I don't know how to get rid of her. All she does is as soon as she comes she says she'll put the kettle on and make a cup of tea. And then when she's done that, she sits and chats for two hours. She used to be very good, but now she doesn't do a blind thing except have a quick run round with a duster, ask me if I want any shopping bringing in, go and get it, and then she's off and I don't see her till next time. Once in a while she'll take my washing to the launderette, but it's God's honest truth that's all she does mostly, spends all her time talking to me. Not talking with me, or letting me talk to her: that wouldn't be so bad, but talking to me all the time, do you know how I mean? A lady came from somewhere once and asked me was everything all right, was I satisfied with the home help. I said I was. Well you have to don't you when it's somebody's job, you can't complain about them because they might lose it and nobody wants to put somebody out of work do they? I mean not except this Tory government we've got, they enjoy doing that, they're wicked; but nobody else would.

There's somebody called a voluntary visitor or something, she comes in as well. I think she's an old age pensioner who's got nothing else to do with her time, she comes about once a month. I don't know her name; but she's another of them, she wants to tell you what she's been doing, her ideas about this that and the other, she's another one gets on my nerves. Apart from her, that's the lot for my visitors. Mr Cross might call in now and again and make me a cup of tea if he happens to be passing, but no one else.

A typical day for me would be that I usually wake up about six o'clock, and I have my wireless on the table by the bed there and listen to that till about half past eight or nine. Then I get up and get dressed. I've got this very bad rheumatism in my hips and arms, so usually it'll take me an hour and a half to two hours to get dressed. I have to keep stopping for a rest. Then if it's the day for the home help she comes, and if it's not I'll make myself a cup of tea and start making my dinner. I don't like these things you get in packets, I don't think there's any nourishment in them: I'd sooner have a few potatoes and carrots with a bit of gravy. I might have a piece of meat, a sausage or something of that sort, or an egg, but not every day. In the afternoon I listen to the wireless again, I might have a doze until it's my tea time. Then I have something on toast as a rule. I like cheese or sardines or a tomato. Round about seven o'clock I'll have a cup of cocoa and a biscuit, then I go to bed and usually I drop off to sleep about nine.

But it's no use us going on talking about that subject, because I don't care what you say, I'm not having those meals on wheels. I think they're disgusting – all that white sauce over everything so you can't see what you're eating. I had one once six or seven years ago. I don't mean to be rude dear but if you go on until you're blue in the face I shan't change my mind. I'm not having them.

– Last night I had a dream, I dreamed I was out shopping. I was along the precinct there at Robins Walk, I was walking about and people were coming up and speaking to me and chatting, it was lovely. Then when I woke up and found it was all a dream, I started to cry. It's five years, no it must be more than that now, since I've been along there or anywhere else on the estate.

Sometimes one of my sons will come for me on a Sunday if it's a nice day in the summer and take me out for a little ride in his motor car. There's two of them live near enough to do that. The other two, one's in America and the other one I don't know where he is, I haven't seen him for years. The two that do come, Michael and Charlie, they're good boys but they've got wives and families and children of their own, they don't want to be bothered with an old woman and you can't blame them, not really.

The vicar used to come, but he seems to have dropped off lately. He told me off once for swearing, I do say 'bloody' and that; that might be why he doesn't come. Sometimes the chiropodist comes, she's another one spends all her time talking, I can't be doing with people like that. I don't know why people can't leave you alone; if they don't want me to talk to them, I'd sooner they didn't come and talk to me.

The person I like best is my neighbour next door, the one who goes and gets my pension from the post office for me. She comes and knocks on the door every two weeks for my book. She never says anything apart from 'Good morning' and she's never away more than half an hour because she knows I worry. Then she comes back and comes in and puts the money on the table and says 'Good morning' again, and then out she goes. That's it then, and I don't see her again for another two weeks.

It does get lonely sometimes, and I do sometimes I do have a bit of a cry about it. But I think to myself 'Well Clara' I think, 'Well Clara there's no use crying about it, you're getting to be an old woman now and you can't expect any different.' I used to be such an active person you see, never had a day's illness, brought up all my kids on my own, never asked anything from them since they was grown up and with families of their own. It's not as though I've been used to being a person who couldn't get about until these last years.

One of my boys, Charlie I think it was, he came to me one day and he said him and Michael and their wives had all been having a talk and they all thought it would be a good idea if I had a telephone. He said then if there was ever anything wrong any time, I could ring up and they'd come over; or if I like wanted the doctor I could call him. So they had this telephone put in for me.

It was, it was bloody awful. I said I didn't care if they were paying for it, it was more trouble than it was worth and they were to have it taken away. One thing was they used to ring up and tell me they couldn't come over at the weekend to see me, so they'd rung up for a chat instead. You can understand it, it made things a lot easier for them. But it got to be none of them came for weeks on end – as soon as I heard the phone ringing on a Friday night I knew who it was, it was either Michael or Charlie or their wife to say they were sorry they couldn't come.

The other thing would happen would be you'd be on the toilet or something and the bloody phone would start ringing. It always did it: I knew for sure if I went to that toilet the phone would ring. It was never anybody proper – it'd always be someone like the electricity people ringing up to say they were checking everything was all right, did I have any problems; or the home help woman would ring up, 'It's all right Mrs Williams it's only me, I thought I'd ring up to see how you are since I'm not going to be coming in tomorrow.' I used to feel like shouting I'd been all right till she rang up, why the hell didn't she push off. Only I didn't say push off, I used another word I won't say to you.

And a couple of times, this happened without a word of a lie, this is God's honest truth this is – twice it started ringing in the middle of the night. I switched my light on to see what time it was, and if I hold my alarm clock under that lamp and put my face right to it, I can see what time it is: and both times it was two o'clock. I didn't have my name in the telephone book, so where they'd got my phone number from I don't know: but it was a man, or it could have been a boy even, a young man. In all my life I've never heard anything like it, he said such dirty filthy things, over and over he kept on repeating them. I didn't know what to say so I didn't say anything, I couldn't think. You know you should put the phone down, but somehow at the time when it happens you stand there and you can't move. I nearly fainted with it. I let go of the hand thing, what do they call it, receiver, and I was, I was trembling so much I could scarcely get back to my bed.

I didn't dare put my light out and I don't think I slept any more. But I sort of drowsed off some time though, because the next thing I knew it was daylight and the telephone was making that whirring noise it makes when you haven't got it put down properly. I was very frightened but I didn't tell anybody, I didn't ring up my sons or anything. I wished I had, because the next night I've gone to bed again and the same thing happens, in the middle of the night it starts ringing again at two o'clock. I thought if I didn't switch my light on and didn't answer it, they might think I'd gone away and there was no one here. So I left it, I let it ring and ring. I don't know how long it went on, it seemed like hours but I swore I was never going to answer a telephone again, and I didn't.

Next morning I rang them up, the telephone people at the post office or wherever it is. I said I was an old woman on my own and I was frightened of electricity and they were to come straightaway that day and take it away. I don't remember if they did come that same day or not, but they did cut it off for me there and then until they could come and remove it. I never told them the real reason it was all about, and I never told my sons. I don't know who it was, for all I know it might have been the telephone people – but then somebody told the social I wasn't having the phone no more, so the next thing is they came round to see what was the matter and what it was all about. I never told them either.

That woman from the social, she was another of them, another bloody do-gooding cow. She said how was I going to let anybody know if I felt ill any time and needed help. I said if I did I'd shout; but oh no she said, that wouldn't do, I must have one of their cards to put up at that window there. It had got 'Help Wanted' in big letters on it so everyone could see it and come to help me. That's the sort of thing they do these people, they think up ideas and tell you to do this that and the other, and then they're surprised when you've no time for them afterwards.

What happened you see was that a few days after she'd give it me I did feel a bit queer, so I thought I'll ask someone if they'd go to the doctor for me and get me some medicine. I put the card up behind the curtain there against the window where anyone passing could see it, then I went and lay on my bed and waited for someone to come. Well no one came, did they? I dozed off, I went to sleep, and when I woke up in the morning there was nothing wrong with me so I carried on as normal. Only I'd forgot to take the card down: a day went by, two days, and I'd still forgotten all about it. Then on the third day in the afternoon I'm sitting in my chair having a doze, and there's a hammering and a banging on that door, and people climbing up on the ledge outside and trying to get their hand inside the window and open it. I was frightened out of my life. This is God's honest truth, I thought it was a gang of burglars or something trying to break in and kill me and steal my money.

After that I threw the card away. I thought if anything happened to me I'd sooner lie there on the floor I would for a couple of days, rather than something like that. That's the social for you.

– It's been a pleasure to talk to you dear, you call in when you're passing any time you like. Only you will promise me now won't you, you're not going to send anybody round from the meals on wheels? I mean it, I'm trusting you about it, all right?

RIVERS

'A woman ripe for liberation'

Alison Shaw

– Sherry, whisky, gin, rum, Cinzano . . . Christ it sounds as though I'm an alcoholic doesn't it? I think I'm going to have a gin and tonic tonight, what about you?

A small dark febrile woman, her hair neatly styled and cut smartly short; a navy-blue dress, plain except for thin white piping at the collar and cuffs of the threequarter-length sleeves. She sat on the edge of the settee, chain-smoking. Green eyes, pale face, thin lips; her voice was low and husky, her smile frequent and direct.

– I'll tell you the typical story of a working-class woman, right? I'm one myself, very much so, with the big difference that unlike a lot I can step back and look at myself from the outside, see what I was and how I became it, and see how I've changed into what I am now: a woman in the second year of doing social studies at a polytechnic, not yet a totally liberated woman, but certainly a woman ripe for liberation.

I'm thirty-nine and I was the third of four children, girl boy girl boy. My father was a vegetable market porter, and my mother went out cleaning: she had to, because in those days my old man's job was a very irregular one and she never knew how much money she was going to have at the end of the week, if any at all. Not to put too fine a point on it, he drank. He used to come home some nights and thump the first person or thing he saw – sometimes it'd be her, sometimes one of the kids, and failing that it'd be the dog or the cat or the goldfish.

He was a second-generation Irish Catholic immigrant, she was a good Catholic girl from Birmingham. How they met and when they came to London to live I've no idea, and I can't find out now because neither of them's alive. My eldest sister or brother might know more about it, but I've never bothered to ask.

Being brought up a Catholic didn't mean a great deal. My first communion at seven, church every Sunday, going to confession and having to think up things to confess, because a child of that age doesn't have any idea what it's all about. An ordinary uneventful childhood: no particularly terrible deaths or disasters that I can recall. A bit of playing truant from school, hopping the wag as we called it, but nothing very serious – everyone did it. I was the dunce of the family. The others all passed their exams and went to the prestigious local school. I didn't, and had to go a long way every day to a convent school.

The only thing I learned there was what a load of nonsense religion was – that was the only lasting effect school had on me. I didn't hate the religious instruction which made up such a large part of the curriculum, it just bored the pants off me: by the time I was fifteen and due to leave I'd spent more time daydreaming than I had thinking about the subjects I was supposed to be learning about all put together.

The height of my parent's ambition was that when I left I should get a nice job. That meant not going in a factory but into a shop. One of the chain stores had what was known as an apprentice scheme: they took girls who were school leavers, gave them lots of perks like a canteen lunch and ten per cent discount on purchases in the store, free medical attention, a hairdressing salon for the staff, and all sorts of other goodies which got them out of any obligation to pay a decent wage. I joined them and worked for them for four years, during which time I learned how to press buttons on a cash register. I also learned from the other girls an extension of my vocabulary, words which hadn't been taught us at the convent school such as 'shit' and 'fuck' and 'bugger' and 'sod'.

Little though the pay was, I always saved up enough money to go for my holidays once a year. To be fair to these chain-store people, they did give the staff a fortnight's holiday with pay, so I have to say that. I used to go with one of the other girls to a holiday camp. One year we picked up with a couple of boys. At the end of the holiday she and hers finished with each other, but I went on seeing mine after we came home because he lived not very far away. We were courting for about a year, and then when I was twenty we got married.

Nine months and a week later I had my first baby; two years after that I had my second; two years after that the third, only that one died when he was only a few weeks old; and then another two years and I had my third. So there I was, three kids and still under thirty; and for five years after that I lived in a council house – cooking, cleaning, dressing the kids and seeing they got off to school in time and went to the doctor's if they'd got a temperature or were being sick or had spots. A husband who was a telephone installations engineer, who gave me housekeeping as though it was some kind of prize I'd won for being a good girl, and who was having it off on the side regularly with any woman whose house he went to who gave him the eye. He didn't make any secret of it, he was quite proud of it: he never told me directly, but once a week on a Sunday he used to have his mates round for beer and games of cards, and he'd tell them about his week's adventures in a loud voice that wasn't difficult to hear whenever I was in the kitchen making sandwiches and pots of tea for them.

One day I was hanging the washing out and so was my next-door neighbour, and I started complaining about it. She listened for a while over the fence, then she patted my arm and said she'd got to get on; and without a trace of bitterness, absolutely and totally acquiescing to it she said 'Well dear mine's the same, that's men isn't it, it's only natural; they have to have their little fling.'

I stood there with my washing basket under my arm after she'd gone back inside her house and I thought: that's it is it then, that's my lot, Alison Shaw This Is Your Life? And then I thought: Shit, no, oh no I'll be buggered if it is. When my husband came home that night I told him I didn't know what he was going to do with his evenings from now on, but I knew what I was going to do with mine: I was going to go to night school and catch up on my education, with a view to being able eventually to earn my own living and live my own life, and never have to be dependent on him for anything again.

– My husband and our break-up: yes. Well, I was determined and he knew it. The result was that in less than two months he told me he was moving out and going to live with a young girl he'd met of nineteen; she was going to look after him and devote herself to him in the manner to which he felt he was accustomed. The house we had at that time was in Gorrivale Square over there. The girl was round in a flat with her sister and mother. He said it'd be handy for him coming round to see the kids; I said it'd be handy for me going round to get the money for their support if he forgot it.

I've got to be fair to him and say that he never did forget except for the odd time or two, and when he did it was usually a genuine mistake. The one thing I put my foot down about was the kids going round to where he was and seeing him there with this girl. Thinking about it since I'm not sure that that was the right thing to do. When I was asking my eldest daughter a few weeks ago whether she felt it was, now she was grown up and could look back on it, she said they used to go round there anyway without telling me, which I suppose is no more than I deserved.

My mother and father nearly died when I told them what had happened, that Reg had left and why, how I'd more or less thrown him out. My mother went on telling me women didn't do things like that, they put up with it. She said Reg had given me – that was the word she actually used, 'given' – he'd given me three lovely kids and a nice home. I blew my top: the kids were ours, neither of us had made a present of them to the other, and the nice home was rented from the GLC. I might as well have saved my breath. My father was worse: he started talking about women's place and quoting that thing 'The rich man in his castle, The poor man at his gate: God made them high or lowly, And ordered their estate.' He went chalk white when I said that had got fuck all to do with anything, and was an absolute load of balls. He was so horrified at hearing any woman, let alone his own daughter talking in that way that he turned round and walked out of the house.

It was a traumatic time, but it was a very exciting one for me too. I'd suddenly come alive, I'd realized there was still a person underneath the layers of outward conventional acceptance. One strange thing was that it started to show up quite literally: I was eleven stone when I made my decision, and without dieting or cutting down or anything or making any kind of conscious effort about it, went down to what I am now, a few pounds under eight. Not going thin with worry and strain as people suggested. I'd describe it as fining down myself.

Despite all their disapproval and prophecies of disaster, I must say my parents were very good and helped me out with money for the first year or so until I'd got a few 'O' levels together. I was determined I wasn't going to do my own thing at the expense of my children having to stop doing theirs, and leave school to get jobs. And they haven't. Nick the eldest has gone on to teacher-training college on a grant; Shirley the oldest girl is still at school doing her 'A's, and Lisa the youngest will be taking 'O' levels in a couple of years. Shirley said a little while ago she thought she'd like to be a nurse; I asked her what was wrong with being a doctor, why didn't she set her sights on that. I hope she will, because I think she's got it in her to do it: I think it's criminal the way society as a whole sets lower targets for girls, and the girls themselves accept them as a matter of course. It's a self-perpetuating educational system, designed by men for men: things are getting better slowly over the years, but I'd like it all to go much faster. I can't see either of my daughters growing up into a world that accepts women as complete equals; my hope is they'll be among the fighters who try to bring it about for other younger women in their lifetime.

There are a few good signs. Shirley for instance at school is getting exposed to ideas about women's liberation from her history teacher: she teaches the social side of history to her kids, and exposes them to suggestions that would never have seen daylight when I was a girl. There's always a danger of a backlash of reaction – naturally men will fight back when they really begin to find all their assumptions of superiority coming under question. But it's exciting to feel you're in a society which is changing: it must be rather akin to what some of those women involved in the suffragette movement experienced.

The expression you asked me about last week, 'hopping the wag', that I didn't know where it came from? If you're still interested, I looked it up in the library at college and I've written it out for you.

– We moved to this flat seven years ago. I liked the Gorrivale Square house, but it was too big and anyway the council were going to refurbish it and turn it into two maisonettes, so we'd have to have moved out of it before long. This is smaller, more compact and easier to run. The girls have to share a bedroom which isn't good, but otherwise it's fine. Sherry?

But nostalgia isn't something I've ever suffered a great deal from; I don't look back to the past and wish I was a child again. People who talk about 'the good old days' usually mean they were happier then than they are now, not that conditions were better. Socially they weren't, they were a damn sight worse. They say vague things like there was much more of a spirit of neighbourliness or community feeling. It's not true: people in these flats couldn't have been nicer to me when I came, a woman with three children separated from her husband. They were kind and they were friendly and they went out of their way to be helpful. The kids made friends with other kids each side; that was a great help to them in settling down. It was a big upheaval first to have their father leave and then not long afterwards to change their home.

One of the best things about working-class people to my mind is the way they accept people as they are. Even the woman I was telling you about who took her husband's infidelities without protest was doing that, even if she was going too far to my mind and accepting the unacceptable. People on this estate, and on most others too, live much more on a day-by-day basis than the middle class do; they have a short-term view of life, money's something to be earned and spent, not something to invest. Most working-class people are financially better off now than they ever were, in so far as money's spread about more and they get better wages and can have their share of consumer goods and luxuries like anyone else. And well why not? Nothing gets me madder than hearing people talk about how working-class people nowadays have all got cars and colour televisions. It's not true, but even if it were you can't argue there's any reason on earth why they shouldn't. There might be in heaven, if God's the sort of person my father described him as, picking out some to live in comfort and others to work hard to keep them comfortable. That sort of country-shires view of society is one I find very obnoxious; and I know it's still quite prevalent in some quarters, especially the church.

There used to be a vicar on that other big estate over the other side of Tullbrook Road. I remember being at a meeting he was at once over there, I think it was something to do with getting up a pedestrian crossing on the main road where a lot of kids crossed it on their way to school. He was telling everyone they should organize themselves into a pressure group, have a committee on which the officers were locals and not outsiders like himself, and that they should stand on their own feet. Then there was another meeting a month later – by then there was a dock strike on, and one of the fathers there was a docker who was on strike. The vicar took it upon himself really to upbraid this man after the meeting in front of everyone else, telling him he was being selfish, he should think of the national interest and get back to work. I've often wondered if he went to the dockers' employers and told them to think of the national interest too, and give the men the wage increases and security they were asking for so that the strike could be settled and the men go back to work. He was obviously all for people standing on their own feet so long as it was something he agreed with and wasn't caused inconvenience by; but not when it meant them having ideas of their own.

When it comes to myself and you ask me how I see the next seven years going and where I think I'll be then, all I can say at this stage is I don't know, nor am I going to make up my mind yet. For the next couple of years at least I'll still be at the Poly. When I get my diploma I'm not sure what use I shall put it to in getting a job and going to work. I shall do something which I hope will be useful as well as earn me money. At the moment I'm drawn towards trying to get into something like mental health and be involved with psychologically disturbed or handicapped children. But that's probably because what most of my reading's about this term: I'll change my mind half a dozen times yet before I decide.

One thing I am fairly certain about is that I shan't marry again. I've had one or two affairs in the last couple of years, and I've enjoyed them; and if I met a man and we both felt there was something more to it than going to bed together, I'd be happy to live with him. But it would have to be on as equal a basis as we could possibly work out: I wouldn't give up thoughts of career and a job, and stop at home and cook and housekeep for him. I've had enough of that for one lifetime – I'm never going back to being a paid housekeeper or a paid mistress, or a combination of the two.

I can't properly work out what I am yet, but I will. By that I don't mean what sort of a person I am, because I think I know that by now: put shortly it's an independent one, even a selfish one. What I mean more exactly is whether I'm first a mother and second a person who's got something to contribute to society in general, or the other way round. Men have been telling women for hundreds of years that being a mother is the greatest contribution to society they can make. It wouldn't be a bad idea if they were challenged on that, and asked whether being a father wasn't equally as important a full-time job, or even a more important one. Psychologists in recent times have been telling us how vital the father's role is in child development, but they've always defined it from their own masculine viewpoint. A definition of what being a father really is is getting overdue now.

So where will I be in seven years? Answer: come back in seven years and see me and ask me where I've got to. In some ways I hope to be a bit more settled than I've been trying to sound: in others, I hope I'll still be in a state of finding life as interesting and exciting as I do now.

Wag. *Verb*: to play truant; often 'wag it'. Dickens, 1848. From late 16th. cent. 'wag' = go, depart. Standard English, until colloquial by mid 19th. cent. Also 'hop the wag': perhaps a pun on literal sense of 'play the wag', be amusingly mischievous.

Eric Partridge, *Dictionary of Historical Slang*, 1972

RIVERS

'Prawns Woz Ear'

Ian and friends

Ian was twelve, and we talked several times in his bedroom in his flat, his mother providing tea and biscuits and then leaving us on our own. He also arranged two group meetings with his friends: one in his room, the second at six o'clock in the evening in an unused garage under Cramner, one of the long flat blocks.

– I like living on Providence Estate because I was born here in this flat and all my mates are round about. We all go to school together at Tullbrook Road, and there's loads of places round here to play. In the summer you can ride your bikes on the grass and the little hills round the tower blocks, or you can go over the park. In the winter there's the youth club in Robins Walk, two nights a week and Sundays, and you can go there. I think Providence is a good estate apart from all the blacks coming in: the big coloured boys mess you about if you're trying to play football, they come and push you around and take your football.

The thing I don't like about the coloured boys is they all carry knives: they come up to you and ask you to lend them 10p and you've got to give it them because they've got a knife. They'll do it anywhere, in the school playground or outside school times as well. Some of the coloured girls have got knives too. I've never seen one with one, but somebody told me they had.

The games I like to play best are cricket, football, Cannon, and Knock Down Ginger. Cannon is where you count up to ten and everyone runs away and hides: you have a ball, say a tennis ball, and you run round looking for them and if you see someone you throw the ball at him and try to hit him. You get right up close to him and you throw it at him as hard as you can, so that it goes a long way after it's hit him. Because then he's got to chase after it, and try and get it and hit you with it before you get back to your base; otherwise then he's it, he's the one who's got to count and chase everyone.

Knock Down Ginger is where you go into one of those big blocks like Foxman or Vernon and you ring people's doorbells. Then you run as fast as you can down the corridors, so when they come and answer the door there's no one there. You do it to make people shout, it's good fun because sometimes they run after you and you have to get away down the stairs. It's a good game to play in the tower blocks too. I know a boy in our school who did every bell in Kendal from the tenth floor downwards, that's forty bells. It isn't in *The Guiness Book of Records*, but I think it ought to be.

I can't have a skateboard, my mum won't let me, she says it's too dangerous. She says she won't let me have a motorbike either when I grow up. My brother Terry's got a motorbike. He doesn't live here now because he's got married, but he says when I get older my mum won't be able to stop me if I'm working and paying for it out of my own money. He gave me that poster of Barry Sheene on the wall. He gave me the one of Elvis Presley too, I think Elvis was the greatest. Terry gave me all his Elvis Presley records when he got married.

When I grow up I'd like to be an architect or an actor or someone like that who earns a lot of money. Or I might like to be a plasterer like my dad, he wants me to have a trade, he says people will always want tradesmen and it's something for all your life. When I'm twenty-five I'd like to emigrate to New Zealand. I met a New Zealand person once in the library, he saw me looking at a book of pictures of it and he told me he came from New Zealand. He said it was a great country for young people, and I should get a trade like my dad said, and then I'd be able to get a good job with it in New Zealand. He might have been a schoolteacher, but not one from our school – ours don't talk to you about things like that, they mostly swear at you and hit you round the ear.

One of my friends who's in my class, he hadn't done his homework last week, or he'd done it but he hadn't written it out neat enough in his exercise book. The teacher kept going on at him in front of the whole class, and Danny said 'Oh fuck off' under his breath. The teacher heard him and he got hold of him by his ear and lifted him up out of his desk like that. He said 'Don't you talk like that you little black bugger.' I thought that was just as bad as what Danny said to him, yet he was telling him off for using bad language.

My three best friends in my class are Kevin and Julian and Danny. We all sit together in class, we play together in the playground, and we go around together after school. I've only ever heard Danny get called black by a teacher, none of the rest of us do it. There are five black boys in our class: they're just the same as the rest of us, nobody cares if they're coloured or not, it's no different from anyone else.

– I told them I knew this author who was writing a book, and they all said 'Pull the other one.' So now you can all see it's true.

Stacey: I'm Julian's sister and I'm thirteen and a half. I think living on the estate's boring and horrible, and when I leave school I want to go and live somewhere else and be a nurse.

Julian: I think it's better for boys on the estate than it is for girls because there's more for boys to do, boys like me anyway. I'm twelve.

Danny: My name's Danny, I'm nearly twelve. My best mates are Ian and Kevin and Julian. I like living on Providence Estate because it's nice: I don't know why I like it, but I do like it and I wouldn't want to live anywhere else.

Kevin: I'm Kevin, I'm twelve. I don't like living here because I want to go and live in Brighton with my dad.

Ian: We're all going to say what our favourite game is. Mine is bombers, that's when you go dropping empty milk bottles off of balconies and making people jump.

Julian: Mine is 'Hot Bottle'. That's when you nick a full bottle from someone's doorstep and you take it somewhere and you all stand in a big circle and you throw it round. When someone drops it you all shout 'Hot Bottle'. It was funny one day, one boy was just going to catch it and the cap come off and the milk went all over him. He had to go back home and change all his clothes; he told his mum a coloured boy had threw it at him.

Kevin: The best one I like is playing tennis: you have a milk bottle each and a stone, and you try to hit the other person with the stone after you've hit it like that with the bottle. It's very exciting because it's dangerous if your bottle breaks, but if you drop your bottle you're a coward.

Stacey: The game I like best is wars. You can have the reds and the whites, or you can have girls against boys. You throw stones and old cans and things like that. We go over and play it round about Vernon or Foxman because it doesn't matter if you break the windows there.

107

Ian: Wars isn't really a proper game, you can have that any time.

Stacey: All right then, what I like best is skateboards down the garages. I'm not allowed to have one, my mum and dad won't let me, they say it's not for girls. But I go down to the garages and do it down there, some of the boys let me have a go on theirs. I like doing handstands best.

Danny: My favourite is going over the park and seeing if we can find any drunks on the benches. There's one with big whiskers all round his face and long hair, they call him Billy Bottle, he's my favourite one because he's the funniest. You take his hat or one of his boots and he swears and tries to run after us. One day he fell down when we were all running round him in a circle, he was swinging out at us with his fists and he got dizzy and fell down.

Julian: I think that's cruel.

Kevin: I don't think it's cruel. I think they should go somewhere else if they don't want it to happen to them, they shouldn't sit on the park benches all day.

Julian: Another thing I like to do is Prawn writing; I like that, I think that's good fun.

Kevin: We said we weren't going to talk about Prawns. It's secret so I don't think we should talk about it.

Stacey: What is it, what's Prawn writing?

Ian: It's right what Kevin said, we all said we wouldn't talk about it. Let's talk about something else instead. I said we'd talk about thieving so who'll talk about thieving?

Kevin: I'll talk about it, I don't mind talking about thieving. Milk bottles is the main thing I'd say: milk bottles, bicycle lights, and sometimes sweets from shops.

Julian: Bubble gum's the easiest thing to thieve. You go and buy a comic, and you put it down on the bubble gum: then you pay for it and when you pick it up you can get a couple from underneath.

Danny: That fat woman at the shop in Robins Walk though, she's twigged that one. When you put the comic down she straightaway picks it up again and holds it in her hand until you give her the money, then she hands it you like that over the counter.

Stacey: I don't think thieving's much fun, you can get into too much trouble for it. I went with a girl once, she said she was going to go in the chemist's and get a lipstick. I got frightened, I run out before she took it.

Ian: I don't think thieving's a game, I think it's serious. If you're going to go in for it when you grow up, and be a proper thief, well that's all right. But I don't think kids should do it, you can get caught too easy.

– I bought my skateboard off of a boy at school, I have to keep it down the garages because my mum won't let me have one. I pay him for it out of my pocket money, so much a week plus an old pair of football boots I had and a table tennis bat. All parents are a bit funny like that, you can have this but you can't have that. If you really want something there's nothing else you can do, you have to hide it. A mate of mine who's older than me, he's fourteen and he's got an air rifle: his mum and dad would go spare if they knew, so he keeps it down the range.

The range is like a shooting gallery, it's one of the empty garages under Cramner House. There's a gang of boys there, they've all got air guns and they shoot at bottles and cans. They've got it set up like you see on a fairground. None of their parents would let them have guns so they keep quiet about it. I've been in once, my mate took me in to have a look at it when there was no one there, it's a garage further along from the one we have.

Ours is our club, it's like a camp; we've got furniture in there that people have thrown out. In the blocks like Cramner and Foxman, if people don't want things they tip them out round the back of the blocks: I've seen people taking things there from other places too. They leave them there and everyone thinks it's the people in Cramner and Foxman. We've got an old settee, three old armchairs, a kitchen table, two kitchen chairs, and a lot of pans and a kettle and spoons and forks. We collect sticks and bits of wood and make a fire outside on the concrete: not outside our garage because then people would know where it was then, but further along. Someone'll bring bread, someone else some potatoes, and someone might nick a tin of beans from home: then we all have a good feed. We put candles in bottles because we always keep the door closed and it's dark inside.

We call ourselves Prawns but it's not really a gang; there's only a few of us, and now and again we do Prawn writing on walls. I don't know whose idea it was first that we should call ourselves it: it started about two years ago one day after we had a biology lesson at school. Prawns hide under rocks and things like that, no one knows they're there; they creep about and hide, as soon as they see anyone looking at them they disappear and no one knows where they are, there might be a prawn there or there might not. And they've got sort of feelers on their heads like that that they wave at people. We decided we'd be like prawns and no one would know who we were. Here it's a school thing at our school. By that I mean there's probably others besides us at other places, all in little groups being Prawns; but it's not one great big gang from all over.

You only do Prawn writing on walls that have already got writing on them. You do it to show you've read the other writing, and to fill up the spaces so that no one else can write anything else, to make it more fun. You don't write rude things. You try and think of funny things to write. All Prawns carry their Magic Markers with them all the time: they have a little write whenever they see the chance. Another thing you have to do is spell words wrong if you can, because that makes it look more funny.

The one I like writing best is 'Prawns Woz Ear'. Big boys will give you a belt round the ear if they see you doing it on their wall. Other ones I know are 'This Wall Az Bin Prawned', 'Prawns Are Hear To Stay', and 'Don't Read, Write Prawnography'. One I thought was very good said just 'Prawns', and then after it there was thirty-five what do they call them, exclamation marks, then 'Wozere'. It looked like this:

'Prawns !!!!!!!!!!!!!!!!!!!!!!!!!!!!!!!!!!!!! Wozere.'

The idea of that was whoever wrote it had been very brave: he'd stayed there all that time doing all those exclamation marks before he signed off. Kevin thought of a good one once. It said, 'Watch Out Prawns Is Cummin: Look Back, Prawns Is Goin'.

I'll ask the others and if they say you can come and have a look at the garage I'll take you there.

Julian: There was a fire once in one of the other garages along here. That was because they was stupid and lit it inside and all their stuff caught light. They all ran away and the fire brigade came.

Kevin: Yes and the next day the police come poking round to see who else had got furniture in garages. We knew they'd be coming so we'd moved most of our stuff out and left only a few things piled up at the back like rubbish, then afterwards we put it back again.

Danny: The police watch you if they see you round the garages to see which one you go in. If you want to be naughty you go in someone else's and then come out again, and the police go in and make them take everything out.

Kevin: The police is always onto you all the time. One of my mates, they drove their police car round and round on the grass after him. They said it was to give him a fright and let him know they had their eyes on him.

Julian: Some of those that walk about are not too bad. That one Mr Davidson, PC Davidson, he's all right so long as he's not in a bad mood. But the ones in motors, they pull up next to you when you're not doing anything but walk along the pavement. Who are you, what's your name, where'd you live, where've you been, where are you going. I don't think they should be allowed to do that.

Danny: I don't think they should be allowed to hit people in police stations. They took my brother in Tullbrook Road police station and he come home with his eye all swollen and a big graze on his arm he had to go to the doctor with. When my mum went and complained to them they said he'd fallen down some steps.

Ian: It's all true what people say about the police. They did all that Starsky and Hutch business with me once, right out in the road in front of everybody: made me put my hands up on the car roof and spread my legs out, then they patted me all over like they were searching for a gun.

Kevin: You haven't done anything but they treat you like a criminal, or like they thought you was a criminal and there must be something you've done.

Julian: When Mr Davidson comes and gives a talk at our school, he's always making out what nice people they are, policemen. He's all right, but a lot of them aren't; they're what people call them, which is pigs.

Danny: When my brother came home that time, my mum said the police were chicken shit. That's the only time I've ever heard my mum talk like that.

– A lady came to our school once from the social services. She said she was going to start a scheme for young people to help old people: do their shopping for them, mend things, do some gardening or whatever they need. The old people tell her they want something, then she comes and sees your mum and dad and asks if you can go and do it; and if they say you can she tells you the name and address of the person.

I do it, Danny does it and Julian does it, but Kevin doesn't. So far I've put up some polystyrene tiles that had fallen down in a lady's kitchen, painted the outside of a back door, and mended a leak in a drainpipe outside someone's house. Julian's done a lot more than I have, he can do things like put washers on taps, mend holes in a bath and things like that because his dad's a plumber and he's shown him how. Danny mostly does going errands.

You don't get any money for it, and I think it's a good idea for people who need help. One old lady said to me when I did something in her house that she used to think children nowadays were all bad, but it had made her change her mind.

RIVERS

'Not very good about medical things'

Doreen Church

The mornings when the sun was shining she put Gavin her ten-year-old son on the sun lounger out on the tiny balcony. He lay there dozing or disinterestedly looking at a comic. She sat near the window where she could see him, glancing towards him every few minutes while she talked. Small and thin, she had short straight dark hair and blue eyes; her voice was dry and tearless, and she gave an occasional little laugh of embarrassment, almost in apology for what she was saying.

– I'm thirty-five, and my life's been nothing but a rotten mess. I know there must be a God but I do wonder why he's so hard on me, it's not as though I'm a specially wicked person. I once read a book that said we were all reincarnated and had to suffer for what we'd done in previous lives. I don't know what I did, but it must have been very dreadful then.

I'm illegitimate, but I wasn't told that until I was fifteen. All up till then I'd thought the lady I lived with was my mum. I called her mum and she never told me any different, and I was always called by her surname at school. She didn't have any other children except me. It sounds an awful thing to say about your mum, but by the time I was eleven or twelve I really hated her – she was always slapping me and shouting at me for not using my handkerchief, or for wearing the wrong dress, or not changing my underclothes. Or sometimes it'd be having a bath and using up all the hot water, and other times not having a bath and taking advantage of it that we had plenty of hot water. Whatever I did, it was always the opposite of what I should have done. She was a big woman and I was frightened to death of her. I can still see her in my mind's eye looming up in my bedroom doorway, coming to give me a whipping for whatever it was she'd sent me upstairs for. She had one of those shiny black patent-leather belts and she used to use it on my legs.

I didn't understand why I hadn't got a dad, but if any of the kids at school asked me about him I'd made up a story about him being in America where he was working for the British government trying to catch spies in the atom factories. I was a terrible liar, I made out he was someone who was very brave and led a very exciting and dangerous life, but he couldn't come home because he was doing this secret work. I almost believed it myself in the end.

I've forgotten how old I must have been, but one day I asked my mum where he was and why I didn't ever see him. She gave me a very cold look and said he was dead, he'd died when I was a baby. You don't think about these things when you're a child, it never crossed my mind to say had she got any photographs of him: the expression on her face frightened me off the subject, and anyway I didn't believe her.

Eventually I found out what had happened from an auntie. It was just about the time I left school and was going to apply for my first job and I had to produce my birth certificate. There was a big row: when I told mum I had to have it she said she hadn't got it, and it wasn't right that whoever the people were who wanted it should go sticking their noses into things, I should try and get another job somewhere else. I'd already started work, it was in an office as a filing clerk; but there were about six other girls there the same age as me and I liked it, I didn't want to leave. Only the boss kept asking me and asking me to bring my birth certificate.

I'd guessed by then something was wrong somewhere. I didn't dare ask my mum about it again, so I went to see her sister who lived down the road from us, and who was my favourite auntie. She sat me down and she said she thought I was old enough to know something now, and if my mum wouldn't tell me, she would. She said my real mother had been a young girl who a man had got into trouble and then disappeared and left her on her own. She couldn't afford to keep the baby, which was me, or have me properly looked after and so on, so she'd put me for adoption. My mum, or the woman I'd always called my mum, she hadn't been able to have any children of her own so she and her husband had taken me from the adoption people when I was a very little baby only a few weeks old. Then about only a year after that her husband had gone off with someone much younger than she was, and he hadn't been seen or heard of since.

If I'd liked my mum better, when I think about it now I think I would have tried to talk to her about it, but I never did. Soon after I went to another job somewhere else, in a cardboard factory where they made shoe boxes, so that meant the subject of the birth certificate was dropped and there wasn't any more opportunity for it.

Once or twice I've had thoughts about it since. Two main ones: one was that it might have been my auntie who was the young girl who had the baby before she was married and had her own family, and her sister took me over to look after me. Or I was really my mum's illegitimate child, and the story about her adopting me was all completely made up. Sometimes I've thought I'd go into it. I read somewhere you can do that now, they can't stop you if you want to go and look up your own birth certificate. But I've had so many things have happened since that have given me a lot more to worry than that, it hasn't really seemed much worth bothering about.

– The first thing was I got pregnant myself when I was sixteen. It was one of the men from where I worked, in the back of his car one night, the first time and there it was, I fell. He was married, he didn't want to know. I know it was my own fault but I was disgusted with him about it. At that time things were so bad between me and my mum I wasn't living at home any more, I was living with another of my aunties in Croydon. I told her about it and she put me onto one of those societies that do with moral welfare. They were very nice, they said I could go and stay in one of their mother and baby homes for six weeks before I had the baby and for six weeks after, and they'd help me decide what was best to do. What I liked was that they didn't try and press you to make up your mind there and then, they said after I'd had the baby would be the time to talk about it.

I stayed the six weeks before the baby, then I went to hospital to have it and it was stillborn. It would have been a little girl. There was nothing to go back to the mother and baby place for afterwards, so I went back to my auntie's and I went to work again in another factory. I think it was one where they tinned vegetables, carrots and peas – you stood there all day long and pulled a lever, that was all there was to it.

Then when I was eighteen I got married. It was a boy who was the same age as me, we'd been at school together. He'd got a job with London Transport, not a very good one but sufficient for us to live on if we were careful without me needing to work. My auntie said we could have a furnished room in her house to start off in, which is what we did.

I fell pregnant in only a couple of months of us getting married;

115

and I think it was when I was six months that I found out he was going with someone else. I didn't want to have a baby that was his, and I tried to get rid of it – all the things you do like hot baths and drinking a bottle of gin and jumping off chairs, but I couldn't stand the idea of anybody poking about with knitting needles inside me so I wouldn't have that.

None of it worked, and when the time came I went into hospital again. It might be I'd done harm to it when I was trying to get rid of it: anyway that one was born dead too. It would have been another little girl. After that I got very depressed for quite a long while, all I did was sit in a chair and cry all day long. They wanted me to go into hospital and have that electrical treatment but I didn't want to. The doctor kept giving me different pills – some of them made me feel better and some made me feel worse, but in the end I got a little job in a tobacco kiosk at a station and gradually got over being depressed.

There was a divorce some time during that time too, I'm not exactly sure how old I was when it was all finished, about twenty-two or -three, I suppose. It made me feel I never wanted to get married again. But then about two years after, I met this man who was a good bit older than me – twenty years, he was forty-three then. He'd been married and divorced too, his wife had gone off with someone and taken his children. We started going together, and he came to live at my auntie's. When we found I was pregnant again, I thought that was a chance to have a new start with everything, so we decided to get married.

That was the worst mistake I ever made in my life that was.

– My second husband's name was Bill. Like I told you I was pregnant when I got married, and it was six or seven months afterwards that I had Gavin. Because I'd had two babies already that had been born dead, the doctors said they were going to be very careful with me, and they had me in hospital five weeks before the birth was due. They were all very delighted when Gavin was born with all his hands and arms and legs and things.

Bill's job was he was a gas fitter. I'd told him before we were married about my babies being born dead; I told him everything I knew about myself, being illegitimate, not knowing who my real mother and father were and all the rest of it. I think he should have told me everything about himself too, but he didn't. I'm not saying I would have done any different if I'd known: I probably wouldn't, I'd still have married him. But I would have gone into it more, especially about having children: I'd have tried to get advice about it from someone.

They rang up from work one day and told me Bill had collapsed, and he'd been taken to hospital in an ambulance. He was unconscious when I got to the hospital: no one could tell me anything about what was wrong with him. They let me sit with him for a while, then when I went back the next day he was still unconscious, and the day after that. When he did come round he didn't remember anything about it himself, so he couldn't tell me anything.

They kept him in hospital for six weeks. I tried to get to see a doctor. When I did, all he'd say was they wanted to do a lot of tests, Bill had had something like a kind of stroke but he was going to be all right. What I didn't find out until a long long time afterwards was that Bill knew what was the matter with him: but he'd told them at the hospital they weren't to tell me, he said he would tell me himself when they sent him home. What he knew he'd known since long before we'd even met: only he hadn't said anything to me, and he still didn't even after he came home.

I'm not very good about medical things, well I wasn't in those days. What he'd got was some very rare form of a bone disease and blood disease that can sometimes go together. When they do there's nothing can be done about it. It's very painful and gradually leaves you helpless so that someone has to nurse you all the time. In the end you die from it: it can take a short time or a long time, but you can't be eased of it. It's something like cancer. I've had it explained to me, it's got some special name which I can't pronounce.

You see though the thing is that he'd known for years he'd got it, and that it's a hereditary thing and his own father had died from it when he was a quite young man. I dare say he was very frightened about it and tried to pretend it wasn't going to happen to him; but I think if you're going to marry someone and have children with them, then you should tell them about something like that. I got to feel very bitter about it before he died: I was at the far end sometimes with him. I felt he only married me because he knew what was going to happen, and wanted someone to look after him and nurse him.

He never went back to work after he came home from hospital. He stayed at home and wandered round the house in his pyjamas and dressing gown all day. Even then he was too ill for us to go out anywhere or for people to come and see us, except one or two of my aunties or his brother and his wife.

Altogether it was over three years that he was at home, slowly going worse and worse until he died. In the last six months I can't describe how horrible it was. I know it was awful for him too. I

117

suppose some people would say I was heartless. But what got me down most was the way he begged and pleaded with me to keep him at home and not let him be put back in hospital: he used to sit in that chair crying and shouting, and he'd make me get the Bible out and swear on it on my bended knees in front of him that I wouldn't let it happen. It didn't matter if I'd sworn it only the day before, once he was in that state there was nothing to do except put up with it.

He had a lot of pain, and towards the end the drugs they were giving him for it weren't having any effect. It made him very peculiar. You've got to say he didn't know what he was doing, but it killed whatever feelings of love I might have had for him. I got to the point where I used to go to the bedroom and shut the door and cry and cry. Sometimes I hated him so much I was certain if he did not die soon I was going to kill him.

He couldn't move or be moved, and I put his bed there along that wall. As far as he could go was to sit in the chair for an hour and then he had to be helped back into bed. He couldn't control himself, so I was having to wash and change him sometimes two or three times in one day. He didn't thank me for it, he'd shout and swear at me and tell me really I was enjoying seeing him in that state. He said I was a whore and a tart, he knew I'd been with lots more men than I'd ever told him about; and the two babies I'd had that had died, I'd probably killed them myself. There was nothing he wouldn't say.

And because we couldn't have sexual relations any more, he used to make me do things, I won't describe them. I know he was very very ill and had awful pain for the last few months so he must have been somebody who was mentally sick. I can't ever forget those times, days and nights on and on when I was terrified what he was going to say or make me do next, or what he might not do to Gavin if I didn't keep him in my sight. I can't say any different, because it's true: but it's terrible to say it, that you were glad when somebody died. I really was though, even if God won't forgive me for saying it.

– My husband died when Gavin was four, six years ago. And by only another few months afterwards, I knew. I'd suspected it, I'd seen it coming for more than a year before that. I'm sure Bill had too, even though we never talked about it. It was about six months after he died or a bit less: Gavin had started being sick, having restless nights and a lot of high temperatures, more than he'd ever had before. I felt I might as well face it if it had to to be faced, so I took him to the hospital and told them what I was worrying about. They did a lot of tests, and it was quite a good few weeks before they had the results and sent for me. When I did they said they were very sorry to have to tell me, but Gavin had got the same thing his father had, only in this case it was almost sure that he wouldn't live anything like as long. I said to them not to tell me exactly how long: I'd sooner go on till the time came, not be planning how long there was still to go.

He's got much worse in the last year to eighteen months. He's not well enough for me to send him to school any more now. We go to the hospital once a fortnight, they're very good; they give him things to help with the pain and to help him sleep at night, and other things to help him keep his food down.

They've explained to me how when someone's like this they catch other illnesses much more easily as well – even colds and minor things can turn to pneumonia if you're not careful. Whenever he has the slightest thing, I either take him to the hospital or send for the doctor to come at once. The doctor's sometimes said he'd better be in hospital until his fever went down, so he gets him admitted then. I stay with him most of the day when he's there and everyone's very kind to me. But as soon as they say it's safe to, I always bring him home again. I think it's much nicer for him being here rather than in hospital.

I sleep in the same room as him in the night; I want him near me so I can hear his breathing or if he calls out and wants something. As time goes on you get used to doing without things. It's like that with sleep, I mostly doze through the night but don't actually sleep. The doctor and the hospital have said they'll give me pills if I want them for my nerves, but I don't want to start that. There was a time last year when I was crying a lot, I was frightened that the depression I had before was coming back. But I got over it, the crying stopped and I pulled myself together.

I wonder sometimes why this is all happening, and why it should happen to me like this, one thing after another. I say my prayers to God to help me with it: if it wasn't for Him I don't think I'd have the strength to bear it.

If you don't mind now I don't want to talk any more.

CAVENDISH

'I am what I am'

Paul Porter

– I am what I am. I'm a homosexual, and while I wouldn't go so far as to say I don't care who knows it, because that'd sound a bit like flaunting it, on the other hand I don't make any secret of it. We've lived here almost two years now. I live with my friend Chris, and if neighbours inquired about us getting married when we first came I used to tell them there'd be no question of that, we were living together and we were gay.

After so many years and years of unhappiness, and feeling guilty and ashamed of myself for being homosexual, at thirty I've gradually found out who I am and what I am, and am starting to enjoy life. I'm very lucky in having met Chris, we love each other very much and we complement each other in almost every way: we're happy together, and we've lots of non-gay friends who accept us exactly as we are. But if you'd come to see me five years ago, all I'd have been facing was what I thought was an endless future of loneliness and misery. And I wouldn't have talked to you, I wouldn't have dared.

A tall broad-shouldered man in slacks and an Arran jumper, with short neatly cut and parted fair hair. The walls of the sitting room were lined with bookshelves, the three-piece suite and dining table and chairs were reproduction mahogany antique with grey-green upholstery that toned with the plain olive-green carpet and curtains. An Athena block reproduction of a Matisse abstract at one end of the room, Gainsborough's portrait of Sarah Siddons in a gilt frame over the sideboard.

– My father worked as a clerk in the docks. I'm the second youngest of four boys. My mother died very young when I was six and my father died when I was thirteen. We had a big house at the far end of Tullbrook Road, and my father had had an insurance policy which paid off the mortgage but didn't leave us anything else. My eldest brother called a council of war of the four of us, and asked us what we all thought we should do: should we sell the house and divide up the money or should we stay where we were. He was eighteen and he'd just started work. The other three of us were still at school, although Steve the next eldest was sixteen and could leave if he wanted. He decided he would; and he and Pat, the eldest, reckoned that between them they could earn enough for the four of us to live on, while me and my brother Greg stopped on at school. There was a nice middle-aged woman who lived a few houses further along. She came in and made a hot tea for us each evening, but the housework and washing and shopping we did ourselves.

It worked very well. Pat was very sensible and responsible, and a good manager with money. We each had our own bedroom, and there were two big downstairs rooms so we weren't on top of one another all the time, and we had as stable an existence as was possible under the circumstances.

The agreement was I would leave school as well and start work when I was sixteen, which I did. Then finally Greg left and got a job too when he was old enough. Pat had left to get married a few years earlier and gone to live in Yarmouth. Not long after, Steve wanted to get married as well. The four of us decided that by then the best thing to do would be to sell the house and divide up what we got for it. House prices had gone through the roof around that time: it was in good condition, it sold for £80,000, so that meant we had somewhere near £20,000 each. Not a fortune, but enough for us all to think in terms of buying our own places if we wanted to.

I'd never been academically bright at school. I left at the time when the colour-television market was at its peak, and I got a job with a rental firm which put me through a series of courses in maintenance and repair. I'm still with the same firm – I'm now a fully qualified engineer, I earn a very decent salary and I like the work so I can't see myself making any change in the immediate future. Unless they give me the sack, I'll stop where I am. I'm happy and I'm not the sort of person who enjoys change for change's sake. In that sense I'm very much a conservative with a small 'c'; but not politically, in politics I'm a keen Liberal.

When we sold the house I was in my early twenties and as I say in a good steady job. The family was split up because my elder brothers

were both married or about to be; and Greg the youngest was working, had met a girl and was wanting to set up in a place with her. I
wanted to stay in the area because of the job: but I couldn't get
anywhere to live except furnished rooms. I lived in a whole lot of
different ones one after the other, and although I had my name down
on the GLC list for housing I knew realistically there wasn't going to
be much prospect of a place unless I was going to get married.

And that was something I knew wasn't going to happen. I didn't
know I was gay: all I did know was that there seemed to be something
disastrously wrong with me sexually. As we'd had our own house and
no parents to consider, it was a regular thing that we should all take
girls back there. In all I'd been to bed with seven or eight, and with
not one of them had I been able to do it. It wasn't that I found them
physically off-putting, but they definitely weren't on-putting: I
couldn't get an erection however hard I tried, and the harder you try
the less chance you've got of succeeding. Most girls I found to be
very understanding and sympathetic, they said they didn't mind, it
was only a matter of being patient, if we didn't worry about it it'd be
all right between us in the end. From all I've heard and read since,
as a rule most women are like that about it; often to a certain extent
some of them feel there must be something wrong with them, they
can't excite the man enough.

So time went by and time went by, and I was getting more and
more worried about myself but still hadn't a clue what it was that
was really wrong. I didn't feel any attraction towards men, which
might have given me some indication if I had. It's a very strong
tradition in the working class that you prove you're a man by laying
as many girls as possible. All you ever hear about homosexuals is
them being referred to as 'nancy boys' or 'poofs'. That's the extent
of your knowledge, apart from seeing the drag queens on television.
In my case I've always thought they were ludicrous and repulsive,
and still do. They were the sort of 'public' homosexuals: people either
laughed at them or thought like I did 'Christ, I'm glad I'm not like
that.'

That was the full extent of my knowledge of the subject: total
ignorance combined with distaste for transvestites. So eventually
when one girl I'd taken to bed with me wasn't sympathetic like all
the others, and started sneering at me and asking me what was the
matter with me, was I a poof, I was absolutely horrified. It upset me
so much I made up my mind to do something about it if I could. I
wouldn't have dreamed of going to see my own doctor about it – I
made an appointment at one of the big teaching hospitals on the

other side of the river and went there to what they called their 'Sexual Problems' clinic.

I was seen by psychiatrists, psychologists, therapists, God knows what: they asked me hundreds and hundreds of questions about my childhood, my mother and father, my early sexual experiences with girls and the usual playing about with one another that boys do. I did tests with diagrams, saying what they reminded me of; and those other tests where the therapist says a word and you answer with the first word you think of that comes into your head. This went on for weeks, and then finally I went to see one of the high-ups who'd got all the test results in front of her. As soon as I sat down in front of her desk she said 'Now Paul before we go any further, the very first thing I want to say to you is that if you're worried you might be homosexual, well don't be because you're definitely not.'

I'd no way of knowing she was wrong had I: and I remember my reaction being one of mild relief. It hadn't been one of my great worries, so while I was glad of her reassurance, it didn't do anything for my impotence except increase my worry. I went on going to the hospital, and then in the summer of that year I went on holiday for a fortnight to Majorca with a friend, a chap of my own age whose name was Doug, and our respective girlfriends. It was one of those free-and-easy beach-camp places where nobody bothers who sleeps with who. He had his girl and I had mine, and as usual all she got from me was a lot of effort but nothing that could have been all that exciting for her. But she was nice about it, she didn't try to make me feel embarrassed or anything. Then one day, it hadn't been pre-arranged but the girls had hired scooters and they went off on their own. Doug and I had rather too much to drink with our lunch, and afterwards we staggered back to either his tent or mine, I can't remember which, and we made love.

It was fantastic for me, for the first time ever in my life I experienced full and satisfying sexual pleasure. Then we both went to sleep, and I remember crying because I was so happy. But it didn't last long: a couple of hours later when we woke up, Doug went nearly berserk. He said he'd been drunk, I'd taken advantage of him, it was the most horrible and disgusting thing that had ever happened to him, he wasn't staying there a minute longer, as soon as his girl came back they were moving out of the camp. I was absolutely horrified, I was petrified with fear at what he was going to say and do; and I was disgusted with myself. One of the things he'd said I was was a pervert, and my feeling was it was true, that must be exactly what I was.

He didn't carry out his threat, but the rest of the holiday wasn't much fun for any of us. The girls kept asking us what had gone

123

wrong, why Doug and I were barely speaking to each other, what had we quarrelled about. Fortunately it was only a couple of days before we were due to leave, but I felt utterly wretched.

As soon as I was home I went back to the hospital clinic and told them what had happened. They told me to try not to worry about it: the doctor assured me yet again that I wasn't a homosexual, and said she was going to give me active sex-therapy treatment which would cure me. It consisted of showing me erotic pictures, telling me erotic stories, and even indulging in some pretty intimate contact, all in an effort to get me sexually excited by females. None of it worked. I got more and more despairing, I stopped going to the hospital, and I ended up by taking an overdose and collapsing at work, and waking up to find myself in the casualty department of another hospital having my stomach pumped out. You often hear expressions like people being described as 'in the pit of despair': that's where I was then, without any doubt at all. They asked me to promise them at the hospital I wouldn't make another attempt at suicide. When I said I wouldn't promise, they kept me in for a few days until one of the other doctors there could see me. He asked me what my trouble was, and I don't know what possessed me but I suddenly started crying – I poured it all out to him, how wretched and unhappy and disgusted with myself I was. All he did was sit and listen and nod to encourage me to go on talking. When I'd finished, he simply wrote a phone number down on a piece of paper, gave it me and said 'When you go out, try ringing that number.'

He saved my life.

– It was a social club for homosexuals of both sexes. They have a meeting once a month in this rather posh hotel near Victoria. It's very formal, you mix with people, have a chat and a drink, and that's all there is to it. I was scared to death of going, and the first time I did I wasn't sure if I was in the right place. There wasn't a single effeminate-looking man there nor a single butch-looking woman: all my preconceived ideas had to go straight out of the window. Everyone was very informal and pleasant, there was no rowdiness and no one tried to force themselves on you.

It was there that I first met Chris. I'd been going for about six months, and I could tell it was something completely new for him by the way he stood on his own in a corner and didn't talk to anyone. I went up and introduced myself, we started to chat, and for several months afterwards the only times we met were when we were there. Then we went to the theatre to an ice show, to a couple of films, to a restaurant for a meal and so on: and after about a year we were seeing each other regularly twice a week. There was nothing physical between us at all – we liked each other's company, but that was as far as it went.

The next thing that happened was I got a letter from the GLC saying they had a flat vacant and my name was on the list as due for it, but it was two-bedroomed, did I have anyone I could share it with? Ironic: and I was terribly nervous about suggesting it to Chris in case he turned the idea down. He didn't though and so we moved in. I'd already told all three of my brothers that I was homosexual, and without exception they were fantastic about it, apart from my older brother who'd been a bit worried at first because he and his wife had got two young boys of their own, and he thought I might make a pass at them. When I told him, which was true, that I didn't fancy children and his boys were in about as much danger from me as Steve's daughter was from him, he came round to seeing things in a clearer light and now he doesn't worry about it at all.

Chris's parents were very middle-class respectable though, he didn't. tell them what the relationship was between us, and he still can't bring himself to. We play ridiculous games when we go to see them, being very very careful to avoid any physical contact between us. That's a bit of a strain, because here at home we're always touching each other like other people who love each other do. And when they come to see us, it gets even more absurd: we put books and things in the spare bedroom, make up the bed and so on to try and make it look like his own personal separate room. I used to wish he'd be as open about it with them as we are with everyone else, but I've accepted now that he can't. He says he's sure they know, but so long as he doesn't force them to admit it, it won't cause them any pain. They still sometimes ask us hasn't one or the other found a girl he wants to marry and settle down with yet, but that's getting less frequent now.

We're happy living here. I never thought we'd ever find a community as tolerant of homosexuals as the people here are. Perhaps it has something to do with both of us being quiet and not a bit outrageous, not limp-wristed queens like the public expects and like the media usually portrays gays. We went on a march last year, Gays Against the Bomb: there were about 3000 of us in our column, but the only ones who were shown on TV were three freaks who'd dyed their hair and were wearing frocks. This is the sort of thing which is not only no help to homosexuals in general but is downright harmful to them. I often wonder if some of the stage people who make a very good living out of camping around and making people laugh at them ever stop and ask themselves how much damage they are doing to the great mass of ordinary everyday homosexuals, who've got enough problems coming to terms with their own nature without being made out to be a bunch of fairies.

But coming out and being frank about it isn't easy for everyone. I have a friend in the police force who's frightened to death of anyone finding out about him – he swears he'd lose his job if anyone knew. Another friend's a teacher, and he's in the same position. And I know a doctor who works in a hospital who'd like to be a GP but says his practice would always be at risk if he did, because any male patient could make an allegation that would drive away most of the rest of his male patients immediately. People accept that doctors don't interfere with their female patients as a general rule: but we're still a thousand light years away from agreeing the same standard of professional conduct would apply to one who was homosexual. All these three people I've mentioned come to the club that Chris and I go to, the one we first met at. We keep on going there once a month because we know there are so many lonely and frightened homosexuals who need to see happiness is something that isn't necessarily out of their reach for ever.

– I would say I'm definitely working class in background, and I hope I've stayed working class in my outlook and attitudes. I get a bit stroppy with Chris sometimes about having to play games with his middle-class parents. I say what's true, that we have our neighbours from each side in for a drink or a chat sometimes, husbands and wives together or separate, and we never feel we have to make the slightest effort to pull the wool over their eyes, nor have we ever had to from the day we came.

They're more tolerant of us than they are of blacks for instance: you don't see 'Gays Go Home' written on the wall inside the entrance-way downstairs like you sometimes see things written up which are aimed at the blacks. Nobody ever says to us stupid things like 'I've nothing against gays so long as they're good gays,' like a black woman further along on this floor told me one day had been said to her face about blacks by someone. I've made a conscious effort I must admit to keep my accent working class, and I suppose the fact I don't walk along with one hand on my hip or speak with a lisp is a help to people in talking to me as though I was not all that different from any other man, which I'm not.

Because they all know what my job is, I often get kids knocking at my door and saying their mum's sent them to ask me would I mind going and having a look at their telly, there's something wrong with it they can't fix themselves. If I can put it right for them, I do; and if I do, invariably afterwards that same kid will be sent along with something for me in the way of a return favour – a cake or some scones or a pot of home-made jam, something of that kind. What pleases me most is the parents feel they can send their kids, because a lot of people are generally ridiculous on the subject of children where gays are concerned.

Chris wouldn't go as far as I do. He's too shy to talk about the subject with anybody, and wasn't prepared to meet you even, when he knew what we were going to talk about. I don't mind, it doesn't worry me. Why should it, what's there to worry about? Everyone knows, which is why I wouldn't ever go and live anywhere else but here in Cavendish on this estate.

CAVENDISH

'Senior unretired citizen'

Percy Collins

*Ringing the front doorbell halfway along the first-floor balcony always
brought a prompt shout in response from inside. After a few weeks he
was laughing each time he opened the door: 'Look, there you are see,
I've gone and done it again, can't remember to leave it on the latch for
you like I say I'm going to every time. You must stand there saying to
yourself "Stupid old fool's gone and forgotten again, he's losing his
memory." Ah well come on then come in, how's things going with
you, all right?'*

*On the oak drop-leaf table in the sitting room of his two-room flat
there was a chenille cloth and a tray ready laid with gold-rimmed
porcelain cups and saucers; usually by it were a bottle of milk and a
packet of Maryland Cookies or Coconut Crisps. The electric kettle was
ready boiled; tea was made immediately, the pot put under a cosy for
a few minutes. There'd be chat and questions about the news in the
world, drinking tea and crunching biscuits. Then he'd clear the table
and sit ready at it in a dining chair, his hands clasped in front of him
on the cloth.*

*A tall thin spruce man smelling faintly of coaltar soap; pink-cheeked
and clean-shaven in a collarless open-necked shirt and trousers and
braces, his short sparse white hair carefully combed and brushed, his
eyes borage-blue and clear. He seemed quietly amused at the idea of
what he said being recorded; when he talked his voice was unhurried,
his words thoughtfully chosen and almost savoured. Though he lived
alone he talked without the anxiety of someone uncertain whether he
was being listened to.*

– It's my ambition to be a writer myself one day. I've never written anything so far in my life, not except letters; but the last two winters I've been going Monday nights to Wilbraham College to a course called 'The Modern English Novel'. Our tutor's that chap whatsisname, you know, you'll have heard of him, he wrote that book what was it called, there was a bit of a fuss about it because people said it was dirty. What *is* his name? Anyway never mind it'll come. He's a good teacher, he's opened my eyes a lot I can tell you. He's put us onto books we'd never have known existed if it wasn't for him. Don't be afraid, he's always telling us. Don't be afraid of trying new things. There's people writing today who are trying to do things in writing, tell a story but not only tell a story: trying to find a new style or a new way of putting things, or perhaps even just a new way of seeing things.

There was one he got us onto last term, it was very very interesting I thought, a novel about a homosexual; but it wasn't about homosexuality as such, if you understand my meaning. The main person in it was a man who'd been like that all his life and he couldn't see anything wrong with it. But the clever part was how the writer got over to you that to that man, people who weren't homosexual were somehow peculiar and he couldn't understand them at all. It made you see things through someone else's eyes; and it wasn't asking you to feel sorry for him, it tried to get you to put yourself in his place so that you looked at things from a different standpoint. It made me think – about how many people I must have met through my life who were homosexual without me knowing it, and how I always took it for granted everyone was the same as I was. I must have said things and done things that perhaps hurt them, or at least made me seem very inconsiderate about them. Like telling a dirty joke perhaps, like men do; and taking it for granted they were going to enjoy hearing it, when it must've seemed very, well very distasteful to them.

The classes are not about how to write, I don't think anyone could teach you that. They're more about how to try and be aware of things, make your choice of material broader as you might say, if you ever were going to make a start. He says you've got to know what it is you want to write about first, then if you can see it clear enough and want to do it enough, you'll do it. Only don't write about yourself he says: he's always hammering that home to us. Yourself, if you're an ordinary sort of person with no education and who's never done anything with his life – well that's not a very interesting subject you see, unless you've got some unusual way of looking at things. Even if I don't ever actually write a novel, I'll always look on going to the classes as very important, something I enjoy doing a lot. That one whatsit called *Ulysses* by James Joyce, do you know that one? He had us nearly half the term on it, reading it ourselves, reading bits out that we didn't understand and then all of us talking about it. Someone would say, 'Oh, don't you understand that? Well I understand that, but I'll tell you the part I don't understand and that's this bit.' It's very interesting and it all makes you think. School never made you do that or at least mine didn't, school did nothing for me. I left it when I was twelve, I suppose it wasn't until I was about my middle fifties or somewhere around there I started being interested in being educated again.

A few years ago, about the week after my seventieth birthday I think it was, I went to the Education Department people and asked them if I could go to school. 'Yes' they said 'Of course you can, here's the list of all the night classes we've got.' I said I didn't want night classes, I wanted proper school; there were a lot of things I'd like to know a bit about to begin with, and then go on further with one or two I fancied to follow up.

'Well go to the library' they said. 'They've got books there about every subject you could think of, have a good look round and see what takes your fancy.' I said I thought going to the library was all right, but you needed somebody to guide you with study; and anyway I didn't want to read a big book about something to find out whether I was going to be interested in it or not. Then they said well what sort of subjects did I have in mind; I said that was the whole idea, I couldn't tell until I knew what there was. Geography, history, French, sums, which I think they call 'number' now, plants and animals and stars and English and so on – what I wanted was to go to an ordinary school where I could learn first of all what there was to learn. I wanted to do it full time, all day each day – proper school. No they said, they were very sorry but they didn't have anywhere like that. I said 'Yes you do' I said, 'there's a school over the road there. Let me go there like the children do, and be given homework and have my books marked and everything. Only I'd have to be excused the PT in the gymnasium.'

First of all they laughed. But I said 'Look I'm serious.' When they realized I was, they thought I must be mental. They said I couldn't do it, it wasn't allowed. So that was that, and I was very disappointed about it.

– I've lived here on this selfsame spot near enough almost all my life, for seventy-five years. Where these flats are used to be little streets of grubby terrace houses. I've worked it out: the one I was born in stood almost exactly here. I lived in it all the time I was a child. I left school when I was fourteen, and I was a good big lad for my age. I joined up in the Army in 1916: they were so short of men they didn't bother too much about your age. I never went abroad except to France after the Armistice; and when I came back I met Molly and we got married, and we came to live back here in the house with the rest. When we were rehoused twenty years ago it was from there to here. It's unbelievable nowadays, but there was eleven of us in the old house: my father and mother, me and Molly, and I had four brothers and three sisters.

As the others grew up and got married themselves, they moved away. In the end there was only us and my parents, and Molly looked after them for the rest of their days as well as bringing up our own two boys. I never had much of a job, because of no education you see: in my time I've been a sewerman, a boilerman, a storeman, and a brickmaker. Like they say, a Jack-of-all-trades and master of none. But I've tried to see to it my sons did better, and I think I succeeded in that. Edgar's worked all his life for an engineering company in Scotland, he's got a nice home and wife and two children. I say children, one of them's married and lives down here in London. He's got a boy of his own, that's my great-grandson Arnold who's eleven. Then our other boy Cedric, he's in Australia, he and his wife have got two boys too. They came over three years ago and they're coming back again next year. They asked me last time would I think about going out there to join them; but I don't know, I enjoy life too much here to want to go over the other side of the world and leave it. They keep on at me about it being a great place for retirement, all I'd need do is sit in the sun all day. Well I might be a senior citizen as we are called, but I haven't retired from living: I'm a senior unretired citizen.

One of my greatest joys of my life is going in the summer in the holidays to the Oval to watch the cricket with Arnold. He's mad about cricket, it's all he thinks about: a lovely lad, and he's got me almost as keen as he is now. We've had some great days together. It's a hard thing to try and explain, but him and me seem to understand each other without speaking about all sorts of things. I feel more close to Arnold than I've ever felt with any of my own children or any of the grandchildren either. I think it might have something to do with the fact he's the only other one in the family besides me whose got this thing that I've got of being left-handed.

You couldn't call it an affliction exactly, but it does make you feel that bit peculiar and odd, and not quite what you ought to be in comparison with other people. They call it 'sinister' don't they: I read it in a dictionary when I was a boy; it's something I've never forgotten, that to normal right-handed people it's a thing they find a bit frightening. It makes you feel lonely, especially as a child: you stand out, and in my day you got made fun of for it, though I expect they're more enlightened about those things now.

When I first realized Arnold was left-handed was when we were at a cricket match and he was writing something on the scorecard. I couldn't help it – it's daft but I was thrilled about it. I said 'Well God bless my soul Arnie, you're another one like me!' We both had a big laugh over it; he thought I was joking and having him on, so I had to do some writing for him to prove I couldn't write with my right hand either.

– We were very lucky, me and Molly. You read about so many marriages breaking down, or you meet couples and there's no other word for it they seem to downright hate each other. It seems to be their whole lives for them, they're forever trying to find nasty things to say to each other and ways to hurt each other. But Molly and me we were, we were very lucky. What I mean is we really liked each other, all that long long time, fifty years. What I mean by liked is we always fancied each other, sexually I mean. Right from when we were youngsters up to when she died, we were both always ready for it with each other: never ever less than twice a week, I don't think there was a week we missed in our whole marriage. And of course with it being like that, I was never once unfaithful to her. I never felt the slightest thing physical towards any other woman, she satisfied me completely and I think I did her.

Afterwards, after she died, it took me a long time to get over it, that feeling of being unfaithful to her every time. It must've been four years you know before I got over it. It's all right now though; what I had with Molly was something that nothing'll take away. I've never felt the desire to get married again. I still enjoy the sex. I wouldn't want to live with anyone again though, not one person.

I don't know why it should be, and I wouldn't want to particularly, it must be something biological: but I've not got like those men you hear about who go you know 'off' when they get old, and start to mess about with girls or little boys. One really big piece of luck for me is this thing I've always had that whatever age I was all through my life, the sort of person I've been sexually attracted to has always been someone my own age or a few years younger. I've never felt the need to look at sexy pictures or read books either, I've not been able to get any excitement or pleasure from them. A nice woman my own age, an hour or two in bed together with someone like that, that's always been the thing for me. And so long as it's regular, once a week or so, I'm perfectly content. It doesn't have to be what they call the full thing every time either – I enjoy the love-making and kissing and cuddling as much, or more even sometimes, on its own.

I've never been with a prostitute, I don't somehow fancy that, it's got to be someone I know and like. There again you see I've been lucky, there's any number of ladies around who're my age, widows or single most of them: I don't think it's right to run the risk of perhaps someone's husband finding out and making trouble about it. Most of them seem to feel the same way I do. I usually say something like 'Well shall we try it and see how it goes, and if you don't like it we'll not go on with it.' But there's not many that don't. I think there's something about sex that's really nice, it's fun but it's more than that, it gives you a good warm feeling inside of you, you're being absolutely natural. It's giving somebody pleasure, it's you giving somebody pleasure. I think that's very nice and very good. So long as you don't get jealous about them and they don't get jealous about you, it's not doing harm to anyone as far as I can see.

I suppose there must be about twelve or so ladies that we're on that kind of terms together. Most of them like myself belong to the church – it's a very good meeting place to come into contact with other people who're on their own. And if someone goes to church you know she's got what you call a level-headed approach to things; she's not going to be like somebody you might pick up casually in a pub. I don't like the sort of coarse jokes you sometimes hear women making in pubs. If I'm love-making with someone I prefer her to be a conventional sort of person like myself.

– Changes, yes oh there've been a lot of them. This nice modern housing estate, after the last war it was a terrible slum; people living in conditions that were appalling, I'd hope we never see a return to times like that. The biggest change I've noticed without question is the health of people, particularly the children: nowadays you never see ragged kids running about without shoes on their feet and no bottoms in their trousers. Most of them look well fed and well nourished; and despite what a lot say, I think people are far happier now than they used to be. You'll get the few unfortunate ones here and there who can't manage, who life's given some hard knocks to. And there's still a lot of inequality, too few at the top having too much of the country's wealth. But the middle band of people, money's spread out far more among them than it used to be, and it reaches further down to what used to be the very poor and deprived. More people have more comfort, I think that's what I'm trying to say.

The one big change that I don't notice, and I'm looking back over seventy years when I say this, is the one so many people are always going on about, the increase in the coloured population. We've always had people who were coloured, I can remember plenty of them round here when I was only a child. A lot of them were seamen and people from the docks in those days, that's how they came to be here. To my mind the British government ought to be ashamed of itself, the way it's treated the West Indians in particular. Right after the Second World War there were big recruiting schemes in Jamaica and Trinidad and those places, to get people to come and work over here. They'd always been brought up to think of Britain as their home country even if they'd never been there, so they were really pleased to come, especially as they were told the living standards were much higher and the wages far better than anything they could ever earn in the West Indies.

And what did they find when they got here? That what they were really wanted for was only as cheap labour, to run the buses and trains and work as cleaners and cooks in hospitals. They got the worst jobs, the worst houses, and poor education for their children. There's still hardly more than a handful of black people in top jobs anywhere in the country: not only them but their children have been exploited and taken advantage of. And this is after twenty-five to thirty years of them being here. I think it's disgraceful what's been done to them, I lose my temper.

I get short-tempered when I talk to people about that and other things, that's one of the penalties of getting old. Old and fractious you get, that's the expression isn't it? It's funny though how people will put up with things like bad behaviour from those who're old, yet they won't tolerate it for a minute from kids. 'You're old enough to know better' they'll say to a kid when they're telling it off for something, but you'll never hear that said to an elderly person. They've got an excuse for anything they do at all, rudeness, bad temper, carelessness. I think old people get away with murder sometimes, people fall over themselves to be understanding towards them when really by all logic what they should do is shout at them for their bad behaviour.

You get stupid about being old sometimes; I know I do. A young man on the bus the other day, he got up and gave me his seat: do you know, it was all I could do not to lose my temper with him, specially as he said 'Here you are grandad.' You know it's meant kindly but a lot of people treat old people all the same, as though they were infirm. And stupid with it, that's the most common of all: when they start to say something to you they lift up their voice, speak loud and slow and clearly, making it plain to you they're ready for you not to understand. Funny isn't it?

To my mind there's far too much fuss made of old people: they get cut-price fares, cut-price meals, social clubs all over the place, special trips out. I'm not saying they shouldn't have them; but I do think they're a very privileged section of the community, and at the expense of others who're more in need. I'm thinking of mothers on their own bringing up kids, or single parents: they're the ones life is hard for, and they're the ones who should have a few treats out of the taxes.

My God I go rabbiting on don't I, you should tell me to stop, you must get bored to death. We must have one day when you do all the talking and I'll sit and listen; you tell me all about your life and your ideas, you think this is wrong and that's wrong, and it ought to be put a stop to. I don't know that it's good for me to do all the talking: I enjoy it though, I'll not pretend I don't. When I told Arnie about it, what I was doing, talking to you about things I'd never talked about to anyone before, I said to him to keep it a secret and not say anything to anyone else in the family about it. I told him perhaps one day he might come across it in a book, and find out a lot of things about me he didn't know. I wonder if he might one day read it and think 'Cor that must be my old great-grandad that must.' You never know do you?

Crumbs, you know some secrets about me now though all right don't you? But it's been very good having someone to talk to over these last weeks – ten times has it been, eleven? I've had the feeling often after we've been talking that I ought to get down to it myself you know, and try and write my autobiography. But it's not just a question of skill, it's a question of time. I don't mean I don't have the time, I do of course. But at my age you start rather living day to day, you're what they call 'at risk'. There was Bernard Shaw though wasn't there, he wrote quite a few things when he was getting on; and H. G. Wells, and that Victor Hugo. So you don't know eh, one of these days I might do it.

Part Three

OUTSIDERS (1)

'I'll be Jack the Lad'

PC Jack Farmer

The first time I saw him he was walking along the pavement in Gorrivale Square in torrential June rain, the collar of his uniform mac turned up high and his helmet pulled almost onto his nose. He walked slowly and methodically, as though to demonstrate that it would take worse than a monsoon to deter him from following his predestined beat. At the time I was sheltering in the entrance to an alleyway; he joined me, gave a nod and then stood by me silent and aloof. Forbidding, six foot four, fourteen stone, fair-haired, blue-eyed; heavy-featured and square-faced.

It was a surprise the first time we talked afterwards in a café, when he was in civilian clothes and without his uniform and helmet, to see how young and fresh-faced he was.

– I'm twenty-three, I've been in the Force just on five years now. I don't live on the Estate, I live in a house with my parents about ten miles away, and come here each day. I'm what's known as a temporary Beat Officer. But the real Beat Officer for this part is PC Arthur Davidson. This has been his patch for years, he knows a hell of a lot more about it than I'll ever do. Come to that, he knows a hell of a lot more about everything than me; but he's twice my age and has been a copper five times as long.

I don't mind talking to you, but I must check it out with Arthur first. I haven't been attached to Tullbrook Road station very long and I wouldn't like him to think I was treading on his toes. He's been very good, very helpful to me since I came. Knowing the sort of man he is I'm sure he won't have any objection; but all the same I'd like to make sure. If he says he doesn't mind, then fair enough, I'd be glad to help you.

– As I think I said to you when we talked before, I'm only attached to this area temporarily. In a few months I shall be moved on to somewhere else, somewhere different: it may be quieter or it may be busier, or if I'm lucky it might even be back driving cars again, which is what I like best. After a while, when I've got a bit more time under my belt as they say, I may start specializing in some particular aspect of police work; but at present I'm getting as much experience of as many different things as I can.

What I'm here to get experience of is what could roughly be described as community policing: that means the bobby's beat is the same beat all the time. The idea of it is that he gets to know the area and the people in it, and they get to know him. It's really the old idea of policing, trying to put the policeman forward as an individual who's known to people by name; but whether it's something that works in a high-population inner-city area like this is something I personally am rather doubtful about. To take Providence Estate as the example, it doesn't seem to me half the people who live on it really feel they belong to it: it's somewhere that they eat and sleep and go to work from, and that's all. It could be anywhere as far as they're concerned, it wouldn't matter.

Whether it was more of an individual place with a character of its own in the olden days I wouldn't know, because I wasn't here then. But I do feel when I'm walking round that it hasn't got much character to it, no personality of its own. I've been on three other London housing estates and they're all the same, so I'm not making a criticism of Providence in particular. It may be if I spent more time here and had more opportunity to get to know people it'd look different. But I can't see myself how it could. Arthur will perhaps give you a different opinion, he's very enthusiastic himself about the system, but I can't say I am. In a way the estate kind of overwhelms me I suppose.

Take the towers over there, Darwen and Bolton and Kendal and the rest. There's six of them in all, with twenty floors each and four living units to a floor; so that's a total of 480 living units with an average at very least of two and a half inhabitants per unit. That gives you something like twelve to fifteen hundred people living in just that small area over there where the towers are, with only at most no more than five per cent of them at ground level. So what hope have I or anyone else of ever getting to see and be seen by other than a tiny proportion of the people who live there? I can't very well go walking up and down the stairs all day long in the hope that now and again someone might open their door and see me passing by. So where's your community policing then, when the majority of the community's not even ever seen you or is going to? You could apply exactly the same argument to the big blocks, Vernon and Foxman and Cramner, and to the flats, and so on and so on. Whoever designed this estate in the first place one thing is for sure, and that's that it never crossed their mind there might be a problem policing it.

There are parts of this estate, large parts of it, that are nowhere near a road at all and they can only be reached by a policeman on foot. You get a call on your radio that someone in number such-and-such in so-and-so block of flats has seen someone suspicious hanging about, but there's no way at all that you can get there quickly. You can be seen coming from miles off, and so naturally you get no chance of an arrest or even making a stop-and-question. It makes you feel a right Charlie when you stop the first bloke you see as soon as you arrive on a landing and ask him what he's doing, and the answer you get is 'I live here mate.' Which he does, and it doesn't exactly put the efficiency of the police in the forefront of his mind.

Mind you, no one could say there's very much crime on the estate. That may be one of the reasons why I'm not too keen on being on it myself. I like to be where the action is, I don't much care for being just Mr Plod. My ambition is to get up the West End eventually, or into plain clothes, where I'll be Jack the Lad.

– I suppose the most common crime there is on Providence is what we call domestics. That's where a husband's knocking his wife about, or the woman he's living with. Policemen don't really like domestics very much, because they can be very very dodgy and there's all sorts of things can go wrong. You'll get a report comes into the station over the phone from a neighbour: quite often he won't give you his name or anything, but he'll say he's just walked past flat number so-and-so and it sounds like somebody's being killed in there. Maybe you'll decide to do something about it, maybe you won't: but if you get say two such reports not long after one another, then you don't have much choice but to go along and have a look.

Knock on the door, ring the doorbell or whatever: Good evening sir I've just come to give you a call because we've had a report of a disturbance here. Nine times out of ten you'll get the innocent look: what sort of a disturbance officer, there's no disturbance here, it must have been the flat up above or the one below. You wonder whether to push it or not and say can you go in and have a look, but if you do that you're more than likely to get a lot of lip. And more often than not too the man'll bring his woman to the door anyway, or call her: Elsie there's a policeman here says there's been a report of a disturbance, have you heard any disturbance? And she'll come to the door and she'll stand there and look at you with half her face swollen up like a football and an enormous black eye, and she'll say No she hasn't heard no disturbance. So what can you do? About all you can do is hope the man'll take the hint and lay off of her.

Now and again you'll get the one who will say Yes he's beating the shit out of me and I want to lay a complaint. Here again, it's not wise to think you're treading an easy path, because you're certainly not. Most of them by the time it's come to court they've had another think, and you're the one who's got egg on your face. Well Your Worship we did have a bit of a squabble yes, and he gave me a bit of a push But I tripped over the edge of the carpet and fell and hit my face on the sideboard, he certainly didn't mean it. The beak says to her but the officer says when he arrived you said to him, and so on. Oh no Your Worship I never said nothing like that, no the officer can't have heard properly, I'd never say a thing like that, not about my Georgie oh no, he'd never hurt a fly.

You hear about these women, you know in battered wives' refuges and that sort of thing. Well, it's my opinion most of them could have prevented themselves getting into that sort of situation long before, if they'd only done the sensible thing in the first place. It would be to say to her husband the very first time he lays a finger on her, that if he ever does such a thing again she's straight down to the law shop to lay a complaint about him. And the next time he does, to do it: without hesitation to do it. She can take it back again when it comes to court if he's shown signs in the meantime of changing his ways. In fact, she can make a good drama out of forgiving him for it there and then in the court if she wants. But that'd be my advice to a woman: give him a warning, but only one and then the next time report him without listening to an apology or anything. But to go on and on staying there and taking it, and then suddenly one day deciding you've had enough, and perhaps sneaking out to a wives' refuge with the kids and a handful of clothing: well, it seems to me you should never have let it get as far as that ever, you should have put a stop to it long before.

– We were talking about crime on the estate before; I was saying the most common was men hitting their wives. I don't want to give the impression from that which I might have done, that knocking women around is a sort of hobby that's very popular amongst the people who live on the estate, because it isn't. I think I said when you asked me that it was the most common crime there was: which may have given you the impression there was a fair amount of it. When I was thinking about it afterwards, I thought it would have been more true to say it's fairly common only among a very small number of families on the estate. We get so many reports come in, and they're all about this one group of say ten families all together at most. The reports come in once a week or more, and it's bound to be one or other of them. So that's the only sense in which I meant it was common: regular, but only among the same group all the time. It's not common in the meaning of widespread, not at all.

The most widespread crime of course is petty thieving. Not so much burglary and breaking and entering, but nicking things that are left out in the open: motorcars or parts of motorcars, contents of vans and lorries, goods left in packing cases in yards, that sort of thing. It doesn't seem to matter what it is – if you leave it in view, some people take it as a challenge to them to try and nick it. I remember a young lad I took once, only about thirteen or fourteen: he nipped over the wall at the back of a shop and lifted a big cardboard carton that big of sixty-watt light bulbs; about 500 there must have been in it or somewhere near. I said to him how did he think he was going to sell them, who was he going to get rid of them to? Do you know what he said? He said he wasn't going to sell them, him and some of his mates were going to take them up on the roof of one of those big blocks and drop them on people. I think it was true too, that was really what he had in mind. Amazing.

And there's a certain amount, a small amount but not as much as you might expect, of mugging. You'll get five or six youths, nearly always black, who stop people and make them give up their handbags or wallets. Sometimes they get a bit violent with it, but not unless the intended victim starts it first as a rule by shouting or screaming or something.

Blacks make me very uneasy, they're a new factor in crime nowadays. They always say the police are picking on them, but it's a fact that in ninety per cent of cases when someone comes in to complain they've been robbed in the street, they say it's by black boys. So quite naturally, it stands to reason if a day or two later you see a group of black youngsters standing around in the very same place you've had a report someone was robbed by a group of blacks a couple of nights before, what else do you do but go up to them and start questioning them? They complain about it, the race relations people say you're harassing blacks, but I don't know what they expect, do they expect you just to walk on past them and pretend you haven't heard about what was done by a group of black youths in that same spot not all that long before? I think any policeman would be failing in his duty if he didn't question them, and OK if they're polite and they've not done anything, they've nothing to fear.

The trouble is, and this is a fact, that most of them are not polite. Whether it's their upbringing or what, I don't know; they don't exactly jostle you, but they very often do come on, moving round and round you, and I don't mind admitting it's something which can be very scary. They do it because they know it's not easy for you to tell the difference between one black face and another: you'll start questioning one, and before you know where you are one's moved round to the side of you and you're talking to a different one without realizing it. You start getting a bit rattled and you show it. That makes it worse: they'll laugh at you right in your face, while those behind you'll be saying out loud things like 'fucking pig', 'white bastard' and the rest of it. You turn round and of course then it's, No, it wasn't me said that not me, I didn't hear no one say that. Well, they talk about police harassment, but there's a lot of black harassment of policemen too, and that's a fact, as any policeman on the street will tell you.

The other dodgy thing about the blacks as well is that a lot of them, far more than white boys, a lot of them do carry knives. They reckon themselves to be in a permanent state of being threatened, and to some extent if you pay attention to the antics of the National Front, they are. So they can justify to themselves the need for them to carry knives for protection. They know it's an offence, and any policeman questioning a group of them will know that half the members of that group have got knives on them and are therefore committing an offence. But it's got to be a very brave policeman indeed if he's on his own, who's going to insist on them all turning out their pockets. But your only alternative to doing that is to close an eye to the fact they're flouting the law. So naturally what you do, before you even approach them, is to ask for assistance on your radio: if you're lucky a mobile'll be there in two or three minutes, and then at least you can take some of them in and get them to empty their pockets at the station. But of course they know the game just as well as you do, and by the time they're in the station anything like a knife has long since disappeared into thin air.

This whole business with the blacks is steadily getting worse, and I don't know what the answer to it is.

'Going home to worry'

Miss Hancock

I used to see Miss Hancock somewhere on the estate at least once a week nearly every week. A small slight dark woman in her late thirties, hatless in a neat dark coat and with a crammed shoulder bag, she would pass me with a polite smile, coming out of a block of flats as I was going in, or give a little wave from the other side of the road when she was walking one way and I another.

For a long time we never exchanged more than 'Good morning' or 'Good afternoon', and I didn't know who she was or what she did. It was several months before the opportunity of a chat occurred.

– I'm what's called an Estate Officer; I'm one of nine hundred employed by the GLC, and myself and three others are responsible for Providence Estate.

I've been with the GLC for three years, but I've only been one year of it so far here. Before, I was on another estate, and I came here because travelling was easier. I live out in the country, in a small village just outside one of the dormitory towns: it's twenty minutes walk for me in the morning to thestation, then just under an hour on the train if it's a fast one, plus another ten minutes or so to the Housing Department offices on the tube. So all in all it's an hour and a half's journey in to work and the same out back home again in the evening. I live with my parents; I like the peace and quiet and cleanness of the countryside after being in town all day, so I put up with the travelling because of that. I'm not really a town person: here is where I work and earn a living, but I'm glad to get away from it at the end of the day and at weekends. I don't think I could stand working here and living here as well.

I have one section of the estate to look after entirely on my own, and my three colleagues each have their own individual sections too. But we don't absolutely strictly adhere to boundary lines: I might ask one of the others to make a call for me one week say in Jesmond Close, the posh part of the estate, if I know he's going to be somewhere near there. In exchange I'll do one for him that's handy for me on one particular day. At holiday times we cover for one another, so it's useful to get to know as much of the whole estate as possible. I think I could say by now there isn't any part of it at all I haven't been to at least once: as soon as I read an address, I find as a rule I know exactly where it is.

My job is really two jobs in one: one is to control rent arrears, and the other is to maintain relationships with the tenants on behalf of the GLC. I have some but not a lot of power to take decisions on my own: I'm more a communications channel between landlord and tenant, or in the opposite direction between tenant and landlord. I might be the only human face connected with the GLC that a tenant ever sees apart from the mobile caretakers, so I'm very conscious that the impression I make is the one they're going to keep, and I try to keep contact with tenants as friendly and polite as possible. With one side of the job this is fairly easy to do and I thoroughly enjoy it: the other is not as easy or pleasant, but I do the best I can. On the whole rent arrears control is nothing like as awkward and difficult as a lot of people might think.

– When the GLC offers someone a tenancy, if it's in my section it's my job to take them to have a look at the property so they can decide if they want to take it or not.

As you'd expect, there's a tremendous variety of reactions, ranging from those who're really desperate and are perhaps having somewhere of their own offered to them for the first time in their lives, to those who put on an act of being almost affronted at you for even suggesting they might want to live in such a place as you're showing them, because it's of far lower standard than they want you to feel they expect. There's just no satisfying some people. But you can only keep your patience and explain this is all that can be offered just now; and they don't have to take it if they don't want to, their names can go back on the list until something else comes along.

I won't say it very often happens, but it does happen sometimes that you'll get a person who's persuaded her doctor to give her a letter saying if she isn't adequately rehoused, and very promptly, she's likely to end up having to stay in hospital and her children be taken into care. So you go along with her to show her somewhere, say on the fourth or fifth floor of one of the tower blocks. And she says Oh no, she couldn't possibly live somewhere as high as that, she'd be frightened to death all day long of one of the kids falling over the balcony. You think Well there are people like that who really can't stand heights, so you go to a bit of trouble to make sure when a ground-floor flat becomes vacant she gets the first offer of it. Along you go with her again: Good gracious she says, you don't seriously expect her to live there do you, with all the traffic going past fifty yards away and kids running round and shouting and yelling all day long? So you grit your teeth and go back to the office and have a chat with your colleagues – maybe one of them has got something that you feel will be ideal for her. You offer him one of your vacancies in exchange, for one of his people who wants to live in a tower or on the ground floor or wherever. Since you're the one who's now in a way got to know the woman, you take her yourself even though the property's not strictly speaking on your section. It'll perhaps be an old house that's been modernized and done up and converted into two maisonettes in a quiet part, well kept and not noisy. Just the job you think: but she takes one look and says how do you expect her to live that far away from the shops, if you were really any good at your job you wouldn't be wasting her time like this going on showing her ridiculously unsuitable places.

I suppose you shouldn't really, but you can't help it, you tend to get a bit cool with people like that. They're very few and far between thank goodness, but especially when you know there's someone much further down the list who'd give their eyeteeth for any one of the places you've shown them, you have to bite your tongue off nearly sometimes. I suppose the worst I've had is a lady on the estate I was on previously, who kept me on the go showing her place after place for almost a whole year. She'd got a doctor's letter saying she was in a crisis situation and if she wasn't rehoused he wouldn't be responsible – and it had been written over a year before, but she still seemed to be surviving.

On the other hand, completely opposite is perhaps the old person who thanks you literally with tears in their eyes, as though it was you personally who was responsible for them being given the offer of a place. You take them along to have a look at it, and they're saying how lovely it is before you've even turned the key in the door. You feel a bit of a fraud because you've had no say yourself in the process of the place being offered to them: their name has come up in strict rotation on the list as it should do, and you're only the person showing them over it. But to some of them, they make no secret of it, they think you're an angel sent straight from heaven. I think it's sad that people should sometimes be in such desperate straits before they get somewhere. You can't really claim any credit for it, but all the same you do feel the job's rewarding when someone's so obviously delighted at what's happening for them.

– The other side of the job, the one I said wasn't by any means as easy or pleasant, is the rent arrears control part of it. I sometimes get the feeling when I've had a particularly sticky week that there's hardly any other side to the job than that at all. I don't know why it should be that rent arrears seem to come up in batches, but they do. Weeks'll go by and no one's falling behind, then suddenly you'll have perhaps fifteen all at once and you know you're in for a hard week that week.

The GLC system is that if someone's two weeks behind with the rent, they get a letter; if another week goes by and they still haven't paid they'll get a second letter, much stiffer but also saying if there's some particular reason for non-payment like someone being in hospital, the Housing Department must be told immediately or else. If that doesn't produce results, then I have to go and visit the tenant: and if I get nowhere, then two weeks after that they'll receive notice to quit.

I look on it as a distasteful but necessary chore: I don't enjoy it, but on the other hand I try as far as possible to be detached about it and not let it get me down. I don't know whether being a woman, and for that matter a small woman and a quiet sort of person, is an advantage or not: I think it probably is. I shouldn't imagine when someone opens the door and sees me they think I'm very threatening, and I don't go barging in and blustering or making a fuss. As far as possible I stay affable and pleasant: I try to give a smile and get a smile, but at the same time make it clear the situation's serious and I mean business. No one would be any good at getting in rent arrears if they were utterly soft-hearted, so I hope that I'm both fair but tough when it's necessary to be.

I'd say we never have any trouble with perhaps eighty to eighty-five per cent of our tenants; perhaps another ten per cent'll get behind maybe once or at the most twice during their tenancy; and then there's the final five per cent who always owe not just their rent but perhaps a couple of hundred pounds here and another couple of hundred there for other things, electricity, HP and the rest of it. They've been like that all their lives and they're never going to be any different. It's a small handful of people, those I think no one could ever get anywhere with. In cases of that sort where I know the people concerned through contacts with them before on the same subject, I pay my visit but don't get disappointed if I don't achieve a result.

Keeping in mind the figures I've just been talking about, I try to remember when I get a note to go and see someone whose rent's in arrears and I don't know their name, that this could well be the first time in their lives they've ever had a visit of this kind. They might be frightened, they might be angry, they might be deeply ashamed, they might feel that everyone in the world's against them: so it's going to be no use me making up my mind beforehand what sort of person I'm going to find myself face to face with, the only thing to do is go along and see, and try to react appropriately. If they're frightened I'll do my best not to be a frightening sort of person; if they're angry I'll try and mollify them, and if they're something else again then it's up to me to find the best way of responding to it.

The basic purpose of my visit is to get them to pay the rent they owe, and in most cases while I'm there to impress on them that the situation really is serious and they must put it right. I'll ask them what offer they will make; to pay it all off in three days' time, to pay half of it this week and all the other half next week; and in one or two particular circumstances, to ask my superiors if the repayment time can be a little less inflexible. I've some latitude in making decisions, but anything which involves a large sum or a longer time than usual, I have to refer to higher up.

I regard it absolutely as part of the process as well to try to find out why the tenant has fallen behind in making payment. In the great majority of cases it's a one-off, there might have been illness or unemployment or some kind of domestic upset, and in many instances the tenant really and truly can't pay rather than won't pay. I always carry with me a supply of rent-rebate application forms; and it's my duty to point out to someone that they're entitled to a rebate if they are. Quite a lot of people can't cope with forms of that sort, so I very often sit down at the table with them and help them fill the form in. I won't take it away and post it for them, but I'll do everything else that's necessary; all they have to do is sign it and send it off. I also carry rate-rebate applications as well. Most people who are in trouble with money want to tell you how it's come about, and if what they say sounds as though it's honest and correct, as I say I think I have a duty to try and help them get sorted out.

There are some who are downright cheats, who'll spin you a fantastic tale. Like anyone else I can be taken in, and have been a time or two. But not very often, and of course never twice by the same person. What they're telling me the second time might well be true, as it happens: but if they've lied to me once, as far as I'm concerned that's it and I'm not going to believe them. I leave the wheels to go on turning, and they pay up quick or find themselves in court. We have an arrangement with the social services people by the way, that if proceedings are going to be taken against someone and it looks like they're going to be evicted, we tip off the social services in advance if there are children in the household who are going to need to be taken care of.

Court cases and eviction orders, I'll say quite clearly that I regard these as the failures of my job. I don't feel bad about having failed, but all the same I do think of it as having failed. On the other side of the coin, a success to me is where someone has paid off arrears: perhaps with a bit of help in the way of claiming a rebate, perhaps with a bit of tact and moral support. The main thing is they've paid it off; and as I think I said to you before, that's usually the end of it and you don't find that person ever falls behind again in most cases.

– There are sometimes occasions when you get very much drawn into a situation, you get far more involved in it than you could ever have dreamed of when you first knocked on the door to say you're from the GLC and you've come about the rent arrears.

I remember one quite elderly man I went to see a few months ago. He'd been a tenant living in the same flat for more than twelve years and then suddenly one day after all that time a ticket came through to say he was owing over four weeks' rent. Off I go to knock on his door. When he opens it I say who I am, and it's Oh yes we have had a letter about this, please come in. He was a very quietly spoken old gentleman, and he had a very quiet polite wife of about the same age. Please sit down he says, and he'll explain to me how it's come about. The opportunity had occurred a few weeks ago, he says, for him to buy some very rare old books: they were very expensive, but even so at the price he paid for them he was going to get more than double that back again. It meant using up his savings and his wife's savings as well, but it was such an opportunity as he'd get only once in a lifetime and he couldn't miss it.

He showed me his bank savings book to prove he'd drawn the money out like he said, and his wife's bank savings book the same. Between them it amounted to every penny they had. Then he showed me the books: I'm not an expert on the subject, but they were certainly old leather-bound books and for all I could tell they might well have been worth what he said. Just for a minute I thought he might be going to ask me to take one or two of them instead of the actual money, but he didn't. He had a well-known West End book dealer coming round the next morning to buy them he said, and so in two or three days at the most all his temporary difficulties would be over. I said all right, well he should ask the dealer to pay him partly in cash at least and I'd be round at the same time the following afternoon for the money.

It was really quite heart-rending when I went. The dealer had been, as he said he would: and he'd told the old boy he'd been diddled, the books weren't even worth a tenth of what he'd paid for them. He was shattered. I think it was a genuine story, I think someone had tricked him wickedly, and it needed a big effort to say I still had to insist he paid the rent. How he did it eventually I don't know, but he did pay it within the next week or so. I suppose he borrowed it, and I was quite upset about it at the time because he was such a nice old man. I told him to go to the police, but whether he did or not I don't know. For quite a time afterwards I found myself doing the one thing I'd always said I'd never do, which was leaving work at the end of the day and going home to worry. I've often thought about how he was getting on and how long it took his pride to recover from that rotten thing that had been done to him.

The other sort that I get sometimes rather too personally involved with are the people who get in a mess but won't apply for rent or rate rebates that they're entitled to because they think it's some kind of charity. This is not all that uncommon among older people: you really have to sit down and talk to them, sometimes for an hour nearly, to get them to see that there's nothing to be ashamed of in applying.

– In the year, or almost a year, that I've been on Providence, I've only had one person I've been to see who's been in any way rude or aggressive to me. He was a man who I think was a bit mentally unstable and he did make rather a lot of extravagant threats about what he'd do to me if I didn't clear off, though that wasn't the actual expression he used. Luckily for me his wife was there and she knew how to deal with him: she shouted at him and bullied him off into the kitchen or somewhere, and then she sat down with me and told me what a hard time she was having, which I could quite believe. But that was an exceptional case.

There's a very strong tradition among the working class that whatever else you go short of, you pay the rent. In the old days when people were paid mostly in cash it was the first thing you put aside out of the pay packet, and most people seem to budget for it still in that same way, rent first and everything else has to come after it. This applies to far and away the greatest proportion of the people who live here.

'Passing time till life begins'
Clifford King

Riseborough Secondary was a sprawling characterless redbrick 1930s building in the middle of Tullbrook Road on the eastern perimeter of the estate. Clifford King, its headmaster, was a small bald-headed man in his late forties, his brown eyes flicking restlessly behind his steel-rimmed spectacles and his hands clasping and unclasping nervously in front of him on his desk as he talked.

– I've been in charge here for three years. Before that I was Deputy Head of another Inner London Education Authority secondary school in north London. I live at the moment in a house in one of the southwestern London suburbs; a detached house, quite a nice area, my wife and I have lived there for ten years. We have three children, two girls and a boy. The youngest is eighteen now and is just going on to university. Our two daughters are both married, so there's only the wife and I now. I think perhaps we'll sell our house within the next year or so, when I hope to get a job back in the Midlands somewhere, Warwickshire or somewhere like that, which is where we both originate from. All in all I've worked in London now for close on twenty years: that's long enough, I don't really like the south very much and I shall have no second thoughts about leaving it if I get the opportunity.

The school has just under seven hundred pupils, almost exactly half and half boys and girls. My deputy is a woman, Miss Phillipson, and although we share the work of running the school between us we try to avoid a situation where the boys feel I'm in charge of them and the girls that they're in her charge. She and I take morning assembly on alternate days, and in that way we try to get over to the children that the school is totally cohesive and there are no sex differences. Most of the classes too are pretty well equally divided, although naturally cookery and home economics classes are mainly made up of girls, metalwork and woodwork of boys, and so on. And there's a division between the sexes too where sports are concerned: the boys play football, the girls hockey, the boys cricket and the girls tennis or rounders. The divisions are what you'd expect them to be, what you would call the perfectly natural ones.

There would be no bar to a boy taking cookery or a girl doing woodwork or metalwork: the reason that none of them do is that, in the time I've been here at least, none of them have ever asked to. I'm sure they're more influenced by the other children in this respect rather than by anything else. I think most children like to conform, to be like the other children and not seem to be odd or peculiar in any way.

The age range is between eleven and sixteen, and the educational standard is up to GCE or 'O' level. I don't believe in forcing children educationally: I think they should find their own level during their formative years, so we don't lay any great stress on academic achievement in the sense of making special announcements at assembly for instance, if some particularly bright boy or girl gets three or four 'O' levels. We did have a girl last year who got four 'O's, and I think that's the most anyone has ever got in recent years. CSE's are rather different: we had one boy last year who got nine and a girl who got eight. But as I say, we're not the sort of school which judges success by how many certificates the pupils gain or exams they pass. Our aim is to give them the opportunity to find their own level and open their eyes a little, to start them thinking about what they're going to do after they leave school. Very few of the girls think much further than leaving, getting a job for a few years and then settling down into marriage and children. The boys' thoughts run mostly along practical lines; they come from families with deeply ingrained traditions about being wage-earners rather than salaried people, skilled or semiskilled artisans rather than professional people. It's possible for particularly bright children to go on from here at fifteen or sixteen to grammar schools if they wish to: more importantly I should say it's a case of if their parents wish them to. I would say that in the three years I've been here a total of about only eight or ten children have done that.

Schooling you see in a working-class area like this, is largely regarded as a necessary evil rather than as an aim in itself. It's looked on rather like a way of passing time till life begins; the time that life begins and you enter adulthood is when you're old enough to leave school. Nearly everyone is waiting impatiently for that moment – they don't see school and grown-up life as part of one continuing process, but as two entirely separate states. In the first you're an underprivileged person, a member of a downtrodden minority almost; then you earn your freedom after you've served the requisite number of years. You become an adult, an accepted and respected person, and you've served the unavoidable apprenticeship and come through it, and no one can force you back into it again.

I know this sort of thing isn't what educationalist-theory sort of people like to hear, but it's reality. I often think the people who do the most preaching and philosophizing about education are those who've got least practical experience of teaching. They postulate ideas which they've dreamed up themselves, and then tried to sell them to other people as being good ones. But there's nothing which says that they are any good in fact, and they're impossible to prove or disprove with facts. To give an example of what I mean? Well, history in the sense of the history of English monarchs is supposed to be of value in a child's education. I can't myself see any way in which it is, unless that particular child is going to go on and study history for the purpose of continuing the whole process by eventually teaching it to the next generation of children. This is perhaps an oversimplification, but I'd venture that a knowledge of the life and times of James the First was going to be of no earthly use whatsoever to any child who's in this school at this very moment. It's being taught because it's on the curriculum to be taught, and without wanting to be rude to anyone I'd say it's very likely being taught by a teacher who's swotted it up only the night before he or she is talking about it in the classroom. The teacher doesn't really care much one way or the other about James the First, so it's unlikely that there's going to be much enthusiasm put into getting him over to the class, or that they'll ever regard James the First as someone who's got or has ever had the remotest connection with their own lives at all.

I hope I'm not sounding unduly cynical about this, but I think there's something wrong with a system where pupils spend large parts of their schooltime trying to remember facts and figures about subjects which they're not interested in, and which are being drilled into them by teachers who aren't interested in what they're doing. Neither pupils nor teachers can see any point in the exercise. And the fact is that there is no point in the exercise. But the years go by and the system is perpetuated and perpetuates itself; and it's all a total waste of time and money. Eventually when exam time comes round there may or may not be a question in the history examination about James the First. If there isn't, then God knows how many hours of teacher and pupil effort have been wasted on the subject: and if there is, the pupil will do his or her best to answer the question and then forget the matter for ever. If he or she should ever want to know something about King James, there are encyclopaedias in libraries which can be consulted; and various worthies have written whole books about the gentleman, all of them far more informative and detailed than the few lines devoted to him in school textbooks. So it's no wonder to me that this kind of knowledge-gathering is just looked on by children as a way of passing the time until they get involved in the realities of life.

– Without having it properly checked I couldn't tell you with any great degree of accuracy how many of the children in this school live on Providence Estate, but I would say it was less than a quarter of them. This is because there are quite a large number of schools in this part of the world, there's a variety of choice, and some of the children who are here come from long distances away for no other reason that I know of than that their brother or sister is here, or came here before them, or they have a friend here. I would say it has a reputation of being neither a particularly good nor a particularly bad school, nothing very marked one way or the other. In working-class areas I don't think the notion of schools as good or bad has a very strong hold: education is compulsory so you send your child to school, and it doesn't go much further than that. If education wasn't compulsory, I think a lot of parents wouldn't bother.

I would substantiate that by saying that we have a high truancy rate, or what I would define myself as a high truancy rate. I'd say on average each child truants about one day per fortnight throughout the school year. By this I don't mean every child is away one day a fortnight: some never miss a day in the whole of their school lives, others never have a full week's schooling in the whole of their school lives. I'm merely averaging it out and making a rough calculation, and the calculation is perhaps more of a guess than anything. The Inner London Education Authority I'm sure would deny that the figure was anywhere near as high as that; but I do know, as every teacher does if he or she is honest, that there is far more truanting than is ever actually recorded. A kid will quite commonly come in for the first half hour or so of the day, long enough to get himself marked as present, and then disappear for the rest of the day. There's no way of knowing very often in a school of this size whether a child is here for the rest of the day or not.

Again this is a matter of tradition, this truanting. You'll hear it said that it's a problem, but I don't regard it as such: as one of the facts of school life is how I think it should be regarded. I think if a child comes to school four days out of five, that's quite good really: I think it would be hard to prove that it made any great difference to them in real-life terms, and I'd almost go so far as to say that so long as what they're doing isn't downright criminal, they're probably learning as much that'll be of value to them while they're away from school as they are while they're here. I would sooner my teachers taught the children who wanted to be here than tried to teach those whose minds might be hundreds of miles away even if their bodies were in the desk in the classroom.

To get back to the subject of the estate, although we're the nearest to it in physical terms, we're not in any way connected particularly with it. Between where we're sitting now here in my office and the actual geographical boundary of the estate is only a matter of fifty yards: you can see the tower blocks out of that window, and the entrance to one of the blocks of flats is only just across the road there. But we're light-years away in every other sense: I think only about two or three out of our total staff of forty-odd teachers live there. And I for one, for instance, never have occasion to set foot on the estate. Once last year I had to go and see one of the domestic staff about an urgent matter, but that was the last time I was there.

I suppose it could be argued that the estate should have its own school, actually on the estate, to give it more of an identity and community sense of its own; but I personally wouldn't say the argument was one which had much validity. The boys and girls from Providence who come here are coming into a quite different community to the one they live in, and that's not necessarily a bad thing for them at all. And they go home from here at the end of the day. They're experiencing two different communities instead of one, so I think it could be argued that was a good experience or at least not necessarily a bad one.

It may be the geographical location that we have, being over across the other side of quite a wide and busy main road with a lot of traffic, but I think to a lot of people on the estate whose children come here we seem further away than we actually are. I'm surprised, to be frank, how few parents we ever see on open days and school occasions like the annual play and so forth. Here again I think it's something where tradition plays quite a large part: 'teacher knows best' what's good for children so you don't interfere, that sort of thing. But there's less interest by parents in their children's schooling here than there was at the previous school I was at. There are exceptions, but on the whole parents seem to send their children to school and leave them to it. I suppose this is all tied up with what I

157

said before about education not being regarded as something of great importance, more just a necessary evil.

If you leave out truanting, which as I said I don't to be truthful regard as all that serious, I would say our biggest problem in this school at the moment is concerned more with staff than with pupils. It's very difficult to get staff to come and teach here. Fewer and fewer people want the expense of living in an area of London which, let's be honest about it, has hardly anything at all to offer. If you live within easy reach of the school in order to cut down on what nowadays are inordinately high travelling expenses, then that means that if you want to take advantage of what London has to offer in the way of concerts and theatres and that sort of thing, you're letting yourself in for quite hefty travelling costs every time you have a night out. But no one in their senses would want to live in such a highly overbuilt and overpopulated area such as this unless they had to; and when applicants for jobs do come for interviews, I usually feel quite embarrassed at how little I can show them which is appealing or attractive. A very unimpressive and slightly squalid collection of school buildings in a somewhat rundown area of London is about the truth of it. The GLC will give them priority on the accommodation list; but not all that many people are keen to live here, or at least not keen enough to make it an added attraction to the job.

So we do get a rather high turnover of staff – there's this distinct feeling among most of the teachers that this is only a kind of temporary stopping-off point in their career. They're thinking in terms of two or possibly three years at the most, which means that if you extend that over the five-year period which a child spends here, then during the time he or she's at school nearly every single teacher who was here when they first came will no longer be here by the time they leave. This is something again which affects the children; they're well aware that to the teachers too, or most of them, being here at this school is a temporary state.

It has its effect also on the quality of the staff there is here, and I can say this without denigrating them, I hope. Putting it bluntly, it would have to be a very dedicated teacher indeed who wanted to stay here permanently. I certainly don't myself, so I don't see why I should criticize staff who don't want to. They want to move on to somewhere better: and accepting that there are better schools is again I think only being realistic, it's not anything that anyone should be criticized for.

To turn to the pupils and our problems with them, I would have said a few years ago, as I think most teachers would have, that the thing that worried us most was drugs. Whether these things go in fashions or waves or whatever, I don't know; but the whole thing about drugs seems to have died down a lot in the last two or three years. Not only do you not read about it very much nowadays in the newspapers but there isn't much talk about it either. It used to be quite a popular subject for class discussion among the older pupils, but for reasons I can't fathom none of them seem all that interested now. I'm quite sure there's a certain amount of smoking of marijuana among the older ones, but I wouldn't think it could even be put in the category of 'problem'; either it's diminished or teachers aren't as worried about it, or the police aren't, but we certainly don't hear very much about it at all.

Having said that about 'fashions', I've got to stress that the next thing I say may therefore be just a fashion too, and in a few years time might also be nearly completely forgotten about. But just at the moment, or I hope just at the moment only at least, the thing which is exercising us most is the problem of lunchtime drinking of alcohol by the older pupils. There's a pub up at the top of the road, and it's very much the 'in thing' at present for quite a number of them to go there to have a snack for their lunch. The snack tends to be a bag of crisps, and the rest of their lunch money goes on beer or cider. The publican's breaking the law of course in serving them, most of them being fourteen or fifteen, but when one of the staff tackled him about it one day he said he was tired of asking them how old they were, they all of course always said they were eighteen, and what's more he couldn't tell the difference nowadays, especially with the girls. About the only thing he didn't say was that if he didn't serve them he knew they'd just go on further up the road to the next pub and the one after that until they found one which would serve them; and of course if he had said it, it would have been absolutely true.

There've been several instances this term of older pupils actually falling asleep in class as a result of drinking too much at lunchtime, or being sick and having to be sent home. I don't want to exaggerate it, but it is happening often enough and frequently enough for the staff to be getting a bit concerned about it.

Colour I would say is definitely not a problem, no. We have no figures, but roughly a quarter of the children in this school are coloured. There's a certain amount of shouting in the playground, exchanging of abuse between white and coloured, but I think that's inevitable with children. If you've got red hair you'll be called 'Carrots' or 'Ginger', so it'd be unrealistic to expect the word 'black' not to be thrown around. Those who are coloured give as good as they get though, and I don't suppose I or anyone else would ever have imagined twenty years ago that we'd hear an expression like 'white

159

pig' being used in a school playground as a term of abuse. We have seven black teaching staff and about twelve black domestic staff, so this helps all the children, both black and white, to accept coloured skin as a feature of ordinary everyday life.

'What should I say, "Yes" or "Perhaps"?'

Joyce Nicholson

The health clinic was a converted old church hall, large and high-ceilinged, partitioned off at head height round the sides into several small rooms with a bare wooden-floored open area in the middle. It was empty and deserted after the afternoon clinic; Joyce Nicholson's quiet voice echoed up in the roof while she talked. A tall fair-haired young woman with a friendly smile and cornflower-blue eyes, she sat on the edge of the examination couch with a tin ashtray by her side, swinging her legs and chain-smoking under the prominent anti-smoking campaign poster on the wall behind her.

– I'm twenty-nine, I'm married with two small children and I live about twenty miles away, in a small modern house on an estate of small modern houses in what could only be called typical commuter-belt country. My husband works in the City and for our age I suppose we're reasonably comfortably off; but of course we've a fairly hefty mortgage, and if it wasn't for my salary we probably couldn't afford to live where we do. My parents live in the same town, and the children's school is very near to them. In the mornings we take them over there in the car, my husband drops me off at the bottom of Tullbrook Road as he's on his way in to work, and then I make my own way back at the end of the day by train. I work full time and so does Miss Bennett, my superior, who's in charge of the clinic; and we have two part-timers, Mrs Cartwright and Mrs Foster, which gives us an establishment of three Health Visitors plus two or three part-time ancilliary clerical staff.

I've been a fully qualified Health Visitor for just over a year now;

before that of course I was an SRN, then I did a year specializing in midwifery, and also I did some fieldwork training in a psychiatric hospital. I've always wanted to be a Health Visitor. Marriage and children meant I had to have a few years not working, but I think I'm finally on course now. At least I don't have any more exams to face which is a blessing.

We divide the area up into patches between us, largely according to streets: most of Providence Estate is my patch, or most of my patch is Providence Estate, depending on which way you want to put it. I suppose at any one time I'll have up to 500 families under my care, as well as taking two clinics a week here. We're notified of every birth and every arrival of tenants with children under the age of five. I have a statutory duty to visit within ten days of a birth or two weeks of a move-in, but I keep well on top of it and it's not usually that length of time, on the whole I manage to get a visit in within eight days or less.

I try to persuade my mums to bring their children here to the clinic for the regular periodic checks which we do at six weeks, nine months, eighteen months and three years. These are weight, size, sight, hearing and standard development checks, and of course immunizations. It makes it easier for me if they come here, and the majority of them do once I've established contact on my first visit. But a proportion of mums can't come: they may be bogged down with looking after their other children, or their own health may not be good. In those cases, if they don't put in an appearance when they're due to, I go to see them. There are a few, but it's only a very few, who won't and don't have anything to do with our service: but they are very rare exceptions. Most mothers want their baby's health to be looked after even if they're neglecting themselves.

I've no statutory powers of entry: it's up to me to sell myself on my first visit, to say who I am and why I'm there, and ask may I come in and see the new baby. Just now and again I'll meet an aggressive person who wants to know how the hell I knew there was a baby there; but once I explain that it's standard procedure that we're notified of all births either by the hospital or the local midwives, or if they're new tenants with children that we're notified by the GLC Housing Department, and that this doesn't apply just to them but to everyone, as a rule there's no more aggravation or hostility. It's not difficult to explain that the system is after all for the benefit of babies and children, because after all it is.

The only difficulty comes with squatters. Whether they think the GLC doesn't know they're there or what, I don't know. The GLC usually does, and will inform us of the presence of young children while they're meantime putting into motion the machinery of trying to get them out. It can sometimes take a long time so we don't wait, we don't presume the family won't be there the following week. We go ahead just as if it were a normal move-in.

The other source of information is neighbours. A mum may not know that the new people in the flat next door are squatters. But she'll know that they've got a baby or small children and mention it in conversation. What I try very hard to get over to squatters is that my only interest and concern is the child and its health, and that's all I'm there for. And I am after all offering a free service, so the mother isn't being put under any financial burden or obligation. It's mostly a matter of tact and friendliness: most people respond to it, and initial hostility doesn't last very long as a rule.

– Since I finally became fully qualified I've not worked anywhere else but here, and as far as I can see I'm not going to want to for a good time yet. I like it very much, I like the atmosphere of the area and I like the people. I might feel the same about somewhere else if that was where I was; but I'm not anywhere else, I'm here and I do feel very possessive about it and about the people. One of the things that makes it specially enjoyable is that nearly all the people I come into contact with are roughly of my own age. We're all young or youngish mums, we're all interested in babies and toddlers, and so this makes for a nice feeling of oneness. The fact that I'm better educated than most of them are doesn't seem to make any noticeable difference in our relationship: I call them by their Christian names, and most of them soon start calling me by mine. Another advantage which I think I have too is that I'm not quite so remote as a doctor: I'm not male nor in the mum's eyes anything like so clever as Dr Gray, so that's another obstacle I don't have to overcome and nor do they.

I suppose the most important thing to them is that I'm concerned with health, with preventive health care. People only go to Dr Gray when they're ill or their child's ill. Going to him's bad news, coming to see me's usually good. Tell a mum her baby's doing fine, its development is exactly normal and everything's just as it should be, and it does her a power of good psychologically. It's not that it's one worry the less for her, it's usually that it's the most important concern in her life: and it's going on all right, and so it's a relief to her that she doesn't need to worry about it. Her husband might be out of work or paying attention to some other woman, but at least her baby's the stable thing in her life and in that area the knowledge that everything's fine is profoundly important.

If we had more time and more staff and more money, there are a number of things I'd like to do here; and I think when Miss Bennett retires, as she will be doing in about four years time, I shall probably be in charge of the place myself, and maybe I'll be able to put at least one or two of my ideas into practice.

So far I've only been able to introduce two. One is the slimming club on a Monday afternoon. I got together with about six of the mums to set it up, and it was amazing how quickly the idea caught on. There aren't all that many very fat young women, but what I did notice was that the subject of weight was one which concerned nearly every mother who came here. She might not be all that overweight, but she was constantly worried that she might be getting overweight if she didn't watch it. The club is mostly just a talk-shop: they discuss weight, they weigh themselves and each other, they congratulate those who've lost a few pounds and commiserate with those who've gained a few. Of course it's not really a way of losing weight, it's more a way of getting people to keep an eye on themselves and take a certain amount of pride in themselves. Somebody cares, I think that's the thing that's important about it.

The other thing that I've also started is a mum's luncheon club on a Thursday. They bring sandwiches or fruit, make their own tea and coffee, and all sit around in the central part of the hall at tables and chairs which we bring in from the back. There'll be about twenty mums all together: they bring their kids with them, and they're all put down that end. Each week two of the mums take their turn to look after the kids for an hour while the others sit and eat and have a natter: then the next week it's another two. What surprised me at the start was the subjects they talk about. It's a fault of my upbringing I suppose, I'm as much conditioned as the next woman to thinking that what they'd mainly be interested in apart from children was things like sewing or cooking or family budgeting, or any of the ordinary everyday subjects women are traditionally supposed to be interested in.

Well, far from it: those are the very subjects they hardly ever talk about. Politics, religion, women's rights, what's wrong with education, how people live in other countries: you name it, it'll come up. I was quite amazed at first. I think a lot of the women themselves were too, they'd almost all got the attitude at first that because they were women they had to talk about the trivial things women are only supposed to concern themselves with. In a thoroughly traditional working-class area like this, I think some of them felt they were being very wild and daring indeed in expressing their own opinions about anything. That attitude has worn off now and everyone's very relaxed. And it does make you realize that when they're left on their own to bring up their own subjects for discussion, they've been consistently underrated all their lives and they've constantly underrated themselves all their lives too.

They don't have any leaders, no one draws up a list of things to talk about, they just talk and see what comes up. They all seem to enjoy it, they all seem to want to think of ways of extending the idea to two days a week before long. I find it very interesting to see and to listen to, I hope it's something that's really going to grow.

I wouldn't pretend it's anything very marvellous, but at least it's a start. I occasionally have flights of fancy about starting a library, getting women to bring in books of their own that they've read and liked, and perhaps talk about them a bit; or encouraging them to bring newspapers in and talk about those, or all watch the same television programme and then the next week discuss that. But I don't want to start imposing my own ideas on the group; I'm trying hard to keep in the background and help them think of it as something entirely their own. The idea of taking it in turns to look after the kids was something they worked out themselves without any suggestions from anyone else.

I'd very much like the place eventually to become a sort of daytime club for as many of the young women on the estate as possible; somewhere where they could come and do things on their own or with a group of others, rather than purely and simply as a place where they brought their babies to be weighed. I don't think I'm being unrealistic in feeling that it could well be moving slowly in that direction. This has been the most exciting thing in the year to me so far, and I don't see any reason why it shouldn't go on and develop.

– I must have sounded last week like a very domineering bossy sort of person who thought she knew exactly what was right for other people. Perhaps fundamentally I am, but I hope not. Perhaps one of the problems is being someone with authority, someone who's in charge in a work situation. I may as well be honest I suppose and say that's one of the parts of the job that I do like. One way or another I've been a student, someone taking orders in my work for almost the last nine years, so it's not surprising perhaps that I do to a certain extent relish the freedom and power however small it might be, that I have now.

But after all, all one's training is towards this sort of position. You're working on your own, you're advising other people what to do. When you're a student Health Visitor you're very much under supervision; then there suddenly comes the day one day when you're on your own, you've no one to go back to and ask questions about what you should do. You have to decide for yourself; and it's no one else's fault but yours if the decision you make's the wrong one.

I'm thinking of the basic situation where a mother asks you to tell her what to do. It could be about something simple, or it could be literally a matter of life and death. But whichever it is, she's asking your expert advice and opinion and she expects an answer, and what's more in all probability she's going to act on your answer.

An example of a fairly straightforward matter would be on something like whether she should have her child vaccinated against whooping cough for instance. She'll ask you straight out what you advise: and you say Well on the one hand this and on the other hand that, but what she should really do is talk it over with her husband and then decide. More often than not though she'll know that you've got children yourself, so she naturally asks you what you've done. I've had mine immunized, I say: so of course she's taking it that I'm personally recommending it. Which of course I am, but even so I'm never entirely happy about taking that kind of decision for other people. Another and more difficult example would be when you look at a baby which some mother's brought into the clinic, and some sixth sense tells you there's something wrong with it but you don't know what. As tactfully as you can you advise the mother that there's nothing to get alarmed about, but you feel she should perhaps go to the doctor and say the Health Visitor has suggested he should give his opinion about whatever it is; perhaps its failure to put on weight or constant attacks of diarrhoea that's caused you to feel it should be checked. Sometimes it can happen that the doctor examines the baby and can find nothing wrong: there *is* nothing wrong, and all you've done is worried and upset the mother. It'd be much worse if there was something wrong and you didn't spot it; but all the same, after an incident of that kind when you've been unnecessarily cautious, it almost invariably weakens your future relationship with the mother.

More seriously, to give an example of something which really is serious and really is to do with life and death, the one that's on my mind most because it only happened quite recently is the subject of cot deaths. I have a young mother who's twenty-three who lost her first baby three years ago as a result of a cot death. When I saw her three months ago, which was the first time I'd met her, she'd just had her second baby. She told me all about what had happened with the first one, and she was desperately anxious for reassurance about the second: could it happen again, could it happen again? I thought what should I say, 'Yes' or 'Perhaps'? Eventually I decided the most reassuring thing I could say would be the second, 'Perhaps': so that's what I said to her. Two weeks later her baby rolled over on her face and suffocated in her cot.

I felt absolutely terrible about it, I still haven't got over it by any means yet. I feel if I'd only said to her very firmly and positively 'Yes it could happen again and you must be very careful indeed' the baby might be still alive. I blame myself for not having seen the need to warn the mother to be extra careful, and I regard it as a mistake on my part not to have impressed it on her. This was an example to me of a situation where I should have been more positive and directive: it might not have made any difference, it still might not have avoided it happening, but I think I'd have felt less guilty about it. I suppose when you get older and more experienced you put things more into perspective, but that kind of incident has an effect on you which it's not easy just to shrug off.

I don't want to dwell too much on that though: it's one case out of five hundred, and I wouldn't want to give the impression that it's something which hangs over me every day. I hope I don't sound callous if I say it's over and done: it's an experience I'll remember and learn from, but it wasn't something which I let affect me in my relationship with my other mums for a week or even for a day. I keep it in proportion, or I'm rapidly learning to, I hope. And the enjoyable things about the work far outnumber that.

'Missionary Worker'

Mr Nunn

The public library in Robins Walk shopping precinct was a modern single-storey building. Light and airy with broad high windows, it had light blue carpeting, old gold curtaining and matchingly upholstered comfortable chairs at the tables in the reference section. Mr Nunn the librarian was a gentle-spoken man, an enthusiast about his work: his eyes shone with pleasure as he talked about it.

– This library was planned and built twenty years ago as an integral part of the centre of Providence Estate. It's unusual but not unique; I think I'm right in saying there are three others like it in south London that were similarly conceived and constructed as focal points of the community they were intended to serve.

I myself have been in charge here since a fortnight before the first day we opened twenty years ago. Many people in the library service regarded it almost as an outpost of civilization. It was somewhere which was intended to encourage reading and book borrowing among the sort of people to whom, it was presumed, it wasn't part of normal everyday life. When I first started I thought of myself as a kind of missionary worker, but over the years I've come to realize that was not really a very accurate basic concept. Working-class people seem to read no more and no less proportionally than any other part of the community: our reading patterns might be slightly different from those say of the inhabitants of Cheltenham as far as subject matter goes, but our actual number of registered borrowers is only slightly under the national average of twenty-five per cent of the residents of the area. And we have something in the region of almost half the population, if you include children, taking books out from here.

There's a deeply rooted myth that working-class people don't really use libraries, but this hasn't been our experience at all here. As I say, we're not really all that different from any other public library anywhere else, except in the type of books that are borrowed. Fiction comes at the top of the list as far as popularity's concerned, but that applies to all libraries everywhere. The only way in which we're different is that the majority of our readers are practical people who broadly speaking earn their living by doing rather than thinking. This reflects itself in the sort of books they're interested in: they tend to like books on practical subjects, books which are about doing rather than learning for the sake of learning. But this is a very broad generalization and is only based on my own subjective impressions over the years.

It never fails to amaze me how at meetings of librarians other people in the service take it for granted that mine must be a rather depressing and unrewarding job. That is very far indeed from the truth of the matter. I enjoy coming here to work every day, even though I live outside the area with my family in Kent. As a place to work it's grown on me tremendously over the years and I wouldn't want to be anywhere else. There's a great feeling of warmth and affection among the people, and it's mutual. It's taken time to grow, but it's now not just a job but the major part of my life to me. I'm sure I should feel very much a stranger and completely out of place anywhere else.

There's a sense of pride in knowing that the library was actually opened and in use before any other shop here in the precinct had started business; only a minor point, but I think it helps people to look on us as an integral part of the estate, as something they take for granted as always having been here, literally since the year dot. I was a fortunate man to be given the job, and I'm a happy man to have been in it for so long.

– When we first opened we had a book stock to start with of about 10,000 adult titles plus 3500 children's books. Over the years that's increased to a total of somewhere in the region of 20,000 titles in all: we're now in the position that we haven't a spare inch of room anywhere for any more books to be put. If we add a new title to the permanent stock we have to remove an old one, and it goes into the centrally held reserve stock. We can of course get it at any time for anyone who specifically requests it, but it's no longer on display on the shelf. You have to think very carefully before adding a new book and removing an old one; you try to keep a balance between subjects that roughly matches what it was previously, and yet takes into account changing tastes. There are many authors, too, who seem to enjoy a vogue for a few years and then suddenly for no discernible reason no one seems to want to read them any more. And they're just as likely to come suddenly back into fashion again, though no one seems to know quite why. Perhaps it would not be wise of me to be too specific here, but doubtless you can think of writers yourself whose popularity fluctuates in this fashion.

Despite what many people feared in the early days of it, in my opinion television has not only not discouraged people from reading but has actually encouraged them to. You only have to think of the very popular serializations in recent years of books by such writers as John Galsworthy, Tolstoy, Dickens, J. B. Priestley and Arnold Bennett. In every single instance the showing of their work or adaptations of their work on television was followed by a huge upsurge in demand for their books, and I think no one would contradict the statement that it was largely from people who had no knowledge of their work at all before. Television, in my opinion at least doesn't stop people from reading books at all: quite to the contrary, it arouses their interest and gets them reading other things by a writer who they feel drawn to. I remember only a little while ago a lady bringing one of Galsworthy's books up to me at the counter and asking me if he was the same person who she'd seen a serial by on the television last year. I said yes he was, so she took the book – which wasn't the one that had been serialized – off to read; and the following week she was back asking for other things by the same writer. I think anyone else on the staff here would bear me out about this, or for that matter any other librarian. So in a case like that, what happens is that a lot of people read Galsworthy who wouldn't otherwise have ever been curious enough to take his books off the shelf and look at them. In this respect I think television is a very good and encouraging influence on people's reading habits.

I hope that my library looks like a friendly place, a place that doesn't give the impression that reading is a serious matter and isn't something to be enjoyed. The days of notices saying 'Silence' or 'Quiet please' have long since passed, and I think it's very good that they have. The hour immediately after school in the afternoon is usually a very noisy one of course with all the kids in the children's section – if you want a quiet browse that isn't a good time to come in, but neither I nor my staff want to give children the idea that a library is a stiff and starchy place, so we do put up with quite a high level of noise. We don't mind children chattering and raising their voices, but we do discourage them from rushing about. Very few do that actually, so I wouldn't say we get a great deal of trouble in that respect.

We have the odd miscreant who comes in to be deliberately provocative, pushing the other children about and trying to stop them looking at books; even occasionally one who'll sit at one of the tables and very ostentatiously light a cigarette. But these are few and far between, and more often than not they only come in on one occasion. What's triggered them off is probably something which has happened at school or perhaps on the street. It's not a serious or a common problem. I think most of the children who come in here look on it as a nice quiet place to come. We keep it tidy, we display the books as variedly and interestingly as we can for them, and they respond to that: most of them are very meticulous about replacing books they've been looking at in exactly the same place they got them from.

We have one girl, whom I perhaps really ought to refer to now as a young lady, since she's probably fourteen or fifteen, who comes in regularly two or three days every week, and sits very quietly over there in that corner by herself, reading. She hardly ever actually takes books out: she just stays there with them for perhaps up to two hours at a time. Mostly she reads nonfiction books of a historical type, and she's also very interested in costume and historical fashions. I can only presume she finds the library a quieter place and one more conducive to reading than her home background, and I would imagine by now she must have a really very wide knowledge indeed of her subject. She doesn't sit at one of the tables or make notes, so I conclude it's just a hobby with her and she's not for example studying for an exam or something like that. It's strange how that kind of thing can go on over a long period of time, too. We should miss her if she wasn't there, even though she never speaks to any of the staff or requests a particular book; we don't trouble her, we just leave her to it. One day perhaps I'll try and get into conversation with her, but obviously it's reading and not talking that she comes for, so it wouldn't be right to try to intrude on her.

There are other people on the other hand who quite definitely come in much more for a chat, either with me or another member of staff, than they do to look at or borrow books. To a lot of them it's almost a regularly weekly social occasion. They'll discuss at great length the book or books they've brought back, ask you what others you've got of a similar kind; and quite often the conversation then goes on into much wider areas, sometimes of a quite personal nature. There's a sort of companionship that develops between a reader who likes some particular kind of book, and us who are on the staff here.

We take it as part of our job to keep him or her supplied with a constant stream of reading matter in the field they're interested in. It can get quite comical sometimes, because more often than not they seem to take it for granted you know much more about their subject than they do, and you seem to be proving it as far as they're concerned ever more clearly whenever you show them a new book that's come in. It doesn't cross their mind that you haven't read the book yourself and most probably wouldn't understand it if you did.

One young man in his thirties who comes in once a month for example, he's very keenly interested in cybernetics. The first time he took out what was then probably our one and only book on the subject; and just for the sake of interest after he'd gone I looked it up in the dictionary to see what it would be about. As a result, when another book which had something to do with a different aspect of the subject came in with other new titles a fortnight later, I kept it aside to show him when he next came in; he was very grateful and took the book. And I suppose from that day to this, on perhaps two or three more occasions I've drawn his attention to books that have since come in which I've thought would not be too far away from the subject. He's now convinced he and I share this common interest; and what's more he speaks to me in a very deferential way as though I'm almost his leader and mentor about it. Perhaps it would be unkind of me to tell him I'm only a librarian who can identify the subject matter of thousands of books but really can't make head nor tail of cybernetics at all, nor have any great desire to. But I'm doing my job and he's happy, and that's as much as I would ever want.

It always fascinates me what subjects people are interested in, particularly when you could never dream it just by looking at them. We have one lady who at first sight looks slightly forbidding, she's a very tall and rather stout person with an abrupt manner and a rather commanding sort of tone in her voice. Over what must be the last two years or so she's now had every book we've ever had or could find for her on the subject of banking, no matter how abstruse or technical. I was convinced she must be at least a chief cashier or something like that and one day not long ago I asked her what her job was. She hadn't got a job she said, she lived at home and looked after her invalid mother. Was she perhaps going eventually to go in for banking, I inquired. No she said, but it was a subject that had always fascinated her and she enjoyed learning about it, though she'd never taken or had any intention of ever taking any examinations in it. I thought that was amazing: it was the pursuit of knowledge for its own sake, just for the enjoyment of acquiring it.

Another reader who comes to mind when we're talking about this subject of how impossible it is to tell anything about people simply by looking at them, is a young man who I suppose is about twenty. He has very long wavy hair which used to be the fashion among young men a few years ago; and his great passion in life is horses and horse breeding, he never reads about any other subject at all. I wouldn't have thought there were all that many places around here where he'd see thoroughbred horses or be able to come into contact with them. As far as I can tell he's not at all interested in the gambling side, it seems to be purely and simply horses as animals. He's had several books about the horses of the Camargue, and he told me once that his great ambition in life was to go there one day and actually see them with his own eyes. I remember he asked me one evening with a rather anxious look on his face if I'd ever been there myself. I said I hadn't, and he said did I know anyone who had, who might be able to tell him whether the bulls that lived there ever attacked the horses. I said I was sorry I didn't know anyone who could answer that, but I'd keep my ears open and if I ever heard anything about it I'd let him know. So far I haven't had any luck; but he was someone else you see who was investing me with far greater breadth of knowledge than I deserve, just because of my position.

And mentioning him reminds me of just one other person who I think, every time I see him, serves as a very good example of how you can't judge from outward appearances. He's a very tall very powerfully built man who comes in regularly, who's got the most ferocious face I think I've ever seen. You could only describe his as something like everybody's idea of the last person they'd like to meet in an alley late at night. Not only does he have the look of a sort of battered heavyweight boxer, but he's got a long scar from his ear almost all the way down this side of his face to his chin. I know it sounds ridiculous, but the first time I saw him coming towards me when I was on duty at the desk I really did for one moment think there was going to be some kind of trouble, because he was looking at me with the expression which you usually associate with those who are about to complain about something. All he wanted to ask me was something quite trivial, like where could he find what books we'd got on whatever the subject was he was looking for; but he really did make me feel uneasy that first occasion because his appearance was so disturbing.

I gradually got used to the sight of him because he was a regular borrower: he still is now, for that matter. We've got to know each other and we quite often have little chats. His scar's the result of a motor accident: he's got quite a sense of humour about it, he told me once it had been a stroke of luck for him because before he used to

173

be rather ugly looking, he said. But what I was really going to say is that he told me one day what his job was; in every sense of the expression you could have knocked me down with a feather, because he makes his living breeding budgerigars.

– Since we last talked has been a typical week here in the library, and I've kept a note of some of the things we've been asked to get by borrowers just in this one week alone.

Any book of patterns of corn dollies; *On Liberty* by John Stuart Mill; *Oliver Cromwell* by Antonia Fraser; anything about shire horses; a biography of Charlie Chaplin; *Family and Class in a London Suburb* by Willmott and Young; a beginner's guide to coin collecting; anything about Ethiopia; a guide to antique furniture; any book about the Great Train Robbery; a book on how to adopt; anything about flying saucers; a book on jury service; a book on computer programming; anything recent about Tibet; and a biography of Lord Southwood.

I would say that's a typical week's requests.

– The thing I like best about my job is the contact with people which it brings, in very nice surroundings and for a very nice reason – that basically they like books as much as I do, and look on them in the same way, as interesting and rewarding things. We have a wide selection of picture books for very young readers in the children's section, for children as young as eighteen months old. It's always a great thrill to me to see a young mother come in with a toddler and start showing it them, and choosing one or perhaps two to take home. You know that the habit of reading is being instilled into that child, and you think it's a priceless gift its mother is passing on – the enjoyment of books, which I think is one of the things that you never lose once you've got it.

It gives me a lot of pleasure too, having been here as I have for more or less two whole decades now, to see young adults in the library with their children, whom I remember first coming in here when they were children themselves. It makes me feel our library has been a part of their everyday life, which is exactly as it should be.

'Billy Bottle'

Norman Leonard

On top of his short thin body his head, surrounded by a shaggy mass of unkempt dirty ginger hair streaked with grey, looked incongruously large. His pale green eyes were red-rimmed and watery, his cheeks were scrawny and pale; he wore an old shiny black suit without buttons on his jacket or flies, a collarless striped serge shirt, a greasy mac which was always unfastened and battered shoes with flapping, gaping soles. He looked to be, I thought, about in his early sixties.

The degree of his intoxication varied from the catatonic to the mild; and there was only one day when I met him when, for some inexplicable reason, he seemed completely sober. Sometimes he sat on one of the benches in the park drinking cider from his bottle, wiping his coat sleeve across his mouth, staring at nothing; at other times he was in one of the shelters near the bandstand. He was around somewhere every day, and he was always there on his own. He made occasional brief begging forays out onto the path if he noticed someone coming, and occasional trips to the gents' urinal near the park gates; and sometimes, ran away if he saw schoolchildren approaching.

It was not easy to have many conversations of length with him. More often than not, after only a few sentences, or even after only a few words, he lapsed into vacant silence, his eyes unfocused: a quiet belch now and again was the only sound.

– Excuse me sir could I trouble you for a couple of bob for a cup of tea? I'm much obliged to you sir, thank you sir, and good luck to you. Yes it is a bad cough I've got, it is indeed sir, I got very wet last night with the fucking rain.

– I come from Newcastle.

– Sometimes you'll find me here like, and other times you won't, if you see what I mean. Sometimes I'm here and sometimes I'm not here, I'm somewhere else. I go to a lot of places, there's a lot of different places I go to like, over there, or over there, or in that direction over there, depending on how I'm feeling like. Only most times I'm somewhere round about here. Are you a drinking man yourself?

Good, I'm glad of that because I'm not a drinking man sir and I don't like the company of drinking people. This bottle I've got now, I've had since the first thing this morning; I just have a little drink from it now and again like when I'm thirsty, but I'm not what you'd call a regular drinking man. I'm not saying I don't like a good drink now and again, I do like a good drink now and again but not as a regular thing if you follow my meaning. I don't do a great deal of drinking, I just have a – excuse me – I just have a sip now and again when I feel like it, but this bottle will last me all day, I've had it since the first thing this morning and I don't drink it all the time, just a fucking sip now and again when I'm thirsty like.

It is, it is a nice day today yes, it's on a day like this that I like to sit here for a while and I don't bother no one. Excuse me sir but am I bothering you? No well that's all right then because I don't like to bother – excuse me – people. And it's been a great pleasure to me to meet you sir, and good luck to you.

– Excuse me sir could you spare a few bob for a cup of tea? Yes I do have somewhere to live sir, I am living at Row Green House. It's like a hostel for working men, you can go and stay there for a while if you're down on your luck until you get back on your feet again. It's run by some very Christian people, I'd say they were very good Christian people most of them, but you get a few daft cunts among them like you do anywhere else.

I've done all sorts of jobs in my time, all sorts. No I don't mind telling you about them, I don't mind telling you at all. We could go and sit in the shelter over there out of the rain. It looks very likely that it will rain and so if it does and we was in the shelter we'd be out of it.

You may not believe this now to look at me but I was at one time in Her Majesty's Navy, I was a ship's cook on the destroyers. I've also been a pastry chef in some of the best-known hotels in the West End of London, but I liked the Navy best. I'll tell you now, if I could get a ship tomorrow I'd be off, I wouldn't be hanging round a shitty place like this. My home's Newcastle, I shall be going there next week to stay with my sister and while I'm there I'll have a good look round and see if I can get work. This is no kind of an existence for a man such as myself who's got a trade in his hands. But things are very hard at present, there's no work going you see. I went to that place the other day in Denmark Street where they have all the jobs for cooks and chefs and so on in the hotel trade, and they said Fuck off they had no jobs at all, not a one.

Other jobs that I have done are I've been a hotel porter, a hotel kitchen porter I should say. That is the worst job there is, is kitchen portering. You show me a man who's a kitchen porter and I'll show you a man who is up against it. It is a very evil world we live in that there are such jobs as that, well they're not jobs at all if you want my opinion. The dregs among the dregs, is kitchen portering.

You couldn't spare me a quid could you? They're holding this bed for me you see, only I've got to take them the money by four o'clock else I lose it. It's all just one fucking great big racket is that fucking place, when you're down they'll screw the last drop of blood out of you that they can, the cunts. Ta very much, I'll let you have it back when I see you.

– My name is Norman Leonard. At least as far as I know that's my name. What I mean is it might be Norman Leonard something if you get my meaning, but most times I just say my name's Norman Leonard.

I've been in London quite a few years now, quite a good few years. My home's really Newcastle but I've not been up there now for a long while. I think I might have some family up there somewhere but I'm not sure. I left home when I was fourteen or fifteen or something like that. Well you couldn't really call it leaving home in the true sense because it wasn't home, it was a children's home. There were about thirty kids there to my recollection, something like that. I think I'd been there since I was little, I don't remember parents or anything of that sort. There was a girl there in the home with me, and I seem to have the idea she was my sister or something; my elder sister perhaps, something like that. When you got a certain age you had to leave the home, and that's what happened to her, she left it; and then not long after I left myself, if you follow me.

I went through to Hartlepool and I got taken on a ship there as a deck hand and galley boy on one of the coastal steamers. We used to go up to the Clyde or down and round to Tilbury. I think it was mostly general cargo we had on board, things like that. For a few years I was a cook; well first I was assistant cook, then I was a cook, and when I was about twenty or twenty-one I got my ticket and went to the Merchant Navy. My mind's not all that good about those times, I was invalided out almost as soon as I got in. It was my nerves, nervous trouble that I had. I was in hospital quite a bit; I don't know what the name of it was that was wrong with me, they didn't tell me. Yes a bit of prison I've been in too, a month or two months at a time like, nothing big. Some thieving, nothing serious, perhaps a bit of lead or copper tubing, things of that sort. But that was a long time ago that I've been in for anything like that. Now it's only seven days drunk or fourteen days for not paying the fines.

I spent a bit of time in Birmingham a few years back, I was doing labouring work before my health got bad. I had an injury to my leg. I was working with a labouring gang on a motorway construction site and there was an accident, a load of wood from a lorry fell on me. I think my leg was broke in two places, I was a long time in hospital with my leg in plaster and up in the air on one of those pulley things to keep it straight. Several months it was, I'm not sure exactly how long.

After that I'm not sure where I went after that, in a hotel in the Midlands somewhere, I think it might have been Coventry or somewhere like that. I was a chef, a vegetable chef, and I did some pastry work too. I always had to lie about my experience, where I'd been and what I'd done and say I'd had my references stolen but I was going to get copies for them. Once they'd let me start and I could show them what I could do, I was all right if you get my meaning: my work was good though I say it myself, they were always quite satisfied with me.

I suppose I never stopped anywhere longer than three months at the outside. The trouble was the you-know-what, the drink, the bottle you see. As soon as I'd got my wages I'd go out and spend the whole lot whoomf like that, I'd go on a blinder. Well no one was going to stand for that were they; so I'd get my notice and I'd have to move on. I had some good jobs too, you could say I was a fool to myself more than anything.

I never got married, perhaps if I had done I sometimes think if I'd come across the right person they may have been able to keep me on the straight and narrow. But you can't tell about things like that, eh? They say what you've not had you don't miss don't they? I can't say I've ever thought much about women one way or the other. I've met a lot of men who've been married some time in their lives, I used to ask them now and again about it, what it was like and things like that. None of them seem to miss it very much from what I can tell.

I suppose I must have been in London for a few years now, quite a good few years if I was to add it up. I think I came here looking for a job, I think that was why I first come. One of those big hotels in the West End, I went there to ask them if they'd got any jobs, they said they wanted a second pastry chef I think it was. I was only there for a few days, I hadn't any money and I asked them for a sub. As soon as I'd got it I went out on a big drunk, when I went back they said my job wasn't there for me any more. You can't blame them though can you for something like that, they were entitled to do it.

Living, well I live all sorts of places. I'll never go in the spike if I can help – that's the government place, the reception centre they call it. If you've had a drink they won't let you in, you have to stand outside in the street until they say you're sober enough to be admitted: then once you're inside they order you about, you've got to do jobs before you can go out in the morning. Things like washing the corridors, cleaning the latrines. And most of the men who're in there are nut cases as well, they'll come and kick your bucket over or pick you up and throw you against the wall, and then you get banned seven nights for fighting and things like that. You might just as well be in the fucking nick.

I'd sooner skipper, which is living out and about, living rough. In the summer in the parks, in the shelters if it's wet or in abandoned cars. In the winter I like to get a proper roof over my head, say in one of the garages under those blocks of flats over there, or somewhere like that; or sometimes you can get a good place say in an underground carpark under a hotel, near where the heating pipes are. Or there's derelict land, or quite a few houses in this part that are up for demolition, that sort of place. I keep my places to myself, I move around. I don't tell anyone about them because if you do you'll find in a few nights every dosser in town knows about it

The police is very good round here, they don't give you any trouble. If you don't bother them they won't bother you. Sometimes they have a night and they decide they'll go out and pick up a few of the jake drinkers, but on the whole if you keep out of their way they're OK. I've got the advantage you see that I keep myself to myself. I'm not in no school or nothing, I keep myself away from all that sort of thing. It stands to reason you see, if the police see someone's got a fire that they've made and there's half a dozen or a dozen men round it, well that's six arrests they've got for the price of one if you follow my meaning. But a man on his own, they're going to leave him on his own on the whole. They'll tell you to move on, they'll tell you they're going to come back in an hour and not to be there when they come back, but that's about the extent of it. So long as you don't stand in the road pissing in the gutter they're pretty reasonable.

There's some of them mind you who'll nick you as soon as they
see you. There's one, a ginger-headed one from Tullbrook Road
Station, everytime he sees me he nicks me. Next morning in court he
says Your Worship I saw this man go up to three people and ask
them for money. He's a lying cunt – when I see him around I never
ask no one for money. But there's another one, now he's a gentleman:
he's stopped me a hundred times and never nicked me once. He says
Come on Billy he says, let's see if we can't find you somewhere warm
and dry. He says I was down the bottom of Absalom Road tonight
he says, that house number three there, there's no one in it, why
don't you go and kip down there and then none of the lads'll bother
you eh? I think he's a good man, he's never done me no harm and
I speak as I find.

I used to be with some others over London Bridge way. They had
a good place to stay under the railway arches there, but there got to
be too many of them. Some nights there'd be as many as forty or
fifty men there; the Law used to come with vans, that's no exaggeration, there was that many men the Law'd bring two or three vans
and take everyone in. Operation Dragnet we used to call it. But I
got fed up with that, I don't like drinking with other people, everyone
gets stupid and they're always trying to bum money off you. They
say it's friendship but I don't reckon it is, not what I'd describe as
friendship in my book.

I suppose I'm a London man now, I suppose this is where I'll stay,
I'm getting too old for moving round the country. Well sir I must be
forty-three now, forty-four. I used to have a picture of myself when
I was a young man and it had a date on it, so I could work it out
from that. I used to have a picture from the children's home too but
I lost that a few years back. To tell you the truth I fell in a puddle,
I think it was when they were putting up one of those blocks of flats
over there. I'd gone one night looking for somewhere to sleep and it
was dark, I missed my footing and I fell in a hole they were digging
for drainage. It was full of water, I think it must have been raining
or something. I was right up to here in water under my chin, I thought
I was going to drown. I'd had a drink and I didn't know where I was
or what was happening to me. Then the police come, they must have
heard me shouting, and they took me to Tullbrook Road and gave
me a blanket while they dried my clothes out. Then the next day they
gave me some different clothes and I never saw the ones I'd had
before again. That was where the picture was you see from the
children's home, like in this pocket here; so that was the end of that.

If you could give me a quid or two I'd say that was fair enough, I'd
be very obliged to you. I might go and get myself a bed for the night

or I might have something to eat, or I might go and have a good drink somewhere. I have a store of drink that I keep where nobody knows. When I feel like a drink I go and help myself. I can get maybe fifty or sixty bottles of cider a week from what I get from the social; the rest I either nick from the supermarkets, or I find things and sell them. Mostly I find things in wastebins: you'd be surprised what people throw away in their wastebins, tins of soup, old clothes, a writing case I found once, things like that. All these are things you can sell for a few bob. But mostly it's anything that's going. For myself I think the supermarkets are the best: you can get perhaps a half pound of butter or something like that, and someone'll buy it from you. Or they'll give you things: if you don't do it too often you can go to the supermarket round the back and you say you haven't had a decent meal all day. They'll usually give you something, say an old pie that's got the wrong date stamp on it or something like that. Then you can sell that to someone and that's the way you go on, you get money to keep yourself going in drink.

Yes well I expect we shall meet again if you're round here. I'm always round here, you ask anyone where I am and they'll tell you. Just ask them where Billy is and they'll tell you. I'm always round about here somewhere. But I don't think the people are very friendly round here in my honest opinion. I've never had a friendly person come up to me and give me a few bob without me asking them for it, if you follow my meaning.

Yes, good luck. If anyone asks you, you can say you've talked to Billy Bottle, there's not many can say that.

– Excuse me sir could I trouble you for a couple of bob for a cup of tea? I'm living at Peter Street hostel sir and if I don't get there for four o'clock they won't have my bed for me. You're a gentleman sir and good luck to you, I'm obliged to you.

I come from the hostel at Peter Street sir, I'm a London man.

Part Four

HOUSES IN THE SQUARE

'The local sex symbol'

Susie Moore

Barefooted in a sky-blue jumper and bib-and-brace denim overalls, she sat cross-legged on the floor smoking and drinking coffee from a red enamel mug. Not much more than five feet tall, her straight long dark-brown hair fastened in a ponytail with an elastic band reached down her back to her waist; her eyes were brown and small and almond-shaped, slightly slanted in her pale thin face.

She lived in a three-roomed flat on the top floor of one of the old houses in Gorrivale Square, sharing the bathroom and toilet down on the first-floor landing with the three other families who lived in the same building. The green-painted walls were dark and depressing, and the small windows looked as though they hadn't been cleaned on their outsides for a long time.

– I've been here six months now. The GLC has a single-parent family accommodation list which my name was on for a year until they offered me this. It's a bit small really; well it's very small actually. My little boy's almost five now and quite big for his age: it would have been all right when he was one or even two, but it's getting to be a strain now when he's all the time wanting to go out and play. I take him in the park on the days when it's fine enough, and he goes to the nursery school most mornings for a couple of hours. But he's got a lot of energy, he needs to work it off. I went to the housing people and they said they'd nothing else they could offer but as soon as they had they'd be in touch. The doctor's given me a letter, but he says there's not much else he can do, I must try and hang on and keep taking the pills.

I don't think I'm going to have a lot to say to you that you'll find interesting. I suppose there must be thousands of girls like me all over London, all over the country for that matter. Not married, having a kid, living on Social Security and wondering what the hell's the point. Seeing the future as a long stretch of nothing much.

I'm twenty-three, I'm a born and bred London girl, but from a suburban part of it, a very suburban part of it, where a girl who got herself pregnant at eighteen like I did was lowering the tone of the district and should be made to understand that she was. Sorry if that sounds a bit bitter; if it does, it's because I am.

I was an only child, and although I say it myself I think I was quite bright at school. I'd got a few 'O' levels and a couple of 'A' levels, English and Economic History. I was at a grammar school for nice girls and the idea was I was going to go on to teacher-training college. Only I never got that far: I had a boy friend who was very what's the word, importunate. Anyway, the usual story: parents away one weekend, a party, waking up next morning thinking Where the hell am I, what happened last night, oh Christ did I really have Dave in bed with me, was I that drunk? Yes I was, yes I did, oh well what the hell it'll probably be all right. You get a shock when it gradually dawns on you that it won't.

The bloke, well he wasn't a bloke, he was a boy, he was still at school too. What we were doing was experimenting I suppose. I should think it was the first time for him just as it was for me. God, I was so ignorant it's frightening. I didn't like him all that much either, it was no schoolboy–schoolgirl romance; so I didn't even tell him I was going to have a baby and it would be his.

I told my mother quite soon afterwards, I think I was only two months. She was fantastic, but I don't mean fantastic wonderful. She only said one thing: immediately straight off she said 'Oh God, we mustn't let your father find out.' *We* mustn't, that was the part I like. So I said well what did she suggest we should do about making sure he didn't; I was thinking probably she was going to tell me about how to get an abortion. Not a bit. She'd ring up my Auntie Cissy in Worcestershire she said, see if I could go there to have it and then give it for adoption.

I thought Well fuck that; it was really true, all she was worried about was my father and what he was going to say. So I thought that in that case the sooner he found out the better, so I went and told him.

When I say he went through the roof that's putting it mildly. You hear about people going purple, he really did: quite literally he went about that sort of colour that that curtain is there. He kept opening his mouth and gasping; it must have been nearly five minutes before he could say any proper words. When he did they were ones like whore, tart, slut, dirty bitch: all the terms of endearment fathers use to their daughters at such times. Then next came the horsewhipping scoundrel bit, who was it, wait till he got his hands on him, he was going to pay for what he'd done. It was real Victorian melodrama stuff; and I had a sneaking feeling that when he was talking about someone paying for it he meant just that: in cash. His daughter's honour was worth X thousand pounds to him and he'd settle for that but not a penny less.

I'd never had a very high opinion of my father; and I felt he'd really touched rock bottom then. I didn't want anything to do with him and nothing to do with my mother either. After the big bust-up scene she told me I was feelingless and selfish to tell him, it could quite easily have killed him. All this, all this shit from both of them: nobody gave a sod what I thought or what I felt or what I was going to do. Oh no, all it was was how much it was upsetting them.

But in a way it made it easier for me to make up my mind about some things, well two in particular. One was that not only wasn't I going to say anything to the boy who was the father, it made me determined too that I wasn't going to tell my parents or anyone that it was him. And the other thing was that I wasn't going to stop at home a minute longer. I'd got a friend, a girl who lived over the other side of the park: she was a couple of years older than me, she was separated from her husband and she'd got a baby a few months old. She'd only been on her own a few weeks, and she quite liked the idea of having someone else there with her so I moved in. Somehow or other, I can't properly remember how it came about now, but I was put in touch with a woman from a welfare agency, I think it might have been through the doctor. Anyway she came round to see me; she was very good, she explained all the options to me about keeping the baby or placing it for adoption, but she didn't try and persuade me one way or the other.

I talked it over with Sandra, the friend I was living with, but there was no great debate really in my mind about it. Somehow I just felt all along that after I'd had it, I wanted to keep it.

– Look, I'm sorry about last time. It wasn't as difficult talking as I thought it was going to be, but afterwards I thought all I'd done was have a long shitty moan about my parents and generally give a picture of someone who spends her time sitting around feeling sorry for herself. I don't spend all the time doing that, now and again I quite enjoy life even though I'm a long way from sorting myself out.

I've got a few friends. The people on the floor below are very nice
to me, they're a West Indian family. And I've a good friend called
Peter who lives in one of the houses in Absalom Road scheduled for
demolition. I don't know how long he'll be there because he's a
squatter; he's very nice, he's got two kids. He's quite a lot older than
I am and he's a really nice guy, he's done more than anyone to restore
my faith a bit in men.

The problem's the old one of a girl living on her own who's got an
illegitimate baby. That seems to be a kind of signal to men: they take
it for granted that you're free, you're available, you're an easy lay.
That's bad enough in itself; but the really arrogant ones, and there
are plenty of them, take up the attitude that you must be missing it,
so they're doing you a favour in offering to screw you. Peter's the
first man I've met for a long time who's not like that. I can sit down
in his place or he can come round here and I don't have to be saying
to myself Wait for it, watch out, it's bound to start any minute now.
It's quite extraordinary: the man who comes to read the electricity
meters, the insurance man, a plumber who came round to fix the
water heater in the kitchen – they all start chatting you up, it's
pathetic how they've all got the same idea and yet it never seems to
cross their mind that they're not the first or the tenth or even the
hundredth who's tried it. It works the other way too, because you
presume every single man you meet, young or old, is going to start
eventually. The first time you came round and said you were doing
a book and could you come and talk to me, I thought Well now,
there's a novel approach. I get the feeling that around here everyone
talks about me as the local sex symbol: I'm not quite a prostitute,
more an enthusiastic amateur. Yet Christ knows, if the GLC have
got their special one-parent family list which they have, I can't be
that unusual.

However to get on with my life story. I went into hospital to have
Danny, it wasn't a bad confinement and I was only there under a
week before I went back to Sandra's. By then my mother'd come
round a bit and accepted the thought of me having a baby. So she
was good, she turned up there nearly every day for the first couple
of weeks. Whether I'm a bit soft in the head or what I don't know,
but when she said she and my father missed me and they wanted to
let bygones be bygones and have me back at home again, I agreed.
Sandra and I weren't getting on all that great together, so about a
month later I moved out and went back to my parents.

God when I think about it, it is it's chronic that I can be so stupid,
it really is. I shouldn't think I'd been back at home a week before
the rows started. Susie do this, don't do that. Where are you going

Susie? What time'll you be back Susie? Don't use words like that in my house please. Don't speak to your father like that. Why's the baby crying? Why's the baby not crying? Can't you stop that baby crying? Jesus.

I went out one day and went into one of those private employment agencies. I said I don't care what it is, just give me a job: never mind the salary, anything you've got, send me now, I'll start today. What they offered me was what sounded a good idea at the time, a living-in mother's help with my own room and no objection to me having Danny. I went to see the woman, she was a bit rich and snobby for my liking, but she'd got a little boy of about a year and I thought you never know, it might work. First of all there was a big drama to go through at home, how ungrateful I was for what my parents had done for me and all that stuff: it wasn't quite Never darken our door again, but it wasn't far short.

So I moved into this big detached house as mother's help the next day; and the day after that I got her kid firmly dumped on me at nine in the morning, told to keep him amused, put him to bed at six in the evening and have a meal ready for her and her husband at seven. There'd been nothing said about me being a cook in the original arrangements, but I thought I'd take it easy at the beginning and not start being awkward till I'd given it a proper go. Nothing had been said about time off, let alone a day off. It was my own fault, I should have got it sorted out before I began. But after eight days I was getting fed up to the back teeth with the woman never being there and never getting even so much as a couple of hours on my own. When I plucked up courage and asked her about it the silly bitch said what was I complaining about, I had nearly all day off every day with nothing to do but play with the kids and keep the house clean and cook.

I couldn't bear the idea of going crawling back to my parents, so I went back to the agency again and said I didn't like that job, had they got another one similar. They had and so I went for an interview for that. The same thing, mother's help again, only this time a woman with two kids, a big house right out in Surrey, swimming pool, two cars, and already installed there was a cook and a housekeeper. I think the husband was in the pop-music business.

I'm not going to bore you with all the details of it, but after six months I got the sack, the wife threw me out because of what was going on between me and her husband. If I'd been her I'd have thrown me out, so I'm not blaming her. Her husband was one of those men who can't look at any woman under forty without trying to get into bed with her, and I'm not pretending I put up much of a struggle. I wasn't engaged with him in my feelings though: he'd bring other girls back when his wife wasn't there, he made no secret to me about it. I was more regular than the others because I was living in the house.

Funny, it was one of his other girls that I'd got friendly with who I teamed up with when I left. She had a flat near the West End. She wasn't a model but she worked as a secretary at one of the big model agencies. She had a kid, and she said in return for me looking after it I could share her flat. It all worked out quite well: we sat down and wrote it out on paper before we started, we'd take it in turns to look after the kids alternate Saturdays and Sundays, she'd pay everything and make me an allowance as well. It was good, I enjoyed that; or I enjoyed it for a while, six months about.

But I was worrying about myself and the kind of existence I was living; it all seemed so unsatisfying somehow, and I started to get very depressed. I kept bursting into tears when I was on my own, not about anything in particular but I'd suddenly just find myself crying. I was having well having quite a few love affairs if they were worth calling that. None of them lasted more than a week or two, I don't know if it was me or them; each one I used to think was terrific for about three days, and then it'd all disappear as quickly as it had started. I was in a right mess all round. Finally one night I was in on my own, I found a bottle of aspirin and I remember I sat at the kitchen table taking them one by one with sips of some cheap Spanish cooking wine we had in the cupboard. I didn't count them, I went on till I'd finished the bottle: about thirty I suppose I took altogether.

Viv came in to find me staggering about being sick all over the place, and called an ambulance. You don't think at the time, but it was a terrible thing to do like that on the spur of the moment. Viv was shouting and screaming at me, she was bloody furious and she'd every right to be: she said what about Danny, was she the one who was supposed to look after him when I was in hospital, what if her little girl had woken up and come in the kitchen and found me dead on the floor. She really ripped into me, but I couldn't take it in properly because my head was spinning and I kept sort of swimming in and out of being conscious and unconscious.

They took me to hospital and pumped me out, and a really nice psychiatric doctor guy came to see me. He didn't give me any lectures, he just said after I went out would I like to go and see him once a week for an hour on a Thursday afternoon as an outpatient. I said Yes I would, I'd like to have someone to talk to. Life was really pretty bloody awful by then because Viv said she wasn't going to have the responsibility of me going back to her flat; and so I had to go to the only place there was, which was back home with my parents again.

I went on going to the hospital as an outpatient for something like a year. He said the only way I could cope with living at home with my parents and not working was to take tranquillizers when things got too much for me, so that's what I did. I had a time last year when I was off them for quite a while, but I'm back on them now since I've come here. It was his idea for me to go and put my name on the housing list, and that's how I got this place. I only go and see him once a month now instead of once a week; but if I feel really down I can ring him up and get an appointment for sooner, only so far I haven't needed to do that.

– I'm not mad about this estate. I might like it better if I felt I was more a part of it, living in one of the nicer places round near the shops or somewhere like that. The woman who brought me here to show this flat to me said she knew it wasn't much, but at least it was a start and she'd move me to somewhere nicer in perhaps about a year. Not having been a GLC tenant before didn't put me very high on the list to begin with, but maybe being one now will help me later on. Sometimes I look round and I think that grotty though it is I've got to look on this as a sort of halfway house. Not long after I'd come my mother came to see me: Susie you can't possibly live here she said, now let's all be sensible and put everything that's happened behind us and start all over again. Come back home with Danny and we'll see if we can't make it work this time. Jesus I'm twenty-three, how much longer is she going to go on pretending for Christ's sake? I told her I'd give her a ring sometime, but in the meantime it would be better if we all forgot about one another.

Where will I go from here, well I can only go up or down can't I? Perhaps one day I'll sort myself out about men: the guy at the hospital, the psychiatrist, said until I could come to terms with my father I was never going to let myself have a proper relationship with one. Oh well Carl and Ella the West Indian couple downstairs, they say any boyfriend I have I'm to let them look him over first and they'll tell me whether he's good enough for me. They're a lifeline to me you know, those two: anytime I'm feeling low all I have to do is go downstairs to them, they can always make me laugh. They've a little girl a few months older than Danny. She's called Lena and they don't know it yet but we've already got the two of them married off to each other when they grow up.

'A certain amount of satisfaction'

Stanley Huntley, JP

– I started without a penny to my name, I had no education and I was a nobody. Yet now I am one of Her Majesty's Justices of The Peace, I have been on the local council for twenty years, I have a highly responsible position with British Rail, I am an official in the Trades Union movement, I'm well known and respected in the Conservative Party in this area, and I have recently been accepted into membership of a Masonic Lodge. There's surely nothing else that a man could want. I have this lovely maisonette in one of the most pleasant parts of the estate, and not forgetting the most important thing of all the very dear lady who has been my wife for forty years, without whose support and companionship I would have achieved nothing. And our two very dear children and our three very dear grandchildren, they must not be forgotten either, even if we don't see a very great deal of them because they live so far away. So at sixty, as I shall be in a few months time, I think I'm entitled to look back on my life with a certain amount of satisfaction.

I am very pleased indeed that you've come to see me; and it's something of a coincidence really, because I've been thinking increasingly of late, as you inevitably do as the realization increases that your life cannot go on for ever, that I should really make some effort to find the time to set down my biography, as it were, in some form that other people could read. I feel there's a great deal to be learned from my story, especially for the young people coming along. Not least it shows how in this wonderful country of ours, it doesn't matter who you are, if you buckle down to life and work hard the rewards will be yours. Our democratic system as we know is the envy of every country in the world and rightly so, and my own particular story shows very clearly why it should be. I am pleased to be able to tell it, and I think it's one of those nice coincidences that there are that you should have come along when you did.

The floor-to-ceiling curtains at the first-floor sitting-room window were olive-green flecked with gold; the thick pile carpet was a lighter green, and the huge three-piece suite was upholstered in shiny teak-coloured buttoned leather. In one corner a modern reproduction mahogany grandfather clock ticked quietly, in another a big glass-fronted display cabinet was crammed with silver dishes and candlesticks, jade figurines, Staffordshire pottery carthorses, crystal decanters, a line of seven onyx elephants in descending order of size, and a hand-painted porcelain cock pheasant.

A heavily built florid-faced man with iron-grey hair and horn-rimmed glasses in a neat dark lounge suit, he sat with his arms resting easily along the sides of one of the armchairs, drawing reflectively on a slim panatella cigar. In silence his small fair-haired wife brought in a silver teatray with china cups and saucers and silver teapot and sugar bowl and cream jug, and put it down on one of a nest of mahogany occasional tables which she placed within his reach. In silence and without looking at anyone she went out again. He stood up and went over to a cabinet with an inlaid decorative door and opened it.

– At this time of day it's my habit to have a small brandy as an aid to digestion. So please help yourself to the tea, it's all for you, have as much as you like.

– I've always thought you know that one of the most unusual aspects of my life is that I never took to crime. We hear an awful lot these days about poor home circumstances, about people who've never had a chance and all that sort of thing. But if anyone could ever have said that about himself, I could myself, of that I'm very sure. My poor dear mother God rest her soul, she had eight children to bring up almost single-handed. I don't wish to say malicious things about my father, but there's no use in beating about the bush about it, the fact of the matter was and there's no escaping it, that he drank. If you were to ask me what his job was I couldn't tell you: my only memory of him is my mother sending me to the pub along the road to tell him his dinner was ready and waiting for him. To tell you the truth I don't know what became of him, he was never a proper father to any of us, and then one day he was no longer there and we never

193

saw him again. I have the idea in my mind that he could well have gone off with some other woman perhaps; but I was only a boy and children don't understand these things. I never asked my mother and when I was fourteen I was told he'd died, so I'd no opportunity then to find out.

Coming from that sort of background, we were not a particularly close-knit family. My brothers and sisters were all older than me except one. Most of them got married, or so I believe: one of them is in Canada now and I hear occasionally from her, but more or less we've all drifted apart. This is a great pity, because family life is of great importance. But there it is, and it affected my good lady and I to the extent that we were determined our own children should not suffer from an unstable home, and thanks be to God they never did.

But you know, when some young Probation Officer stands up in front of me and my colleagues in court and starts to tell me of some fellow who's stolen a lady's handbag and knocked her down, how his childhood background has been such a terrible one, I'm often very tempted to point out to that young Probation Officer that there are other people in the courtroom at that very moment who have had the same or in many instances worse experiences when they were children; and if he wants to know who they are, he should look for them not in the dock but in a somewhat different position.

When I was fourteen and my father disappeared, it was necessary for me to leave school and find work to bring some money into the house to help my mother. She poor soul had had a terrible time and her health was not good, and it was typical of her that she wanted me to stay at school because I was showing signs of making good progress in the academic world. But children know things you know. I was well aware of the sacrifices she had made for me, and I was determined even at that young age that the time had come for me to start to repay. Work was not easy to come by: it was in the middle thirties and very many men, let alone boys, were not able to get employment. However, I persisted. One of the characteristics I've always been blessed with is a quiet determination, once I set my mind to something, to stick at it. I worked in a wholesale greengrocers in Covent Garden market, I did a short period in a tannery near Shoreditch, and then very briefly just for a few months I worked as a station boy for the old Southern Railway, as it then was.

It was sad, and there was no means of telling it at the time, but my dear mother had burned herself out you know, and she passed away the week after my sixteenth birthday. That gave me a terrible knock, I'd loved her dearly. As you can see, I'm not a person who makes a great show of his feelings but I have difficulty in speaking of her without a lump in my throat even to this day. She was a very lovely woman, one of God's chosen people as the saying has it.

Well now however, then we could all very clearly see couldn't we, in those days, what was coming along with old Hitler up to his tricks so I there and then volunteered for the army. It was both a mother and a father to a boy you know, was the army: a very fine life for any young man, and I think there wouldn't be half the trouble we have with the youngsters of today if they all went into it as a matter of course. It gives you something of what we call the eternal verities, that will stand you in very good stead all your life: love of your country, discipline, pride in your appearance and an ability to bear reverses with fortitude instead of whining to everyone who'll listen about your personal misfortunes.

A couple of years of that, no I tell a lie it must have been more; anyway, however long it was to bring us up to the correct time, I was a corporal and as soon as the war broke out off to France we all did go, as one of the very first units of the British Army to go to the aid of our allies. Long before Dunkirk we were in action somewhere in the region of the Maginot line, I don't exactly recall the name of the place, and we were captured by the Germans. So hardly had we started when it was all over, and I spent all of the war in a prisoner camp in Germany.

We were in a forest in huts. It was a very well-run camp, all very clean and though you couldn't say the conditions were those of a life of luxury, they were of a better standard than most. The purpose of the camp was to be a showpiece for visiting army generals, visitors from the Swiss Red Cross and other organizations, to show them how well the Germans treated their prisoners. And so that was our very great good fortune and we had no complaints whatever. I was a camp leader, it was my job to see one particular section which I was in charge of was always neat and tidy, and to keep the men's morale up by encouraging them to observe standards. Towards the end of the war we went out in parties to work on a nearby farm belonging to one of the big German aristocratic families, and we were doing that until our American friends came and liberated us. Not at all a bad war from my experience, I was exceptionally fortunate in that respect. I came back to quite a handy little sum of money, my pay and gratuities that had been building up while I was away; and I was lucky in one other respect also, that Southern Railways as it still was in those days were ready to take me back on their staff again when I came home and came out of the Army.

My goodness, have we really, have we been talking for an hour? It goes so very swiftly doesn't it, such enjoyable reminiscences.

– As I believe I mentioned to you on the occasion of your previous visit dear friend, I'm a true-blue Conservative and have been all my life. There are people who say to me very frequently at work, how can I be both an active Trade Unionist and a Tory at one and the same time? My answer to them is this: I think the Union Jack is the best flag in the world, I'd like to see it flying outside every house on this estate – and I think the Conservatives are the party of the Union Jack, they're the best people to run the country and look after it, because they put the country before any ideas of political dogma. Conservatism you see isn't really a political thing at all, it's a way of life. We believe in reward for effort: the handicapped should be looked after, but the rest should work and stand on their own feet. To me there's nothing wrong at all with the idea that a man is entitled to the rewards of his labour, and if I work that much harder than the man next to me, then I feel it's only right and proper I should have a little bit more of the fruit off the tree.

I think unions are, or they should be, in one big wonderful partnership with the employers. There's far too many today who have the attitude that the workers and the bosses must always be at each other's throats, if one says this then the others must oppose it. I think this is very wrong indeed, we should work together to put this country back on its feet again. The trades unions have far too much power, and I'm sorry to say that many of them are entirely in the hands of what I call anarchists and lefties. This can't possibly be good for this dear old country of ours, surely everyone would agree with that: what we want is a return to the old days of stability and peace. I'd even go so far as to say that if that means a period when the constitution is suspended, and we're ruled by a monarchy until the disruptive elements can be brought to order, then so be it. What we have in this country is the finest way of life in the world, and it must be protected from the moral corruption of foreign socialist ideas.

I regard my work as a sector supervisor for British Rail as an illustration, fundamentally and in real terms, of what I'm saying. My job is to control my sector: I'm responsible for every thing and every person in it, down to the last man and the last nut and bolt. So what am I doing, well I am making sure that you and hundreds upon thousands of people like you who cross my sector pass freely from one side to the other, across my province and into the next, freely and without let or hindrance. If a signal fails, if a rail is bent, if for any reason at all there should occur anything which prevents the free passage of the individual, it is my responsibility to attend to it at once. To see it is put right, the bent rail is straightened, the failed signal is replaced. And this is just how it is in society: we have the right of the individual up to a certain point, but if that right is abused, if that individual whoever he may be is hindering the smooth going about its business of the rest of society, then he must be corrected and if he cannot be corrected he must be removed.

I see myself as a magistrate as one who helps in this process in society in a larger way. I was honoured in being put forward by my party as their nominee for the bench, and I look upon that as a sign that I'm regarded by my fellows as someone of impeccable character who has been chosen as a fit and proper person to administer the law of the land. If someone has broken the law, he should be punished: I can't see that there can be any argument about that, and I've no time for these societies of what I call do-gooders such as the Howard League who are all for the criminal and without thought for their victims in the slightest. Their opinions are not even worth listening to, they've no knowledge of human nature, they're not representative of anyone but a small group of fashionable lefties; and that they should have government money given to them to make nuisances of themselves, as I believe they do, seems to me to be scandalous.

Our whole legal system has become utterly soft, I'd say to those who defend it. Well where has it got us? Has it reduced crime, has it stopped the perpetration of anarchy among football crowds, has it reduced immorality among young people? The answer is most emphatically that it has not, and the time has come to cry 'Stop!'

For young offenders we should have the birch back immediately: it won't kill a lad, but it will shame him, and I think a good thrashing is the only answer to violence, to make it clear to the offender that there still exists such a thing as retribution and there are those who will not shrink from calling it down upon the miscreant's head. Similarly with sending a man to prison, it never worries me when my colleagues and I put a man there: it's only done on the occasions when he truly deserves it. I regard it as my duty when someone has done a bad crime to give them a prison sentence; if nothing else it takes a man out of society for a while and teaches him a lesson. These social reports which we have to have nowadays on offenders, they're all complete rubbish you know, written by young women who get a kick out of associating with criminals, or effeminate men who'd be more usefully occupied playing with children in a school playground. They know nothing of life, they've been to school and university but they've never known real hardship. I have had to earn my position as a magistrate as a result of the fruits of my labours in the field of life; they've come straight from college and yet they have the audacity to try to tell me how a man should be dealt with. They themselves

197

would be the first to run away crying with self-pity if that man's offence had been perpetrated against them.

In my opinion, the worst offences of all are those that are committed far too often these days, the assaults upon the police. Our police force is one of the most envied ones in the world; but there are some elements in society I'm sorry to say who take advantage of the consideration the police extend to them and try to turn it to their own advantage. I know many of these young policemen myself as personal friends, and they all know they can rely on me if anyone says so much as one word in my court which reflects badly on them all he's doing is making more sure than ever that punishment will fall on him. This is to me only a matter of plain common sense, that those of us who are selected as society's representatives in these matters must unhesitatingly support those whom we employ to keep the peace for us. Common sense, that's all that's involved in being a magistrate, all along the line. That's why I've never for example been on any of these training courses for justices which they're bringing in now. It's surely self-evident that if you require training to exercise your common sense properly then you shouldn't ever have been made a magistrate in the first place.

I could go on in greater detail about many other things and would very willingly do so if it would assist you in your endeavours. Now please don't hesitate at any time, whenever you wish, to come back and see me: whatever help I can give you I'll be only too happy to oblige. I've lived here on this estate for almost twenty years, here in this house, and I would say that there's very little to do with it that I'm not familiar with. I may not work here, I may work twenty miles away as I do, and my wife and I may spend most of our time in our social activities, as we do chiefly with political and union functions and so on, in other parts of London. But that doesn't alter our belonging here in every sense of the word and being, I would say, very truly representative of the majority, not only around here but in our dear old England as a whole.

'I can get a bit hostile'

Anne Knowles

Green-eyed and with short fair hair, she sat on the sun lounger on the small paved patio outside the ground-floor sitting room's sliding glass windows. She wore a royal blue off-the-shoulder sun dress with a long pleated skirt down to her ankles, and flip-flop sandals. She spoke in a quiet rapid confident voice, laughing often, and with a look of self-assurance.

– I got two of your books out of the library, I thought I'd better see what I was in for. Interesting. One was about a prison and the people in it, another one about lighthouses and lighthouse keepers. Two different kinds of societies of captives. And now a housing estate, so do you think we're prisoners of our environment too? Perhaps we are, the idea of it hadn't struck me before. But no, right, who isn't, yes quite. By all means we can talk, once a week, twice a week, as often as you like for the next two months. In September I'm going to Germany, but I'm completely free and on holiday till then.

– I'm eighteen, and last week I left school with six 'O' levels, two 'A' levels and a couple of typewriting certificates. In some ways I'm sad to have left, it's the closing of a chapter in your life. And I did, yes, I enjoyed school. Naturally, a lot of friends and shared experiences, plenty of good times. But I'm not heartbroken about it, I'm looking forward to what comes next whatever it is. I think I'm a reasonably grown-up person for my age, I'm not frightened of the great big wicked wide world that I'm now going to enter. For two years I've had a Saturday job, so that's been a help. How can I put it? I've been a weekend adult, a part-time adult, so what I'm going to be now is only an extension of it to full time. One of my jobs was as a shop assistant in a dress shop, then last year I changed to being an assistant in a local home for children so some of the resident staff could get a Saturday off once in a while. I liked that better than the dress shop, I'm much more interested in children than in clothes.

I would say if I had to describe myself that I'm a very ordinary girl, a typical eighteen-year-old schoolgirl of today. Or at least I'd like to think I was typical, in the sense of being modern and up to date. The last class I was in at grammar school, the upper sixth, there were only twelve of us in it. But I should think if you talk to any of the other girls you'd find them all more or less the same as me in their attitudes and outlook and ideas. It's true I'm the only one of them who lives on this estate; but I think three of the others or maybe four live on other GLC housing estates, so I'm not unusual in that respect. It might be true that I'm a bit different from a lot of girls of my age who live around here, but I don't think so. I go to the youth club most Saturday nights, and though a lot of the girls who I know there left school at sixteen or younger, I don't think we're all that different underneath.

The school, which is eight miles away, is a girls' grammar school, and it has a reputation for being a bit posh. Only two others besides me got in from the local junior school. It's supposed to be of a high educational standard, which means they cram you through your exams; and it does have a bit of prestige, without any justification for it that I can see. If you're a St Mary's girl you're supposed to be somebody special, or at least that's what they tell you at St Mary's. Green and gold striped blazers, straw boaters in summer – so you'll be recognized, so you'll be on your best behaviour because you know you'll be recognized. It's not exactly a snobby thing so much as a trying to get you to take a pride in yourself thing. We have long class discussions about it, whether it's good or bad. Some of the younger teachers are dead against uniforms and things like that, and one of them told us last term we were brainwashed into conformity before we'd even begun our adult lives. It was good stuff, we had a very lively discussion. The school's going comprehensive though at the end of the year; and there's even talk it might become coeducational, which would definitely improve it.

When I was younger there, I was very gauche and awkward whenever I was with boys at the youth club – like all girls I used to giggle a lot whenever I was in their company. It's only in well the last year or so I suppose that I've got over that – this time last year for instance, I couldn't have seen myself having a conversation with you or any man, I'd have been far too shy. Which at seventeen would have been ridiculous; but it would have been so all the same.

It was probably the final year in the upper sixth that helped most of all, I should say. There isn't quite the same pressure on you as a pupil, you've more time to develop as a person. Smaller numbers in the class, more opportunity for you to get on with work quietly on your own, and the teachers start to treat you more as an adult, they ask you to do things instead of telling you to do them. They even ask you if you want to do them today, or would you sooner do them next day, or they did at St Mary's. There wasn't a timetable, you made your own. If you didn't feel like French one day for instance you could put it off to the next.

All the kind of non-school things were very good, very helpful to a young person I think. We did all the usual visits to art galleries and museums and concerts and theatres, but the part I enjoyed most was the Friday afternoon discussion groups. We could talk about any subject we liked, or we could ask visiting speakers to come in and talk to us about their work or their ideas. It was up to us to arrange it all, to approach people and invite them. Let me see, I can't remember all of them but we had a doctor from one of the big mental hospitals, we had a journalist from a Fleet Street paper, an actress, a social worker, a priest who was a worker priest in the docks, someone from the Socialist Workers' Party, an architect from County Hall, someone who talked about mentally handicapped children. Those are about all I can think of off the top of my head, but there were lots of others too if I could remember them.

Most of all what that sort of thing does for a young person is it gives you self-confidence in talking with adults, and even in disagreeing with them out loud if you don't like what they're saying. My only criticism of it at my school would be that it should have been started at a much younger age, say fourteen or at the latest fifteen. So should the talks they give you about things like sex and birth control: on that score I think the school was really abysmal. All we had was a film in the third year about VD, and one in the lower sixth about how easily you could get pregnant. Every girl in the class at that time knew far more about the subject than was told in the film; I'd say more than half of them had practical experience of different methods of birth control. It was a subject everyone was interested in and talked about at great length. A lot of us felt it was an insult to our intelligence really, to treat us as though we were simple-minded children who could be scared off something.

It's funny isn't it how I spend the whole time talking about school? It shows I haven't really left it yet. I expect it will sink in gradually that I'm not going back there in September, but so far this seems only like one more school holiday.

– I was born and brought up in this house here. It was one of the first ones on the estate to be modernized by the GLC and converted into two maisonettes. That was about twenty years ago, and my parents moved here from the next borough where they'd been living in property that was going to be pulled down. We have what's in effect two floors, the ground floor where there are three bedrooms and a sitting room, and the basement where there's the kitchen, dining room, bathroom and loo. Obviously I'll always think of this as home wherever I go; and I expect next year when I come back from Germany this is where I'll come back to. I might feel then like moving away from home to live, but if I did I'd still like it to be on the estate.

I'm going to Essen for six months to work in a private nursery school. I've taken German as one of my 'A' levels, so I think it'll give me good experience in speaking the language properly if I live there for a while. I'm going to live with a friend of my mum's, she's English but her husband's German, and they've two daughters of about my age. The idea is that I should live with them as one of the family. The job part of it's a bit of a wangle, because the nursery school is run by a friend of this family's. All the same I shall enjoy working with small children. None of them will speak any English at all, so that should really stretch my vocabulary.

I think I am as I said to you before, very typical of most teenagers on this estate. I might have had a bit more education than a lot of them, but that doesn't make me fundamentally any different or set me apart. I think whether you're working class or middle class has much more to do with your home background than your education. I've one brother who's older than me and married. He and I have talked about this more than once. We both agree we've been very lucky though with having parents like we have. We've always been a close-knit family, I don't ever remember rows or shouting matches; and come to that, I don't ever remember being hit by my parents either, not even a little smack when I was tiny. As long as I can remember they've always seemed more like friends than parents: I mean all my recollections are of being asked to do things and treated as though I was sensible and responsible, not being told to do things and being punished for what I'd done wrong. I suppose I must have been punished when I was younger, but I don't remember having my pocket money stopped, being sent to bed or anything of that sort.

If this sounds as though I've always been very well behaved and perhaps even a goody-goody, that would be true: I have. When I was at the estate junior school I didn't mix very much with the ones who got into trouble, but looking back on it I couldn't tell you why that was. I think I must have always have been the one who hung around on the outside of the group, I was the one who shouted 'Look out, someone's coming!' I was never a vandal and I was never a thief: a lot of the girls were, so that separated me from them rather, insofar as I wasn't a member of gangs or cliques or anything.

I understood them though, I didn't think of myself as being really any different from them. I still do understand them, I don't go along with my mum for instance when she starts generalizing as she sometimes does about young people nowadays, that sort of thing. Sometimes she says she's pleased I'm not like that. I'd like to try and explain to her sometime that I am, I'm just like that; but I don't suppose I could begin to make her understand what I'm talking about.

What I mean when I say I'm like that is that I'm like that inside me, I'm at one in my feelings of annoyance and irritation at the grown-ups' world. I knew some boys and girls a couple of years back, we were all from the estate and we used to hang around at the youth club, go to the Saturday night discos when they had them at the social club, stand at street corners and skylark and talk and all the rest of it. The great fashion at that time, and these things do seem to go in fashions and be very short-lived, was to go up on the top of one of the big flat blocks and drop electric light bulbs either down the inside stair wells or off the highest balconies. A completely pointless occupation; and I'm sure from the quantities of bulbs that there were available that they must have been stolen, a lot of them. Anyway as I say, that was the thing to do at that time. 'Coming bombing tonight?' was the question at least once a week.

It was daft, it was stupid, in a mild sort of way I suppose you could say it was destructive too. You'd get ten or a dozen boys and girls spending a solid hour or more leaning over and dropping light bulbs on to the ground far below. A satisfying little bang as the end product, but nothing more. It was an outlet for something though: partly energy and partly anti-authoritarian, though when you talk about it it seems an extraordinary feeble gesture. I remember a man coming out of his flat one night and ticking us off; and I remember he picked on me and another girl, presumably because we were the oldest and biggest, and said he couldn't understand us doing something so utterly useless and pointless. When I thought about it afterwards, I thought how utterly and completely he'd missed the point. The point being that there was no point, the complete unreasonableness of it was the whole reason for doing it. You tend to think when you're a teenager that grown-ups never do anything unless they think they've a reason for doing it, so the light-bulb thing, potty though it might sound, was a kind of gesture against that.

There's something, well actually there's quite a lot really of what I'm trying to say, in pop music. One of its great attractions is that it's not the received acceptable traditional standard of grown-ups, it's something that's our own. We're the ones who judge whether it's good or it's bad, we don't measure it by whether it's acceptable to adults or not; and if they disapprove of the punks and the rockers, all that's more likely to do is make us cling on to it even harder.

It doesn't seem to me that there's a very big difference between being a sort of mental vandal like that and an actual physical one, someone who really does it. Why I don't, why I didn't, I don't really know at all.

– On the working-class thing, and being working class, and saying my attitudes are the same as everyone else's even if I do think I've had more education: well I suppose the two most obvious examples would be in my views about money and my views about marriage.

To take money first, I'd say I've been conditioned by my parents into believing that if you haven't got something and you can't afford it, you do without it; or if you really feel you can't do without it, you save up for it. I think perhaps a big thing like a car or a dining-room table and chairs, all right that's justified on HP but only so long as you can afford the weekly payments. I know with any of the things we've had on hire purchase in our house, there's always been big discussions first. Dad and mum have worked out what the repayments were and made sure they could be met. It's never been a case of having something and hoping for the best when it comes to paying for it. My dad's in the print and he earns good money; but ever since I can remember, he's had a savings account with the Co-op and paid into it regularly. Rent first, savings second: that's been what he's drummed into me, and I think I'll not change from that myself ever. He doesn't mind dipping into the savings for holidays and Christmas and so on – that's what they're for. He's always said that there are plenty of troubles and difficulties in life that you can't avoid and you can do nothing about, but being short of money shouldn't be one of them because that's one of the things you can control. If you haven't got it don't spend it – that's another of his phrases. I think they're all very good and sound.

Regarding marriage, well this is even more theoretical and outside my experience than money is. So far I've never been in love with anyone properly: by that I mean I've never been to bed with a boy, nor have I ever met one who I thought I'd like the idea of settling down with. I know this isn't a very common attitude among a lot of girls of my age in the world in general, but I do think it is among working-class girls. I've read a few things by women's libbers, chiefly some of their magazines, and although I can see what they're getting at, myself I think they've done a great deal to help girls and women be aware of male chauvinism and be much less ready to put up with it. But I'm not anti-man, I expect some time someone will come along who I'll fall for and it might be that I'll change all my ideas then.

It's difficult to be definite about something you haven't experienced. My best friend has had three quite serious love affairs already, and sometimes I start wondering if I'm quite normal because I've never really felt about any man like she does. I've had boyfriends, but none of them's ever stirred my feelings to the point when all I want to do is make love with them to the exclusion of everything else. So as I see it, I'm just going to wait till it happens to me; but when it does, falling head over heels in love I mean, as I am now I still can't see myself running away with someone or rushing into marriage with them without having a good hard think about it first. It's a dangerous thing to say that, isn't it? Maybe I'll make a bigger fool of myself than most when it comes to it.

This idea of marriage being permanent, though; I think I'm typically working class in that. Not all but most of the girls I know on the estate feel the same, I think. I can get a bit hostile when outsiders suggest as they sometimes do that because there are more illegitimate babies in social groups four and five or whatever they are, then that shows working-class people have lower sexual moral standards. I'd say myself that nowadays almost the reverse is true, permissiveness is a middle-class invention. Another thing I can get a bit hostile about too, and do, is when people generalize about working-class people. I think they're as much a group of individuals as any other type or sort of people.

I hope I've been a bit of help.

'When the fourth brick came through the window'

Timothy Rodgers

Tall, dark, young-looking, bearded. Before he sat down he took off his cassock; underneath it he was wearing a sweat shirt and jeans and suede desert boots.

– My wife and I have been here for over eight years now. I never had any hesitation about coming. I can't really explain why, it just seemed to me after I was ordained that that is where I would like to work. I didn't mind where it was: about all I knew was that I didn't want to stay in my first parish, which was a very middle class and slighty arty and intellectual place. Perhaps it was because I recognize a tendency in myself to be a sort of arty intellectual, and I wanted to avoid being that.

I was very bright at school; it would be wrong of me to say anything else. I think I was the only one in my sixth-form year to get to Oxford. Mind you at that stage I had no particular desire to be a clergyman; that only came during the year I did between school and university when I worked as a labourer in a brickyard and then after that I went for a time on a farm in France. Sometime between school and university I was converted to Christianity. It was an experience which I'm sure is a traditional one; I'd never thought a great deal about religion, and then suddenly one day I found myself thinking about it and realized not only that I had had an experience of meeting with God, but that I wanted to devote my life to working in a religious vocation. I never doubted the truth of that experience, and I was very enthusiastic about it and about wanting to try to work to spread Christian ideas. But I was also well aware, and indeed I am still very much aware, that the enthusiastically proselytizing Christian is or very often can be the person who puts more people off Christianity than anyone else. So I tried then and as I say I still try now, to preserve a decent reticence about my religious feelings. Perhaps that's a very English sort of thing to say, but what I chiefly mean by it is that I try to channel my enthusiasm into hard work rather than gabbling about how marvellous Christianity is and how much it means to me.

I did geography at Oxford. I'd have liked to have read theology, but it was linguistically based and I was poor at languages. Latin was Greek to me, and Greek was double Dutch. Although it isn't necessary to have a degree to be ordained, I thought I would go on and take mine, which I did; although whether having a first-class geography degree will ever be of any help to me in the future I don't know. I spent nearly all my time at university involved in theological societies and things to do with religion, and after I left I spent two years on a post-graduate course in it. At that time there was a considerable public revival of interest in Christianity – it was the days of John Robinson's *Honest to God* and all those things, which made it a very good and exciting time to be involved in the Anglican church. My parents were quite pleased I wanted to be a priest, I think. I know that my mother was delighted, though I think my father was not quite as pleased about it as she was. But he wasn't in any way actively hostile to the idea, he accepted that it was my own choice. Most of my friends I think were surprised – I hadn't been all that much of a rebel as a young man but I think to some of them actually going so far as to enter the church as a lifetime's work was taking things a bit far. I did really want to work rather than go on studying for longer than I had to, and although I enjoyed the academic life I wasn't wanting to stay in it.

About the only slight little doubt in my mind concerned not my belief in Christianity, but whether I could accept being part of the Establishment. The Anglican Church is part of the Establishment and I didn't like then and I have never liked the pomp and ceremony, the ornate vestments and all that sort of nonsense.

When I left school and before I went to university, I became a determined socialist. There has always been a fairly strong radical element in the Church, and I identified myself with that. I think Christ was obviously a socialist, someone who was on the side of the poor and the oppressed, and who was himself very much against authority and the Establishment.

To me it's difficult to accept that there are people who are Christians and who yet are Conservative. I don't see how you can be

207

Christian if you don't care about social inequalities, poverty, poor housing, lack of education for the underprivileged and so on. Conservatives in the Church would argue that they are concerned, but they feel change should be brought about in a different way. I can only look on it that their rhetoric very often protects the desire of the rich to preserve their richness. I absolutely don't believe that our society which is still fundamentally divided into haves and have-nots is a truly Christian one; and I think it is the duty of every Christian to work towards a society in which wealth is much more widely and equally distributed. But for all that I have to say that I'm first a Christian and only secondly a socialist. My religious beliefs are fairly orthodox, and I don't go anything like as far in radicalism of belief as a lot of my contemporaries in the Church do.

When my wife and I first met, it was her radicalism which first attracted me to her; I think she's had quite an influence on me in that respect, though our views were the same in many ways. I think she was not as keenly Christian as I was, and I feel that had a good influence on me too. It made me think about my own beliefs. Here was someone with whom I saw eye to eye on pretty nearly everything in the world around us, but she wasn't as convinced as I was of the world after this; and that did cause me to ask myself questions. The single greatest thing that she contributed to my development was making me face the fact that by no means everyone thought the same as I did, and she taught me to respect other people whose views were not necessarily the same as mine.

The other great thing she did was that she saw that although I was very enthusiastic about being in the Church, I was not going to be attracted towards or satisfied with the outward trappings of it. She knew that if she married me it was not going to be a very comfortable existence; I mean comfortable not only in a material sense but also in a mental one, because it was plain to her – before I'd even properly realized it myself I think – that I was quite often going to be at odds with the hierarchy. I wasn't going to be done any favours to help me on in my career. She accepted that; in fact I'm pretty sure that she wouldn't really have accepted anything less, she wasn't the sort of person who would settle for a comfortable existence.

When we first married and started our family, things were hard: we were living in very cramped conditions and had very little money between us. Over the years things have got better financially, not because I have a particularly well-paid job but because Judith can go out to work. We have this house where we live rent and rate free, and I also get some help with expenses to do with my job. But of course the house is not ours and never will be. It's the Vicarage and it belongs to the Church. Where we go next, if and when we do go, we may well be in nothing like so nice a house; and wherever we go, if I were to die, my wife and the children would then have to find accommodation of their own. The Church wouldn't provide it for them, and they wouldn't own anywhere themselves and it would be very difficult.

The house is the thing that worries me most about my position here. It really is far too grand, in fact I was almost going to say grandiose. I think it symbolizes to a lot of people the difference between them and the Church. This is the largest house on the estate, I don't think there's much doubt about that, and certainly the one thing that couldn't be argued about at all is that it has far and away the biggest garden of any on the estate. It's ludicrous when you think about it: it's the best and most prestigious accommodation for miles around. It looks like the home of affluent people, and it gives a totally false impression of the clergy. I think it should look like and be no different from any of my parishioners' houses. Some of them have no garden at all, and yet I've got one which can only be called enormous. I'm not surprised that some of the local lads take to lobbing bricks over the wall: we're in a very exposed situation in the centre of the square, a sitting target. In the last few years I don't think I'm exaggerating when I say that nearly every single one of our windows has had a stone through it. We've had to replace them all with polycarbonated glass substitute. When the fourth brick came through the window I thought something drastic would have to be done, and decided from then on that as each one got broken it would have to be replaced with unshatterable material. Now if anyone throws a brick it just bounces off: so they express their feelings that way, the lads, but no great harm is done.

– I really don't have the faintest idea at all how long I shall stay here. I believe the average length of stay for an Anglican clergyman in any particular parish is about six years. We've been here a good deal longer than that, but I could stay here for twenty years if I wanted to and I wouldn't say that such a prospect appalled me. I'd be quite happy to do that, but I think it wouldn't be good for the parish or for me. But I can't say what would tempt me away: I've no strong sense of wanting to be in a different type of parish altogether, and it maybe that if I got the opportunity I would move on to another one that was very similar to this. But I can't envisage myself at this moment going anywhere, though by next week I could well have heard of a living elsewhere and decided I would like to apply for it. If it was some sort of job I hadn't thought before of doing, but which when

I heard of it appealed to me, I'd move. But I don't think I would want another inner-city parish for a few years. I'd like to broaden my experience by going perhaps to a suburban place, but working-class suburban. I might even be tempted by the idea of a team ministry somewhere.

Wherever I did go though, I'd want it to be somewhere challenging. Not that I think I would have much difficulty in persuading myself that it was that. I'm very well aware that the majority of the population wherever you are don't deeply believe in Christianity except as a fundamental, and not as an everyday way of life. In most communities the church is used for weddings and funerals but not a great deal else. There'll be good attendances at Christmas, Easter, Harvest Festival and perhaps the big state occasions like the Jubilee and weddings, but otherwise people on the whole don't go to church. The only time I've ever had the church remotely full is at Christmas time for the nativity play, when everyone comes to see their children. So wherever I went I know I would feel one of the things I had to do was to go on trying to get more people to come to church regularly.

To a Christian of course church-going is an integral part of life. In this respect I feel a large part of my ministerial work should occur in the church. But it's hard work getting people in the parish to see it like that. They have a basic kind of theistic belief: they say they don't come to church but they do say their prayers. I'm sure this is very true, and I don't know how you can get people into church when it really isn't a part of their habitual way of life. All the same I want to keep on trying.

– Strangely, coming to live and work here in a working-class parish which was what I'd always wanted to do, has made me since I've done it into less of a theoretical and radical socialist than I was. Principally I've got reservations about public ownership, particularly in working-class areas. The philosophy of corporate ownership, if it is a philosophy, hasn't caught on. What you do get exemplified here on Providence Estate is bureaucratic corporatism: the people have what's best for them decided on their behalf. And I know it's not possible that on an estate of this size the people who live here can be managed by anything other than a bureaucracy. The GLC owns nearly all the buildings, is the largest employer of labour, even organizes leisure; and it's a large and impersonal organization, and not at all what I think of as a socialist idea. People, for instance, are not allowed to choose the colour that their own front door should be painted. This seems to me ridiculous; but it seems it's quite unavoidable.

I do feel that undoubtedly there's less freedom and opportunity for people as individuals when they're herded together like this. I think one of the mistakes that was made when this estate was built, and I hope it will be learned from and not done again, is that nothing like enough provision was made for the people to have their own gardens. There are public green spaces – and the result of that is that people don't regard these spaces as belonging to them. And they don't, they belong to the GLC. I think this feeling of 'It's not ours' is at the bottom of a great deal of the vandalizing of buildings: people regard themselves as transient travellers striving to reach somewhere better, and so don't have much concern about their immediate surroundings.

And while they're here they think of themselves as little more than ciphers. The housing was designed and built to provide better conditions. Yet it completely missed out on the fact that it was for people. I don't see how you can encourage people to feel pride in an area that they're determined to get away from as soon as possible; and it becomes a vicious circle, people don't care, they don't look after the area, the area deteriorates and becomes shabby, and that makes the people want even more to get away. Somewhat to my own surprise I must confess I'm beginning to think the Tories' idea of selling council houses to tenants might be a way of encouraging people to make an area much more a place which they looked on as their own.

I suppose the other major way in which I've changed since I came here is that I've set my sights a lot lower: I'm talking now about evangelizing, about bringing God to people and bringing people to God. The majority of people are not really terribly interested in Christian theology. It's quite clear that as a clergyman you're looked upon by most people as someone slightly peculiar, as someone who is to a certain extent wasting his time with things that don't greatly matter. Kids will shout at you in the street. One of the most popular things at the moment is to repeat the supermarket advert joke. This is something they've seen on TV. There's a list of price cuts, and then a chorus at the end of delighted shoppers shouting 'I don't believe it.' So at the moment what kids round here do is they chant various phrases which they think are particularly Christian such as 'Jesus was the Son of God,' 'God is all-forgiving,' 'The life after death in heaven,' and then they all shout, 'I don't believe it.' When you have things like that shouted after you in the street it doesn't annoy you so much as remind you that you really are living among people who are going to take nothing for granted, and they're not going to be impressed by fancy words and a good education. Unless

Christianity can find some way of getting itself into peoples' lives on a more day-to-day level, I don't think it will ever really get anywhere.

I'm regarded by a lot of people in the area as some kind of authority figure, but on the whole I hope a benevolent one. People will from time to time come round and ask me to help with their problems; but they're mostly their practical problems rather than spiritual ones. Will I help them fill in a passport application, that sort of thing. I had a man came to see me a week or so ago, he was having problems with his income tax. The usual thing, he hadn't filled in the forms in the right way, and he was frightened of the Inland Revenue authorities. He knew that I would have the self-confidence to tackle them which he hadn't got. And I occasionally have people asking me about their children's problems at school; they say they're unhappy at their child's lack of progress, or they don't feel the teacher understands their son or daughter as the case may be, and ask me if I'll have a word with the teacher for them. When I say that as the parents of the child, the teacher should really hear their point of view, they become very reluctant. They say things like 'The teachers will pay more attention to you because you're better educated.' It's tempting to say 'Yes all right, leave it to me' – and you know that if you don't do it, the person will feel you haven't been of any help. But it's a difficult situation and one in which I don't have any hard-and-fast rules. I'm being asked to provide a service for people who haven't had the benefits of a first-class education; and yet to provide that service is not going to help them really in any way at all, because it isn't guiding them in the direction of self-help. It's difficult not to impose one's own middle-class ideas of the way people should behave. I've talked with Judith quite often about the idea of trying to set up local discussion groups, in an attempt to encourage people to stand up and express their views or even at least see that they have views which are worth expressing and which other people will listen to. But when this kind of thing is done under the aegis of the Church it doesn't prove very popular with the people as a whole.

My biggest worry, without the slightest hesitation, is the way intolerance of coloured people is on the increase. Perhaps one can only try to spread the Christian creed and hope that it infects and affects people; but I'm very unhappy indeed about the way racialism is spreading. We are getting very rapidly into a 'them and us' situation, particularly in this part of the world. I feel that a lot of the black community workers are not improving the situation either. Many of them have gone into community relations or race relations because they feel the blacks are underprivileged and are a minority group threatened on all sides. They may well be right, I think they are right in many ways; but unfortunately they bolster the very feelings in black people which make any kind of rapprochment more difficult than ever. They seem almost to be encouraging the black people to keep themselves separate.

But it's easy for a white person to say that the blacks ought to be more forthcoming and friendly and ready to integrate; and it's easy for the blacks then to answer by pointing out that it's the whites who greeted them in the first instance with hostility, and they're only reacting to that. What I am saying I think is that the problem is getting worse, and what efforts there've been so far to improve the situation not only failed but actually seemed to worsen it. I have to say I see very few hopeful or encouraging signs of a solution being discovered: I don't. I feel that the Church should be a good deal more forthright than it is about this subject, and I try to do my bit by making my views known.

Part Five

ABSALOM ROAD

'This year next year or when'

Ben and Sheila Longman

The room was tall, empty, derelict and echoing. The floorboards were broken and rotten, and a steel girder supported the sagging plaster of the ceiling. In one corner near the window a small desk was piled high with books and papers: on it an angle-poise lamp, a telephone, and three old tins full of pens and pencils. Scattered around haphazardly on the floor were some hessian-covered cushions.

A tall woman of thirty, thin and with long dark hair, Sheila Longman gently swivelled to and fro in the old office chair at the desk. A pale high-cheekboned face, dark eyes and hands that rested relaxedly in her lap as she talked in a low quiet voice.

– We've been here about a year now. Ben's a teacher. I am too if and when I can get work. Mostly I spend my time helping out at the local children's nursery.

I'm not quite sure whether we're supposed to be here or whether we're not. I know that sounds a funny thing to say, but we're definitely squatters insofar as we were not allocated a house or a flat on the estate by the GLC. They know we're here though: we pay them a nominal rent, and in return they allow us to use the electricity and gas. What we don't pay – I think I am right in this – is any rates. It's one of these curious arrangements that I think quite often big local authorities enter into that's a kind of turning of a blind eye to something. Perhaps I'm a bit cynical when I say that as long as it doesn't get known about too widely and too many people don't start doing it, they use it as an example of showing what they like to call the 'human side' of bureaucracy. Maybe I'm up the spout about this

217

though, maybe I've got it wrong. Ben knows more about it than I do.

How long we shall be here I've no idea: I expect we shall move on this year next year or when – I don't know. Ben and I've been together a couple of years now. We're not married but our relationship does seem a fairly stable one and I suppose how long we're going to be here is going to be affected chiefly by how long we stay together. I don't really want to go into a lot of personal details about my life. I've been married before – officially I'm still married – but I don't think of myself as divorced or separated or anything like that. One relationship didn't work, so now I'm trying another one.

I think I've always been the sort of person who's rather vague and unsure of myself. One of the things that I think's good for me is that Ben seems to be more sure of me than I am. He says just because I've had one personal relationship that's broken down, it doesn't mean I'm never going to be able to build up another one which will last. This has been a problem to me for a large part of my life. I've never really got on that well with my family – my parents and my brothers and sisters. I'm a kind of a loner, which is really ironic because I don't like being on my own at all and I never have done since I was little.

Anyway, I said I wasn't going to talk much about my personal life, so we'll leave that subject there. You'll have gathered though from what I say that my name isn't Sheila Longman – it's Sheila something else, but I prefer people round about not to know that. I'm wearing a wedding ring as you can see and everyone takes it for granted Ben and I are married. I think the working class are very conventional people and I think they'd be shocked at the idea of two people living together who weren't married. Maybe it's my middle-class upbringing and background, but I do think working-class people are a long way behind the times when it comes to morality nowadays. Ben and I are both what is – well let's be honest about it – not in the same class as they are and we don't come from the same kind of background. I'm not saying we're better or different, but it is a fact that we're not the same.

I'm most conscious of it in our way of life, what you might call the furnishings and trappings of everyday existence. My clothes are different, my voice is different, and I surround myself with books and magazines and newspapers and do a great deal of reading. I live mostly inside my head, whereas all the other people round here are extroverted and spend their lives in a completely different way. I hope this doesn't make me sound a snob – I think it's realistic.

I keep talking about myself don't I? I said I wouldn't so I'll tell you something about the road instead shall I? Its name 'Absalom Road' is very ironic: Absalom was supposed to have been very good-looking wasn't he? He was a son of David, and I can't think who thought up the name 'Absalom' for such a shitty-looking road, even as it must have been in the days when it was in a good state of repair. It's being allowed to stay like it is because all this is scheduled for demolition: they're going to build a new block of flats everywhere, so everything is being allowed to crumble. This end of the road where we are – I think it used to be about number sixty – is quite quiet and deserted, but down at the other end where the Rastafarians and people like that are is a different picture altogether. This is definitely the posh end, oh yes.

I've heard there's a man somewhere around one of the middle numbers who's got an injunction against the council to stop them pulling his house down, so what the outcome of that is going to be I don't know. It could well be one of those situations when everything else in the road is flattened he sits there in the middle of total desolation refusing to budge. I don't know the guy personally, but I hear about him from time to time: he's the sort some people think of as downright bloody-minded, and others admire his tenacity and individuality. I rather envy someone like that.

I know when the GLC tell us it's time for us to go, we'll go. Neither Ben nor I is very much of a fighting person. We look upon ourselves as birds of passage. And we don't really belong to this community, we came here because it was somewhere for us to live, so we shall move on when the time comes. Anywhere where we have a roof over our heads we'll be quite satisfied.

We haven't much money – well to be honest about it we haven't any money – but our needs are not very great. Ben does his two and a half days a week teaching at a technical college – he teaches engineering – and what he earns there just about keeps us going, supplemented by what I can bring in now and again. To be perfectly honest with you, although I was brought up as I told you in Lancashire, I certainly don't have what's often referred to as the 'Protestant work ethic'. Perhaps it's because I come from a good family, but I certainly never had it instilled into me that there was any particular intrinsic value in work as such. I'm quite happy to potter around here with my writing, and earning a few quid now and again. I definitely don't feel that I have to go out and get a proper job which will bring in a steady and regular income. Now I come to talk about it, I'm not at all sure that my parents would approve if they knew about it – in fact I'm bloody sure they wouldn't. So I suppose that lets me think I'm being a bit of a rebel in my own quiet way.

He sat cross-legged on a cushion which he'd brought up to the ground-floor front room from the basement kitchen, hand-rolling one cigarette after another, biting off the loose straggly ends of tobacco and spitting out the fragments as he talked. Red-haired, thin, pale-skinned and with long sensitive fingers. The first time, it was evening and the light was going: his voice was flat and shallow.

– Sheila said after she'd talked to you last week she thought you must have thought she was a terrible snob. I said that I knew she wasn't really a snob, but it is the impression she sometimes gives to people. She does actually come from quite a well-known family up north, and it seems to have given her a terrible hang-up about what people think about her. She wants to live a bohemian sort of life and yet at the same time she's concerned about the impression she's giving people. I'm not like that: I don't give a shit what other people think. When we came here it never crossed my mind to take steps to stop people getting the impression we weren't married; but to Sheila it was important that people shouldn't know. Not long after we arrived she met the local vicar in the street: he's quite a nice reasonable tolerant sort of person obviously, you find that out as soon as you talk with him – but Sheila came back in a great tizz because she thought he might find out we weren't married. If it would affect his attitude towards us, then he's not the sort of person I'd want to know. But I don't think he'd give a damn one way or the other really.

She'll have told you how we got this place, how we came to be here and all the rest of it I suppose. I don't know there's going to be a lot I can add to that. She's a very private self-contained sort of person: she doesn't go out much and she finds it difficult to mix with people. I don't. In my part-time teaching job I mix with people, but when I get home here all I want to do is get on with my own painting and designing. I've ambitions one day to become an interior decorator.

When I'm here I hardly ever go out, we neither of us really meet local people. Sometimes I've thought we ought to get to know other people in the street but we don't make the effort. The particular people I would like to get to know are the Rastafarians: their culture and life style is so different from ours, but they keep themselves to themselves. I think they regard themselves as some kind of chosen people and they're not going to approach us, that's for sure. But I do sometimes have this niggling feeling that I ought to try at least to approach them.

Yes and our attitude is just the same to be honest about it, towards everyone else in this part of the world. We don't try very hard to mix. Perhaps that's because we don't feel we're going to be here for long, and aren't thinking of putting down roots.

I look around this dump where we're living and I have to smile sometimes. I'm a working-class lad from Birmingham and – at least so he always told me – my father must have lived in somewhere very similar to this when he was a child. If he could see me now, and where and how I'm living, he wouldn't be all that sentimental about it though. He worked hard to bring his children up well, and gave them a good education, all the things he'd never had himself and so on. So maybe he wouldn't be keen to know that his youngest son was back more or less at the point he himself had started from. Mind you there's other things he wouldn't be all that keen on either, like me living with a woman who's really married to someone else. Sheila and I sometimes have a laugh and imagine inviting our respective parents to come and visit us. Being the sort of people they are, they wouldn't say much but by Christ they'd think a lot.

– I think the most obvious way in which coming here to live has broken the mould of my previous experience is that although I don't know any of them very well, I never could have imagined when I was a nice clean-washed little public school boy that I'd ever live in a street in which every other person was black. I pass them on my way out, I pass them on my way back to here, and of course it's now got to the stage that it doesn't even register on me. I think it always registers on the Rastas that I'm a white person passing them; there's always a kind of look in their eye, and it's not a very friendly look either. But as far as the colour of people's skin is concerned, I certainly now hardly ever notice this. When I was a kid in the Midlands, I'd certainly have noticed proximity to a black person – I used to be frightened of black people if I saw them. Now I don't notice, so I have to say that's the thing which strikes me most as a change in my way of life.

And there's one other thing too, which had never occurred to me before we came here, which is that it never struck me we ourselves could ever be considered as quote outsiders end quote. I took it for granted, in my middle-class English background, that I was one of the people who everyone else was like or would like to be like. I was the official version of a person: or perhaps I should say I was my idea of the definition of a person. But here, there's no getting away from it, we are not by any means or in any way accepted as official persons. We're not working class, and we don't belong: not just on a class basis, but because we're squatters into the bargain. Kids from round

about now and again throw stones and shout rude words at us. We're
interlopers into their world, and like all kids they'd prefer it if we
went somewhere else. I remember a few weeks ago coming home one
evening along the pavement outside here, and there was a young
black kid of I suppose about eight or nine standing watching me from
the other side of the road. When I was safely past him he shouted at
me, then turned round and ran away. What he shouted was 'Fuck
off, squatter!' I thought it really was ironic: I didn't resent it, it just
amused me that he should think quite rightly that he belonged here
and I didn't.

– Have we changed very much since we came here? I don't know
what you think Ben, but I don't think we have.
– Yes, I think I've changed quite a lot since we came here. Though
whether it's anything to do with the area or whether it's just something in myself, I couldn't really say. The change I'm most aware of
in myself is that since we came here I do seem to have become quite
a lot more confident as a person. It may be just that I've got more
used to the idea of living with you, it may be that now I'm fairly
confident about my ability to be a teacher and hold down a part-time
job. And I do feel living in this area has had at least something to do
with it. In a curious kind of way I get a feeling now and again that
if we really wanted to we could eventually almost belong here. If we
put our names on the waiting list for council accommodation, made
a statement of that kind that we intended to stay here, and put a bit
of work into getting to know the people in the area – then I really do
think we might eventually in a year or two's time come to start
thinking of this area as our home ground.
– You've never ever said anything like that before.
– No, well I suppose that's because I've never thought about it,
the subject's never come up.
– Do you really mean that?
– Yes I do. I'm not saying it's something I'd want to do, I'm merely
saying it's something that to me isn't totally out of the question.
– Would you really like to go on living around here?
– I don't know, I'd have to think more about it.
– Well I don't think it would ever work. I don't think I could ever
feel I really belonged here at all. Ask me where I feel I do belong,
and the answer has to be that I don't know. All I do know, or think
I know, is that it isn't here. Ben – we're not the same as all the other
people living round here, we could never fit in. We dress differently,
we speak differently, our tastes are different. We've both had an
education, whatever its faults might have been, and we have got some

kind of intellectual prospects. All the people or at least nearly all the people who live on this estate haven't. The concept of being able to make what you choose out of your life to any degree at all is outside their experience.

– So what're you saying? That because we're as we are, they'd never accept us?

– Yes I am saying that, very definitely. I think the vicar is a perfect example of that. He's had a good education, but he's a middle-class person and however hard he tries to take his responsibilities to the community here they just don't accept him because he isn't basically one of them. He's a middle-class person who's come into the community from outer space as far as they're concerned, and the poor sod just hasn't got a chance.

– Well perhaps we shouldn't give just our opinions of the position of the vicar. What we were asked was how did we feel living here had changed us. I said I thought it had been at least a contributory factor towards making me feel somewhat more independent and grown up. This might have happened wherever I'd gone, but I do feel living in a part of the world like this has done me some good.

– Yes well it's broadened my outlook on life a bit, I think. I was in one of the local shops the other day and I saw a woman at the counter with a black eye. The man serving her said something like 'Oh are you and Stan having trouble between you again?' The woman just nodded and said 'Well, when he's had a few he always gets like that.' The sort of background and surroundings I come from, it would have been impossible for a woman to admit her husband had hit her; and it would have been inconceivable for a shopkeeper to have asked her the question about it like that man did. I think it makes you realize what a sheltered kind of life you've led when you hear people talking openly to each other like that.

– Perhaps this sounds rather pretentious to say, but I feel that in some way I can't properly explain we've both got more idea now of what life is really about. Somehow people round here do seem to lead lives that are more real than the lives of those people Sheila and I were brought up among – well she was, though I never really came to live amongst them until my teenage years when I went to boarding school. It's ironic, my father sent me away from a working-class background because he thought it would give me a wider perspective on life – and in fact I had to come back and live in a working-class area to get that perspective.

'Trying to stop the rot'

Colin Taylor

– To describe me you could say I'm one of a drug-taking, promiscuous and non-law-abiding group of about a dozen people who live a thoroughly irresponsible life in a couple of adjacent run-down houses in the middle of Dereliction Row, which is our name for this street; but I believe it was originally known as Absalom Road. I don't know if that name is on a wall anywhere, I've never seen it myself; but one of the girls said one day somebody'd told her that's what it used to be called before the particular house at the end with the sign on it fell down. We've been here between eighteen months and a couple of years. Some of us have jobs, some of us live on Social Security, some of us live on one another from time to time, and a few of us work here at this place.

'This place' is an empty shop near the end of Tullbrook Road, which we rent from the GLC for a nominal sum on a purely temporary basis. What's meant by 'temporary' I don't really know: so far we've been here six months and there's been no suggestion yet of us having to get out. If I wanted to be grand about it I'd say we were running a community resource centre, but that's stretching it a bit though it's what we'd like it to be eventually. We have an old printing press where we run off leaflets for people: someone who's trying to form a housing association say, or ones giving information to people who are on Social Security telling them about their rights. We also do a bit for the gay rights people, for the claimants' union, and for the women's lib group which one of the girls in the commune where I live is very keen on trying to get going.

We try to keep the shop open for anyone to drop into at any time for advice or just a chat, and we have a rota of people taking it in turns to be here. We don't have anyone who's the leader of the group; you could talk to anyone, male or female, and that person would be the spokesperson for the whole group because they were the one you happened to meet. I'm saying this as a preliminary to telling you a few personal details about myself because I want to make it clear that who I am really isn't greatly important as far as this place is concerned. If you'd come this afternoon you'd have met Jean and you wouldn't know of my existence, and that's how it should be.

He was twenty-five, small and slightly built, with long straight black hair down to his shoulders. Brown eyes, a ready smile, a friendly manner. He sat on an unstable old bench underneath the pay phone on the wall at the back of the shop, with a tin mug of dark brown tea which he sipped at as he talked.

– It might be obvious from my accent where I come from, which is Australia. Sydney to be exact: you usually find most Australians are very particular that you have the right town or city or area. God knows why this should be – to me Australia was just one big arsehole. I left when I was fourteen: I was sent by my parents to England to get educated, and I came to stay with my aunt in Cheltenham. For Christ's sake – Sydney to Cheltenham at fourteen! I'd always hated Sydney because it seemed rough and uncouth; but if being couth was being like Cheltenham, then I didn't want any part of that, that was for sure. Maybe I was a bit precocious for my age, but I hadn't been there long before I took up with a girl of sixteen from a café, and the pair of us lit off on a hitchhiking tour of Europe. We took a day-trip ticket from Dover to Boulogne, walked off the boat and headed south. I suppose kids get away with things which adults wouldn't even dream of trying, but we went all through France and Spain and Portugal then across to North Africa, then along the coast and over to Italy, up Italy and into Yugoslavia – and all in all we must have been in and out of ten or more countries without ever producing a passport.

That was certainly an experience of life for any young person. The girl I was with – I seem to remember her name was Nicola or something very 'Cheltenham' like that – suddenly ditched me in Dubrovnik. She explained to me that we'd had a good time but now it was over. She hoped I'd enjoyed the times we'd had together as much as she had, but we'd had an agreement that there were to be no strings

225

attached and either of us could go our own separate way whenever we wished. I hope I don't sound a bit sour about this, because I really don't mean to. Experience of Nicola, and experience with Nicola, had certainly done a great deal for me and helped me to grow up.

So I made my way back to Portugal and bummed around there for several months. Portugal? I loved it. It must sound a daft reason but the truth was I felt at home there in a physical way. I don't know if you've ever been to Portugal but nearly all the men are short and small like I am, so I felt very much as though I was among similar people. Also I found Portuguese a pretty easy language to learn, so I felt at home. I got in easily because it was around the time of the revolution and the whole of the bureaucratic system was totally disorganized. I moved around from place to place picking up casual work as I went, and I must have been one of thousands who was wandering around without the proper papers because nobody bothered me at all.

While I was there my political ideas began to clarify or solidify or whatever the appropriate word is. It was a very exciting time: the country'd never had any kind of freedom before, they'd had God knows how many years of Salazar's dictatorship, then Caetano – and then suddenly and finally a chance to become democratic in the sense of having a say in their own affairs. Wherever you went people were having animated political discussions in the cafés or bars, or just standing in groups at street corners. It was very exciting to be there at that time and to join in with complete strangers who were ready at the drop of a hat to ask you your ideas about government, and tell you about theirs.

I stayed around in Portugal for a few months, then I went into Spain and from Spain into France, and then I came back to England again. I can't explain why I came back to England. It's never been a place I'm particularly fond of. It might have had something to do I think with the fact that in Paris I shacked up with a girl called Marian who was English, and she wanted to come back here. I'm still living with her, she's a member of our commune.

And that's about as much as I can tell you about my past. As for the future I'm well aware I'm really only at the beginning of my adult life.

I'll ask the others in the commune whether you can come to the houses where we live. We have this rule that nobody brings in anybody without the agreement of all the others. You see not to put too fine a point on it, some of those who are living there are wanted by the police for minor infractions of the law, and they could well think you were either a plain-clothes policeman or at least an informer. But anyway leave it with me and I'll see what can be done.

– Marian and I have this first-floor front room, and we pay a nominal rent into a central fund which the commune administers. This central fund pays a small rent to the GLC, and in return they don't cut off the water or electricity and they collect our refuse once a week and so on. Even though we're here illegally I think they have to provide basic services because we have small children here. Some of the commune members feel that in return for what we get, and being left alone until the houses in the street are all finally pulled down, there's a certain obligation for us to keep up some kind of standard. So we do minor repairs, replace tiles on the roof and that sort of thing.

Health Visitors come regularly to keep an eye on the younger kids of whom there are three. Two of the mothers resent this very strongly and say the Health Visitors shouldn't be admitted. So we've discussed it at our weekly meetings and the general consensus is that as it's for the children's good in the long run, just because the Health Visitors are part of the State apparatus that doesn't mean we should spit in their eye. Some members feel this is a betrayal of our principles, but by a majority we've agreed that for the moment at least they can come.

We don't want to get into a confrontation situation with the authorities if we can avoid it. There have been instances in other areas in London where squatters have been very militant, have refused to pay any rent, stolen electricity and water and other things by connecting themselves up to the services. Then they've boarded themselves in, got a lot of publicity, and made inflammatory statements defying the authorities and more or less inviting them to come and try to chuck them out. That seems to me crazy. If the GLC would leave us alone permanently and let us stay here as long as we liked, I think most of us would opt for actually improving the premises ourselves. But this is a scheduled demolition area, so there's not much point in doing anything much on a large scale in that direction.

– I suppose most people think we're a group of weirdos because we reject the conventional way of life. We none of us do any regular work, most of us do odd jobs or live on Social Security. But we try to do things for the community like running the centre because after all, as people rightly say, it is to some extent their money which we're living on. At the shop we never charge anybody for any poster or leaflet printing that we do for them; we leave it to them to give us a donation if they want to. We also run a bit of an advice centre: it's

227

what some people would call an 'alternative advice' centre, in that we give out lots of information about Social Security rights and claims. Two of the men run an adventure playground on that waste ground over at the back of one of the blocks there. On Saturday mornings we have football coaching in the street, on Mondays two of the girls run a playgroup for any of the local mums and kids who want to go along, and certain individuals in our commune do a bit of what you might describe as unofficial night-school teaching. By that I mean they run classes about citizens' rights in empty shops and unused halls and places like that. Those are the more politically aware members – they feel their purpose is to arouse or increase political conscious-ness among the inhabitants of the estate, and to a certain extent I think they do make a bit of an impression.

Two of the girls, Adrienne and Jenny, are also trying to get a feminist group going with some of the housewives on the estate. But that's bloody hard work. I don't know that it's ever going to be a viable thing, because it seems to me that all the women on the estate are so conditioned by their upbringing they're never going to go into anything as way out as women's liberation. Adrienne and Jenny get the women who come to write things and read them out, and then the group analyses them and talks them over, and they concentrate on the feminist aspects which come up. It's all very loose and informal and it's their thing so it's not really right I should talk about it.

I've said to you before that each member of our group tries to play down his own personal contribution and think in terms of the group's activities as a whole. But if you don't want to have a whole series of eleven or twelve interviews with everyone, then it's unavoidable that I should mention some of the others and summarize what they're doing. A guy called Mike for instance is a trained teacher but dropped out of the educational system a year ago because he so totally disa-greed with it. He didn't just pack it in though. What he did was to go along to the education people and say that having worked for a while in a local school he'd come to the conclusion that the most important problem concerned truancy. He asked if he could set up a sort of alternative school for kids who didn't want to go to ordinary school to come to as an alternative if they felt like it. The education bloke said he thought it was worth a try and Mike should go ahead. He did, and he now sometimes has as many as twenty kids in a house just over the park there on any one day. These are children who are truanting: they are there because that's where they want to be, they accept a few formal lessons, and Mike feels that's better than them just roaming the street.

– I was talking to you last week about the way we look at things. I've talked to some of the others, and they're not all that keen that I should say anything which could be taken in any kind of sense as a statement which applies equally to us all. But I'd say the general opinion is fairly unanimous that we all think of ourselves as socialists or anarchists or communists, in the broadest sense. We don't like the present set-up in society, we'd like to change it, and we hope that what we do and say might be giving it a small shove in that direction. Another way of putting it might be to say we felt we were trying to stop the rot. We all feel that our present society is a rotten one, with its emphasis on material possessions, individual success which is always defined or at least measured in financial terms, lack of any kind of feeling of responsibility about the state of the rest of the world where people are starving and have nothing whatsoever in comparison to what western society has. The money spent by America and Russia on sophisticated weapon systems with which they're going to obliterate not only each other but a good part of the rest of the world's population. . . . Well, I could go on endlessly about all those sorts of things. So what we have here for ourselves is an alternative life style in which we don't go out of our way to offend people, but we don't go out of our way either to go along with what they consider to be right and proper. If we want to smoke, we smoke; if we want to trip, we trip; if we want to sleep with a different member of the commune on each different night of the week, we do just that. It's a matter for the two people concerned, and as nobody owns or has any rights over anybody, on the whole it seems to work out pretty well. From the outside, as I think I said to you the first time we talked, this makes us look and sound like a group of non-law-abiding, drug-taking and promiscuous people. Perhaps by the majority standards we are but I'm not apologizing for it.

'Several thorns in the side'

Oliver Ash

– If you were going to give any piece about me a title you'd have to call it 'the thorn in the side' or something like that; maybe several thorns in the side if you were going to be accurate, I think. I'm sure that's how the local authority regard me. Ever since I've been here I've been a bloody nuisance to them on every possible occasion, and I intend to go on being a bloody nuisance for ever if necessary. This local authority as you know is socialist and I'm a Tory; but it isn't a political thing, or at least it isn't as far as I'm concerned. I'd be just the same awkward bugger with a Conservative council as I would with a Labour one. This is my house and I bought it with my own money, not even borrowing a penny from a building society or anything of that sort. And this is where I want to live, and come hell or high water or local authority council or whatever, this is where I'm going to stay. Have another sherry. Yes I'll be perfectly happy to tell you about it.

Oliver Ash was about forty, lounge-suited, with his hair short and neatly parted and brushed. He had a habit of tapping the tips of his fingers together as he talked, and he sat in the bay window of his book-lined front room and surveyed his golden velveteen curtains and his orange coloured carpet with all the confidence of a professional man who knew exactly what he wanted and what he was doing. A solicitor in the City, a bachelor, an upper-class isolate in an area where his presence was an enigma: and he enjoyed creating the effect. At times he almost parodied himself and his background, speaking with an exaggerated drawl and laughing softly and sarcastically at everyone, including himself.

– Is your infernal machine switched on? All right, let's make a start then. You asked me to think about a description of myself to begin with. First and foremost a Tory, coming from a landed-class background. But a damnably determined radical Tory: I've no time for the huntin' fishin' and shootin' crowd, I despise them even more than I do the reddest of red communists. I think – I know – that I was born a member of the ruling class of England: there's no way that could be altered, but I think it carries with it a great deal of responsibility. Primarily in one's attitudes I mean. I think one should have a care, as the Quakers might put it, for those less materially fortunate than oneself. I don't believe, as very many Conservatives seem to these days, in devil take the hindmost. I believe in charity and good works and giving a helping hand to the underdog and all that kind of thing. If this sounds like some sort of parody of an Evelyn Waugh character, I assure you it's not. I'm not a Roman Catholic, so I only use Waugh as an example of someone who creates the sort of characters which appeal to me socially. I certainly don't mix with very many people round here – they're not my type and not my class, it would be very dishonest of me to pretend they were. My social life, such as it is, largely derives from my work. By that I mean that if I want an evening out I'll have it with my friends in my profession, we'll go out for a meal up in Town somewhere. Now and again I bring a lady back here for the night, but she is a lady of my own class and I could never envisage myself for instance screwing someone from this street, this area, or even anyone with any sort of cockney accent or anything like that. No, I don't want to get married. I do a lot of divorce work in my practice, and nothing could be more calculated to put one off marriage for ever. I try to cultivate a slightly effete attitude, and I wouldn't be in the least surprised if some of my colleagues didn't think that the reason I was unmarried was that I was queer. It amuses me that they might think that, and it doesn't worry me in the slightest. I don't feel that I have to prove anything to them about my masculinity: it's something which is a purely personal and private matter.

I was born in one of the shires thirty-seven years ago. My parents are not exactly nobility, but they're not all that far short of it. Frankly we don't get on and I haven't been home to see them for years, so there's not a lot I want to say about them that might be put in a book. I have an elder brother and sister and there's even less I want

231

to say about them, since we've nothing in common whatsoever. My brother in fact is a doctor in the north of England, and my sister is married to a university lecturer and has become what one might call a typical trendy leftie. Uncle Oliver is not a welcome guést in her house: she has two small children, and I think she fears the Fascist Beast might have a very bad effect on them if they ever got to know him.

I went to a private preparatory boarding school for little boys, naturally. Then from there I went on to one of the better public boarding schools, and thence to university. I took a law degree, and then through a friend of my father's I was taken into a law firm in the City. Up to there, it was what you might call a fairly orthodox and uneventful background. But after only a short time I was offered a much better position with a company – a very well-known company, so we'd better not mention their name – as one of their legal advisory staff in Johannesburg. I'm not going to say that my job was primarily one of trying to find ways of avoiding the results of international sanctions, but that certainly did come into it quite often. It was an invaluable experience: I learnt how to be devious, which is a very useful asset in life. And I also learnt how to never give up, whatever the odds facing you seemed to be. Sometimes I felt that what I was doing would, if it were known about, bring about an immediate emergency debate at the United Nations. But that was my job, that was what I was there to do, and I did it.

After two or three years, I don't know at all how it came about, but I suffered a sudden and violent change of heart. From a position of temporizing and feeling extremely pleased with myself whenever I helped my company to evade the consequences of some sanctions law or other, I suddenly found myself to be totally out of sympathy with what we were doing and with everything we stood for. It would make a nice romantic story if I could tell you of some incident or other which converted me from one point of view to another exactly opposite to it: but alas, there isn't one. I never saw a poverty-stricken African woman collapsed by the side of the road out to one of the townships, I never saw a starving child with a bloated belly looking at me reproachfully or anything like that. I don't mean that I never saw such things, because I did – you can't avoid seeing them in Johannesburg if you move out of any of the white enclaves. But it wasn't as a result of sights of that kind that I underwent this change of attitude I'm telling you about. I seem to remember I simply woke up one morning and while I was sitting on the end of my bed shaving myself with my electric razor I suddenly felt the whole way of life I was living, the whole thrust of the job I was doing – these were totally and completely immoral. and I should have no further part in them. I went into the office that morning and handed in my resignation. By lunchtime I'd started making the necessary arrangements for coming back to England, and by the time I went home at the end of the day it seemed to me that I was merely completing a process which I had begun months before.

I sent off a rather swift airmail letter to the firm in the City whom I'd worked for before I went to SA, asking them if there was an opening for me to come back to them. They replied equally swiftly that there wasn't, but they put me in touch with another firm who were looking for someone and within a very brief period of time, only a matter of a couple of weeks, I had a job waiting for me to come back to in England.

My main problem when I did get back was the liberals – and I'll say that with a small 'l', because that's what they were. I was showered with invitations to go to people's parties and confirm for them how awful life was in South Africa. But I didn't want to do that, I never greatly fancied the idea of proselytizing on any subject at all, and I hated all the gush and flannel. It wasn't that I was ashamed of what I had done, any more than I was proud of my recantation. I just wanted to forget about the whole thing and resume my profession again. Even now, when people do occasionally find out that I did work for a period of time in Johannesburg, I can see the look coming into their eyes that I know is a prelude to their asking me how it was. I lead off the subject as quickly as I possibly can, but if they insist on bringing it out I usually say I don't want to talk about it and leave it to them to draw their own conclusions from that remark.

This sherry is quite diabolical. I got it at one of the supermarkets in Tullbrook Road because it looked to be a bargain, being about half the price I usually pay at my wineshop in the City. I think after you have gone I shall probably use it to strip some of the old paint off the back of the kitchen door.

– Last time we were talking about what? My own legal background I think, yes, and my time in South Africa.

Well when I came back to London I soon afterwards inherited a little money from one of my uncles. I didn't quite know what to do with it, because although I've always been fairly comfortably off I've never had anything in the nature of a capital sum. Then talking to a colleague one evening in a pub in the City after work, he told me that he knew of a number of very cheap houses in this part of the world which he understood could be bought up and 'gentrified' by people who might be inclined to take the trouble to do that with them. I made inquiries from the local councils in south London, and those inquiries eventually led me to here. I bought it very cheaply and thereupon spent a great deal of money in doing it up. Beginning with the basics, I put in a bathroom, a hot-water system, central heating, even a damp course which it didn't have, had it repointed and the staircase taken out and replaced because all the wood of it was rotten, and had most of the roof tiling replaced too. Then I got someone in to turn what was the back yard out there into a small patio garden – nothing very grandiose as you see, but rather pleasant I feel, and I designed it myself. All in all I would say I spent somewhere in the region of £30,000 on top of the purchase price, including having it replastered inside and decorated throughout.

I'd hardly been here a year when I suddenly received notification from the council that this street was scheduled for demolition and my house would be compulsorily purchased. Like fuck it will I thought, if you'll pardon the expression, particularly as the council's idea of the compulsory price was what I'd paid for the shell of the house in the first place. Of course, like all these vast bureaucratic organizations they thought they were going to have to deal with some old uneducated and inadequate illiterate who they could bully into submission, and it was their misfortune that I didn't happen to be like that. I have colleagues and friends who know as much or more about housing and local authority law as almost anyone you care to mention in the GLC. So I have now made my life's work the preventing of them getting me out of here by every legal – or for that matter near-illegal – loophole in the law that I can be certain they can't quickly brush aside. It's going to be a long process, but they are simply not going to get me out of here. I could of course afford to go somewhere else, particularly if I went to litigation on the subject of compensation. I think I'd get a fair old sum, and it would be enough for me to get another place. But as I see it, this is my place, this is the place I choose to live, and I refuse to move for any Jack-in-office who decides that as a result of the deliberations of a road-widening committee everyone who stands in their way must be removed from their home. It doesn't seem to me that this is just sheer cussedness on my part either. There was never at any stage any consultation between the GLC and the people who originally lived in this street. I'm not referring to the squatters, but to the old indigenous people whose homes those houses were. They were moved out without any choice and put into different accommodation because it had been decided on high that this street was going to be pulled down. I think this is an obnoxious practice, and I think that people like myself who have had the benefit of an education and a training which has taught them how to resist this kind of bureaucratic behaviour have an obligation, I'd almost say a moral obligation, to take a stand.

– In answer to the question you asked me to think about just as you were leaving last week, I'd say that I most certainly do think of myself as very much a person of this area. I live here, this is my home, this is where I'm determined to go on living, and in that sense I am much more someone who has a right to be here, who belongs here and has the right to belong here, than a lot of the people whom I'm sure you'll talk to. I'm sorry if I'm not making myself clear, so I'll try to be more explicit. The people I'm referring to are the social workers and the general do-gooders who infect any area of this kind. They're mostly young and earnest; many of them are dropouts or semi-dropouts from society who have come into areas of this kind to give the poor downtrodden working classes the benefit of their superior standards. They're the so-called 'community workers', and I say 'so-called' because they really are not of the community at all. They come here and do things to the members of the community rather than for them; and then at the end of the day they go to their homes in Kensington or Bayswater or wherever, before coming back the next morning and resuming their social work. I find the very name itself distasteful. 'Social work' suggests to me – and indeed is, I think, if we're going to be realistic about it – no more or less than interfering with the lives of people and trying to help not so much the unhelpable as those who really would be far better off if they were left to work out their own solutions.

A lot of these people are young women, many of them with university degrees in sociology or some other such non-subject; and a large number of them, ironically, are people who have had some kind of relationship in their personal life which has failed and so they come to a working-class area like this rather in the way that Charles de Foucaud went into the desert to live with the Arabs. It's pretentiousness of the most distasteful kind. In a few years time these young women, or most of them, will be married or at least in establishments in maybe the outer suburbs, or they'll be at Keele University or somewhere like that doing 'research'. I really do think that they are inexcusably presumptuous, and that what they are doing is almost totally useless. They theorize and dream, but they have no idea whatsoever about the true feelings of people they're spending their time among.

As you probably know in this area there is a Community Development Project. Some ten years ago or more the government in its wisdom decided that this was a deprived area and could benefit from

235

a CDP. It's a government-funded agency which operates to give the impression that the government really cares about improving what I believe is sometimes arrogantly referred to as 'the quality of life' in areas such as this. The fact is there is nothing whatsoever wrong with the quality of life here. It has a long tradition, it satisfies those who live it – it manifestly must, otherwise they would move away – and it seems to me entirely wrong that anybody should have the sheer nerve to think they are able in any way to decide how it should be improved. It might not be their way of life, but it apparently suits thousands of people in this part of the world and they should be left alone to get on with it.

I don't want to give the impression that I'm a completely *laissez-faire* doctrinaire person because I'm not. There are of course areas in which people need help. One of them is the jungle of tenancy laws, and the rights of citizens who are in conflict with huge bureaucracies. I'm actively engaged now in the process of starting up a law centre, and I'm hoping to run it on a rota basis with a number of my colleagues from the City. We have the knowledge and the ability to impart that knowledge, and it's knowledge which I feel we have an obligation to share. But I do not feel that we or anyone else has an obligation to start trying to tell people how they should live their lives and improve them. At a law centre you can actually start legal action, so long as you are advised by properly trained and qualified people. The Community Development workers can't do anything of that kind at all: they can only advise people who are in legal trouble to come and get legal advice, but they are qualified neither to give it themselves nor to instigate action where necessary.

– I suppose in principle I'd like to be married; I think one should be because it's the conventional thing to do, and I'd quite like to have children. Unfortunately as far as I am concerned I find the idea of giving a great deal of oneself – if not all of oneself – to someone else is one that I don't greatly like, it has very little appeal indeed. I suppose you could say this is because I'm a very cerebral sort of person. If that were said I couldn't disagree with it but I'm in no way apologizing for it. I very much enjoy being the person that I am and I really wouldn't like at my time of life to have to start making some kind of adjustment to someone else. Yes, I would say I'm a very happy person. I enjoy living here, I enjoy – and I intend to go on enjoying – the battle to stay here.

Not at all. Would you care for another glass of sherry?

'The Dangling Conversation'
Peter Block

Of all the houses in Absalom Road, the one at the very end on the corner looked to be the most derelict and the least likely to be inhabited. All its front windows had been smashed and were covered over with sheets of rusting corrugated iron or weather-beaten unpainted hardboard. The steps of the stoep were cracked and slanting, the front door was a mosaic of hammered-together pieces of planking: some new where the old ones had been ripped off, others rotten with the effects of rain. Incongruously, there was a small cheap plastic bell-push hanging at the end of a loose wire down one side of the door frame, just visible in the beam of a flashlamp. It would always have to be after ten o'clock at night when we talked, he said.

– Can you see? I'm afraid I've forgotten to bring my flashlight down. Just on the right along the hall here there's a big hole in the floorboards, but if you keep your left hand on the wall as we move along you ought to be all right. OK so far? Right, well we're now at the bottom of the stairs and the third and seventh ones are the tricky ones: your foot could easily go through them so it's best to jump. . . . Now this first landing here is in fairly good condition, and the second lot of stairs we're coming to are quite safe. . . . But it's up at the top that things start getting a bit dodgy again. . . .

He lived in the two back rooms on the third floor at the top of the house. One was a kitchen with a small chipped formica-topped table, three chairs, a sink with a cold tap, and some old paint-peeling cup-

boards. It was heated by a small portable gas fire and lit by a single low-wattage electric light-bulb hanging shadeless from the ceiling. The other was the bedroom. It had a wardrobe, a single divan bed covered with old blankets, and a two-tier bunk bed in which slept his two sons, eleven-year-old Barney and seven-year-old Philip.

A tall good-looking man in his thirties, brown eyes and short black curly hair. His voice was soft and quiet, and often when he talked there was a faraway look in his eyes as his hands lay clasped, fingers twining, on the kitchen table. We drank mug after mug of strong coffee.

– Sorry about asking you to come so late, but you know what kids are. Barney and Philip won't go to sleep unless they've had their evening television session with some of their mates in one of the flats over the other side of Robins Walk. Perhaps I'm not firm enough with them about going to bed. But I wouldn't like them to have a life like I had, with grown-ups always breathing down your neck. I tell them they have to be in by nine and they're good boys, they always are. But by the time I've got them washed and in bed and read them a bit of a story, most of the evening's gone.

Well, I don't really know there's very much I can tell you. Susie said you were trying to get a cross-section of the sort of people who lived on the estate, and I said I'd be willing to talk to you. But afterwards I thought 'Well what the hell am I going to talk to him about?' I mean some people lead interesting lives, others don't. So maybe you might be able to use me as an example of one of the really uninteresting ones.

I've lived here at the top of this house two years now. When we first came there were people down below on all the floors and in all the other rooms. It's so empty and quiet now it's hard to believe at that time there were fourteen inhabitants and the place was really jumping. But one by one they've all moved away, gone into better places I suppose, and we're the only ones left. The housing department have got us on their waiting list, and there's a social worker comes round now and again. They know we're here, but nothing much seems to happen about us being given somewhere else. I'm not a very pushy kind of a person: if I was I suppose I'd be raising hell at the Housing Department. But I don't seem to be able to raise the energy for it somehow. I think it might be that I'm ill in a way – I don't mean physically, I mean mentally. Everything in life's too much for me and I don't have the drive or energy to make much of an effort to improve things. I keep the boys fed and clothed, see they get off to school in the mornings and that sort of thing, but that's about the limit of what I can manage. During the day while they're out I'm afraid I don't do much except sit around and read and smoke. Rather a spineless sort of existence, and I don't even try to do anything about it. The social worker used to try and talk me into going to see someone – she meant a doctor I suppose. But I think he'd not have done much except give me a few pills for my nerves. Actually my nerves are OK. I don't like the idea of swallowing pills. Here's not a good environment for the boys though is it?

We talk about it sometimes. They're both grown-up for their age and I ask their advice, and I think they know that if they really pushed me to do something, I'd do it. But Barney says while things are as they are he's quite happy to stay here with Philip and me. You know it gets a bit of a laugh sometimes: anyone'd think on the face of it that I was looking after them, but I don't know – sometimes I think those two boys are looking after me. They know their dad's rather a useless sort of character and they talk sometimes as though they're protecting me from the harshness of the outside world. They tell me I don't need to go shopping, they'll do it on a Saturday morning. And sometimes when I'm not feeling so good, that's what they do. I have to go to the Social Security office to get the money once a week for us, but Barney is the one who divides it up. This much for food, that much that we pay to the GLC by way of rent and electricity and so on, that much that I can afford to spend on cigarettes. . . . He's a proper young economist, is Barney.

– To all intents and purposes I'm a local boy. A bastard of course: I never knew my father, I think he was Spanish but I couldn't be sure. My mother had six kids altogether, and I was the first. I think she was only fourteen or fifteen when she had me, because for as long as I can remember I lived as a child with my grandparents just by the park there. Then – well it's the common story – she got married when she was around sixteen or so, and the bloke naturally enough didn't want to know anything about me. I stayed on with my grandparents until I was eighteen, then I went to sea for a while. A deck hand on a cargo ship, an assistant cook; once I think I even got up to the dizzy height of steward on a very small passenger ship. But the sea wasn't in my blood and I came home after only a couple of years or so. I haven't had much education. What am I saying? I haven't had *any* education, I was an ignorant illiterate yob. Quite big and strong for my age: I worked as a hand in a circus for a bit, then I worked in a slaughterhouse, then. . . . Christ what else have I done? I think it would be easier to tell you the things I haven't done: all my life I seem to have spent my time going from one job to another, and never settling down anywhere.

I got to twenty-five and then I got married. She was a local girl who used to live further along our street – I mean my grandparents' street. She was very pretty and I know I fancied her a lot. Her name was Peggy. One night we were in bed together at her parents' house while they were out, and I asked her if she would marry me. Ludicrous. I think I meant it as a matter of interest: not will you, but would you be prepared to if it ever came to that sort of situation? Anyway, she looked at me and she said 'Yes,' and then she started reeling off a whole list of terms and conditions. If we married, she wasn't going to give up her independence; if we married she wasn't going to give up her job; if we were married she wasn't going to have any children and be tied down. I can't really see what possible advantage there could have been to her in us being married at all. However, there it was and there we were, and a few weeks later – at her instigation of course – we found a furnished room in Battersea which we moved into together. I stayed there and did the housework and the cooking, and Peggy went out every day to work. It's incredible now to look back on it, but that situation lasted for quite a number of years. We had Barney and then we had Philip – or rather, she had them and then handed them over to me to look after while she went on with her independent life. Susie once asked me a little while ago what it was kept us together, she said had I been a super lover or something? Oh boy, I certainly wasn't that to be honest I'm surprised I was ever capable of producing two children. They were produced though to order: Peggy decided when we were going to have them, like Peggy decided everything else. It's still a mystery to me why she wanted to go through all the agony of physically producing a child. But there it is she did, and Barney and Philip are the result.

One time Peggy was ill, she had one of those painful skin things, shingles yes. It meant she had to be off work for weeks on end, and she told me to go and get a job which I did, as a bus conductor. It was shift work but the money wasn't too bad. The moment she was better though she told me to stop at home again because she was going back to work. She was a very bright and well-educated girl: she had all the 'O' levels and I think a couple of 'A' levels as well, whereas I have nothing. She worked in a travel agent's, and a few times she went abroad for a week or ten days on her own for her holidays. She got concessionary trips because of her job. I remember once she went to Barbados, and another time I think it was to Morocco. There was never any question of me going too. We had the kids and it was taken for granted that I would stay at home and look after them. Anyway she always used to say that I wouldn't like the sort of travelling she did, she said it took me all my time to get from Sidcup to Bromley, which was true. If she'd ever sent me out to get something in the market or something like that, I know she used to get exasperated at how long it took me to find my way there and back again.

– I think it was the third holiday abroad she had on her own that she came back at the end of it with this very good-looking New Zealand bloke she'd met. She brought him into the flat with her where we were living then – having the two kids we'd had to move out into a larger unfurnished place which she'd found only a few months before. Anyway as I say she came back with this man, I didn't know who he was or what he was, but she just told me that he was moving in with us. He was installed in the spare bedroom only it wasn't a spare bedroom, it was their bedroom. She slept with him every night, not with me. He used to go out every morning with her, sometimes they'd come back for a meal that I'd prepared for all of us, and other times they'd go out to a restaurant or a theatre on their own.

I've always been a weak person, I used to cry a lot at that time; and when the boys asked me what was wrong I used to feel very ashamed that they should see me like that. I used to tell them I wasn't feeling well, but I never had the guts to say what the position really was – that their mother was carrying on with someone else, and I in my weakness was prepared to put up with it. I suppose a lot of men would find this very hard to understand, but when I think back on it I can only come to the conclusion that in my own silly stupid inadequate way I loved Peggy very much and would take anything from her, however far she wanted to go. Or perhaps I didn't love Peggy at all, and no matter what she did it didn't really affect me enough to stand up and make a fight about it. She told me – she was always telling me – that I was weak-kneed and lily-livered and all that sort of thing, and that I was incapable of loving anyone except myself. I don't know, perhaps she was right, perhaps she wasn't. I've puzzled over this a lot.

Anyway there was one thing that was perfectly obvious, and it was that that New Zealand bloke was a very positive and active and virile and good-looking sort of man. I don't know what his job was or his prospects were, but I could well see that Peggy or anyone else would find him a much more interesting and attractive proposition than the husband she'd got. So I can't say I was really exactly struck dumb with surprise when she told me one night that she was going off to

New Zealand with him, and wouldn't be coming home any more. She said they'd made all the arrangements, got the tickets and whatever else was necessary, and would be leaving the following day.

I'm always a bit slow on the uptake, I've already told you haven't I that I think I'm a bit dim. So it was a few minutes before something else struck me and I asked her was she taking the boys to New Zealand too. I remember her standing there in the middle of the room and giving a little laugh as though what I'd asked her was the most stupid question anyone could have thought of. What on earth would she want with them she said; she was going to start up a new life on the other side of the world and she'd have no hope at all of it working if she had two kids hung round her neck. They were mine she said, and it was up to me to get them put in the best possible home I could find.

She turned round and walked out of the door and shut it behind her; and I've never seen her or heard from her, and neither have the kids, from that day to this.

I didn't know where the hell to start about getting the boys into a home, as she'd said. They were then both very young – Barney was six and Philip was two – and I just sat down on the floor and put my face in my hands and cried, because I was quite sure I wasn't going to be able to find anywhere for them to go. It was very late at night I remember, and there was a pop music programme on the radio. Simon and Garfunkel were singing that song 'The Dangling Conversation'. Whenever I hear it now as I do now and again, it always brings that moment back to me very vividly because it seemed to me that what they were singing about was what had just taken place. I don't remember the words exactly now but it's something about saying things that have to be said. . . .

– I get up in the morning at half past six, give the boys their breakfast and take them to school. Then I pick them up again at 4.30 and bring them home and we have our tea. Then they go out to play or whatever if it's light, I do a bit of reading and tidying up until they come home again, and then I put them to bed. And that's about it really.

It's not much of a life for the boys. Susie said once I ought to think of getting married again, if only for their sake. But I don't see how you could say to anyone 'Please would you marry me because I've got two kids who need someone to act as a mother to them?' And Susie once said how about me and her, but I'm sure that wouldn't work. She's a nice girl and she's got a lot about her, plenty of character and personality. Someone like that would soon get fed up with someone like me.

How can I put it? I live a lot in my head – my friends are books, and the writers of them. Mostly I like semi-philosophical things, and political and economic ideas. Sociology is something I'd really like to study one day if I ever got a chance. I think it keeps your mind alive, and I also think it somehow links you up with society all around you.

My main worry is Barney and Philip. They're not having a proper life, and sometimes I wonder if I really ought to have done what Peggy said and put them in a home, have them taken into care. It might have been better for them, there's an awful lot of things they miss. I don't have any family or relatives myself now and so they don't either. Not long ago Barney asked me hadn't he got any aunties or uncles anywhere, and I had to tell him no. I can only put it that it must make them feel like guests in life in comparison with other kids.

Christ, you must find this boring, me going on and on about the kids like I always do, and yet never really doing anything about it. But I get very tired in the evenings and I'm not a good talker.

Part Six

THE POSH PART

'Staying quietly nameless'
Nancy and Haley Dickinson

Jesmond Close, a cul-de-sac. 'One of the snobby parts' . . . 'the posh part' . . . 'it must be quite pleasant to live there'. In a quiet corner of the estate the large bungalows with their front lawns neatly laundered and open to the road seemed to be slightly withdrawn from its everyday life. There was never noise or rowdiness there, and the eighteen bungalows grouped together were unnamed and without numbers. Living there it was not difficult to keep yourself to yourself, which was what Nancy liked about it, she said. She'd stayed on because she'd had a cruel hard vicious blow and it was a good place to lick wounds, to retire from the fraying of living, to recoup, rethink, and eventually perhaps come to decide what came next.

A slim short blond-haired woman with blue eyes and a clipped voice, dry and quiet. A heavy smoker, and her hands restless and thin.

– Being widowed at forty so suddenly and unexpectedly like I was, I can't describe what it does to you. It was nearly two years ago but it still feels like somebody came up behind me and hit me over the head with a cosh and I never knew what hit me. I don't think yet I've really grasped it you know. It's hard to remember any kind of life before that, and I don't really remember things very well since either. It slowed me down like well I suppose like being in a car crash would slow you down. You think you've had a narrow escape, you've only just got away with your life and you were lucky too. Which sounds strange doesn't it: I wasn't in any danger, it was Howard who died. But it's like, it's as though I was with him when it happened though in fact I wasn't; and it was something we both experienced, but he got killed by it and I didn't. I don't suppose that makes sense.

People who know me will tell you I'm very hard because I don't cry. I never have cried, not once since Howard went. It was on a Saturday, and I was back at work on the Monday morning. The people I work for were very good, they said take as much time off as I wanted: but apart from the day of the cremation I never took any time off at all. People say it's a hard attitude to take, my own mother said that. But all right that's me, I can't help being as I am; I don't want to sit around and cry. I know Haley cries but she does it in her own room, not in front of me. She's never seen me cry. Everybody else cried but I didn't, I didn't shed a single tear at the cremation. It's not that I didn't love Howard: I did, but when he went I like seemed to freeze up. I seemed to stop being a person, do you know what I mean? It was like being in a road accident and it paralysed me. I'm still paralysed now, I can't move, I can't feel any emotion. Not a proper person any longer, that's how I feel. So I stay on here, living very quietly, not going out anywhere except to work, not doing anything except smoking and watching the television. It's not really living, but then I'm not ready to come to terms with that yet because I don't feel I'm a person with any character or personality any longer. It's just living, that's all, just about living; staying quietly nameless in the middle of a great big housing estate with life going on all around me, but not being a part of it in any way at all.

This is a nice part of the estate, it's definitely the nicest part I'd say. It's the most recently built, and all the people who live here are just that little bit different from the rest, do you know what I mean? I don't want to sound snobbish about it, but the council won't let just anybody have one of these bungalows. They go very carefully into your background and your financial state, and if you don't come up to a certain standard you're not allowed to be considered for one. When we applied, Howard and I were living in Gorrivale Square. We had to show the housing people that we had a certain amount of money in the bank, we had to show them Howard's payslips and mine, and we had to make it plain we were not the sort of people who were ever going to fall behind with their rent. These rents are the highest of anywhere on the estate, and so it wouldn't do if people were not going to pay their rents regularly, look after their property and so on. They're beautiful bungalows: they've all got a big through sitting room like this, a nice piece of garden at the back, three bedrooms, a dining room, kitchen, two toilets. Yes let me show you round.

– We came here ten years ago now, when Haley was six. We had another daughter Christine who was then twelve; she's married and she and her husband live in Bromley but they don't have any children yet. Howard had a good job. He was a sales manager, actually an area sales manager, with an engineering firm. It was a very good job with good perks like a motor car, a pension scheme and all the rest of it; and his firm have looked after me pretty well since he died. To be honest I don't need to work, but I go on because it gives me something to do. We both of us came from very humble backgrounds: Howard's father was a bus driver and mine worked in the docks. I suppose it's unavoidable when you get married that you grow away from your parents, but I do feel a bit bitter about Howard's family. They've hardly had anything to do with me at all since he died. I think to be honest about it they thought I wasn't good enough for him really, his mother's quite a big snob. They live over at the other side of the estate, only about ten minutes away but they hardly ever come here and I don't get invited there.

One of the things they're not happy about, if I'm going to be honest about it, is that I do have a boyfriend who comes round to see me sometimes. He is a boy *friend* and nothing more, we're not having an affair or anything. He's a man I know from work, he's a bit younger than me, and it's very very difficult. Haley doesn't like him coming at all; he usually comes once a week on a Thursday in the evening, and stops for about two hours that's all. She always makes a point of going out – and it's the one time when she does go out when I know she'll be back early. I never have to say to her to be back early on a Thursday, she's always in by about half past ten whereas other nights she'll stop out until midnight or after. There's absolutely nothing going on between me and this man, but she behaves as though there was. Always after he's gone she says very cruel things to me, like have I forgotten Dad. I find it very difficult to talk to her about it because she gets in a temper and lets me see that she is: she starts banging things about and getting all huffy, and sometimes I really don't know what to do. When I told her one day that this man was married but was separated from his wife, she put on a terrific scene and almost accused me to my face of having caused the break-up of his marriage. It's very painful, and I wish she wasn't like that. But still, she's at an awkward age I suppose.

Another thing that I'm not too happy about is that I think she talks to her gran about it sometimes. That's Howard's mother; she goes over to see her once a week. One day unexpectedly my mother-in-law came round to see me, she said she was just passing so she thought she'd pop in. It's the first and only time she's ever done it.

I didn't know what she wanted; and then just as she was going she turned round in that doorway there and said 'If my husband died I'd never look at another man.' Then she went straight out before I could think of what to say. It seemed very odd to me that Haley had been there at her house only the day before, and then she'd come round and said a thing like that. It was very very upsetting.

All in all I'd say Haley was my biggest problem in life. You read about mothers and daughters who have a good and close relationship and are good friends with each other. I wish we could be like that, but to be very honest about it I don't think Haley really likes me at all. I keep telling myself it's something she'll grow out of. She doesn't approve of my way of life, though God knows there's nothing very outrageous about it. But she makes it quite clear there are all sorts of things she doesn't approve of: the obvious things like cooking, or she says I don't keep the house tidy, or she says that I'm always onto her. I don't think I am, I think I'm nothing like stern enough with her because of her father dying so suddenly like that. After all it was Haley who discovered him. He dropped dead of a heart attack in the bathroom there, and she went to go in and he was there lying on the floor blocking the door.

Really, she's a big problem and a big worry altogether is Haley. It was after her father died that she started drinking. I don't mean at home, I mean at school. She's very bright and she's in the top form, and when you meet her as you will you'll see she looks very grown-up for her age. She and some of her friends – and sometimes I suspect one or two of the teachers too – they go into pubs at lunchtime and they drink. I don't know where the money comes from, I certainly don't give her a lot of pocket money; but two or three times recently when I've come home from work in the afternoon I've found her asleep on her bed, and there's a very strong smell of drink about her. I've tackled her about it, and she says all she ever has is a shandy. But I don't think that would be enough to put someone to sleep: she's really snoring with her mouth open, and to be honest I have to say that she looks very near to drunk to me. I've been to the school and talked with her teacher about it: but she seems to me to be just as bad, she laughs and says it's nothing to worry about. All the same it is a worry, I do worry. Haley's all I've got to live for really. Perhaps I'm not a very good mother to her, but I wish somehow we could be a bit closer to each other.

I mentioned it once to Mr Cross. He's a man who lives somewhere around here, I don't know what he does but he's a nicely spoken man and sometimes he just drops in in the late afternoon if he's passing. I told him about my problems with Haley and asked him if he would try and talk to her, but he said he really didn't feel he could. It's understandable I suppose, but I wish he would. Haley needs somebody to talk to.

Sixteen years old, thin and long-legged and with her long dark hair fastened into a ponytail with an elastic band at the back of her head, wearing faded jeans and a thick grey pullover, she lay stretched out on her bed with her chin on her hands. Her room was a riot of paperback books and posters and record sleeves fastened to the wall with drawing pins. Her taste in reading was almost entirely science fiction; musically her favourites were The Who and Pink Floyd. She smoked cigarettes one after another, talking in a low monotone, punctuating what she said with long silences when she blew cigarette smoke out in long thin streams through her pursed lips.

– The trouble with Mum is she always feels she's got to explain me to people or to apologize for me. She never really wants to let me be a person in my own right. I don't bring any of my schoolfriends home here because if I do she's always fussing and making apologies for the state of the house or the area we live in. This is supposed to be the poshest part of the estate, but if I bring in friends who don't live around here she seems to feel she's got to explain to them that we're only living here temporarily and would like to live somewhere that wasn't on a housing estate. Our house is bigger than the houses most of my friends live in, it embarrasses me when she starts talking to them like that.

The other thing I find very hard to put up with is that she doesn't seem to want to make any effort at all to do anything but sit around and think and talk about Dad. I don't know if you've seen her bedroom, but she's got the top of her chest of drawers laid out almost like a shrine with photos of him in big frames and mementos of him, and she won't let anybody go near it. Just recently she's got herself a kind of boyfriend, a bloke from where she works. But he's a man who's already married so there can't be much future in it for her and anyway he's much younger than she is. I don't feel she's serious about him, I think she's picked him up because he's not the sort of person she's going to have to rearrange her life for. If you ask me I think he's a bit of a drip.

After Dad died she suddenly started taking an interest in things at my school, the Parent-Teacher Association and things like that. Up till then she'd never bothered at all. But then she was up at the school

251

almost every week talking to the teachers and asking them how I was doing, and we had a big row about it. To me it was almost as though she was trying to find a new interest for herself, I didn't feel that it was done out of genuine concern for me at all.

She's also very prissy, or at least I think it's prissy about my language. I don't swear a lot, no more than all the rest of my friends at school; but whenever I do come out with the odd 'shit' or anything she does her nut. But I've heard her when she's in a temper using much worse words than that and anyway I don't think it matters. I'm not a kid any more and I don't think she should treat me like one. About the one good thing that happened at school after Dad died was that most of the teachers suddenly began to treat me as though I was grown-up. My own class teacher, she's very nice and she was a great help.

I shall be sad when I leave school but all the same I hope I can leave at the end of this year. I'm taking three 'A' levels – English, Maths and Biology – and I expect I shall get them because I find schoolwork rather easy. I don't mean to sound big-headed but I'm supposed to be one of the bright ones in the class. The only trouble is that all the other girls seem to know what they want to do, and I'm the only one who doesn't. I think my main thing is to move away from home, I find it too stifling altogether and I want to be somewhere where I can lead a life of my own without Mum breathing down my neck all the time. I suppose all this must sound terrible to you as though I'm not grateful for all the things she's done for me. It's not that I'm not grateful though: it's more that I'm fed up with having to say 'Thank you' all the time. I'm sure she means well, but it's very hard indeed and I wish I was older and knew how to deal with it. We have what's called a school counsellor at school, a woman who comes visiting once a week. I talked to her about it and she said it was something I'd find got better as I got older, and as far as I'm concerned I suppose at the moment I've just got to put up with things as they are.

I think Mum and Dad must have been a very unusual couple in their marriage, at least compared with a lot of grown-ups that I hear about. They seemed to be just for each other; it must have been one of those very happy marriages that you hear about, because since Dad died Mum's never really got over it at all. She seems to be at a loose end all the time. Sometimes I see her looking towards the front door if she's heard a faint noise outside or something, and it's almost as though she's expecting him to come in. I've told her more than once that I think she ought to go and see a doctor and ask him to give her something that would help her over it, but she always says she doesn't want to. Her life ended when Dad died, she says. Well, I don't think that's a very good thing to say when you're only her age. I don't think she'll ever get another bloke while she goes on moping like she does about Dad. She's having no sort of a life and it worries me.

– Haley and I don't really think of ourselves as people who live on Providence Estate, because around here isn't really like the rest of the estate at all. Everyone who lives in Jesmond Close is in what's called a higher income bracket, and we all keep ourselves to ourselves. The neighbours are nice, but we don't go into one another's houses, we're not that kind of people. There is a lot of vandalism on the estate but it's all over the other side. There's nothing like that round here, people just wouldn't put up with it. The mobile caretakers give us preferential treatment, you see them round and about here much more than you see them in other places on the estate. It's their job to keep an eye on things and make sure everything is quiet and peaceful and in order here.

When I said I didn't think of us as someone who really lived on the estate what I meant was that I hope before long I shall be able to move somewhere else. I got quite a fairly large sum of money when Howard died because he'd been with his firm a long time and they had a good superannuation and pension scheme. That money's in the bank now, and when the time comes I want to buy a little house. It will be somewhere further out, not exactly in the countryside but more of a country-town place and definitely not London. First of all I've got to find out what Haley wants to do with her life. She's very unsettled, which is only natural for someone as young as her; but as soon as I can see the way clear ahead, then I shall definitely move. There won't be any problem to me in getting another job. I'd like to go on working because I'm a private secretary and I know I can earn good money wherever I go, and I'd get a very good reference from my firm because I've always been very reliable. I definitely am not thinking that there might come a time when I would want to get married again. I think as far as that side of things is concerned I've had my life. I was very happy with Howard, and I don't think I could stand the idea of any other man messing about with me. I mean physically, if I did marry it would have to be on a platonic basis and I can't see any man agreeing to that. They're all the same at heart, I think it's true when they say all men really only want one thing. Friendship is about as far as I could go with any man now.

I like this bungalow but I shouldn't be sorry to leave the area. I don't think it's a very good area. For instance with Haley, she'll never make what I would call a good marriage so long as she stays living round here. The boys that she knows are nice enough, but for example one works in a greengrocers, another for a butcher, another is in the post office on the counter. None of them have got jobs with any real prospects, and I would like her to take a step upwards when she marries. But if she stays here there's very little chance of that.

I'd describe myself as a very lonely sort of person, but it would be lonely by choice. I tend to keep myself to myself and my thoughts to myself. You're the first person I've talked to about myself since Howard died, and as far as people round here are concerned I don't like them knowing more about me than they have to. I wasn't all that different when Howard was alive; we were both ones for keeping ourselves apart from the common herd. When we did go out, it was up to the West End to a musical or something like that. We never went to the social club on the estate, bingo and things of that sort never appealed to us.

I did believe in God, even though I wasn't a regular church-goer. But when Howard died no one came to see me from the church, and I didn't believe in God anyway after that. I felt very much alone then, I didn't want to pray or turn to religion or anything like that, I felt I could get on with it, and feel I have. I'm not as hard a person as I think I must have sounded when I've been talking to you. But I am a person who tries to get on and make the best of things. I think you have to accept what life brings you, and what it brought me was an early widowhood. I'm not looking for anything else now, I'm going to accept that as I said. I don't cry or feel sorry for myself: crying won't bring Howard back again and although I had a lot less than a lot of people, I know that in some ways I had a lot more. I'm very much an arm's-length person now. I can't ever see myself being any different. I keep everybody away from me as much as I can. I suppose I do it with Haley, and that can't be very good for her. But I don't see how I'm going to change myself now at my age and particularly after what happened when Howard went.

'Second-class citizen, first-class life'

Bert Weir

A white-haired blue-eyed man of seventy, he sat back in the luxury of the large leather-upholstered armchair, lit his pipe, sucked at it until he was entirely satisfied that it was drawing properly, and started to laugh quietly.

– You have to laugh, I hope you'll forgive me laughing. I'm seventy this week, and in all my life so far no one's ever asked me for my thoughts about anything. No one's ever thought I had anything to say that was worth hearing I suppose. Well they were probably right – but it just strikes me as a funny thing that's all, that all the years I was working on the estate no one ever asked me my views about it; and then you turn up out of the blue saying you've heard I'm a retired caretaker and you'd like to make recordings of some of my ideas and impressions. I've often thought it might be a good idea if the GLC sent people round say once every year or so, asking people on the estate what their feelings were. But of course they never did, which is why it's such a sad place now.

Oh yes, it is a sad place now. When they first built it twenty years ago or more it was going to be paradise, wasn't it? For the people who were coming here to live I mean. They'd all been living in very bad conditions, in slums and places like that, and here was this marvellous modern new housing estate which was going to give them all a wonderful new life. It's true, in those early days there was a great sense of community among the people who came to live on Providence. They all knew that they had all come here to have a new start in life. They all knew what sort of background they'd come from and what sort of background everyone else must have come from, and it gave them a big feeling of all being in the same boat. It was a fresh start for everyone.

But it passed. I don't know why, I can't exactly put my finger on it and say to you it happened at one particular time because it didn't, it was more a gradual sort of thing. But people did, they became more and more separate. A lot of the early comers moved away, and new people were brought in, and after ten or twelve years or so it seemed nobody knew anybody any more, and nobody had the same amount of pride in living on the estate that the first people who came here had. Some of the people who started coming around that time, they never stopped complaining. I remember a woman one day, she'd called for someone to go to her flat in one of the tower blocks to fix a water pipe that'd come away from the wall. When I got there, it was obvious she and her family hadn't been in residence very long because there were still packing cases all over the place, there were no carpets on the floor, and none of the furniture had been properly arranged. She said to me that she and her husband weren't going to stop if they could help it – they'd told the GLC they wanted somewhere better. When I asked her what she didn't like about it, she said that it wasn't the sort of place that they were used to. She gave me the impression that she really looked on it as having come down in the world. Only a few days after that I bumped into one of the Housing Officers in Tullbrook Road and she asked me if I knew how this woman was getting on. I said yes, as a matter of fact I'd been called in to fix a pipe for her. The Housing Officer said, 'Oh, I do hope she's happier now. I really had to pull all sorts of strings to get the place for her, you can't imagine what sort of conditions she and her family were living in. I took one look at the two furnished rooms they had and I made up my mind that she was a very deserving and very desperate case.' I didn't have the heart to tell her what the woman had said to me.

When I first came here, it was as a caretaker. I'd been working in the docks, but it was casual labour and you never knew from one week to the next whether you were going to be in work or not. One night when I got home the wife showed me this advert in the paper, it said the GLC were looking for resident caretakers for a new estate, see. The wife said that if we could get somewhere which had a house or a flat going with it as part of the job, that would be much better: we were living with her parents then in Lambeth, and we had our two children who were just starting to grow up and get a bit noisy and troublesome, especially when it came to having to live in someone else's house. So I wrote off, and I think it can't have been much more than two weeks before I'd got the job and we'd been given a ground-floor flat in that first tower over there, Bolton. Good God, did we think we were smart in those days! It was like being put to live in a palace. There was lots of grass all round for the kids to play on, and the wife could keep an eye on them from the windows. In those days they hadn't built the garages; there were only the other tower blocks, I think just three at first and the other three were building. It was beautifully quiet and peaceful, it was just as though we were living in the countryside. We couldn't believe our luck.

The people who lived in the tower were all very nice polite people. I had a little sort of cubbyhole-cum-office next to the entrance, and my own telephone system that the tenants could ring me up on if there was anything they wanted. Every morning there was this constant stream of people going out to work and all of them saying 'Good morning Mr Weir' as they went out and 'Good evening Mr Weir' when they came back in the evening. I think I knew everyone of them by name. It was 'Good morning Mr So-and-so how are you today? Good morning Miss So-and-so what a lovely morning!' Then in time they got to know my name and I got to know theirs. So it was 'How are you Bert?' 'Fine thanks John how are you?' I used to say to the wife that I felt as though I'd got a great big family of my own.

You even got people amongst those first residents who would ring down at four o'clock and say things like 'I've just made a cup of tea Bert, come up if you feel like one.' And at Christmas they'd give you presents; I don't know how many bottles of sherry I used to get, boxes of chocolates for the wife, sweets for the kids. It was a lovely job. People were very good; they never took you for granted, but of course you went out of your way to help them. They'd ring down either to my office or to my flat if something had gone wrong and they were always very apologetic about disturbing you. Even though it was my job, they still asked politely if I could manage to help them. When people treat you like that, you're always ready to go and help them even if it is late at night or at the weekend. But the later people who came, I could never puzzle out why it was that they were like they were. They'd think nothing of ringing you up in the middle of the night sometimes to say that one of their windows was loose and the wind was making it rattle and they couldn't sleep, and would you come up straightaway and fix it. Never a word about them having woken you up in the middle of your sleep or anything like that. Funny how different people can be isn't it?

It was because of that sort of thing that the union eventually got us all together to say that we weren't going to put up with it. Well that was one of the things, but of course the main one was the hooliganism and the vandalism. You'd get youths would come into the towers and they'd kick the door in of your storeroom, they'd even smash the windows of your office – and they just did that sort of thing for the love of destruction. They weren't youths who lived in the tower you were in charge of, you'd never seen them before so you couldn't report them. Then there came the night when one of the caretakers in, well I've forgotten which tower it was exactly now, but anyway in one of them a caretaker was set on. These lads came in one night it was only about half past five but it was dark, it was December, and they started making a noise and I believe one of them was urinating up against the door of the lift. This caretaker came out of his flat and he set about them; or at least he tried to, he got hold of one of them and tried to pull him into his office and told him he was going to call the police. So this youth's mates all jumped on this chap and knocked him down and kicked him and beat him very severely: he was taken to hospital and he had broken ribs and a fractured skull and goodness knows what else. He was off work for months and months and he always walks with a limp from that day to this.

That was the finish of it. Nobody's going to do a job where that sort of thing can happen. We'd all been used to taking a lot of lip, and worse things than that: stuff pushed through your letter box. I don't want to say the word, but you'll know what I mean when I say it was the sort of thing that should have been in a toilet. And you got to the stage when you were in fear for your life. You would go out say in an evening to go round the big containers under the waste shutes at the bottom round the back to make sure they weren't blocked, or you'd go round to where the central-heating plant was – and you'd be scared to go back inside the building again because you never knew who would be waiting for you or what might happen to you. The wife used to say to me 'Please Bert don't go out of that front door tonight.' She got into a right state about it.

So as I say in the finish the resident caretakers was withdrawn and we all went to a central point just round the back of Robins Walk where we worked out from with radio-controlled mini-vans. And we never went out except in pairs. So up to when I retired five years ago, that's what Providence had come to – a very far cry from what it was when it first began.

– I was telling you last week wasn't I about the difference I've seen in the estate since I first came here, and how it's gone down. I've been thinking about what you asked me, and I just can't put my finger on it at all as to why it should have gone like it did: but the community sense has all gone, there's no question about that at all. I was talking to the wife Betty about it, and asking her if she could throw any light on it. Like me she said no she couldn't; but we both agreed that that was how it is now, the sense of belonging just isn't with us any more.

I think one of the things that might have something to do with it is that our children, Joan and Lillian, of course they've grown up now; and so that doesn't bring us into touch with people like it used to when they were young. Joan works at a bank, and Lillian's at a training college in north London, she lives in digs there. We've noticed it particularly these last three or four years since the girls have lived their lives off of the estate, as you might say. Betty and I have been thrown back on our own devices, and we don't have all that many friends around here either. When I retired the Council were very good, they let us have this big bungalow in what's supposed to be the best part of the estate; and we get it at a reduced rent. But we were happier when we were living over the other side, in Bolton. All our friends were round there, and we don't really know anyone in this part at all. It's quite a long walk to what you might call the heart of the estate: very quiet here, perhaps a bit too quiet, which doesn't encourage us to go out to the social club or things like that. We spend most of our time in the evenings now staying at home and watching TV. We're very happy with each other's company, Betty and me. We're more fortunate than a lot of people in that respect. You hear so much these days don't you of people's marriages breaking up, or people not being happy together? We've been very very fortunate in that respect, and that we've been spared too to see our children grow up and start to make their own lives for themselves. I'm contented in my heart, and how many people can say that these days?

Yes, I'd definitely say I was an estate person. This is my home, this estate. Like I told you, it's the only place where Betty and I have lived with a home of our own. It's the people who make it what it is; it's the people who live here who make me like it, and other people who live here who make me dislike it. Most of all I regret they've let so many coloureds in. I've nothing at all against coloured people in their place, but I think old Enoch is right and the time has come to start sending a lot of them back home, particularly the troublemakers.

The ones who give you the worst troubles are the young coloureds. They just don't seem to have any respect for other people, you see them in the street shouting and laughing and making a big noise. Well when I was a young man, I'd never have thought of behaving like that, rushing about and creating a disturbance. And if I had, I'd very soon have got a clip round the ear from my father – or from my mother come to that – and told not to be so noisy. But these coloureds, their parents don't seem to bother to try to discipline them or give them any control, they just let them run wild. I suppose that's because of how they were used to behaving themselves in their own countries.

This is what's the main reason for the estate going down so much, to my mind. It's nothing against the coloureds as such, and in their place; but I don't think their place is being mixed-in like they are with white people. Their customs are different, their whole way of life is different from ours, and if they won't go back to where they came from then I should think they should be made to live in separate places of their own where they can behave in the way they want to without being a nuisance to anyone else.

I think this government or the next government or the one after that is going to have a very serious problem on its hands if things go on as they are doing between the blacks and the whites. It's no good saying everyone ought to live together in peace and harmony, that's just pie in the sky. People of the same race and colour of skin don't all get on together, so what hope is there for people who are so different? It's only the government who can do something about it; we let them all in, and it was a mistake. I'm sure there are lots of people like me who are very fearful for the future. It used to be said didn't it that there was two classes of person – the rich and the poor? That's how it was when I was a boy anyway. And the rich had their place and the poor had their place, and nobody tried to mix them up together and force them to live together. My parents, our whole family, was what you would call working class; and we'd never have thought of trying to live with the rich. We just got on with our own way of life, and it was a good way of life in many ways, even if we hadn't any big sums of money and had to go without things.

I think you'll find going round on the estate talking to people that most people think the way I do. And I don't just mean the white people – I think you'll find the blacks are of the same mind. There was one the other night in the pub in Robins Walk. I don't go there often, but I got talking to this chap and he told me he came from West India, and he'd been here a long time; I think it was fifteen years he said, and he said he was never going to get used to the weather. He was a nice chap, polite and a well-spoken sort of person. So I asked him if he didn't like the weather, if he had ever thought of going back where he came from. He didn't take it the wrong way, he laughed and he said there was nothing he'd like to do more, only there just wasn't the work and he couldn't earn anything like the wage that he could earn here. Well, that man had got children growing up who were born here, he told me that; and he said as far as they were concerned, this country was their home and they'd known no other. I could see his point, but it just goes to prove what I'm saying – that it's been allowed to go on too long, and we should start taking steps now to do something about it.

I don't think a Conservative government will make any effort at all. After all they don't really care about working-class people do they? You don't find coloureds living in the posh areas of the country which is where most of the Conservatives live. So they're not bothered by them. It's us, the ordinary working-class folk who have had the blacks forced on us. I think the next Labour government will do something to help us, because they're for the working class.

Oh I've been Labour all my life. I could never vote anything else. I hate the Conservatives, I really do. They're all for themselves and nothing for the working man. Grab grab grab – that's all the Conservatives are. Yes I'm a Labour man I am. I'm a Labour man because I class myself as a labourer basically, whereas the Conservatives are those who've got something to conserve, which is their money and their property. But people like us don't have money or property.

When I say that I'm Labour, I don't mean by that that I'm a socialist. To me there's no difference between socialism and communism: the communists want to take everything that people have got, all they've worked for all their lives, and give it all to the State. Also they're not for freedom – in the communist countries nobody can do what they want, and they get sent to prison camp if they don't do as they're told. Well that's not the English way. Here everyone has his own allotted place, and that's his and no one can take it away from him.

I've always been content all my life to be what you might call a second-class citizen. By that I mean a working-class man – and we are the second class of citizens, there's no way round that. But I've enjoyed my life: you could say second-class citizen, first-class life; as far as I'm concerned there's no question about that.

'Some kind of feminist'

Sandra Barnaby

– I suppose I'm about five foot five inches high, I've got blue eyes, I've got brown hair, dark-brown hair, and I keep it cut fairly short. I'd say I was slightly thin, too thin really, a bit on the scraggy side. I'm wearing a white shirt-blouse with a high collar and long sleeves, and a plain navy-blue skirt. I've got wedge-heeled sandals on, no make-up, and I've got a gold wrist-watch which was a twenty-first present from my parents and a string of big chunky wooden beads which I got last year when I was on holiday in Greece with my boyfriend. I'm twenty-three. What else can I think of? Well, I'm sitting in the sitting room in my parents' bungalow in Jesmond Close, there's no one here except me and you, Mum and Dad have gone out for the evening to the social club, and my brother's out somewhere but I don't know where. I don't know that there's really a lot more that I can say about myself. I work in a solicitor's office up in the City, I have my own car which I'm buying on HP, it's a Mini Metro. And that's about all I can tell you really about what I'm like.

What am I like as a person? Well, that's very difficult to answer. I suppose my parents would describe me in one way, my boyfriend in another, and you'd probably get a totally different impression from any of them. For myself, I suppose I'd sum myself up as being some kind of feminist. At least that's what I'd like to think, and that's what I'd like other people to think. By that I mean that I'm really still at the stage of finding myself or trying to. Trying to find myself as a person, but with a fairly clear idea in my head of which direction I want to go, which is towards independence, independence as a person. I may get married, I may not: and I'd be quite willing to leave home and go and live with my boyfriend of the moment. But he's a rather conventional sort, though I don't say that in any way to criticize him. I think he's a bit scared of what his parents might say. I know my parents wouldn't like it, they're very orthodox working class. But I'm old enough to decide things like that for myself, and if they didn't like it – well, they'd just have to put up with it. I think they'd get over it and come round to seeing it my way in the end. My way? Well, my way of looking at it is that I don't feel I want to tie myself down to any man at this stage in my life. I know that a lot of working-class girls get married much younger than I am now. I think it's terrible, in some cases tragic, even. A few weeks ago I was down at the shops in Robins Walk and I bumped into a girl I'd been at school with. She's the same age as me, got married at sixteen – and she's got three kids already. To me her life's over. I think it's terrible, what's she going to do for the next fifty years? She's never had any kind of life of her own at all. I suppose you could say it was her own choice, but personally I don't think she's ever had any opportunity to really make any choice.

Anyhow, to get back to me. Let's think. I left grammar school at eighteen, I had nine 'O' levels and two 'A' levels in History and Economics. I was going to go to university but without any clear idea in my mind of what I wanted to do, so I thought I'd read History and take a bit of time to make up my mind. My first choice was Sussex and I didn't really want to go anywhere else, so when they turned me down I decided to work for a year and then try again. I got this job, the same one that I'm still in now, and I liked it and the money was good. So I'm afraid I've rather settled for that. I don't relish the idea of going to university and living on a grant. I've got too many of the good things in life at the moment – the car, the boyfriend, a salary big enough to have a place of my own if I wanted to. On the other hand I know I'm having quite an easy ride at the moment. I pay for my keep here at home, but it's nothing like enough really. I've tried more than once to make Mum and Dad take more, but they tell me to put it in the bank and save it. Sometimes I feel rather guilty about it and think I either ought to make them take more or move away, but it's easy to get mentally lazy and let things drift on.

It's a terrible thing to say, but I sometimes feel rather as though I'm caught between my family and my boyfriend. They know him and like him, they get on with him and he gets on with them. They take it for granted that we're going to get married, so this is what all the 'put it in the bank and save it' business is about. They're trying to push me into it I sometimes feel: for the best of intentions because it's the right thing for a girl to do. And I think he, my boyfriend, feels that if he just hangs on long enough I shall probably give in and agree to marriage. Does this make me sound rather a hard-faced calculating bitch? Perhaps I am if I was honest about it. This is one of the things women suffer from isn't it? If they don't comply with convention and try to lead their own independent lives, being 'calculating' is the thing they're usually accused of.

— Last week it was all the women's lib stuff, wasn't it? I think we were talking on a raw night — raw for me that is, I wasn't feeling too well and I always get very resentful once a month when women's lot descends. To me it's a perpetual reminder, being made aware that in some kind of way we're inferior, 'not well'. I suppose it's something we're conditioned into. Men don't have to put up with it, and like a lot of women I get very grumpy about it.

Anyway, that was last week. This week I'm back in my usual state of enjoying being a woman. This week you can tell that, because tonight I'm wearing a rather colourful flower-print dress and high heels, I've got a dozen of these jangly metal bracelets on my wrist and I feel altogether different from the rather austere person I presented to you last time. Brian — that's my boyfriend — he says he finds these mood changes difficult to keep up with. But I think he likes them really, especially when I doll myself up a bit and put on perfume and play the game of being a bit more like what a woman should be like. Men are funny, at least the ones I know are. By that I mean well take the ones at work for instance, without boasting I can say that I do have a good and responsible job, and that I am quite good at it. But most of the men — the young clerks who are articled but not just them, the older ones as well — they want me to do two things. One is to be good at my job, and the other is not to make it too obvious that I am. Otherwise it worries them. Perhaps they think that a woman should be frail and always teetering on the edge of failing: so I must admit I play the game and try and give them that impression.

We were talking weren't we last week about girls on the estate and I was telling you about the one of my own age I met who'd already got three children. She's not by any means unusual — I'm the one who's unusual. A woman the other day, a friend of my mother's was round here one evening and was sitting in the kitchen there having a cup of coffee when I came in from work. She had the nerve to ask me whether I wasn't worried that if I didn't get married soon I'd be left on the shelf. She actually used that phrase. I was a bit narked with her so I asked her how old she'd been when she got married, and she looked entirely satisfied with herself and the rightness of her answer when she folded her hands in her lap like this and sat up straight and said 'nineteen'. I could have said something very nasty:

I was tempted to, but then I thought there's no reason to, after all she was a friend of Mum's and that's the way her generation thinks. It's a bit frightening though to think that there are still people in my generation who think that way too, and they're not by any means a minority.

In fact I suppose I'm the one who's outnumbered. But even being in a minority of one wouldn't greatly worry me. I'm not particularly concerned to persuade other people to my way of thinking, certainly I'm not militant about feminism. I feel that I don't really belong with a lot of the other young women of my own age on the estate – and it's not just because of this, but also of course because I went to grammar school. There's again this working-class tradition that girls don't on the whole go in for education, their purpose in life is to get married and produce children.

There was quite a bit of radical thinking going on among the older girls at my school when I was there. We used to bat these ideas about women's role to and fro, largely under the influence of one particular teacher. I still feel a certain amount of regret that I didn't keep up my interest when I left school. I suppose that's something which would more likely have happened if I'd gone to university.

I feel very isolated altogether at present. I can't talk very much with my parents about these ideas. My mother is a traditionalist, my father is a Conservative with a capital 'C', and my brother doesn't think about anything much except his motorbike. Mind you I'm not the one to be criticizing them: I don't read anything like as much as I should do, I tend to go out and have a good time at parties at weekends, dancing and drinking a bit and chat.

Where do I think I'll be ten years from now? Well hell, I don't have any idea at all – except that I'm fairly sure I won't be here on this estate. At least I hope to God I'm not here on this estate. Because if I am the only way that could happen would be that I'd caved in and got married and had a couple of kids. Why don't you come round in ten years time and see?

Where would I like to be? Well as I've told you, I've really no idea which direction I'm going in at all. I don't even think I'd like to be living in London by the time I'd reached that age. Maybe I could live in the country somewhere and do the self-sufficiency bit, though I think I'm rather too fond of my own comfort to rough it for very long. This isn't any great ambition or dream, it's just something that comes into my mind now and again: I start to feel fed up with the way my life's going, or perhaps I should say isn't going, and start to wonder what I could change it into instead. I don't actually think I've got the courage to do anything very drastic on my own, I think I'd need somebody's help. Not necessarily a bloke's, though I suppose that's almost unavoidable.

This is what education does to you, you see. You've got a nice working-class girl who's going to settle down and be a nice working-class mother and have a few nice working-class children and have a nice working-class husband. He's going to slog his guts out in the docks or the market until he's had enough, and then they're going to retire to a caravan at Herne Bay. They could go on fifty years or more like that, without ever once questioning what life was about. They'd vote Labour because that's what you do if you're working class, and it would never occur to them that life held anything different for them and their children. In fact if you were to ask them, they'd tell you they had everything they wanted and life had been good to them.

So as I say where does education get you, particularly if you're a girl? It gets you dissatisfaction with your lot. It gets you thinking, and you certainly can't enjoy the sort of life I've been describing if you're going to think. And most of all what education gets you is confused. I'm not saying that I regret having had the education which I did. I regret not having had more in fact, but that was entirely my own fault.

I suppose I'll get it all sorted out eventually. Maybe I'm a bit young yet, or maybe something will happen that will point me in the right direction. Maybe, who knows, I shall go on doing a bit more thinking about it after talking like I have been doing to you. We'll have to see won't we?

'Hoping for a home Christmas'

Tony Allen

His home was the first bungalow on the right in Jesmond Close but he didn't want to talk there. We met on street corners, chatted sometimes in the car, sometimes in empty houses or unoccupied and unfurnished flats, and once at the home of one of his friends. He had a series of alternative meeting places, but they were always cold and lonely and deserted. Between times there was no communication and no telephoning to confirm arrangements: we would fix a time and place for the next meeting a few days or sometimes a week ahead, and I would be wherever it was and waiting. Always within a minute or two without fail he would appear coming along the street with his head down and his hands in his pockets. Always he was reliable and always he was punctual.

A tall and very powerfully built young man, with a punk-style haircut: deep-brown eyes, bitten-down fingernails, a rasping voice and a nervous agitated manner.

– Talking's good, I like to talk. It gets me down sometimes, I don't talk to anyone for days on end. How long I'll be able to go on seeing you I don't know because I'm on bail, I don't know when the case is coming up. Not for a good time yet if I'm lucky. I'm hoping for a home Christmas, but you never know your luck.

I'm seventeen, I live in one of them lovely four-bedroomed bungalows as you know. I've lived there all my life, we were the first tenants. There's Mum and Dad, my sister Annie, my brother Duggie, and Penny who's married and another sister Jean. I'm the youngest, Duggie's the eldest he's twenty-five, Annie's nineteen, Jean's twenty-three. Those who are living there now are me and Annie and Duggie and Mum and Dad. Our bungalow is one of the nicest on the estate.

Look it's going to be too complicated if I don't come out with this right away to start with. The others are all the same family more or less but I'm not, I'm adopted. I think I was about six weeks old when I was brought into the family. My Mum was married and had three children, then her husband died, then she married Dad as I call him, and they had Annie, and then they adopted me. I've always known about it ever since I could understand, from about the age of four I should think. They never made any secret of it, they did all the right things and told me all about myself, they always have done. When I was twelve or thirteen I asked could I see it and they showed me my birth certificate: it had just my what do they call it my natural mother's name on it and no father. They told me like it says in the books, how my mother loved me but couldn't keep me, and they chose me for themselves and all that shit. I've never tried to find my real mother, she didn't want to know me so as far as I'm concerned I don't want to know about her.

My parents – I call them my parents because that's what they've always been – they've been very good to me, and it's not their fault I turned out like I did. God knows they tried their best. And I'm not just saying that as like a phrase: I mean God knows, I used to pray to him and I know Mum and Dad did. We're a Catholic family, they brought me up a Catholic – I think that was something my real mother had asked for. But not God nor the priest has ever been able to make any impression on me. I was a funny kid, I've always been a bit funny. When I was nine they gave up, my Mum got a beyond-control order for me and I was taken into care, into a remand home for a year. It was because I used to do funny things, smash up furniture, light fires in the middle of the room with newspapers and all stuff like that; so I was sent somewhere where they tried to deal with cases like me. My Mum was heading for a nervous breakdown. My Dad explained to me she couldn't cope and said I was going away so that they could have a bit of a change and I could too. He wasn't cross about it: funny, now I think about it I remember there was tears in his eyes when he was telling me. He said I could come back from the remand home at weekends, and I could come back and live at home again as soon as the people there said it would be all right. He didn't want to send me away; I never felt anything of that sort, and I could see his point of view.

I don't know why I was like I was. Something in the blood perhaps, the bad seed and all that business. I think I was more reckless than downright bad. I wasn't unhappy at home, I just did those fucking stupid things.

I was in the remand home for a bit but I was let home at weekends. They tried to find somewhere that would take me, eventually they put me to a school for maladjusted children during the day. My own feeling is that that made me worse. I was in with a lot of other maladjusted boys – whatever maladjusted means. I was a big lad then like I'm a big lad now, I was the top boy – I used to smash anyone in the face if they even looked at me. I was quite violent when I got sent to the remand home; and when I came back I was very very violent.

The school did give me some schooling, they learned me how to read and write, tried to teach me good manners and all that stuff. If I'd stayed there I think I'd be a different class of person now, but I was only there about six months. There was a young helper, I suppose she'd be about twenty-three and very pretty. She ticked me off about something, probably something I well deserved, and I got her in a corner and lammed into her and kicked her black and blue. So they sent me home because they said the place wasn't suitable for me, and after a few months I was put to another home for almost two years.

I was in trouble again there too for attacking someone, so it was back home again. By that time I'd be about fourteen, so Mum and Dad said they weren't going to send me away any more and I could just go to an ordinary local school. I did that, but I got into a lot of trouble, I was always getting the cane and I was dangerous. I do have to say that a lot of the staff was frightened of me because I was big and would punch anybody. At the death I was expelled for I think it was stealing, or it might have been breaking the place up or both. I was sent to a place like a sort of prison, what they call an allocation centre while they decided what to do with me. It was obvious wasn't it? There was only one thing it could be, which was borstal.

I was just old enough, but my Mum came and pleaded with them and they let her take me home. It makes me sweat to think about it, how hard my Mum and Dad tried.

– I've got nine convictions for burglary, the earliest one was when I was twelve. I've always worked on my own; mostly houses but as I got older I started doing shops as well because there's more goods in them. Quite right, yes: because I've got nine convictions it doesn't mean that I've only committed nine offences; there's quite a few – quite a good few actually – that I've never been caught for. And never since I began have I ever offered any t.i.c.'s. Up to last year I never got sent away, all they give me was discharges, probation orders, compensation orders, and CSOs. No I tell a lie. I did do a three-month DC. That was OK, I was at what's supposed to be the tough one at Send. To tell you the truth I quite liked it, I enjoy doing PT, I think it does you good physically the regime, toughens you up a bit.

Last year was the first borstal I got and I came out on licence three months ago. So I'm sure to get sent back this time, there's no way the judge can do anything else is there? He's bound to give me a recall, and probably another whack on top.

What would make any difference to me? Well I don't think anything would: probation hasn't worked, fines don't stop me, I think I'll have to be a Young Prisoner or another borstal. If it's the same judge as last time he said I was a menace and I should go for borstal training because otherwise I was heading straight for a life of crime. I don't think I was a menace, well not in my book I'm not, but I suppose the public might think so. There's one thing I do realize, which is if I'm going to continue I've got to be a bit more clever than I've been up to now. By that I mean cleverer enough to keep just that bit ahead of the Old Bill, because I am getting nicked a lot of times. They recognize my pattern, and they're straight round our house and pick me up; in fact one time last year they was there waiting for me in a car outside when I was coming home.

I shan't mind going back to borstal. It was quite good there, I was baroning tobacco, selling food, selling phone calls out. I was able to do that because I knew how to get around the place and what days and times there'd be no one in the administration offices. I got myself a set of keys I should think within two days of getting there, and I'll do the same again. If you're a hard man in borstal you have quite a good time, you can get what you want. I've even had birds while I was in borstal, but I don't want to say too much about that because if I say how it's done and someone was to read it, it might spoil it not just for me but for others who do the same.

Once you get the flavour for crime, money in your pocket and not having to go to work except when you want to, being able to get anything you want whenever you want it and all that, it's very difficult to give it up. It's a good life, much more exciting than working in a factory or an office or something like that. I mean I suppose I must be lacking in something: I read somewhere that in the old days they used to call it being a 'moral defective' and I'd say that is me. If I was to put it in one word I would say I'm a villain, my job's villainy like yours is writing books.

There's plenty on the estate who are not quite villains; but I know ten doors I could take you to now and knock on them and they'd buy stolen gear from me. I don't know any what you might call rock-hard villains on the estate, though I might start a fashion and end up one myself. Well perhaps to define it you'd say it was someone who regularly carried a shooter. I don't, at least not here on the estate though I don't usually go up the West End without one.

When I was a bit younger, say eleven and twelve, I was one of the biggest vandals on the estate. I had a little team and we used to go around creating havoc. They sometimes say it's because the kids have got nothing to do. All I can say to that is that people who talk about youth clubs, well we kids all went to the youth club at the back of Robins Walk and then at ten o'clock when they turned us out, that was when we went roaming around looking for damage to do. It's a kids' thing and you grow out of it. I don't think you're ever going to stop it, not unless you catch kids at it and give them a thump round the ear.

One of the best things we used to do was ride on the roofs of the lifts. There's a way of opening the first-floor doors and dropping down: there's a control box on the top of the lift and you can switch it any way you want. We used to wait for someone to get in at the bottom and let them press the button for whatever floor they wanted, and then whizz them right up to the top of the tower block and leave them up there. They never knew what the hell was happening because they didn't know three or four of us was on the roof. Stupid, but we used to think it was dead funny. Like most things it goes in fashions, and you don't hear of kids doing that much these days. Vandals aren't like what they used to be in my day. We had the kicking cars fashion, the paint spraying, the gang fighting, and the setting the rubbish shutes alight. Nowadays it's all mostly just tame stuff, breaking glass windows, kicking a few doors in and things like that.

To me the youth clubs are a complete waste of time. Christ, you've only got to look round the estate to see how much fucking effect youth clubs are having on vandalism. It's when they shut down and send everybody home – that's the time that you want to occupy kids. Most of the damage gets done between ten and twelve o'clock at night; at least that was the time when I was a vandal. So what are you going to do? What they do here is to have the police prowl-cars going round the estate, but that's just a laugh. They can't get over the grass and near the entrance to the blocks, they can only stay on the road miles away.

– You're conditioned into your way of thinking just like I am into mine. They've both got a lot in common really. You would write

271

about somebody like me, I would rob somebody like you; and those are our professions.

I don't think you can put it all down to the parents and say they haven't brought you up right. It's the same as would you say you was a writer because that was how your parents had brought you up? You hear someone in a pub shooting his mouth off about young people and he says he blames the parents. There was a geezer the other night up west, he was talking like that. I wanted to tell him in my case my parents was the last people it had got anything to do with. They tried according to their lights, and it's wrong of people like him to blame them. And it's not the environment, it's not the estate. There's lots of other young people on the estate who're my age and have been brought up like me but they don't behave like I do. And it wasn't the influence of other kids I mixed with: I was the one who influenced them towards bad ways. I mean at the age of twelve I was looking in the window of that jewellery shop in Tullbrook Road and trying to puzzle out how to do it.

I always tell the social workers at borstal about how unhappy I am knowing I'm adopted, about how horrible it is to live on this estate, it's so soulless and impersonal and all stuff like that. A load of shit. They write it all down because it's what they want to hear. As far as I'm concerned I'm saying it just to keep them off my back because I don't want to be involved with them. But it is, it's total shit: if there'd been parties in the streets every night when I was a kid I wouldn't have had anything to do with them anyway, I'd have been clocking who was there to see whose homes would be empty and nip round and do them while they were out.

Nobody's ever been able to exert any influence on me, not even older villains. Makes you laugh. One tried in a club one night to talk me out of getting to be like he was. I only like straight girls, but one wouldn't make any difference to me. As a matter of fact I like older women, I mean up to thirty or somewhere around there, that's my sort. I had a Probation Officer once, I suppose she was twenty-six or twenty-eight and I used to go and see her two or three times a week because I really fancied her. I think she twigged it, because she used to talk to me a lot about feelings and not being afraid to say what your feelings were. She'd have been a bit surprised I think if I'd come straight out with what my feelings were about her, but all I was interested in was you know what. But I got fed up of her, she was always trying to persuade me to change my ways, telling me how much she liked me and how she didn't want to see me ending up in prison for the rest of my life. I was interested in the first part of what she was saying but not the second. Anyway it never got nowhere.

There was one last Saturday, she was a straight girl, about twenty-five and we've had quite a relationship these last few weeks. She's another who wanted me to change my ways and we had a big row about it on the Friday. On the Saturday I was supposed to meet her at the club but she didn't show, one of her mates came down and said she'd taken an overdose because she was so unhappy. That's a shame: but who wants a girl like that, she didn't kill herself, it was only a gesture. I can't take things like that, it was fatal to the relationship, she was trying to twist my arm wasn't she? I mean poor kid, big shame and all that; but so long.

You see people think how terrible it is, I'm going to be in and out of prison for the rest of my life. But what they don't understand is I'm not thinking of that. I know I'm going to go away now and again, but it isn't going to kill me. I'm not all that keen on being in borstal or prison, but I can do it; just so long as I've got the time when I come out to look forward to. That's all I think about when I'm in, about what I'm going to do and how I can do it better.

I think the only man who understands properly how I think is Arthur – that's PC Davidson. He doesn't give me any of the sentimental shit, he just comes for me and says 'All right Tony you're nicked.' He takes me down to the station and tells me what they've got and what they're going to do me for, and it's always very very fair. He never tries to fit you up doesn't Arthur. Which is more than you could say for some of the other bastards down there. I don't mind it when it's like that, it's only when they try to swing things on you that you haven't done that I get to feeling a bit stroppy about it. Arthur's a good man: shame he turned out like he did and joined the Old Bill, because he would have made a good villain, he understands how villains think. He's the best of the Law that there is round here.

I enjoy this talking lark, I don't know if it's any good to you but you might be able to make something out of it. It won't help you understand me though. Jesus, I don't understand me, so what hope is there for anyone else. See you, and next time maybe I'll have thought up something with a bit more sense to it to tell you.

There wasn't a next time. He was arrested again two days later, remanded in custody, and sent back to borstal. He didn't get a home Christmas.

Part Seven

OUTSIDERS (2)

'Just passing through'

Mr Cross

He was a small slim thin-faced man in his sixties with his sparse silvery hair neatly parted. He usually wore a single-breasted overcoat; and he usually passed quickly by in a corridor or on a stairway with a nod and a near-silent greeting. I must have seen him six times over a period of three months before he really began to impinge: he always had the air about him of someone who was busily engaged in business matters, looking like an insurance agent perhaps going on his rounds.

One day finally we were standing together in one of the lift lobbies on the sixteenth floor of a tower block. He gave me his usual polite nod, then there was silence for a while. The lift didn't come and his repeated pressing of the call button had no effect. It seemed we were going to be in for quite a wait; and then he suddenly turned and inquired 'How are you getting on, how's it coming along?'

Well, quite well I said; it didn't strike me his question implicitly conveyed a good deal more knowledge of me than I had of him. But he must have been aware of it himself, because when after a few more minutes I started to say something he suddenly said 'Oh hang it, I'm going to get on my way' and made off in the direction of the stairs and disappeared.

The next time we met was in one of the pedestrian walkways between the ground-floor levels of two blocks of flats. My turn to ask how he was. Oh yes thank you very well: but busy and he must be getting along. A week later early one evening, seeing a light round the edges of a doorway at the far end of a fifth-floor landing, and knowing it only led to the subsidiary boiler room of the central-heating system, I tapped on it and pushed it open. Sitting facing me in a large battered

*old upholstered armchair Mr Cross had a paper cup full of coffee in
one hand and a hamburger in a bread roll in the other.*

– Silly of me to leave the door ajar, I'm usually much more careful.
But of course now you're here, do please come in. Only be so kind
as to close the door for me if you would, because I don't like being
disturbed once I'm settled for the evening. If you find it too warm in
here please remove your coat and put it on those packing cases over
there where mine is.

All I know about you is that you are writing some sort of book
about the estate, and I've heard that you are tape-recording interviews with people who live in different parts of it. I believe in fact
that you call on some of the people whom I know and who know me,
and it's through their telling me about it that I know.

You're absolutely correct that I am the person known as Mr Cross.
How much do you know of me? Little. Well I'm relieved to hear
that, though actually there's very little of me to know about. I think
most people would tell you that when they came to think about it
they knew very little about me. I am not in the habit of revealing a
great deal about myself. Not that I have any particular reason to hide
anything. I'm not doing anything very wrong – it's just that I find on
the whole that the less other people know of your business the better.

What is my business? A very good question my friend. I will be
perfectly frank and say I am in the business of existing: that's all, no
more than that. I think therefore I am: *cogito ergo sum* or words to
that effect. And I would add to them on my own account: I am,
therefore I must exist and so I'm doing my best to do so. I think if
you were to rummage among those old newspapers and magazines in
the corner there by the box where you put your coat you would find
a half bottle of quite good brandy which I obtained this morning from
the supermarket; and I would regard it as a friendly gesture if you
were to join me in what is usually referred to as a nip. That's it. I
think you'll find the top is loose, I've already opened it earlier, and
don't bother about wiping the neck of the bottle, I'm not at all
particular about matters of that kind.

Well sir, I don't know that there's anything of particular import
that I could say to you but I would be willing from time to time to
meet with you and attempt to answer some questions if you wish. For
the next two weeks or so you would usually find me here in this room
at this time. It's past the time when the caretakers might come round,
so I may well stay here for a little while. I have three other cubby
holes of this kind in different locations round the estate; if it should

occur that this one is no longer usable then I will let you know where you can find me thereafter. Tomorrow night would suit me ideally for the first of our talks: I have no engagements tomorrow and was wondering what I was going to do in the evening, so if you come that will help to pass the time agreeably.

– I regard myself as as much an inhabitant of Providence Estate as any other person who lives here. It has been my home for almost ten years now, and the fact that I don't occupy a residence – or for that matter pay any rent to anyone – doesn't seem to me of great importance. My needs are simple, my belongings are very few: I am perfectly happy here, I know a large number of people and have many acquaintances of all types and ages, and though I say it myself I do have the great virtue of being a very good listener. My purpose is to visit people, to pass the time of day with them, to talk with them, and most importantly to listen to them when they wish to talk to me. There is a vast number of people on the estate who live on their own or spend most of the day alone who are only too glad to have someone to talk to. One of the important things, one of the very important things, is that I don't attempt in any way to interfere with people's lives. I do not for instance dispense advice, although I am very frequently asked to do so. But that is not my purpose, I am not in the business of telling other people what to do. As I believe I said to you last night, I am in the business of existing. And this I most satisfactorily do. People are most kind – in return for my sympathetic ear they will and do keep me regularly fed.

It may surprise you to know that there are no less than six ladies who give me breakfast. This is a convenient number, it means I need only call on each of them once a week and don't therefore seem to any of them to be taking advantage of their hospitality; and on the seventh day I rest, that is I lie in in the morning. None of these dear ladies ever asks me why it is that I go to her for my breakfast: I think several of them are under the impression that I am some kind of night worker and that I either live on my own or my wife is unable on that particular morning to get breakfast for me. That is the impression I like them to have, though I would like to make it clear that I have not gone out of my way to fabricate a story for them about it. Nor, I would like you to appreciate, do I ever either beg or accept money from people. Food yes, occasionally an item of clothing; but always on the implicit understanding that it is no longer required by the donor. I may say here that it never fails to surprise me how ladies seem able to lay their hands with unfailing regularity on a supply of male garments. Where they get them from I don't know, nor do I inquire; but it may be that they are merely pruning their husbands' wardrobe.

At this point too I think I should make very clear that my relationship with every lady is entirely a platonic one. I can lay my hand on my heart and say with complete truth that I have never had a liaison of any kind with a lady who I have met under the circumstances I have been telling you about. What is more, I am not on Christian-name terms with a single person: they call me Mr Cross and I call them Mrs or Miss as the case may be. I think they would not admit me to their homes unless they were absolutely sure of the innocence of my intentions.

As for a midday meal, the problem lies not so much in getting one as in avoiding one. Without exaggeration I could have at least three main meals a day in the middle of each day. People are extraordinarily generous. Evening meals are a little more difficult, but I usually find that I have had more than sufficient food to last me for the day by teatime. Some ladies are extremely generous late in the afternoon with cream cakes and things of that nature, but if I do require anything additional I usually buy something of a takeaway nature.

Where I get my money is where anyone else in my position gets money – from the National Assistance Board. I don't have the facilities for drawing a state pension because I haven't got a book, and the reason I haven't got a book is that I haven't for very many years paid for any insurance stamps. However the local Assistance are on the whole fairly friendly and helpful. Only one of them has ever reported to me that he could not find the address I had given him. The others seem to be willing to accept my word that such and such is where I live. I think this may be because I am well spoken and modestly but cleanly dressed, and they think that I fall into the category of 'respectable'.

I think this is a very satisfactory way of life. It is a pleasant and undemanding one, it brings me into contact with people and I am never bored. How many people can say that?

– I came to London some twenty years ago. I was a schoolteacher in Yorkshire, and I then had a nervous breakdown and had to go into hospital for quite a considerable period of time. I am married and I have children, but I regret to say that while I was in hospital my wife – and this is the kindest thing I can say – must have come to the opinion that I was never going to be mentally well again. I had, and I will say this without hesitation, given her and the children a hard time. Be that as it may, she took herself and the two children who were then quite young to live with someone else. She stopped coming to see me, indeed she told me she did not wish to see me again and nor did the children. I was in no position to contest that, being as I was then a long-term patient with no immediate prospect of release. I was suffering from – or at least so I was told I was suffering from – schizophrenia. I was very violent, and so perhaps my wife's feelings can be understood.

Then as I understand happens not infrequently with illnesses of that sort, I made a complete recovery. The hospital were not able by then, which was almost two years later, they were not able to trace my family. My own feelings too had undergone a change: I felt very bitter about my wife and very resentful. I was of the opinion that if she wanted no more to do with me then I wanted no more to do with her. I have to say that in the time that has passed since then my feelings have not greatly changed. It has never for instance been an ambition of mine to return to Yorkshire or try to find my children.

When I came to London I took a very menial clerical job with a shipping company, and lived in a series of furnished rooms. My existence was very meagre in every way: there was no light and shade, there was no what might be referred to perhaps as spiritual nourishment, there was no interest or enthusiasm. I became very shut in, very depressed, and on more than one occasion life was really not worth living at all. Anyone who has been for any length of time in an institution will understand the difficulties that one has on release in trying to come to terms with other people and make some kind of relationship with them. An institutional staff pay attention to you, they will ask you every day of your life how you are, they will feed you and look after you. It is very different when you come into the outside world, especially in London where nobody seems to have the slightest interest in you at all.

As I say life had become very meaningless to me. Quite by chance one day I found myself in this part of the world – I think I was recovering from flu or something of that kind and had not yet returned to work. I took a bus ride and got off down in Tullbrook Road there because the area was one I was not familiar with. It was a nice summer's day, the estate looked rather pleasant from the top deck of the bus, and more or less on a whim I decided to get off and walk round it for a while. I was standing I remember on one of the green grass spaces near one of the blocks of flats, when much to my surprise a lady came towards me and said that she lived in a ground-floor flat and had been watching me from the kitchen window, and I looked lonely and unhappy – and would I care to come into her flat for a cup of tea that she had just made. I was flabbergasted at the time; she was a very pleasant young woman and very friendly. So I accepted her invitation and while we were having tea she told me that she and her husband had only recently come to live here, it was their first home; they were very pleased and excited about it, they had two young children who she had found places for in a playgroup or something of that kind, and the whole of life was opening up for her. I have a suspicion that she herself had been a patient in a mental hospital, and that is how she had spotted me because I had the same kind of air about me that many of the people she had been among had had. She did not refer to the subject though, and neither did I.

I went on my way rejoicing: I thought her gesture had been most kind, and when I went back to my very dingy furnished room near Waterloo my mind was full of a feeling that this was where I would like to live. I approached the GLC housing department and asked them what the possibilities would be, but they said they were realistically nearly nil. The following week it occurred to me that if I were to wait, I would in all probability never come to live here. So I sold what very few possessions I had and moved and that's how I came here. I had every intention at first of finding a job and getting my name down on whatever the appropriate housing list was.

I have never seen that young woman again since that day. But what I have seen and experienced is many people like her: I now have a whole network of people like her, whose doors I can tap on or whose doorbells I can ring and say something like, 'Just passing through, I thought I'd call and see how you were.' And I know for certain that an invitation to enter will be immediately forthcoming; if the time is appropriate refreshments and nourishments will be offered, and then after a short stay of perhaps no more than half an hour I will make my excuses and say that I have to be getting on, and leave. In this way I am sure I am always welcome when I next return. I never you see overstay my welcome, I am always scrupulous about expressing my thanks, I take an interest in people and what they are saying to me, I have a very retentive memory and so can pick up a conversation that I have had a week or even a fortnight before at the point where it was left off. So I am never rebuffed. I do occasionally go errands for more elderly people, I offer to go shopping for them, to go to the library and get some books for them, or anything else that they wish. One lady asks my advice on when it is time to have her curtains cleaned, and on subjects of that kind I will give advice. Then I take the curtains to the cleaners for her, and in due course collect and return them.

I hope to continue to lead my very quiet life in this very quiet fashion for quite a long time to come.

'Who wants to know you?'

Phyllis Dawson

– The thing that's most difficult here is the people – they're stand-offish, they don't want to know you at all. I've lived here seven years now and I don't know a soul. The children have one or two friends at school, but not the sort they seem to want to bring home. They were born here in London, but I wasn't, I was born and brought up in Carlisle and I didn't come south till I was thirty. You always find that with southerners don't you? They're a very unfriendly lot all round, at least I've always found them to be. I wish I was back up north.

A school cleaner part-time, three days a week. By half past five in the afternoon she'd have finished her work. She'd sit in a chair at one of the formica-topped tables in the empty dining room, the lid of a polish tin as an ashtray in front of her; a scrap of pale-blue muslin tied round her head to keep her hair in place, an overall which the school provided, thick coarse stockings and heavy shoes. A big woman who smoked one cigarette after another and spoke in a low monotone about the desert her life was.

– I take four or five valium a day; the doctor says not to have more than three, but I find three isn't enough. I'm a divorced woman with an eleven-year-old boy and a nine-year-old girl. Well I may as well say it that I'm not officially divorced: my husband's living with another woman over the other side of the estate, he says he wants a divorce and I suppose one day I shall have to agree to it. I haven't so far because he's treated me very bad and I don't see why I ought to make things easy for him. She's only a girl, half my age; twenty I think though I've never seen her, but somebody told me that's all she was. He just upped one day and left, so I don't see that I've got any responsibility to him. He's supposed to give me money each week for the children, we're supposed to meet in the pub for it on Friday nights at six o'clock. Two weeks out of three he isn't there and I'm just left sitting. If he doesn't arrive in ten minutes I leave, I'm not going to hang around in some pub waiting for him. Then of course the next week he'll be all full of apologies and explanations why he didn't come.

There's often times when I'm glad not to see him. I feel so down and drab-looking like I do, and I know he'll just take one look at me and be glad he's got somebody more attractive to go back to. I wouldn't say that I love him now, I don't think you can when somebody does that to you. But we had been married twenty years almost, and it's hard when someone does that to you. You read about these women who kill their husbands, sometimes I feel I could do that to him. I talk to the doctor but he's not much help, he says I'll get over it and just to go on and keep taking the pills. He said to me last week that I mustn't look as if my life was over. I don't know what he thinks it is then. He said a good-looking woman like me would one day find a man who'd value the things I had to offer. I don't know what he thinks I've got to offer anyone. My life's a wreck, I'm a wreck, I've got depression very bad and two kids I'm always rowing with; I've got no money, and I live in a dirty old place at the back of Gorrivale Square that's due to be pulled down, but not for two years yet the council says. I don't know a person, and no one wants to know me. I mean you've got to be honest about it, if you're like me who wants to know you?

– The only ray of hope I've got to cling to is a doctor's letter for a transfer. He gave it me six months ago, and I sent it to the housing straight away. I've not heard a word about it since, but each day I'm looking for the post. If I could get away and into a decent place that would make all the difference. I used to be very house-proud, you could come in my house and there wouldn't be a speck of dirt anywhere, you could eat your dinner off the floor. The children was spick and span, I had some nice dresses and things and I used to have my hair done once a fortnight. But then when your husband does something to you like he's done, it takes all the stuffing out of you. You've worked all your life to bring your children up decent, you've done his washing and cooked his meals and you've tried to be a good wife to him in bed because that's what men want really isn't it? Even if you don't feel like it yourself, that's part of your duty as a wife. And then he turns round and says there's someone else he likes better. Well I think anyone would feel very bitter at something like that.

I come here three days a week to do this job because the doctor said I should try and get out a bit. I came to see the Head, and I think he knew what position I was in because I know someone else had tried just a few weeks ago for a dinner lady and got told there wasn't any vacancies. It earns me a bit of money, but they deduct it from the social. Still, it's better to be working.

Anything that gets me out of the flat is good. It's a terrible place. It's Vernon, that's one of those big long blocks over the other side of the road there. I told you when you asked me the first time that I lived round the back of Gorrivale Square. Well that's where I used to live but we were moved into Vernon three years ago. Only it's such a terrible hole I don't really like telling people that I live there, and I was scared when I first met you that you might want to come and see me. I wouldn't want anyone to see where I live. Those places are just like being in prison, that's exactly what it's like: you've got a long long corridor down the middle inside, and all these front doors that all look the same. There are forty doors in the corridor where I live and every one looks exactly like all the others. Some days I go home and I'm not sure which number is mine. It might be the pills but I've forgotten what my own front door number is, and I have to stand there and try and think. You can't tell any difference between one and another by looking at them.

Inside there are three levels. They're built like that you see, like an open pair of scissors. This would be mine with my front door down here. Then it goes up to like the middle here which is the level where the kitchen and sitting room are, and then up at the top here are the bedrooms and the fire-escape door. Then my next-door neighbour, hers goes up this way, like across mine.

I wouldn't want you to see it because it's not very well kept, not like I used to keep my home; and I've sold a lot of the furniture and carpets and things to get money for food because my husband doesn't give me enough. It's not the sort of place I'd ever ask anyone to. To me it's a place to get out of and get away from whenever I can. When I'm there the only way I can stand it if I'm on my own is to put the record-player on as loud as it will go. I've only got one record, it's the Supremes, and I play it over and over again. If I don't do that, I find I'm just sitting in a chair and smoking cigarettes all the time, or on the really bad days what I do is lie on the bed and smoke.

I get very frightened to go out to the shops or things like that.

There are kids, really big boys some of them and black. They ride bicycles up and down the corridor, and if you're a white person they come at you to try and make you jump out of the way, and then at the last minute they'll lean over so they just miss you. And the girls are as bad. They write things all along the corridor walls, up and down the staircases, everywhere. Really filthy things they write, I wouldn't repeat the words, I don't know where they learn them from. And they do their business against the walls or in the lifts – sometimes if the light in the lift is broken you step in it. Well that's not the sort of place you'd want to ask anyone to is it? That's why the doctor's given me the letter for the housing, he agrees that living there is making my nerves much worse.

– There's nothing about living on the estate that I like at all. I think it all ought to be knocked down, all of it, and people moved wherever they like. It's a real bad place to my mind. None of the people are nice, there's far too many coloureds, and nobody has any thought for anybody but themselves. There's nothing for the children, the schools are very poor and the teachers don't give them proper attention or make them work. There's nothing good to be said about any of it.

The feeling I've got in myself is one of hopelessness. Just going on from day to day, and having to put up with things because I can't see any way out. I've thought sometimes of putting an end to it, but then I start to think about what would happen to the children, where would they go, who would look after them, and I suppose it's thinking like that which stops me. I don't have any relatives of my own down here, but I wouldn't want to go back up north. It's my home up there but it would be nothing for the children. They're southerners like my husband is, they belong down here. He has relatives, some of them on the estate. They would like to have the kids I know, but I wouldn't give them the opportunity.

Sometimes I think if I had a bit of a holiday that might do me some good, but I wouldn't know where to go. The last time I went off this estate was when I took the children two or three years ago on the coach up to my parents. But we don't get on me and my parents, so we only stopped two days and then I brought the kids back again.

It's all a big mess my life is. I said the doors in the corridor outside my flat made me think of a prison like you see on the films; my life feels like serving a prison sentence. Only people in prison know when they're going to come out and I don't. I feel as though I'm serving a life sentence.

The main thing is that I don't have any friends, and that's because the people around here are all so unfriendly. There was one day a few weeks ago and I'd finished my work and I was taking the cleaning box back to the storeroom. It suddenly came over me and when I got there I sat down in a chair and I had a bit of a weep. After a few minutes another of the cleaning women came in, she put her box in its place on the shelf and then she just said good afternoon to me and went out. She looked as if she was frightened to see somebody crying, and she didn't ask me what was the matter or could she help or anything of that sort, just ran out as fast as she could. I don't care who they were, I don't think I could do that to a person if I saw they was so unhappy that they were sitting crying. But that's the sort of thing you get in the south, nobody wants to know about anybody but themselves.

– I wouldn't want to be thought of as an estate person, not in any way at all. I don't think of myself as someone who belongs here or has their home here. I live here but I'd never say to anyone my home is here, my home isn't here, not what I think of as home anyway. If your book's going to be about people who live on the estate I wouldn't belong in it because I don't live on the estate, I want nothing to do with any part of it. Where people live is in their heads, and where I live is somewhere up north: anywhere up north, but definitely not on this estate which is the most horrible place on God's earth to me and I consider myself to be outside of it completely.

'The amazing maze of class'

Ray Mills

– I'm twenty-nine, I'm a social worker, and I work for the local authority as a member of the Area Team which is responsible for among other places Providence Estate. I've been working here for two years; and before I came here I was doing my CQSW training for two years. Before that I wasn't in social work at all, or not professionally. I come from Cardiff, and when I was there I was a schoolteacher. I'm married to a schoolteacher, and we have a part-share of a rather large old-fashioned house just outside the area with three other couples. So I'm not a very experienced social worker so far, but I think I shall stay in this sort of work because I enjoy it.

It's hard to say what exactly it is about it that appeals to me, that makes me feel that it's a job worth doing. Like anyone else I've had my ups and downs, periods of doubt when I feel I'd do better at something else. But on the whole I usually feel it's worthwhile work and rewarding work. One of the aspects of it that makes me feel like that is that you can get a sense of actually doing something which helps people to do things themselves. My main job in the team is with elderly people, but we all do everything and try not to get too compartmentalized. I've been quite active in helping the setting up of tenants' associations in several areas, and that's something I like too.

I'm a middle-class person working with working-class people, and I don't think there is any point in spending a lot of time thinking about class. It's very much an obsession with English people: there are rules and regulations, expected standards of behaviour both good and bad, and the whole thing is really given far more importance than it deserves. Where I was born and brought up in Cardiff, I don't think it occurred to people to think what they were in a class sense: they were Welsh and that was what mattered – and in many places and cases the bosses were all English. My father worked in a steel works; I was one of six children, my mother spent her whole life looking after us and bringing us up, and we had a very warm family atmosphere. I would say for myself at least a very happy childhood. The unity among us was in our nationality and I don't think it occurred to any of us to compare ourselves with others in our area when it came to social standing. We didn't have a very high material-content background, but then we didn't know many people who did. I'm not suggesting that class is purely a matter of possessions, but what I'm trying to say is that we regarded ourselves as everyone else's equal, no better and no worse than them. We were all of about the same educational level, cultural level, and it didn't cause any great interest that there were others who lived in say the wealthier parts of Cardiff who were definitely higher up the social scale than we were.

It was only when I came to England to university when I was nineteen that I first became aware of the amazing maze of class in English society. I didn't really like what I saw as far as the middle and so-called upper classes were concerned, and knew that if I was going to stay here I would want to work among – again so-called – working-class people. Their values and their way of life was much closer to my own experience, and it seemed to me that they had a more realistic and certainly more pleasant attitude than other people. Though I realized too the deprivation of the working class: it seemed to show up in much sharper contrast than it ever had when I had lived with it all round me as a child.

I don't mean only material deprivation. Working-class people are not exactly kept away, but more kept separate from very many things that the middle class take for granted. I have in mind such things as further education, legal services, concepts such as taste and design and so on. Although I'm not suggesting that they are the essence of good taste necessarily, I'd choose Habitat as an example: the sort of basic good design which they have is really not very apparent anywhere in a working-class area such as this. If you look in the furniture stores along Tullbrook Road you'll see a basic poverty of design, a basic cheapness in the way things are made and upholstered that would be quite unacceptable in a middle-class area. If you were interested in good food or good wine, to give another example, you wouldn't think of going to look for it on Providence Estate. What you could be sure of finding there would be vast quantities of packaged convenience foods and cheap wine – but it wouldn't be cheap

French wine, it would be cheap and nasty British or South African wine. I think if you discussed it with a shopkeeper he would tell you there is no demand for anything better. And well of course there isn't, there couldn't be and there never will be so long as anything is considered good enough for a working-class area. It's this attitude of lack of concern towards the people who inhabit such areas that you see very clearly expressed in the sort of goods which manufacturers provide for them. They don't make the faintest effort to try and give them the best, only the cheapest and most easily produced.

Another difference concerns rights and privileges. The middle class has rights, the working class has privileges – basically I mean, in their own way of looking at themselves as much as in any other. It is the middle class which dispenses charity and the working class which gratefully receives it. And they are grateful, they regard it as a kindness done to them rather than an affront to their dignity. An obvious example is in social security benefits. They know they are expected to hold out their hands and take what's given to them with due deference. There are some are too proud to accept. But it never occurs, or it never seems to occur, to any of them that the under-privileged have as much right to a share of the nation's money as anyone else – after all most of it was earned by their labour, although it wasn't their pockets it went into. As a social worker I find myself in this contradictory situation about basics all the time. Should I get people to accept the unacceptable, to adjust to unfair situations in regard to lack of housing, lack of facilities of all kinds? Or should I really to some extent be trying to increase their awareness of the inequalities in the system and hope they will become more politically active?

On the other hand, although I think a certain amount of prompting is justified I try to draw the line short of manipulation. I don't think committees or associations should be fronts for my or any other social worker's own personal theories. I think it's quite justified to try and get people to alter their attitudes in the hope that they will then do something to alter their personal situation. But realistically, especially with older people, it's important to remember that here and now is what matters, rather than improvements in some vague future which they may well not be around to see.

There's the danger too that a lot of social workers fall into of stirring up or at least starting up political awareness in an area and then moving on. It results often in despondency at failure from the residents who have started to become active, and it's counterpro-ductive in the long run because it becomes that more difficult to enthuse them to try anything again. One of the tenants' associations

– not on Providence but on another estate – withheld a proportion of their rents until certain repair work had been carried out in one street which had a particularly bad surface. Their children were always falling off their bikes, old people were slipping and hurting themselves when they were walking home at night and so on. The social worker who had helped them form the association actually made the suggestion himself that they should take the action they did about rents. In very quick time, the local authority had the road resurfaced and he was able to claim it as a success for his methods. Only a few months after that he moved on to somewhere else, and before long the residents were complaining that the council was victimizing them by being inordinately slow in attending to repairs to plumbing or heating in their homes. Rightly or wrongly they felt that the council was having its revenge and they were in a state of great confusion. They had no one to turn to for assistance or advice, and a woman on the residents' committee said to me 'That's the last time we shall ever do anything as stupid as he got us to do, that time when we didn't pay our rents. Now look what happens to us.' In all probability it wasn't quite such a simple cause and effect, but that was how it seemed and naturally it will be quite a long time before those residents really trust a social worker again.

– I think last week I spent most of the time giving you the dubious benefit of my political theories. I told my wife about it when I went home in the evening. She said you would have got the impression that I was somebody who sat here in the office all day and talked about himself and his own ideas. If you did, then I've no one to blame but myself.

I still regard myself as a beginner in social work and I think – or at least I hope – this period of working here will rub off some of the raw edges. One thing I did forget to mention to you when I was talking about the English obsession with class, one part of which concerned itself with how people speak, what sort of an accent they have and all the rest of it, is that I'm fortunate in having a Welsh accent. It's something I've carefully preserved just because it is a no-class accent, and I do regard this as a great help; people identify me as Welsh rather than middle or working class.

My working week is spent with old people, and I visit on a regular basis. I have somewhere around two hundred clients on Providence Estate alone, and I try to see them all at least once a month. Not just for chat and a few pleasantries I should make it clear, but to ask them what their needs are and to see they get what services we can offer if they want them. This would include meals on wheels, chiropody, a visiting library service, and visits from the Social Security people to check with them that they are getting all their financial entitlements. We – the social services that is – have a good relationship with the Social Security, we don't get into battles over money. The Social Security area manager is a very good and concerned person. He's made it clear to all his staff they are to go out of their way to ensure elderly people get all they should have, and not wait to be asked for information on the subject but give it without delay.

We've also instituted a Voluntary Visitors scheme, utilizing the mobile elderly. This means that senior citizens who can get around are roped in to do something useful, which is to call once or twice a week on two or three people near them who are housebound or nearly so. The scheme has now got something like four hundred voluntary workers, and seems to be proving very beneficial both to those who do it and those who receive it. I think it's far better for someone who has a grudge or complaint or even just a moan to be able to tell another elderly person about it, rather than have some younger person from here go and listen and nod sympathetically and perhaps promise to have it seen to and then do nothing. We encourage our volunteers to come here, or to telephone us, and to complain and to keep on complaining at us on behalf of the person they're acting for.

We get at cross purposes sometimes in the team, particularly with the youth workers. Quite naturally they favour their clients and we favour ours. There was an instance a few months ago when we nearly came to blows: there was a meeting here in this building attended by about forty people, and a right riot is nearly was. We – myself and my co-worker Jean – had had a lot of complaints from elderly people living on Providence in the ground-floor flats at Preston and Lancaster; there were complaints about kids playing football on the small patch of grass inbetween, and kicking footballs into their very tiny gardens or as happened on one occasion through somebody's bedroom window. So without really sitting down and thinking out the situation, we had a notice made and erected on that particular piece of grass saying 'No Ball Games'. The youth workers were incensed at what they considered to be a high-handed action on our part and removed the notice. One of our elderly volunteers immediately informed us that it had been taken away 'by the kids' as he thought. So we put up another one and asked the local police to keep an eye on it, as well as two of the senior citizens who could see it from their window and who had telephones. The net result of that was that when two youth workers who were under the impression the notice had been put up by the council arrived and started to pull up the pole the notice was on and take it away again, a police car was there in two minutes and they were arrested and told they were going to be charged with criminal damage. The police I think were under the impression too that the notice was council property.

It took dozens of phone calls and memos to get it all sorted out. The police were very displeased and threatened us with prosecution for erecting the notice on GLC land in the first place, the youth workers were more convinced than ever that we were a toffee-nosed lot who threw our weight around, and there was general confusion and bad feeling.

It was eventually resolved as it should have been in the first place by calling all the interested parties together, including some of the boys who played football there. And with everyone sitting down round a table to solve the problem, it proved very simple. It was the boys themselves who suggested they should rearrange the lie of their football pitch so there was no danger of the ball going anywhere near the old people's windows.

That sort of thing is a very clear example of social workers taking things into their own hands and not consulting properly with the people concerned, in this case the people concerned being just as much the boys as the old people. Of course it's only possible in an area where there is a fairly strongly developed sense of community among the people who live there. I've been made very aware since I came of how strong that sense is: maybe Providence is particularly fortunate, but it does seem to me to be a place where on the whole people have a great sense of belonging.

'Trying not to be mistaken for God'

Dr Gray

A tall elderly angular man with a thin bony face, long thinning hair and a lock of it occasionally falling forward over his glasses. Pipe-smoking, soft-voiced, paternal, much revered. His surgery was what had once been a shop on the edge of the estate, and its waiting room was always packed full during surgery hours.

– I've been here since the estate was built twenty years ago. In fact I was here a little before that – my uncle used to have a practice in Gorrivale Square and I joined him there when his partner left. I've liked being here and I've never had the slightest wish to go anywhere else. And by now of course I wouldn't and couldn't: I have a deep feeling that I've an obligation to stay here because it would be letting too many people down if I went away to practise somewhere else. Perhaps that's rather an arrogant-sounding thing to say, but I don't mean it though in the sense of suggesting they couldn't do without me. It'd be much more honest to say that I suppose now I can't do without them.

Most practices on housing estates have doctors who are first or second-generation immigrants, and I should think when I go it will be the same here. Patients are very strange about the subject of colour: they will accept a coloured doctor or a coloured nurse and give them the same respect and affection they would to anyone else. In that situation they are literally colour-blind, but it's the only situation I know of of which that can be said. And having said a minute ago that I don't want to go anywhere else, I now have to say also that I don't by any means like all my work all of the time. Too much of it is rather conveyor-belt stuff, giving people sick notes and pills and not really practising medicine at all. I'm not sure how the situation could ever be changed. I was discussing it with my female partner the other day and we both agreed without any argument that in many respects we neither of us found our work entirely fulfilling and rewarding. Yet as I said I do have this strange feeling as well that I couldn't and wouldn't ever move away.

I'm not particularly ambitious either in my profession or financially. If I had been, I certainly wouldn't have stayed on here because although I have a full list of patients I have no others, I'm not in the private sector at all. And equally as I've been saying the medicine aspect is not entirely satisfying: these days it's very much a matter of referring people on if they've got any really serious condition to a hospital where they will be seen and treated by a consultant. I suppose I'm rather mentally lazy in that I don't do anything like moving about it. The time to do so would have been ten or even more, fifteen years ago. I don't think I shall do anything about it now.

I live down in Kent in a little country village, and I find that the hardest time is Sunday evening: I often feel I just can't face coming back into town on Monday morning. Monday is a heavy day – I'm usually here by about eight o'clock and I have three surgeries as well as making calls, and never get home much before ten. I see anything up to thirty people at each surgery, so it does make it a very heavy day. On our list my partner and I have almost the entire population of the estate; there are very few people whom we don't see at some time or another in here or in their homes. Sometimes my ears seem to have lost all power to absorb any more words by the end of a day. I nod and look sympathetic to what people are saying, and I feel bad about it afterwards because I have no longer the necessary physical stamina to take a day like a Monday and be as sharp, and indeed as caring, as I should be by the time it's getting on towards the end of it.

One of the interesting things about being a GP is that you never know what the next person coming in through the door is going to bring. This makes the work varied and interesting, but to be quite honest if I get a succession of say five or six patients who have nothing very much the matter with them I do tend to find my attention flagging. Sometimes you feel that you might just as well be writing out a shopping list – the conventional drugs, bandages, medical aids and so on. This isn't practising medicine in any true sense at all. And sometimes people come in about the most incredibly trivial things: it's very common for mothers to bring their children after they've had a fall and grazed their knee, and they want reassurance that infection isn't going to set in or concussion hasn't been inflicted. I find it hard not to get irritated at trivialities of that kind, and have to keep reminding myself that the mothers are genuinely afraid and have come for reassurance. But I think when I first began in practice, patients were not so ready to do that: they had more faith in themselves and, if you like, more common sense. Of course like any other doctor though I get equally aggrieved with the patient or parent who doesn't come to see me as quickly as they should have done, and I say 'Why have you left this so long before coming?' When I get the reply, the standard reply which is 'I didn't want to bother you doctor' I then get very cross and say things like 'That's what I'm here for.' Doctors are as unreasonable as anyone else, aren't they?

I am a Christian, and I hope without sounding pompous about it that that is what motivates me. I'm definitely not a socialist: I think the welfare state was a very bad idea. Since it began people have been brought up to be dependent and to take things for granted, and to consider they have rights in certain areas which never crossed their minds before. Quite a lot of pressure is brought to bear on me by patients who want certificates of one kind or another, and they have very fixed ideas about when they have the right to have them. Certificates that they are unfit for work, or that they are fit to go back to work; or for their children not to play games at school, or for their children's fitness to take part in amateur boxing; and for what they consider to be good reasons for having a telephone put in their house or flat; or they have bronchitis and their house is damp and they should be moved. On top of all those you get the genuine cases of people who have depression which if it's not actually caused by the bad housing conditions in which they live, certainly isn't helped by them and they should be rehoused. So naturally then I give them a housing certificate. But I don't tell them that the GLC must by now have a stack of my certificates that high, which are worth nothing at all and really scarcely make any difference whatsoever to anyone's chance of being moved and rehoused.

I get rather cross at times with the GLC. I know, and there's no question about this, so many people say it that it must be true and I see no reason to doubt it, that they go to the Housing Department and tell them that they have noisy or unpleasant neighbours and they want to be transferred to some other place. The GLC then tells them that for their complaint to be taken seriously they must have a medical certificate to back up what they're saying about the conditions they're living in being harmful to their state of mental health. So back they come to me and tell me what the Housing Department have said; and if I think that the situation is truly doing them no good and they would be better off if they could move, I can do no other – I give them a certificate. They take that back to the GLC, firmly under the impression that it is going to make a difference to their application. It isn't and it doesn't. The Housing Department puts it in the person's file, but it gets them no substantial increase in priority at all because there are so many thousands of them. It seems to me the GLC are misleading people by suggesting a medical certificate will get them an advantage, and I resent the fact that perhaps because they are unable to do anything the GLC does nothing. The whole operation is a total waste of time, it merely raises the person's hopes for a while. It's a practice which I personally think should be put a stop to because it is, and I use the word deliberately, cruel.

I think the GLC are not very good landlords in any way. The only reason they ever give tenants notice is for non-payment of rent. So long as you pay you can behave in any way you like, and it doesn't matter how much you annoy – or in many cases distress – your neighbours, the GLC are never going to give you notice for it. They're only concerned with prompt payment of money, and nothing else. It would be difficult for them to pass judgement I know on people who are inconsiderate neighbours, but I do feel it shouldn't be beyond their wit to make at least some attempt. I'm not saying they should punish badly behaved people, or at least that's not the first thing I'm saying – but they should protect other people who only want to live in peace and quiet.

The theory which the GLC has, which I'm sure you will have heard about, the theory of 'rub off' which is that if you mix up problem families and ordinary families in some way the problem families will be improved by being in proximity with the others – this is rubbish and dangerous rubbish. I have patients who are justifiably almost hysterical under the stress of living among problem-family neighbours, and the GLC extends no consideration to them at all.

– We were talking last week about the shortcomings – or at least the shortcomings to my mind – of the Housing Department. Well I think another of their failings is not having devoted sufficient thought to the problems which are created by mixing white and coloured people together. I know there's a danger of forming ghettos, but I do think we have a very long way to go yet before integration between blacks and whites can be taken for granted as something which will sort itself out in time. Most coloured people who are given houses or flats on Providence are in a pretty parlous state: I'm not saying they are by definition problem families, but they would not have got rehoused unless they had been living in very bad conditions. Perhaps they were seriously overcrowded or in insanitary conditions or something of that kind; but many of them don't find those conditions as onerous as the majority of white people do, because they have tended to take them for granted. As a result when they get a flat or a maisonette here, they tend to move in their friends or relatives who are in poorer housing conditions and create overcrowding which leads in turn to nuisance to their neighbours, not least because noisiness seems to be part and parcel of their everyday life. However much one wishes it wasn't so, this does nothing for black-white relationships. It causes great resentment. Resentment at the coloured people's way of life, resentment that they apparently were given housing before other people who'd been on the waiting list for years. It is construed as preferential treatment and it causes very bad feeling. It creates the kind of simmering atmosphere that people like Enoch Powell can take easy advantage of, and do. I think the whole policy of housing black or coloured people who are immediately identifiable because of their skins, along with white people who do not want them, needs much more careful handling.

Another point to which sufficient attention has not so far been paid is that black and coloured people regard themselves as a community with similar aims and interests to one another, and rightly or wrongly they very largely keep themselves to themselves. They would say I'm sure that this is because white people are unfriendly; but this is not a one-sided thing, many black people are extremely unwilling to admit whites to their culture and way of life. They group themselves self-protectingly. I can't say that I've any ready-made solution to the problem, but I'm constantly reminded of it. At least once a day some patient or other will say to me in a half whisper when I am enquiring why they are in a condition of extreme jumpiness or anxiety 'It's the blacks doctor.' So what do I do? I say 'There there' and put them on tranquillizers. I can hardly start preaching to them about the evils of colour prejudice, I don't see my work as part of that of the Race Relations Board.

I don't want to give the impression of course that a great deal of what one might call mental ill-health is caused by the subject that I've been talking about. Aggravated maybe, but caused is not something I would readily accept. Nevertheless it doesn't help anybody's anxiety state if they regard themselves as living in alien surroundings where their immediate neighbours are hostile and threatening. They may well not be, but the fact of the matter is that that's how they see it.

For that and many other reasons I do prescribe tranquillizers a lot. I don't think they're of any value and certainly they make no impression on the behaviour of other people: in other words they don't stop the neighbours being inconsiderate, or prevent husbands for example from being cruel. All they do is make the situation bearable or at least less painful. I would say that something approaching fifty per cent of all my patients are either having, or have at some time had, tranquillizers. They don't as I've said do a great deal of good; but I can't see either that they necessarily do a great deal of harm. It's not up to me to carry the banner in the lead of protest movements for better social conditions. I'm afraid I regard myself more as the ambulance following up in the rear and picking up the casualties and giving them what first-aid I can.

I'd agree this is a low-level estimate of my position, my abilities and my capabilities. Patients everywhere all over the world invest their doctors with magical powers, at least as much because they want to believe they possess them as doctors want them to believe that they do. In this kind of situation, which is particularly prevalent in this kind of area, it is almost a full-time occupation trying not to be mistaken for God. I don't know that I am very successful at it myself; and I don't know that it would necessarily be welcomed by my patients if I were. At least as much as any drug I could give them, their faith in my ability to perform miracles is a therapeutic and healing thing. They believe I can make them better: and I wonder when if ever I have the right to shatter that belief if it's all they have to cling to?

'Fuzzer'

PC Arthur Davidson

– You've talked to Jack Farmer, yes. He's a nice young lad and I expect you'd do better with him than you will with me, because he's had a decent education and can put things into words better. Me, I left school when I was fourteen.

I did a series of jobs, none of them lasted for more than a few months because none of them really interested me or had much in the way of prospects: shop assistant, tea boy in a small factory, storekeeper, that sort of thing. It's hard for me to remember all the different things I did do, there were so many I lost count. I went on like that for about six or seven years all told. Then for want of anything better that I could think of really, I applied to join the police: at least it was secure. And that's where I've been ever since. Always a constable, I've never wanted to take promotion. I've been in for twenty-five years now, and I'm happy in the job and I don't want to go any higher up the ladder.

I was born in this area though I don't live here now, and when I joined many of my family looked on the police with a good deal of suspicion. They were not nice, the police I mean, and my family were not great upholders of the law. My mother particularly wasn't a bit keen, not because she herself was on the wrong side of the law but she knew more than one person who was and regarded them as her friends. Anyway it didn't cause the trouble over the years that I sometimes thought it might have done. There really is quite a working relationship you might say between the lawbreakers in the working class and the police. We've got much more in common with one another than either side has with the middle class. We've both got jobs to do and we do them; theirs is to thieve, mine is catch them, and it's as simple as that. Many a time we drink in the same pubs, many a time the barman will put one on the counter for me and give a nod towards someone further along who's paid for it – it might be someone who's just come out, and I was the person who nicked him and got him sent down. What he's saying without putting it into words is that there's no hard feelings about it on his side. The other way round, I've bought plenty of drinks in my time for villains: they'll accept them and at the same time they know that it doesn't mean a thing. I'm merely buying a drink for an acquaintance, but I'll nick him without a second's hesitation when I've got something on him and he knows it.

Kids shout after me on the street. These things seem to go in fashions, but the popular word just at the moment is apparently – don't ask me why – 'fuzzer'. These, or a lot of them, are kids that I know often by name. What they shout is no more than a slightly derisory greeting. It doesn't offend me, I just give them a nod and a smile, and I can't see that this in any way lessens their respect for the police. I've sometimes had a young PC with me who's been very surprised and said that he thinks it's undignified to let it pass. So I just have to agree that's the difference between the old ways and the new. If you were to nick everyone who ever shouted at you, especially kids, you'd very soon have your police station full to the brim.

He was a slight wirily built man, whose appearance hardly matched in any way the conventional figure of a policeman. When he wore his helmet it always looked far too big, and when he walked along the street his steps were short and quick, never at any time seeming stately or plodding. Sometimes he rode an old bicycle, but most frequently he walked; and most of his time appeared to be spent in chatting amiably in shops or with people on the street. He appeared to be on exceptionally good terms with almost everyone. He came to see me whenever he was invited to, in a small ground-floor room of an empty house which I was able to arrange to use temporarily as a meeting place with him and others. It had no more in it than a table, two wooden chairs, a bare electric light-bulb dangling from the ceiling and a power-point where a kettle could be boiled. After a while Arthur got into the habit of bringing a packet of biscuits with him for us to share. I never found him to be hesitant or reticent about discussing any subject whatsoever: he didn't regard himself as someone who should be careful about what he said for fear of being misquoted, and he never asked me for any assurances that I wasn't going to embarrass him. He talked easily and naturally, as one ordinary person to another: he never pretended the

*police were above criticism and he never tried to put himself in a
position where he himself was above it. He helped me greatly also by
introducing me over a period of time to several people who lived on
the estate and whom he thought I might be interested to talk to – not
all of them by any means were people who had reason to admire the
police.*

– I think when you're off-duty you've got to disassociate yourself
from the police way of thinking, which is conservative and very
suspicious of change. The older ones always moan about how things
have deteriorated since their day, despite the fact that they're far far
better paid and the whole job is a good deal more interesting and
there're far better back-up services. In their time a copper was very
much on his own. He might have been able now and again to dispense
rough-and-ready justice in the sense that to quote the old cliché he
could give a naughty kid a clip round the ear. But you've got to set
against that the fact that nowadays if you find yourself in trouble you
can immediately call up assistance on your radio and it will be with
you very quickly, so you hardly ever have to face dangerous situations
on your own.

I'm what is called the 'Home Beat Officer' for the estate. My
number two is Jack Farmer, but that's only a temporary arrangement
and in due time he'll move on to somewhere else and I might after
a while be given another youngster. But they're always temporary
whereas I'm a permanent fixture. I do community policing, to give it
its official title. This means it's my job to know as much as I can
about the estate and the people on it, and to encourage them to look
on me as their local bobby. I go into schools and give talks, and I'm
on some of the local residents' committees which try to deal with
vandalism, and the local community newspaper and that sort of thing.
I see it as very much a public relations exercise and I think it's a very
sound idea. People see me out of their windows or walking past their
shops, and they get the feeling I'm always around. I think that gives
them confidence, because they feel the local policeman is part and
parcel of the everyday scene and their everyday lives. Going into the
schools and getting to know the kids is a good thing too: they tend
to think that because they know who you are and they know your
name that the reverse is true and you know them. The truth of course
is that in the majority of cases you can't tell one from another, but
very often it does make a warning sound a good deal more impressive
if you're able to look the kid straight in the eye and say 'I know all
about you, you know.'

It works with adults too. If you're called by neighbours to for example a marriage dispute, it's a help if you can say to the man something where you can use his Christian name and the same to his wife. It often helps to take the heat out of a situation. These are the two principal areas of my work on Providence Estate – juvenile crime and family rows. There's hardly any real crime at all; on the whole people who live here are respectable and hard-working. There's a bit of thieving, a bit of dealing in stolen goods; but you'd get that anywhere, and to a lot of people it's not even worth giving the title of crime to.

I think I only know one what you might call real villain on the whole estate. There's also a young lad who looks as though he's definitely heading that way; but apart from those two I wouldn't say we've any great problem except the one I've already mentioned, which is kids. I've heard it argued that this is all part of growing up, it's natural for children to go through a delinquent phase to a greater or lesser degree. I think there might be something in that, certainly I do know a lot of kids who I've had trouble with over the years and then when they've grown up there's been no further bother at all. The two things kids do which cause the biggest problems are gang fights and shoplifting.

Gang fights are getting to be increasingly worrying in my opinion. They're usually between different schools, and you can have as many as sixty or seventy kids involved in brawling in the street. The new element which has come in in recent years is the coloured children: you'll have something approaching a mini race riot on your hands sometimes, because they tend to divide up along ethnic lines. What I try to do if the animosity is lasting any length of time is that I go to see the respective headmasters and put them in the picture about what their children are up to after school. I think it's their responsibility in the first place, and I must say that I've always had cooperation. You will get a headmaster who insists that it's never his own pupils who start the thing, but all the same he'll agree that that isn't really the point.

The other thing with kids as I say is shoplifting. Some of them are quite highly organized: you'll get a gang of ten or twelve who will go into one of the chain stores in Tullbrook Road and create havoc. Two or three distract the assistants' attention, another two or three do the actual lifting, and another two or three after that will carry the goods away under their clothing. Any spare members are on hand to get in the way if there's any sign of them being caught. You have to admire the planning that's gone into it very often. It's what you might call professional standard, and of course with the stores' policy of prosecuting everybody who gets caught without making any exceptions at all it can get to be very serious. Myself, I feel the kids do it mainly for the excitement of doing it, but this isn't in any way to excuse it.

If I'm going to be honest I honestly don't know what can be done about it. It's very often said that it all goes back to the parents, they're the ones who are to blame. This is all very well as far as it goes, but very often there's one if not two parents missing when you come to go into it. You go round to see a kid's parents because the kid is going to be done for shoplifting, and if you had any idea of approaching it along the lines that you were going to tell the parents off and get them to do something about it, it's often the case that the door's opened to you by some woman who's got three squawling kids clinging to her skirt, her husband's pissed off with some other woman – and there you are standing at her door looking very stern and telling her that her eldest has been nicked. You'd have to have a heart of stone to say to her 'And I blame you for it, why aren't you keeping the child under control?' You know that your arrival with the bad news is yet one more burden the poor woman's got to bear. If anything you feel like giving the kid a kick up the arse for doing it to her, not blaming her for something which is far too much for her to be expected to do anything about.

– I know some policemen are bent. We've got some who commit more crime in the way of stealing and handling drugs than anyone they've ever nicked. You know that it happens and I suppose if you're really certain that someone has stolen gear in his locker you should shop him. But it's a hell of a thing to do to one of your workmates, and I'm afraid that myself like most others I tend to turn a blind eye. It can't be excused and I suppose it can only be rationalized by asking yourself what other people would do in the same situation and being fairly sure that they'd do the same.

When it comes to the police use of violence, I must admit it does shock me when I go to a school to give a talk and when it comes to questions the first one I'm always asked in nearly every instance is 'Are the police allowed to beat you up when they take you into Tullbrook Road?' If it isn't asked, I've got so used to it now that I bring the subject up myself. I wouldn't for one minute try to deny that there isn't the occasional thumping that goes on now and again, but it's nothing like as common or persistent as is increasingly believed. As far as kids are concerned, I can only say that I've never found it necessary to hit a youngster who I've taken in for questioning in my life, and I don't believe that many of my colleagues have either.

You might get the odd fuzzer who'll take exception to a bit of lip, to being called – well let's face it, you do get called much worse things by kids than you do by adults; and no adult I know would risk in a police station calling a policeman who was questioning him 'a fucking cunt'. But a kid doesn't have the built-in preventive mechanism if you like, and will come out with things often out of sheer fear. As I say, I do know one or two of our blokes whose reaction to that would be to smack someone in the mouth. But the main thing to be remembered with kids is that however tough a lad wants to appear in front of his mates, when you get him in the station he'll often collapse into tears, confess everything he knows including a lot of things you hadn't even thought to ask him about, and give you a long list of the names of his mates as well. The only way he can explain this to them later is to say that the police either threatened him with physical violence, or actually used it on him. So he goes around afterwards telling the tale.

When it comes to grown-ups, of course yes you do get the occasional person who is violent and who gets violence in return. It might sometimes be overdone: I have to say that if you take one swing at a policeman, you're likely to get six put on you in return. And I do know one or two who knowing a man's reputation for violence will very often play on that and try and provoke him; and then once he starts of course that's it, he gets thumped and kicked. But in all my years in the force I've never been present at an incident where there has been violence used by the police without something triggering it off.

And when I'm on duty as I sometimes am at a football match and I have to dive into a crowd of youngsters who're fighting, if one of them punches me what's my overriding ambition? It's to collar him and give him one back. If you put this to kids at school, they don't think there's anything terribly wrong about that either.

– I wouldn't want to give the impression because of what we were talking about last time that all police work is concerned with what you might call the darker side of life. It most certainly isn't, and I think it could be said without contradiction that well over half, perhaps even as much as threequarters of my work, is not concerned with crime at all. The majority of people who come into our station, and there's a constant stream of them from morning till night, are coming not to complain or report a crime but simply to ask advice. Whatever people say to the contrary, in this part of the world we're looked upon almost as what you might term 'social doctors', people you turn to if you want help.

It may not be for anything very serious. In the last few weeks I've had people come up and ask me such things as where they could buy a decent suitcase, was there anywhere in the area where they could get a Father Christmas outfit for a children's party, and did I happen to know anybody who had a white rabbit for sale. I don't think this shows that large numbers of people in this area live in fear of the police. Maybe I shouldn't let on about this, but to be completely honest with you I myself never carry a truncheon. So to me this shows two things: one that it's possible to do policing without ever having to feel you need the back-up of a weapon of any kind, and secondly that by far the great majority of people are law-abiding and I don't need to be afraid that I'm going to be set upon. I can say with my hand on my heart that I enjoy being the local bobby, that ninety-five per cent of the people of Providence are nice friendly people, and that police work in a community of this sort is something which anyone can take a pride in. I think we've got good police here and good policing; but you can only have these things if you've got a good community, which we have.

'Houses for people'

Don Carter

– I am the district Housing Manager who is in charge of Providence Estate. There are eighteen districts and my particular one covers a somewhat larger area than just the estate. I came here six years ago; I was in the GLC Housing Department and was promoted to this job when it became vacant. I have no direct connection with it in that I am not a local resident and I would of course have taken the job of Housing Manager in any other district had that become vacant instead of this one.

I'm a qualified chartered surveyor and I have experience both in the commercial world and with local authorities. First I was involved in the building and management of properties and then I came to the GLC as a project manager working on the development of housing estates. My background is one of buildings knowledge rather than people knowledge.

I'm thirty-three and I have two young children, and my wife and I live in a dormitory town about twenty miles from London. There would be obvious advantages and obvious disadvantages to living actually on Providence. I think it's perhaps better not to live there, because I'm primarily a Housing Manager of the GLC and if I were to move to live to whatever estate I was manager of, I'd be on the move quite often.

My parents were shopkeepers; they had the corner shop in the locality where we lived and I went to the local primary school and then on to technical college. I took only one 'A' level and then started studying for the chartered surveyors' exams. I think what put that idea into my head was that before he took the shop my father had been a plasterer and connected with the building trade. It didn't meet with his enthusiastic approval that I should want to go into it, but he said if I was really determined then I should study and get into the professional side.

I am ambitious, I suppose I always have been; but as I progress I find I get more satisfied with what I am doing. In the fullness of time I would hope eventually to achieve some sort of position such as director of housing – but that's quite a long way ahead. There is a certain sense of vocation in the work as far as I am concerned. I do find it satisfying, even if I am not satisfying every single person who lives in the area for which I am responsible. As people's standards improve, so their aspirations increase and quite rightly. I don't think there is ever going to be any time when everybody is completely satisfied with my or any other housing manager's work.

I'm very much an administrator. I don't really meet tenants of the estate very often, though I do try to get myself involved as much as I can, or at least as much as is compatible with my overall job. I meet the various tenants' associations, and the people who run youth clubs and old people's clubs and so on, and I am – by the residents' request – on a committee which has recently been set up to try and do something about vandalism. I regard myself as being at the service of the community, but in no way a ruler of it. I visit the estate once or twice a month, not on any regular basis but purely when the necessity arises. I find it a very interesting place just to look at. It has a whole cross-section of various types of property – houses, bungalows, maisonettes, those massive linear blocks, the tall tower blocks and the modernized buildings, not to mention the still fairly substantial amount of sub-standard accommodation which there is there. Mind you that's not an official designation: there are certain basic standards which have to be met, and we wouldn't offer accommodation which didn't comply with them.

The people who are in the substandard accommodation are of course the squatters. They are there on a purely temporary basis, and they know that the properties they are occupying are going to be pulled down. We have a fairly clearly defined list of the order in which this demolition work will be carried out, and some of them can look forward to a tenure of a year or possibly more, whereas others will only be able to continue as they are for a period of a few weeks. We do license certain people to occupy properties of that kind on the understanding that it is of a purely temporary nature, and we try to help them to a degree. It seems ridiculous to have habitable property standing vacant, and anyway we couldn't maintain it – maintain the situation I mean – without people going in. But naturally it creates problems. We do actually have powers of eviction, but we don't like using them, and we certainly wouldn't countenance anyone thinking that because they'd taken it upon themselves to move into such a place we wouldn't move them out without offering them alternatives. Some people have had that idea, but it's quite incorrect.

To get squatters out of premises can take as much as three or four months to obtain the court order and all the rest of it. We hardly ever get into an actual confrontation on the street though. It's of no benefit to anybody when that happens, and if there is any way of getting people to move out which doesn't involve that, we're happy to take it. I don't want to sound sanctimonious about this, but our policy is in fact to go as far as we can before taking action. One point which is not always realized is that it's very often people from the estate coming to complain to us about the unhygienic conditions in which squatters live, and asserting that they themselves are frightened to use those streets, that often forces us to take action in the situation where we would have been somewhat more tolerant if it had been left to us.

– Yes I'll willingly answer any of the points you put to me that you say have frequently been made to you.

Right. Well this first one about the so-called 'rub-off' theory is one which crops up regularly. It suggests an all-seeing and all-wise GLC Housing Department which is aware not only which the problem families are but also which the 'good ones' are. I sometimes wish we did have as much information as people credit us with having, it would often help us to avoid making mistakes. But alas we don't. We get families who are in desperate need of accommodation, and we get them either from our own areas or from those of other authorities who nominate them to us. All we know is that they are qualifying for rehousing on the single criterion of need.

We don't rehouse them full stop. What we do is offer accommodation to them which is as suitable as we can find for their needs, and it's then entirely up to them whether they take it or not. We may well make a number of offers to a particular family; and the one which they choose to accept places them let's say for example between two families who are in every way entirely respectable. So what I'm really emphasizing is that the actual location of 'problem' families does have an element of their own choosing in it. It isn't the GLC which decided that if they put them between Mr and Mrs A. and Mr and Mrs B. they'd perhaps benefit from the proximity. I hope this demolishes the idea of any kind of deliberate placing policy by the GLC, but I'm sure it won't. Once an idea of that kind has gained currency, it's almost impossible to stop people repeating it.

309

The second point is a kind of spin-off from this, that we either follow a deliberate policy of mixing up coloured people and white people which is one charge very frequently made, or alternatively that we make ghetto areas by putting all the black people together. The honest fact of the matter is that it's only very recently that we've begun keeping any kind of record of whatever you like to call it, ethnic origin or simply the colour of people's skin. We've done this largely to try and protect ourselves against charges of this kind. You see again the fact is that such details were not in our possession: we really had – and still have as far as a very large proportion of the estate's inhabitants is concerned – no idea whatsoever whether Mr A. is white or Mr B. is black as the case may be. It's only as I say very recently that we have done a study of 1000 lettings in a particular part of Providence on an ethnic basis: and we did it for our own benefit, to see what the result of our random selection policy had been. We were as much surprised as anyone else when it came to analysing the figures in one particular road to learn that fifty per cent were white and fifty per cent were non-white; and again, as much or more surprised to discover that another road had an almost entirely white population while yet another had a population that was almost entirely non-white. I repeat, we first of all rehoused people; and it was only afterwards we did this study of their ethnic origin, not the other way round.

Your third most common point which you say you've had made to you is about the way conditions on the estate have deteriorated since the resident caretakers were removed and the system of mobile caretakers was introduced. Well there's no use pretending that the system can cope with vandalism because it only too obviously can't. On the other hand, I don't see it being quite as simple as that: it's not entirely due to the removal of the resident caretakers that vandalism has become so widespread.

We were getting a lot of resignations from resident caretakers because they couldn't cope with the problem of hostile gangs of youths who were making nuisances of themselves. It wasn't realistic to expect them to either: many of them were elderly men who'd become caretakers in the first place because they wanted a job which was quiet and peaceful and not too taxing. Quite justifiably they didn't see themselves as part of any law-enforcement system; and there were one or two ugly incidents where caretakers were not only abused and threatened but actually set upon and beaten. This made recruiting of replacements very difficult indeed. Naturally a new applicant would ask why there was a vacancy; and if we didn't tell him somebody else would – that the previous incumbent didn't like the work and didn't like being in a situation where he was under threat of physical violence or at least felt he was.

Nor were many of the caretakers fit or able enough to cope with violence which wasn't against them, but which was something like for instance kids smashing windows. Many of them didn't object to being called out at night if a tenant had a burst pipe, or if someone was stuck in a lift. But what they did object to, and I think quite understandably, was people coming knocking on their doors late at night and asking them to deal with boys who were riding their motorbikes round the garages or congregating in noisy groups.

We had perhaps not quite as many, but we certainly did have a fairly constant number of complaints, before the mobile caretaker scheme was introduced, about the resident caretakers. To give only one example, the staircases in the blocks and towers were cleaned by the tenants themselves who worked out a rota system. That was all very well when people were willing to take their turn when it came round; but it created tremendous bad feeling when certain people wouldn't do it. Since we introduced the mobile scheme, it's now the responsibility of the caretakers to clean the staircases, and if it doesn't get done the tenants can and do complain to the housing department.

Another advantage of the system is that we can cover staff sickness or people on leave. This again was something which under the old system couldn't properly be done: if the local man was on holiday, he was very often understandably not willing to have a temporary worker occupying his flat, and the work was frequently not properly done because it wasn't being supervised. This is something else which now doesn't often occur. We may be slightly understaffed at holiday times, but we can and do make efforts to provide a continuous service.

– I think the most serious error which your book could contain would be if it were to paint an exclusively black picture of conditions on Providence Estate. There are aspects of life there, and living there, which are nothing for the GLC to be proud of. On the other hand, I think that a truly balanced picture would be one which didn't present the bad side more than the good. There are many people living on Providence who, if they are not happy, then at least one can say that it's not entirely the fault of the GLC. There are many people there too who are living in much better conditions than they were in before they came and who are reasonably contented. They may well wish to move on eventually to somewhere better, whatever their own personal definition of that is. And that is normal and proper.

We're of course not able to create a paradise out of a desert, but

I hope you'll find or have already found at least some people to tell you that as far as they're concerned life on Providence is not all that bad. This isn't to say there aren't faults in the way the estate was designed and built. One obvious example we're very well aware of is the linear blocks such as Vernon, Foxman, and Cramner, the ones with the inner central corridor and the flat doors opening off it. The original intention was to provide warm and sheltered covered walkways to people's front doors. You could legitimately say that the architects should have foreseen the problems of an almost inevitable nature, when you come to think about it with the advantage of hindsight. I refer to the riding of bicycles and sometimes even motorbicycles along these corridors, and the fears which people have when they're using them late at night and so on and so on. All I can say is that I think it most unlikely we shall ever build to those designs again.

There are complaints too about the tower blocks and the social isolation which a lot of the inhabitants feel. I couldn't as quickly assure you there won't be any more of those; but what I can say is that we're well aware of the necessity of providing people with choices and not just saying it's got to be a tower or nothing. I think Providence is in fact because of its architectural mixture of so many different types of building a good example of this policy. We make from this office somewhere in the region of two hundred offers of accommodation to people per week, and in most cases we are able to offer a choice.

We also have something like six hundred or seven hundred names on the list of people who wish to be transferred off the estate; though it isn't always because they're unhappy, it might have something to do with their work or the fact they want to be nearer their family or things of that kind. We try to keep it as personal as we possibly can. I'm talking now about the offering of accommodation; we do make a practice of getting our Estate Managers to take an interest in applicants when the time comes to make an offer to them. Most of them are very conscientious and enjoy offering choices to people. I would like to have a large notice at the entrance to this department saying 'Houses For People', not only as an expression of hope but as a constant reminder to all my staff that that is fundamentally what housing and rehousing is about. It's not just a matter of buildings and space; it's much more to do with giving people the opportunity to change their circumstances, and that must include both ends of the spectrum. They must have the opportunity in coming to Providence of its being a step forward for them; and it's just as right that they should regard going on from Providence as a further step forward too. The difficulty of this is that there's to a certain extent a changing population, and a consequent loss of a sense of identity with the place and the sense of belonging to a community. But no one is expected to regard this as the end of the line for them if they don't want to. To many it's the place where they have their first decent housing accommodation, and I'd hope that quite a number if they do move on will look back and feel it was a time in which for the first time their standards of living were fairly high.

Part Eight

THE PREFABS

'Love it, this little place'

Barry and Barbara

He was over six feet tall, thin and with wavy brown hair falling down onto his shoulders; she was only a little more than five feet, round and plump and with bright brown eyes. He was twenty-four, she was seventeen.

We usually sat almost knee to knee in their ten-foot-square sitting room which was nearly filled by the brand-new large leatherette settee and two matching armchairs. Grey ex-army blankets on the floor served as carpets; there was a black-and-white television set on a rickety cane table, and against one wall a cocktail cabinet with ornamented frosted-glass doors contained a row of six lead-crystal goblets and nothing else.

– All right well Babs says she's a bit nervous so I'll be the one who makes the start then shall I? Another cup of coffee before we begin? No OK well when you feel like another shout and Babs'll get you one. So right then describe ourselves eh? That's a bit of a stinker for a start, anyhow here goes. I'm Barry, I'm a London lad and I'm an electrician or no well to be a bit more correct I'm someone who works for an electrician. I'm not qualified but I could be if I wasn't too lazy to study for the exams. So that's me. I don't know what to say about Babs, apart from the fact that she's just an ordinary housewife; up to a few weeks ago she did a bit of baby-minding but at the moment she's not even doing that. That's about all I can think of to say about you Babs. Bloody chronic isn't it, is there anything else you want me to say about you?

– No you're doing all right, you're doing much better than I could Barry.

– I'll let you have a turn at describing me later on eh then you can get your own back.

– You haven't said what I look like.

– She looks like a little roly-poly pudding don't you? Isn't that what I've always said?

– Yes, it is – I thought you might say something decent for a change. You haven't said you look like a telegraph pole.

– No you can say that when it comes your turn. Now I'm going to talk about us, us two, the two of us. We've lived here in this what the GLC calls a mobile home but I call a prefab, how long is it Babs just about a year now is it?

– Eleven months.

– Eleven months. And we got it 'cos you were going to have the baby didn't we?

– We was in two little furnished rooms in Streatham, and when I found I'd fallen for a baby I pestered and pestered the housing people till I got what I wanted. Two days a week I used to go up there and go in and see them and the other three days I used to phone. Sometimes they laughed and sometimes they got a bit stroppy, depending on which one of them it was. There was a young one there, she wasn't all that much older than me and she was a right cow she was. She used to say 'I don't know if you think you're the only one we've got on our books, it's not going to make a blind bit of difference whether you keep on like this or whether you don't. You'll get housing when we've got something to offer you when it's your turn.' Silly bitch. But there was another one about the same age as my mum, she was really nice. She used to say 'Sorry love we still haven't got nothing for you, only keep in touch with us every day you never know when something might come along.'

– Yes and I used to keep telling you not to make a nuisance of yourself didn't I? I said if you carried on every day like that they'd put us well down the list just to teach us a lesson. And I have to admit haven't I I was wrong? 'Cos we got this place in just about three or four months, didn't we?

– Yes. One day the nice woman said 'All we've got in so far love is one of them mobile homes.' I said 'I'll take it.' She said 'Well I think you'd perhaps better go along with your husband to have a look first.' I said 'Never mind all that, I'm telling you now we're going to have it.' And we did. I phoned you up at work didn't I, to tell you we've got a place?

– Yes you did. I knew better than to try and start arguing with you about it, I knew you'd made your mind up and once you do that there's no stopping you.

– Bloody Jesus, when I saw it I thought it was a palace this place. I mean the rooms we was living in, well the two of them would pretty near fit in here just in this one room. The windows was boarded up and everything; but that didn't make no difference as far as I was concerned. You see the way I looked at it is this: once you've got a council place you're set up for life. This is like the first rung of the ladder if you like, you can only go upwards, it's only going to be a matter of time. From here there's only better accommodation they can offer us. So long as we keep up with the rent, in the end that's what they'll have to do. Specially now we've got the second baby coming. Oh sorry I said I wasn't going to say that.

– Babs, it was only you said you wasn't going to say it, I've told you I don't mind.

– I don't want him to think we're trying to get him to put a word in for us or anything, honestly we're not.

– He doesn't think that.

– I hope not. Anyhow like I've said we've got number two on the way now so we could do with a place that was a bit bigger. We haven't told the housing yet though so you're the first person to know.

– Mind you I think there won't be any problem about us moving on; we've kept this place nice and clean and I've painted it up inside, I think somebody else would be very happy to have it.

– And it's in a nice part too, I know it's on a bomb site but there's nice flats across the road, and anyhow these are the nicest prefabs on the whole estate. And we've got lovely neighbours and everything: on that side there's Gloria and her husband Warner, they're from Jamaica, and then this way there's Hazel who's from South America somewhere isn't she Barry?

– She did tell me once, I think it's part of the West Indies but I'm not sure. All this stuff about whites and coloureds not being able to get on is a lot of bullshit if you ask me. You couldn't want for nicer people than we've got for neighbours anywhere in the world.

– Love it, this little place. We really do, we've been very very happy all the time we've been here; when it comes for us to move on I'll be quite sad really.

– Here let's have some more coffee love eh shall we? You said you was going to be short of things to say didn't you, well you've not done too bad at all has she?

– The one thing me and Barry've always had was each other, and so long as we've had that we've always been very happy. I know there's a lot of people would say we was very young to get married, particularly me. We've known each other right since we was babies, we lived in houses next door to each other. We've always known we was going to get married, it was only a matter of waiting till the time when we could. Ever since I was ten I told him I wasn't going to marry nobody else but him didn't I?

– Oh you got your hooks in me very early on yes. I never had no chance to look at any other girl. Well although I say that as a joke, it's not true really. Babs won't mind me saying this because she's heard me say it before. But being a bit older than her, there has been one or two other girls that I thought I might be interested in. But the one thing that was different about Babs was that she wouldn't let me, you know what I mean? These other girls they'd have their knickers down and be ready and waiting; but not Babs, oh no. She'd never agree to anything like that and she was different from every other girl I knew because of that.

– I don't know why I was like that, I just was. I knew all along ever since I was little that Barry was the one for me; and I thought it was the right thing to do to keep myself for him. I wasn't going to let him until after we was married, because I don't think it's right. Why did we get married, why didn't we just live together like a lot of people till we were older and knew our minds? Well I suppose it's because of the way we were brought up; at least it's the way I was brought up anyway. It's just that I think if you love somebody you keep yourself for him, I think it's very important to men and I think it's the right thing to do. I'm sure if I was a man I wouldn't like to think that there was other men who'd been there before me, I wouldn't like that at all. They say your life's over once you get married and have kids and that; but I don't feel my life is over, nothing like. I want to have four kids altogether with Barry, and then I want to have lots of grandchildren. And I want to be young enough for my kids to be able to treat me as their sister rather than their mother if they want to. I don't want them to be frightened of me because I'm older than they are, if we can I want us to be real friends. And I'd like it if I was still young enough to enjoy larking about with my grandchildren, I don't want to be one of those ancient grannies who's fifty or more and too old to enjoy anything.

– I think what he's getting at is he's asking you if you don't think there's more to life than just having kids and that. I've never asked you that myself. What do you think about it?

– Well I've always been one of those people who love kids. That was why I did the baby-minding. I know it helped out a bit with the money, but the main reason I did it was because I enjoyed having Robert – my baby – but I felt I'd like more kids around me in the daytime as well. I went to see the Social Services and asked them about it; they gave me a medical and came and looked at this place, and then that was that, they said I could. I had Hazel's little boy and I had Gloria's little girl, and I had two others as well. I enjoyed every minute of it. And I've only stopped now temporary like because Barry's getting good money at the minute, but when I've had my next baby then I can do it again if I need to. I'm very strict with all of them because I think you have to be, but I don't think it does them any harm.

– I don't think you were as strict with them as you are with Robert.

– No well I don't think you are if it's somebody else's child are you? I am very very strict with Robert, I agree with that: it's the only thing Barry's parents and me have ever had an argument about. I smacked him for spitting one day and they was very upset about it, he's their only grandchild. But I told Barry's mum, I said he was my baby and I was going to bring him up my way; so if she wanted to stay friends with me she'd best not start any arguments with me about that. And I must say she was very good, we've never had another cross word since.

– It's true isn't it Babs, we were saying weren't we – we agree on most things really. Amazing isn't it, but it's like you've always said we go well together eh?

– Well I think so. The only really big thing I suppose we don't agree on is religion. We agree about politics, we're both Labour of course like everyone else who's working class is; but when it comes to religion, no we don't agree. We respect one another's point of view though. I'm the one who thinks there must be a God and things like that, and Barry doesn't, but it's a case of share and share alike. When we got married, he didn't want it to be in church and I did. But he gave way to me about that, he said it was my big day and I should have it just like I wanted it. So we had the church wedding and all the rest of it.

Then when we had our baby, Robert I wanted to have him christened in church and Barry said he didn't believe in it. That was all he said, no more than that; and at first I thought that was good because he wasn't going to make a fuss about it. Then the next day after he'd gone to work I started thinking about it; and I thought to myself well he'd let me have my way about the wedding so now it was my turn, it was up to me to give way to him. So when he came home that night I told him I'd been thinking about it and I wasn't all that bothered about christening, I thought it would be better to leave it to Robert till he grew up and decided for himself. Barry said again

321

it was OK if I wanted it, but I said no I didn't. And we've never exchanged another word about it from that day to this in fact, have we?

— Blimey she understands me my wife does doesn't she? I thought you'd forgotten all about that. It's another example of what we were saying though, isn't it? We were saying when you'd gone last week these talks was better than sitting watching the telly. In all the time we've known each other we've never had such good talks as we have on the nights you've come round. After you've gone you know we go on till, well last week it was nearly twelve o'clock Babs wasn't it?

— Yes. It's been really good fun. I don't want to say we didn't know each other before because we did. But there's a lot of things we never put into words. We shall really miss it now. We said last night when we were talking about it perhaps we ought to keep it up after you've finished: sit down once a week and talk to each other, keep that telly switched off and just for an hour once a week talk to each other. It's been marvellous, and if you've enjoyed it too we're glad as well, aren't we Barry?

'They talk to me of "coloureds"'

Hazel French

– I'm a teacher in a girls' secondary school. My parents who live in northwest London come from Guyana: my father is Guyanan and my mother is English, and they came over here when I was ten. My father couldn't get work in Guyana so they decided to start a new life; with my mother being English I think that's one of the things that helped them feel they might have a good chance of settling here. I'm twenty-eight now, but although I've been here for eighteen years I still don't feel English: I feel Guyanan, I feel an immigrant. I suppose language is one of the ways in which I notice it most, apart from the colour of my skin. I tend to speak standard English and be very careful about it, and I use long words and turns of phrase. It shows up particularly in this part of the world. I will say to a girl 'Are you going shopping in the West End?' whereas if I were speaking naturally I would be saying something more like 'Are you going up West?'

Yes I'm very conscious of the fact that I'm not white in skin colour but light brown. I can and do pass sometimes for an English person with a slight tan, but I'm self-conscious about it. A lot of people really don't notice, they take it for granted I'm English; and they talk to me of 'coloureds'. When they do it makes me feel in a way they're almost trying to get me to make some kind of statement about myself. I never know quite whether it's being done without thought, or whether it's a kind of subtle attempt to get at me. I definitely do feel coloured; by that I mean I definitely don't feel Anglo-Saxon.

A tall green-eyed young woman with long black hair, wearing a bottle-green jumper and grey slacks. She usually sat with her legs pulled up underneath her on the settee in the sparsely furnished sitting room of the prefab. She smoked heavily. From time to time she would get up and go off into the bedroom to check that her baby was comfortably asleep.

– My baby's six months now, his father is a teacher, he lives in west London; he's married and he says that as soon as his divorce comes through we'll get married. I'm beginning to be a bit sceptical about that though – he was far more enthusiastic about our relationship until I became pregnant. Then he seemed to cool off rather, and since the baby he's only been to see me four times. He accepts the baby as his and he gives me some money – nothing like enough for us both to live on, but I get quite a decent salary from my job and I think I could probably manage financially even if he paid nothing at all. To be realistic about it, I'm gradually coming round to facing that he's probably going to drop out of the picture altogether; I can't say that I'm heartbroken about it, I think he and I have both grown out of each other. I'm glad to have a baby, and I wouldn't want to portray myself as a woman abandoned by the father of her child. It's nothing like that at all. If we do split up I hope he keeps in touch for the baby's sake; but here again, being realistic, he already has two children of his own and it could well be that he'll drop out of the picture altogether.

Then I'd be faced with the prospect of single-handedly bringing up a child; but I can't say if I were that it'd greatly faze me. Nowadays people are much more tolerant and broad-minded about things like that, and I think it'd be possible to make a go of it especially as I have my teaching qualification which means I should always be able to get work somewhere of some kind. I have no ties, and I don't think that I would go out of my way to marry someone else.

I'm sorry I don't get on better with my parents, but on the other hand it has its compensations insofar as my own personal freedom is concerned. When the baby was born they made an attempt to get me to go and live with them, my mother offering to look after the baby for me. A fate worse than death: it's the last thing on earth I'd contemplate. My father actually is a very conventional man and I know I couldn't bear to live with him and my mother for longer than a week without having a screaming row, because there's simply nothing in the world that we agree about. Politically he's a very right-wing Conservative, whereas I like to think of myself as a liberal; he and my mother go regularly to church, and I'd describe myself as most certainly an agnostic if not an atheist. And he's for ever passing judgement on other people: their moral standards are not high enough, their manners are not good enough, the whole world is populated by examples of bad behaviour of one kind or another.

I sometimes think he'd have a heart attack if he were to come to the school where I work, and see and hear the way the pupils behave. I myself don't consider the regime to be a particularly enlightened or permissive one, but I'm sure he'd think that discipline was nonexistent by his standards. It's an everyday occurrence for most of the older pupils to address me as 'Hazel' just as they call all the other teachers by their Christian names. The headmaster isn't the sort of person who wants a lot of discipline of that kind – his attitude is that it's up to each teacher to formulate his or her own basis on which to work.

A couple of months ago my mother and father came to see me here. My father sat in that chair you're sitting in now, and he wouldn't or couldn't relax, he just sat on the edge of it all the time with his hands on the arms as though he was going to jump up and leave at any moment. I made tea, I'd even baked a cake which is really something for me because I'm not very housewifely, and I'd tried to put on a bit of a show for them, a clean tray cloth and all the rest of it. I could see my father was getting increasingly uncomfortable and when I asked him what the matter was he looked round this room in a kind of bleak despair and said he didn't understand how I could live in such a slum. It may not be exactly palatial, but compared to the furnished room I was living in before it's very spacious. I know I'm not the tidiest of people but I don't think it looks too bad, certainly not bad enough to be described as a slum. I got quite stroppy with him, and of course then it came out, what he wanted me to do was go back there and then with him and my mother and live with them. He meant it well, but he's too blinkered to see that someone of my age is no longer a child who wants looking after.

I'm sorry that I seem to have spent most of my time on this first evening talking about my parents and my father in particular. You can tell from that what a hang-up I've got about him. I'll try and do better for you next time.

– I suppose it was going to teacher-training college that turned me into a socialist, or a liberal as I think I described myself. When I came to live and work in this area that reinforced my views. People say there's no poverty and we live in a society where there's equal opportunity for all. But no one could read Peter Townsend's book *Poverty* and ever say afterwards that we live in anything like an egalitarian society. Even if you define wealth and poverty in terms of

325

having money or not having money, the difference between the privileged few and the nonprivileged many is enormous. I don't understand how any society can allow a situation where a small number of its members never do any work whatsoever in their lives and live entirely on the proceeds from dividends or property which they've inherited. And I even less understand how those people can be put by the masses into positions of authority. It's incredible to me that we have such an institution in this country as the House of Lords and give it the power to alter or delay laws made by the House of Commons. And I don't understand how people can accept that their children will not have the educational and material privileges which the children of the rich will have. And to allow it to continue. . . . Well that's beyond me altogether.

Most people have only restricted choice in every area of their lives: whether it's which schools their children should go to, what jobs they should take, even what they should do with their leisure. On television they're offered the choice between three or four on the whole poor programmes; in newspapers the choice is even less, it's between the right-wing press and the very right-wing press. People are fed from childhood on a diet of misinformation; they're not taught at school anything of relevance to adult life, and of course particularly nothing whatsoever about the built-in inequalities of society. Their aggressions are encouraged to be towards other members of their own class: whites against blacks, the so-called respectable against teenage hooligans or muggers or whatever other hate objects can be defined for them. But all the time this diverts their attention and energies from what is truly wrong with society.

It's something I feel very strongly about, and it's reinforced for me every day I live here on this estate. I see the poor and the underprivileged being conditioned every day into acceptance, being told by the media how lucky they are to have all the things they've got. And most people are content with their lot. Anyone who tries to politicize them like the group in the commune who run the advice centre over the other side of the estate get absolutely nowhere.

I had an incredibly depressing discussion with my fifth formers a couple of months ago about the Royal Family. I was trying to get them at least to question whether it was right that so much wealth should be in the hands of a small group of people who'd done nothing to earn it and were of no real value to society at all. But the majority of kids identified with them and felt they were an important part of their own lives. They didn't see they were parasites who had no excuse for their existence, and they didn't see anything particularly wrong in them owning vast amounts of property and land while tens of thousands of others went short of basic things throughout the whole of their lives.

Oh well, last week I went on and on about my father and now this week I'm belting your ear with my political philosophy. Perhaps you'll be lucky next week: I might talk to you about something which will be of more use.

– This week I promised to be good didn't I and try and talk about life on Providence Estate. You're very patient. Right, this week I'm going to talk about life on Providence.

I got this prefab because I was pregnant. I went to the Housing Department and said I was living in a furnished room in Tullbrook Road, I was a teacher and I wasn't married and I was going to have a baby. I said I thought it would be better if I could find somewhere where there was a bit more room, and I didn't mind what sort of a place it was. The housing people were very good. They treated me as though they were dealing with unmarried mothers asking for accommodation every day of the week, and perhaps for all I know they quite possibly are. After only about three weeks they sent me a card to say would I phone them, and when I rang up the woman said they'd had one of these places that had come vacant and would I like to have a look at it. I came along with one of their Estate Managers and I met her by appointment just outside the front door there. She was waiting when I arrived, and she opened the door for us and asked me what I thought. She couldn't have been nicer: was it big enough, was it good enough, did I think it would be suitable for what I wanted? The rent is amazingly cheap, and there's a list my name has automatically gone onto for better accommodation as it becomes available and my turn comes round. As far as I was concerned it was ideal, and it's amazing how quickly you get attached to somewhere. One of the things that helps a great deal is having such nice neighbours: Barry and Barbara next door are lovely and we're great friends. Barbara offered me anything I wanted out of her house when I moved in, and God knows she's got little enough herself. But she's such a warm open-hearted sort of person, she just came in and said 'Come into my house and see if there's anything that you need and help yourself to it until you've got on your feet.' The truth of the matter is I earn far more money than Barry does, but that didn't matter as far as they were concerned; I was someone on her own who might need help.

Barry's very sweet and very protective. I happened to mention a few weeks ago that some lads had pushed some dog shit through my letterbox one night; and he was all for sitting up all night the next night watching from their front window to see if they came back again and jumping out and catching them if they did. He's got all sorts of ideas about men protecting women and so on, and although he didn't say so specifically I think he thought that it'd been done because I'm coloured. As far as he was concerned he wasn't going to have that kind of thing happening. About all I can offer them in return for their kindness to me is to say that if ever they want to go out together, I'll baby-sit for them. But they never do, they're perfectly happy to stay at home in the evenings and watch the telly together and they've never taken advantage of the offer yet.

I don't know if they're typical of the estate or not. I should think on the whole not – they're far more generous and open-hearted than most, in fact I think they'd be exceptional anywhere. This isn't to say that I find people around unfriendly though because I don't. I'm only saying Barry and Barbara are to my mind rather special people.

The majority of people on the estate, particularly the parents who have children at my school, are extremely friendly. I think or at least I hope their attitude towards me is largely based on what their children tell them about me. I wish some of them took a bit more interest in their children's schoolwork. They have a tendency to think teacher knows best and everything should be left to her. I had one woman assured me very solemnly once that if her little boy wasn't working hard enough, I only needed to mention it to her and she would give him a good wallop.

Well what else can I say about living on the estate? I enjoy it and I feel as much at home here as I would anywhere; when the GLC offers me different accommodation I hope it's still here on this estate. Although I wouldn't like to live here for ever I face the prospect of staying for quite a few years with complete equanimity. It's hard to say exactly why but primarily of course it's due to the people; and also I find it quite pleasant architecturally to come home to at the end of the day. I like the mixture of styles, and the fact that it's not a completely impersonal concrete jungle with thousands upon thousands of houses all looking exactly the same. I'd say I enjoy living here and I'm in no hurry to move on.

'Beleaguered'

Pam Booth

– A northerner, living with Trev, and that's breaking down too; everything's breaking down, me, my life, everything I've put my hand to. Even the bloody alarm clock broke this morning. Living here was going to be a beginning, but it doesn't look like it's going to be that any longer, more an ending. The end of my story, Christ knows what'll happen from now, all I know is it'll be something fucking terrible, that's all I know. Ladies aren't supposed to use language like that either are they, still what the hell? I'm in a state of siege, surrounded by life. It's besieging me, you'd better put me down as under siege – beleaguered, that'd be more appropriate. Beleaguered . . . that's the story of Pam Booth.

I'm not pissed you know, I might have had a couple before you came but I'm not the worse for it. Wait till you get to know me, you'll find I'm like this all the time. It's up to you, but you're always welcome, come round any evening. If Trev's here he'll go out, if he's not here he won't give a shit anyway. We can have long talks about aliens, refugees and all that kind of thing.

Thirty-five, small and thin and with black hair in a mass of tight curls, she usually wore an old plain jumper and an old plain skirt and sat with her bare legs up on the settee, wiggling her feet in fluffy pink bedroom slippers and frowning at them as she talked as though they were a pair of obtuse children whom she had to try and make understand her point of view. Her eyes sparkled, she gesticulated constantly with her hands: always laughing, and always cheerfully bright. She

*drank bottled lager, lining up three or four cans on the floor by the
settee before she settled down and started to talk.*

– Put me down as a working mum. I wonder if there is such a person
as a mum? Since I've had the kids I've often wondered. I take them
off in the morning to the day nursery, I go up to the West End where
I'm an assistant in one of the big stores, I collect them in the evening
on my way home. I do it all myself, because that lazy sod of a bloke
I'm living with doesn't lift a fucking finger. I know I'm damn lucky
to have got them into a day nursery, I know I'm damn lucky to have
got a lovely feller to share my bed with me every night; I know I am
damn lucky – God bless the GLC – to have got this temporary
accommodation in what they call a mobile home until such time as
they give me and the kids a better place of our own. I saw a form
once when I went up to the Housing Department: would you believe
it, they've got me down as the 'common-law wife' of Trev. I tried to
tell them they should alter it to him being my common-law husband,
after all it's me the tenancy's in the name of. But they wouldn't have
it – and it was a woman who I was trying to argue with about it into
the bargain. God help us, what can you do when one of your own
kind is against you? If it had been a man I'd have told him he was a
chauvinist pig. I suppose I should have told her she was a chauvinist
sow, but it wouldn't have conveyed anything to her at all I suppose.

Two kids, Miranda who's four and Susie who's nearly two. Husband's name is Bill, and we've been married for ten years. Off and
on: you can date the break-ups and the reconciliations from the kids'
birthdays. I have a feeling though that there aren't going to be any
more. He and Trev actually had a fight about me a couple of months
ago outside that pub down there in Robins Walk. Imagine that! Two
blokes fighting over you, it ought to make you feel like Helen of Troy
or someone shouldn't it? It didn't me though, it made me feel like a
second-hand piano. That was all either of them really thought of me
as, a musical instrument they could thump out a tune on; not in any
way a person of her own. God, if I go on like this it's a long story I'll
tell you.

I left home in Manchester when I was sixteen and came to work in
London as a waitress. As far as my parents were concerned it was
like an announcement that I was going to be a prostitute. I managed
to fend off the men though until I was in my mid-twenties, and then
when I did get married that was a terrible mistake. Bill did a bit of
painting and decorating, and money was very tight. We lived in a
series of furnished rooms, and we'd been on the GLC list for years.

As soon as I got pregnant that made the difference and they offered us this place. All those years . . . if only we'd had this at the beginning we might have made more of a success of things. But by the time they gave us this three months ago it was far too late. It wasn't his fault, it wasn't mine. Well let's say it wasn't his fault and be charitable about it.

This is the start of the end, I think I've said that to you before haven't I? To some people this'd be the start of a fresh start, but to us it's made it all the more plain we've got nothing left between us to work on. I've taken up with Trev, Bill's taken up with Lorraine, and neither of us wants for us to be back together again. I don't reckon on staying with Trev, but it suits him and I don't greatly mind one way or the other.

He pays the rent of here, Bill does I mean, which is a pretty stupid set-up but I suppose it makes him feel good. He gives me a bit for the kids as well. Trev doesn't pay a blind penny piece unless he's feeling in a good mood. Of course he's got a wife and two kids of his own down in South Norwood, so he's under a good bit of pressure there financially. One of these days I'm going to tell Bill and Trev and every other man in my life to fuck off out of it, and I'm going to go my own way and not have to be grateful to anybody for anything.

Good God what a point to get to, this person that I am.

– When I was happy was long ago. Odd times when I was a young girl perhaps. There've been quite a few men, and I suppose I should've known better. But I've never had all that good a time with any man. I don't know whether there's something wrong with me or what, but several blokes have told me that I'm frigid. I don't know whether it's me or whether it's them when it comes down to it. I've read a few books and things, but they don't help all that much they just get me more confused. Not that I get too worried about it – it's just that some time I'd like to know. I've got a friend Jackie, she says I don't know what I'm missing. So if that's true, well then I don't know what I'm missing and I can't be too regretful about it can I?

I think I must be a little bit of a women's libber; not a hundred per cent but quite a lot, and I often wish I'd learned a bit more about it earlier in life. Perhaps if when I was twenty. . . . But that's a word I'm always using, perhaps. If there was a women's group round here I think I'd definitely join it, but so far as I know there isn't or at least if there is I've never heard of it. I've often thought back to my mum – my dad drank all the time, and I think she should have left him. She died a few years back, he told me when I got married that she'd only stayed with him because of me and my brother. What a waste.

331

– You were asking me last time about books. Now and again I get onto some kick and I read everything I can find about the subject, and I suppose the last one I had was the Rastafarians. I don't know if you've come across them; there's quite a few squatting in the derelict houses in Absalom Road. I walk through there on my way home from work, and I see them standing on their doorsteps sometimes. The thing that always used to intrigue me about them was the way they kept themselves to themselves; if I gave one of them a smile and wished him good evening he'd just look right through me. I wondered what it was that made them like they were, and I asked the library if they could find a couple of books for me about the subject. And I remember a lot of what I read, it's stuck in my mind. They're not only quite different from us, they're completely different from all the other coloured people in this country too.

Their religion has been in existence since nearly the beginning of this century. It started in Jamaica and I think the original inspirer of it was a man called Marcus Garvey. He was the one who first told the people that their saviour would be a king born in Africa. Round about 1930 I think it was, Ras Tafari was crowned Emperor of Ethiopia and he took several other titles like 'Lion of the Tribe of Judah' and 'King of Kings'. He claimed to be in a direct line of descent from King Solomon.

As far as I understand it, the Rastafarians believe in six principles. The first one is hatred for all white people, and the superiority of blacks over whites. Then they believe that one day they'll be able to have revenge on the whites for their wickedness to blacks throughout the world in history; and also they believe Ethiopia will be the centre of black rule and whoever is king there is the ruler chosen for them by God. I don't think that's a very satisfactory description of their ideas, but it's about the best I can do.

They use marijuana in their worship, it's a very important part of a lot of their rituals, and they have their hair in that particular tight-curled style called 'dreadlocks'. The weed was supposed to have grown first on the grave of King Solomon and they believe there are a lot of references to it in the Bible. One or two other things that I remember reading about them is that they distrust men who don't have beards, and they don't make superficial greetings to one another or to anyone else: they rely instead on what they perceive of the vibrations surrounding each person. No white person could have good vibrations, so they wouldn't even ever begin to communicate with someone who was white. Another thing is the woolly hats that they wear: they're red, black, green and gold. Red is for the blood of their martyrs, black is the colour of their African forebears, green is to symbolize Jamaican vegetation and the hope of victory, and gold I think is the colour of the Jamaican national flag or part of it. Oh yes and they don't use 'me and you', instead they say 'I and I'.

I found it all very fascinating when I first got into it, I wished there was some way I could get to know more about the subject. But it's a bit like the Masons, you're not going to learn much about it until you're in it; and if you're white there's no chance of you getting in it anyway. All you can say is that it's a very exclusive sect, and quite an extensive one in Jamaica: there are tens of thousands of them there. They believe that they have to take over Jamaica before they can be liberated properly, and then they or their children will gradually start to emigrate after that and go to Ethiopia. 'Babylon' is their name for the land of oppression which is Jamaica, and they also use it to mean an enemy of any kind.

There's no charge for that lecture.

– Oh when I don't drink I can sound like quite an intelligent person. But I don't think being an intelligent person gets you anywhere, at least not if you've got two kids. You've got to forget yourself and be Mum. If you've got a man you've got to be Mum to him too as well as his wife and his mistress and his cook and his launderer and his listening post and everything else as well. It's been a change for me to have someone as a listening post of my own, but I can't imagine that it'll be much use to you as part of a picture of life on the estate.

I suppose there must be thousands like me on the estate – it's just that we've no way of getting in touch with each other. Sometimes I feel like going outside there in the street and walking up and down in the middle of the road with one of those loudspeakers and shouting out 'If there's anyone who feels like coming out and having a talk please come out because I feel like having a talk with someone too.' All these lives: how do you get in touch with them, how do you communicate? Perhaps I should do what you're doing, spread the word around and say I'm writing a book and asking people will they talk to me. When I saw that card of yours up in the newsagent's window in Robins Walk I thought 'Blimey he's got a nerve, who'll be brave enough to phone up and say they'll be willing to talk to him?' It kept nagging at me, I kept going back to read it again. Eventually I thought oh well I'd got nothing to lose, I might as well ring up and meet you and see what it was all about. I'd guess you must get some pretty strange characters though. Are they all lonely people who just want someone to talk to?

And a funny thing happened: I met a woman I know from one of the towers, and right out of the blue she started telling me she'd got

333

someone coming round to talk with her and her husband once a week about life on the estate. I asked her how she'd met him, and she said it was through the person who lived in the flat opposite her. I didn't let on I was thinking of getting in touch with you myself, but I thought it was funny. All the sorts of different ways that you get in touch with people. Funny yes, and I really ought to do something similar myself shouldn't I? Still.

Part Nine

THE BLOCKS

Vernon, Foxman, Cramner: three gigantic blocks each six storeys high and 600 metres long, some with almost 500 inhabitants. They lay on their sides like prostrate towers, monuments to someone's dreams and good intentions. Designed and built as high-class accommodation for the needy and underprivileged, they were to have central sheltered warm corridors, bedrooms above bedrooms and living rooms above living rooms so no one would disturb or be disturbed by the neighbours above and below.

But after only a few years they had become dirty, decrepit and near-derelict in appearance. The windows in the stairwells were smashed and as soon as they were repaired they were smashed again. The reinforced wired-glass doors to the landings and corridors were smashed; and when they were smashed they were left for the wind to whistle through. The lifts didn't work: they stood with their doors broken open, inoperative on the ground floors. A handwritten notice on a page torn out of an exercise book had been sellotaped in one of them: 'To Whom It May Concern, Will You Please Stop Using This Lift As A Toilet. Thank You.' The request hadn't been obeyed and that particular lift seemed to have attracted more urine and excreta than most. Up the walls of all the stairways there was writing. Large ones done with spray cans – 'Chelsea is Shit', 'Arsenal Are Wankers'; smaller ones with fibre-tips and Magimarkers – 'This is Prawnography'. 'Micky Fucked Chrissy Here And She Sucked His Prick', 'This Wall has been Prawned', 'Stuck It In Her In The Lift Tonite', 'Wogs Are Black Shit', 'GLC Dumping Grund For Rubbich'.

Even in daylight the central corridors were always dark, always had most of their ceiling lights missing. The solid smooth wooden front doors of the flats all had two locks, a Yale and a mortice, and a spyhole. Some had numbers roughly painted on by hand: those which had had more conventional numerals had long since lost them. Wherever there was a piece of loose hardboard panelling near a doorway to a corridor or by one of the lifts, by the next day it was ripped off or torn down the middle. Beneath, the lock-up garages – among the first ever to be provided for council tenants – were equally ravaged, with scarcely a door remaining fitting properly on its hinges. Car owners preferred to park their cars for safety along the side streets where they were at least in someone's view.

The Blocks

The rubbish shutes at the end of the landings were choked and unusable; people on the higher floors merely opened their kitchen windows and emptied their rubbish out. It usually landed in the tiny squares of garden belonging to the ground-floor flats. Talking one day to somebody there, there was a sudden hail of milk bottles, empty tins, a chicken carcass, used condoms, plastic washing-up liquid containers, excrement and a dead cat.

VERNON

'Deep down happy'

Camilla Jones

– I'd say I was, I really would, I really really would say I was deep down happy is what I am. Man, you should've seen the conditions that me and my hubby were living in and with three kids and all before we came here. This is a palace, I'd say that to anyone, it's my pride and joy. We've been here two weeks now and I'm as happy as a lark. I go around all day doing my housework, dusting everything with my little feather duster you know? And I sing and I laugh because after a long time we've at last got a home. My hubby's a hard-working man, he works for the Post Office you know? He has to go off early in the morning, and sometimes he works so hard he don't get home till late at night; but leastways when he does come home we can sit down where you're sitting and he can put his feet up on his own settee. Or it will be his own settee when we've paid off the HP on it man, you know what I mean? And he can look at his own colour-television set in the corner there, which will also be his when it's paid for too, and he's the monarch in the castle. An Englishman's home is his castle, that's what they say isn't it you know? And my hubby's an Englishman and I'm an English woman, we've got British citizenship and our children were born and brought up here and old Enoch Powell can make what noises he likes about sending us blacks back to where we came from. Because where we and my hubby came from was Antigua, but where our children came from was Hammersmith.

Sit there and listen to me white man, I'll go on talking longer than you can sit and listen. I'm happy, I'm happy; I'll go on saying it over and over, and I don't care what becomes of me after this. We've had a not good life up to now since we was in England from ten years ago, but now we're respectable GLC tenants and we can hold our heads up. Happy happy right deep deep down.

Thirty-five, with dark brown eyes and jet black hair curled up in a bun on top of her head, she sat on the edge of a chair in joyful excitement as the words poured out of her. She wore a riotously coloured blouse and purple trousers; her hands swooped and dipped and were never still as she continuously reiterated her enthusiastic view of her new life.

– Oh my children, there's not a woman within a thousand miles who could have three more lovely children. The eldest is Rita, she's seven; then there's Rayda, she's four. And those two girls you know they're my pride and joy, one goes to my heart and the other one goes to my head. And last but not least there's Vincent, he's eighteen months old and he's his daddy's shining light, I don't know a man in the world who's more proud of his son than my hubby is with him.

When we came here from St John's we'd only just got married and we didn't know what we were going to do and all we knew was that there was no life for us at home. My hubby was a labourer and I did nothing but work in the house of a rich French woman. My father and mother had been to England, but they both died within a year of each other and I was very sad. I wanted to come here because my father had written while he was alive that this was a land of opportunity for people who were prepared to work hard.

When we came Reginald and me had made up our minds that we didn't care what sort of work we did but we would not be any charge on the State. I went to work straight away in a laundry, and Reginald worked first of all on a building site as casual labour, then he went on the London Transport underground for a time. But he is an educated man and he applied to the Post Office, and they took him. I think they must have been very pleased with him ever since because he has got steady promotion you know? Now he is a supervisor and we are proud.

I need to earn some more money for us when I can, so now I am a registered home help. I go out cleaning most mornings and I like the work very much. It takes me to people's homes, and most of the people I meet are very nice and friendly. Sometimes you have to laugh you know? The first time you go to someone and knock on their door or ring the bell, they open it and they can't help it when they see there is a black woman standing there they look just a little bit surprised. But I have never had anyone who was nasty to me on account of my colour. Some coloured people you know, they feel frightened and persecuted; but I don't, I can really say I honestly don't. All the people I've worked for and all the neighbours all around, they are all very friendly and nice.

The things you see written on the walls, it's just kids who do that. Let me tell you something that once happened to me. I saw a black boy writing on a wall on one of the corridors lower down here by the staircase and he was writing in very big letters 'NF'. I went up to him and I asked him what he thought he was doing to be writing such a thing. And you know what he said? He said to me what was the matter with it, it was the initials of the football team he supported, Nottingham Forest!

My eldest little girl Rita came home one day and said it was written on the wall of the playground at her school 'Blacks Go Home'. She asked me what it meant, where did people want us to go, did it mean they didn't want her at school? I didn't explain to her, I think she is too young yet: I just said it was silly people who wrote things like that and she should just forget about it. You know I have never met colour prejudice not really anywhere. And that is to be perfectly honest, and neither has my husband. I told you he is now a supervisor, and he has thirty white men who work under him; he says not one of them has ever been nasty to him or anything.

I think the race relations people are not really necessary, I think if you put people together and just leave them to it you will get on. The man who starts complaining about the blacks, he would complain about anything: and if there were no blacks he would find someone else to complain about. You know I truly have no time for black people who are aggressive towards the white people, that to me is colour prejudice. There is a black woman in the next flat along here to me, she told me the other day she did not like white people at all; and she said I would find out for myself what they were like here. OK I haven't been here more than a few days up to now, but I can feel it in the air somehow, I am very sensitive to things like that. I think the white people who are round here are no different from the black people: some of them get on with their neighbours and others don't; some of them will be unpleasant, but far the biggest number I expect will be pleasant as I shall be to them.

– This flat is a lovely lovely home. It is so big you know; the place we were in before we had only two bedrooms for the five of us and the damp ran down the walls. Nobody who has not experienced that could imagine what it is like to be here. I don't care about the outside; all right it looks a mess from outside but who cares about that? When we come inside here we close the door and shut all of that out; we are here in our big big home that is like a palace.

My main wish if I could have one granted would be that my mother and father were still alive and they could come to stay with us in our lovely home. My father would be very proud I think. He was an old-fashioned man and he would not have agreed that I should go out to work as well as my hubby – he would never let my mother go to work. But I think he would see that nowadays things have changed. We need the money, but I would still like to do some work even if we had all the money in the world. I would not like to be like my own mother and stay at home all day long and cook and sew and not have any proper life of her own.

I'm not an educated person, and it is another wish I have that when the children have grown up a bit I might be able to go to night school and study for something. I would like to try to get at least one or two 'O' levels so that I could one day get myself a proper job in an office or something like that. I read a lot, and there is a lovely library here which I discovered just yesterday when I went out shopping. There are all sorts of wonderful books there and I am going to read and read and read. They have records too and I like classical music, Beethoven and Brahms which I've heard on the radio. My ambition is one day to go to the Royal Festival Hall. I think perhaps my hubby will one day take me there for my birthday or Christmas or something of that kind. I just go on – hint hint hint you know?

My nice hubby, a nice family, a nice home. That is everything I want and I am a very happy person. I am sad sometimes that white people and black people spend so much time not understanding each other and sometimes not even trying to understand. I have no time for those Rasta people. I think they are very harmful with their attitude of having nothing to do with white people, I think they can do great harm. I know they are proud and all things like that, but if you are a good person you shouldn't want to think you were either better or worse than anyone else. And you know another thing that I wished? I did, I wished that when Prince Charles got married he had married a black girl, I really did! I think that would have been a wonderful thing for mankind if he had done that, if he had said to everyone that black and white were equal and since half his future subjects are not white it would have been a very good idea don't you think if he had made a gesture of that kind?

It has been very pleasant for me to talk to you. I have only just come to Providence, so I am not what you could call typical of the people who live here. But I hope that I shall go on living here with my family for years and years and years. To me everything about it all, everything about the whole estate, it shines with happiness.

VERNON

'Sit on my arse and take the sick'

Brian Atkins

A burly middle-aged man with wiry, tight-cropped hair and blue eyes; wearing an Hawaiian-style jacket-shirt with a fiery whorl of colour, he stood at the picture windows of his top-floor flat, shoulders bowed and his hands pushed deep in the pockets of his blue linen slacks as he looked out at the sweeping cold summer rain.

– Christ what a summer eh? Really gets me down. Been off bleeding work six fucking months now, it does it really gets me down. Sit on my arse and take the sick, that's all I'm good for. Forty-fucking-two and that's my lot. Gets you down you know, it really fucking does. Bear with a sore head, that's what the wife says I am. And as for the fucking kids, Jesus – they keep right out of my way these days, I'll start screaming at them if they so much as blow their fucking noses.

Sheer fucking frustration in every sense of the expression – you know what I mean? My back's so bad we haven't done it for months now; as soon as I get the urge and turn over a bit sharpish in bed I'm whimpering like a dog. I was reading in the paper the other day about them marriage guidance people and something they've got called a 'sexual dysfunction' clinic or something. Fuck me, I've not got 'sexual dysfunction' I've got sexual nonfunction. I've got this idea in the back of my head see that she'll go and get it somewhere else haven't I? Suppose that's because that's what I'd do if it was me you see. Oh Christ, I get so fucking fed up I can't tell you, I can't put it into words. I almost get to coming out with a whole lot of swearing, honest that's just what it makes me feel like doing. Still you've got to keep a check on yourself haven't you?

Well, I'll make us some coffee and then we'll sit down and have a chat eh? P'raps if I talk to someone it'll raise my spirits a bit, but I can tell you this mate I'm a right miserable fucking bugger most times.

– Where'll I start? No one's going to hear it right? So that means I can be as frank as I like eh, and leave it to you to take out all the effing and blinding and that, if I do happen to forget myself. I don't swear a lot, I don't hold with it; but now and again I must admit I do get a bit carried away. Anyhow I'll leave it to you to clean it up where necessary.

Let's see then, the wife and I came here six years ago. We'd been in a small council flat near Tooting and we had the one girl Ella. Then Rosemary presented me with a son, which is Arnold; and when I went to the GLC they said they'd got nothing except one flat here in Vernon. It was free there and then so I said right we'd take it. The woman gave me a bit of a funny look and said perhaps the wife and I'd ought to come and view it first. I still don't know what she was on about – as you can see for yourself it's fantastic, enormous, four times the size of what we had. Three bedrooms, bathroom, separate toilet, big cupboards everywhere: two bloody great bedrooms they are too, and even the small one has a big built-in wardrobe. Then this massive sitting room, the big kitchen through there. I mean who could want anything better than this? Maybe she thought we'd turn our noses up at the outside or something, the mucky corridors and all that. But it never crossed our minds. Rosemary come with me, we took one look and there was no need to say anything, we both knew we were going to have it and no argument. So we did, and we've been delighted with it ever since. There's some people, her mother particularly for one, who say they don't know how we can live with the kids in what let's face it from the outside looks as though it's one big shithole. But once we're in here we forget about the outside; it'd have to be somewhere pretty good I can tell you to make us want to move now. Even all this time I've been off work it's not the place that gets me down. If you're going to be at home you've got to have plenty of room to move around, and I've got that here all right.

What I was was with a furniture-removal firm, a driver and loader and that. It might've been that that I did my back in with, but they seem to think at the hospital it's more one of those progressive things, something to do with the discs between the vertebrae in the spine. They haven't said so in so many words, but I've got the suspicion I'm not going to get any better I'm going to get worse. I mean I asked them when they thought I might be back at work, because the firm was asking me and I had to tell them something. So the doctor said he thought there wasn't a big chance of me doing any furniture moving for quite a long time. I've had two operations and I don't think I've come to the end of that sort of thing yet. The firm said they couldn't go on paying me full money for ever, which is natural enough; and the hospital said they couldn't say I was entitled to industrial-injury compensation or anything of that sort. So I had to face that, that when it does come to working again it'll have to be something different to what I was doing before. So for now I spend my life in the block.

Life in the block. . . . I see a lot of it I can tell you, being here on my own most of the day. There's a lot of things I could tell you; but I'd have to be careful, know what I mean? I wouldn't want anybody to be able to identify me. Give me a week to think it over if you're coming next week again you say? Let's leave it till then, meantime I'll think about it and decide how much I'm prepared to say.

– OK I said I'd tell you about life in the blocks didn't I? So well here goes then. There's a lot of what I say you'll just have to take my word for it. I mean most of what I'm saying couldn't be supported with facts and figures, know what I mean?

The biggest thing that most people wouldn't realize when they came in a block like this is how many people there are here who are living here unofficially as you might say. There's no way of finding out the total number because people aren't going to tell you are they? But I know for definite for example that there's at least six families along this one bit of landing here who aren't here by rights at all. I wouldn't say they're squatters, because the GLC takes rent from them. But the way they got in in the first place wasn't like we did, by having the place offered to them. They came in and took possession of an empty place, and then the GLC came along so they faced them up and said they'd been here a long time but they'd lost their rent book. If you've got enough brass about it the GLC has to back down and say they must have had a cock-up in their records somewhere. So that's it, you're in.

There's two ways of getting in. If someone's going to leave one of these flats, the current going rate for lending his keys to someone for half a day to get copied is a hundred quid. And most times within an hour of them going someone else'll have moved in with their furniture and the lot. It'll be two to three weeks at least before the housing people have got through all the paperwork and think they've got an empty place to offer; but when they come along they find they haven't.

The other way of getting in is you buy a tip from someone on the landing. The moment anyone breathes a word they're going there'll be six people at least around the pubs that night offering to sell the number and the date it's coming up. Then it's up to the person how they get in. It's very simple, a kid can do it. All you need's one of them wire coat-hangers that you get from a cleaners, and ten minutes on your own at the door. There's one other small ordinary everyday item you need as well, but perhaps I'd better not go any further about that. Anyway like I said a kid can do it – in fact it was a kid who showed me how to do it. I saw him at a door one day and I just stood and watched him and he never batted an eyelid, he just gave me a nod: the little bugger said his mum was out and he was locked out, and just as he said it he got the door open and I could see the place inside was completely empty.

The second thing is the number of people who are carrying on a trade or business as the saying goes, in their homes here. In your tenancy agreement it says you're not supposed to do that, but I should think pretty near one person in three does. There's the obvious ones like women doing machining and curtain and dressmaking and that sort of thing. But again along only just this bit of landing I know one man who's running a motorcycle repair shop, another one who's got a betting shop and I mean actually in his flat, and someone else who's a carpenter and joiner and makes his living out of making furniture for people. There's another family on the floor above, they're Chinese and what they do is naturally Chinese takeaway food. A few of the others I know is an off-licence that needless to say hasn't got any licence of any kind; an Irishman who does dry cleaning and who's got so much machinery in his place you wonder the floor doesn't give way; a frozen-food centre, where all the stuff's so cheap it must pretty near all be nicked; and a man who's in the porno business, he hires out books and blue films and video cassettes which are the booming business these days. I'm not so sure he doesn't film them himself along there as well.

As far as the women are concerned, there's one I know who has a dancing school for kids; there's at least half a dozen who've got dressmaking businesses and upholstery; and any number who're in some part of the catering trade, like baking or cake-making and decorating and that kind of thing. And then there has to be mention of the women who do the age-old women's trade of laying on their backs and taking money for it. I'd say there was at least seven that I know of: some of them do it part-time as you might say while their husbands are out at work, but there's some who have it as their regular occupation. These days you don't have to go out on the street, you just have a telephone number on a few cards around the news-agents' shop windows. Word gets around locally about these things as well. I mean I shouldn't think there's a man in the block who doesn't know where to go if he wants that sort of thing, if you follow my meaning.

– My biggest interest in life, well it's about my only interest in life these days, is to go along to the old baths on a Thursday night and watch the boxing. That's very big around here. I don't know why it should be but there's a lot of people on the estate who give up some of their time to that. Either watching or helping out with the training for the lads in the boxing club, or just generally hanging around. It's all amateur, and I think it's a good sport.

I can't stand the professional game, that's all money money money, and the betting's more important than anything else. You might just as well be a racehorse or a greyhound as far as the punters are concerned. They like to see a bit of blood and most of all they like to see a lot of money, but they don't actually give a fuck for the boys who are doing the fighting. They'll see a lad standing there and getting his face smashed into a pulp, and if he's the one their money's on they'll be screaming at him to make a fight of it. He can be badly injured perhaps even brain-damaged, and not going to be good for anything for the rest of his life – but they don't care not one way or the other.

In the amateur ring you will get a few bets change hands but nothing like on the same scale. The whole thing isn't in the hands of the bookmakers and sharks. It's a sport and it's a good clean sport that a lot of boys like. They're not fighting for money they're fighting because they like the game; and in three-round contests which they all are no one's going to get badly injured. There's very strict regulations about when you can box again if you've actually been knocked out. Sometimes Rosemary comes with me and we have a good evening down there, we know most of the people and everyone's very friendly. I wouldn't mind a bit if Arnold took it up when he got a bit bigger. I've never been a boxer myself but I wish I had been, I'd have liked to have gone in for it.

What I would say about living on Providence to sum it up? Well, I'd have to say that I was very happy here and I think the wife and kids are. I think it's a good place to live; it's sensible and down to earth, people have got their feet on the ground and they don't have their heads in the clouds. But I think the best thing or at least it is to me is that our sort of people have what I think's a very easy-going attitude towards life. They don't rush in and pass judgement on other people; they nearly all seem to regard themselves as being in a way part of one big family. This may be just my opinion but I think it's a working-class thing. I don't think you get it with the nobs, they only stick together when they're closing ranks to defend their wealth against other people getting their hands on it. But the working class don't have any wealth in that sense; they do have a wealth but it's a wealth that's more what you might call the enjoyment of the richness of living. That's something which they share among each other, and I suppose because they're so ready to share it that's what makes it what it is.

FOXMAN

'A very heartless woman'

Rose Doyle

– I don't remember the judge's name dear, but it was one of those up at the Crown Court near the Elephant. He said I was a wicked woman and a very heartless woman. I suppose he said I was wicked because I'd got these rolls of cloth and I hadn't paid for them. I got them from a man but I hadn't sold them, a stall holder in the market said he was coming to collect them but he didn't and so that's why they were here when the police came. So that would be why he said I was wicked I should think. I don't know why he should have said I was heartless though, no. But that's definitely the word he used.

I don't know what he meant by it, because I hadn't done anything cruel or something of that sort. Perhaps he thought I was heartless because I didn't cry when I was in the dock. It might have been that, I know a lot of women do cry and I didn't. Perhaps that's what he was expecting, and because I didn't cry he said I was wicked and then added on heartless as well. I suppose he meant I didn't behave as though I was sorry about it, that's the only thing I can think of. Anyway he gave me two years. Yes, it is a big sentence for a first time isn't it, I hadn't been expecting anything like as much as that. I think I wouldn't have pleaded guilty you know dear, if I'd known he was going to go as heavy as that.

A red-haired blue-eyed Irish woman in her early forties, thin and tall and pale she sat on a packing case in the sitting room which was also her storeroom. Ladies' dresses hung in dozens on mobile clothes-racks and only here and there could a chair or settee be dimly perceived under piles of garments or bolts of fabrics. Off to one side the kitchen

*appeared to be similarly stocked: wholesalers' packs of tinned pet food,
five-kilo drums of instant coffee, cartons of grosses of teabags, display
containers of packet soups.*

– Yes well dear all these things here are things I'm looking after for
people. Someone will come and ring my doorbell and ask me will I
just take care of something for a while for them. They know I'm the
sort of person who'll do a favour for anyone so they bring whatever
it is inside and I keep it until they want it. If somebody else comes
along and sees something in here they think they could find a market
for, they'll very likely sometimes ask me how much I want for it. And
so then if I think they're genuine people I'll let them have it for a fair
price.

I never ask where anything's come from and I never ask where it's
going to. That's nothing to do with me dear. I suppose you could say
I was just running a business, that's the way I look at it. But I don't
buy things off people. If they want me to get rid of something for
them then I'm happy to oblige, but I haven't the money to have my
own stock. I sell it for a fair price and then I come to an arrangement
with the person I'm looking after it for. That way I get what you
might call a commission for my trouble.

I don't look on it that I'm doing anything so very wrong, to my
way of thinking all I'm doing is just providing a service. On the
charge sheet the words were 'handling stolen goods', but I think that's
not a very fair thing to say. I don't know when something's stolen or
not, do I? If somebody comes and tells me his uncle's got a grocer's
and he's a bit overstocked with something I believe him. Perhaps I'm
too trusting.

One thing I didn't like though was when the police came and
arrested me, that same inspector had been here himself only two
nights before to pick up a sheepskin jacket he'd specially asked me
to get for him. He didn't pay me for it or anything, and then two
nights later he's back with a warrant and they charge me with the
rolls of cloth. I don't think that's a very nice person who'd do that.
I'm not going to do any more favours for the police from now onwards
if that's the way they behave.

– It was very awkward when I went to prison because I've got five
children you see dear and I was worried who'd look after them. The
Social Services people were very very good. I was on bail for months
before my case came up and my social worker said she'd made
arrangements for the children if anything happened to me. I had the

351

feeling she'd spoken to my Probation Officer and asked him what he thought was going to happen. I suppose he told her there was a good chance of me having a sentence. So the three young ones went into a home: that's Frank who's eight, Michael who's six and Liam who's four. The two girls were all right: Melanie's sixteen and Marcia's fourteen. They went to stay with an aunt so they could go on with their schooling.

I have one or two previous convictions for the times now and again when I've been in a little trouble, but it's not been anything serious. Once was shop-lifting from Marks and Spencers in the High Road, that was at a Christmas time and I wanted some nice things for the kiddies. I took I think it was a little pair of trousers for each of the boys and some gloves and woolly jumpers and that sort of thing. I believe I was put on probation for that or it might have been bound over.

Then the next one was that I did some damage in the social security office. In those days before I started to take the pills I had a very quick temper; it's the Irish in me I suppose. This woman wouldn't give me my money that I was entitled to because she said I had been what do they call it, cohabiting. I hadn't at all, it was just a friend stopped for a couple of nights. So I swore at her and threw something at her, I think it was a big glass ashtray that was on one of the tables and it went through the partition window. I think that was another binding over, or it might have been a fine.

It makes it very difficult for me to remember things with these pills but I think the next one was stealing again. My recollection is I took somebody's handbag which she'd put down in the ladies' toilet at one of the stores. There was hardly anything in it that was much good, just a few pounds. But that time it was probation too. And I was on probation when the thing happened about the rolls of material. They don't like that – they include the offence you were put on probation for as well as the new one, so you get like a double whack.

Probation has never seemed much good to me. I mean my Probation Officer is a very nice man, he's helped me when I've come out of prison this time and so on. But about the only help he can give you is to talk and I don't see that that's a lot of good. He tried to explain to me if I were to do anything else it would become a very serious matter now. Once you've been to prison you're more or less over a certain threshold and they won't hold back from sending you there again. I suppose he'd have a fit if he came round here and saw all these things I was looking after for people. I expect he'd say it would go very badly for me if the police were to come round again. One of the problems you see dear is the police don't believe you if you say the only reason things are here is you're doing people a favour. They want to know who they belong to and if you won't give them their names and addresses then that's it as far as they're concerned. But I mean you can't do that can you? If you did people would never trust you again would they if they thought you were giving the police information about them? So that's the big difficulty you see.

My husband I'm afraid I have to say isn't very much good to me. He's living over the other side of the estate somewhere with a black woman. I've got nothing against the blacks, I know some very nice ones and some of them are my friends. But on the whole I don't like foreigners of any kind, I only like what you might call ordinary British or Irish people like you and me. This woman that my husband lives with, well the truth of the matter is she's only just over sixteen. I think that's disgusting for a man of his age, he's nearly fifty; but I don't blame her so much as I do him.

Altogether he's given me a lot of trouble and worry over the years. My social worker says she thinks I'd be a lot better off without him. He doesn't give me any money for the children, so I have to do the best I can in my own way. I live on the social security and try to make a little bit extra now and again in the ways I was telling you about last time. But it's not easy, especially as I have trouble with my nerves and have to take the pills all the time.

When I look back on it I don't think I've had much of a life really. I had two children already when I was still a girl in Cork. I've no idea what's become of those, the last I heard from my mother was a few years ago: she wrote they'd got themselves nice husbands in Dublin. Both of them'll be grown-up ladies now, perhaps even with children. It makes me feel funny sometimes to think of the idea that I might have grandchildren who I wouldn't know if I saw them. Neither of those two girls has been at all good about letting me know how they were getting on. It makes you feel bitter, doesn't it, when people are like that.

– The other night there was several of us having a good drink in the pub in Tullbrook Road there, we were all talking and that. They were passing the plate round like they always do because one of the regulars had died, they wanted to give his wife something to help her along. We all of us put something in, even though we didn't know the man. At the end of the evening the landlord counted it up and he announced there was seventy-eight pounds there which was going to be given to the widow. I thought it showed how good people were in their hearts, it's nice to think the widow would get a bit of money in her hand. It won't bring her husband back for her, but it's the only thing that people can do, and it might just help her over some little difficulty or other at a time when she doesn't want to have to be thinking about money.

Afterwards I thought well I'd like to be able to say my husband had died. I don't mean I want him to or anything of that sort, but I've lost him just the same as that woman has. But if I'd said to people my husband had left me, they wouldn't have passed the plate round for me, would they? They think when it's something of that sort it's your own fault don't they? I suppose I could say it is when I come to think about it, because nobody wants to have to tell people his wife's in prison do they? It's not so bad when it's the other way round, I know several round here whose husbands have gone to prison and nobody thinks much about it. But when it's a woman people's attitudes are different aren't they?

I don't want to say though that people on the estate are unfriendly, because I don't think they are. We've been living here six years now and we've never had anything but kindness. The children have a lot of friends and everyone will spare you the time of day to have a chat on the landing if you're passing them.

The corridors and the lifts and things are not in a very nice state, and what with the windows all broken and everything, it doesn't look very good at all. I think something should definitely be done about it, I don't think kids should be let run wild like they are. I know if it was one of mine and I caught him doing hooliganizing I'd give him a good smack and send him to bed. There's no discipline these days though, not like there used to be is there? I definitely blame the parents myself dear I do.

FOXMAN

'Ordered and content'

Mrs Bedford

An old-age pensioner, she lived in a two-roomed flatlet on the ground floor. She had a sitting room with a small cooking area, a single bedroom and outside the garden door a postage-stamp patch of grass. Seventy-seven, heavily built, and her voice was heavy and deep to match. Her great weakness she said was peppermint creams. While she talked she unwrapped and ate one after another without pause.

– I always have been, I've always been passionate about these since I was a little girl. Don't know why but I'm too old to change now: all I ask is when they put me in my box they put in a pound or two of these with me just in case I wake up in the dark and feel lonely. Or what if I get over the other side and then find out they don't have them there? No I can't imagine heaven without peppermint creams though, that doesn't seem possible. The Almighty invented them so I'm sure there'll be plenty in stock. Come on love have another one, it stops me feeling so greedy eating them all on my own.

Well I've lived here all my life. I'm seventy-seven and I was born and brought up as a girl just a few hundred yards away in what was Burley Street in those days. I suppose what it'd be classed as now is a slum but we didn't think so. My mother had eight children and we all lived in a house with two bedrooms and no hot water. When Bert and me got married we went to live next door with my Auntie Clarice because she'd only got four children so she had more room. Then we moved for a while to those old council flats over the other side of Tullbrook Road, and we stayed there for quite a few years until we had another place in that other block, that one Vernon over there.

When my Bert died two years ago they asked me would I mind moving out to a smaller place. I said I'd no objection, so that was when they gave me this place. It's just fine for me. It doesn't take me more than ten minutes of a morning to go round it with my vacuum cleaner so I can keep it like I've always been accustomed to wherever I've lived. I had to get rid of a lot of furniture though because we'd collected such a lot over the years. I told the children and grand-children to come and take what they wanted. I said all I need's a bed and a table and a couple of chairs, anything you don't want will go to the saleroom.

I'm a lucky woman I would say, I've got everything I need; if I'm ill or anything there's always one of the children or grandchildren will come over and see that I'm all right. There's nothing I need and nothing I want for: I have a nice regular life and I'm perfectly happy with it. So long as things go as they should, it seems to me you shouldn't ask for more. My life's ordered and content.

I suppose the one thing I would like is a bit more of a garden, but that's about all. But I'm not much of a gardener; if I had more I'd probably find it too much for me because my knees are bad and I can't bend down. One of my grandsons comes once a fortnight with his mower to cut my grass for me: it takes him less than ten minutes. But I'd like to see a flower or two growing out there; and I'd like to be able to sit out on nice days in the summer when the sun's shining. I don't need to tell you about the problem though: you were with me the other day when we were out there weren't you and you saw what happened. Disgusting. Still that's something you have to put up with, when you get to my age you try to be tolerant. I hope I could say I was that.

– When we first came here, Bert and me joined the tenants' associ-ation straight off because we felt if you were going to live in a place then you should give part of your time to trying to help newcomers, and improve the conditions of your living and so on. We were lucky to live in one of the good blocks like Vernon where there was a good community spirit. I think it's not quite as strong here, but that may be because when Bert went I rather dropped out of things. I keep thinking I ought to go back into it – at my age you've got to fill up your life as best you can otherwise you could easily end up taking pills and tranquillizers and being very sorry for yourself. But I'm not that sort of person, or at least I hope I'm not.

I like to try and keep my mind active by going to the library for books, and I make a point of buying the *Sun* every day to keep me up to date with the world. I watch the television a lot: my favourite programme is the plays, if there's a good play on the box I'm happy. I don't like the historical ones much, I'm more for ones about the present day. History is about dead people and what happened to them doesn't interest me: you can't change it can you? But if you've got a play about as things are today I think it's much more interesting. It might be about a situation where you could say you'd been in one very similar yourself, or one that you could very easily imagine yourself being in. That one the other night about the girl who went round watching darts matches was a very good one, did you see it? She kept taking up with these different darts players, she said she was what they call a darts groupie.

That's a situation which I'm not saying I could be in, I'm a bit too old for that kind of caper now. But when I was her age yes I could imagine I might have been like she was, taking up with this man and that. I didn't do it but what I'm saying is that it's not hard to imagine yourself into a situation something like that. In my day it was the young men you saw at the boxing chiefly, they were the ones who all the girls had got their eyes on. Oh come on do have another of these, you make me feel so greedy.

– I couldn't say I have any complaints about living on the estate at all, I never have had. When I think about the conditions we had to live in when I was a kid, well those days will never come back again and a good thing too. People complain and you sometimes hear them talking about the good old days and that sort of rubbish. All I can say is they must have forgotten what the good old days were like, because for the ordinary class of working people there was nothing that was good about them at all. People expect a higher standard all round these days and it's right that they should be given higher standards.

Outside in that corridor there, about halfway along you'll notice there's a thing on the wall in a box with vents in the side of it. What that is is an automatic switch for the central heating in the old people's flats along the ground floor here. When the temperature gets down to a certain point the heating automatically comes on. One of the estate caretakers said to me one day last winter that there was no old person who would ever be discovered dead of cold on Providence Estate. He was right, and that's a very fine claim to be able to make. It's not a thing even in my mother's day could have been said. Let's not forget things of that sort when we're comparing how things are with how they were in the past.

Another good thing I have is the telephone. It's my children that pays for it and if it wasn't for them I couldn't afford to keep it on;

but my mother never had the chance of anything like that in her day. My children, one or other of them will ring me up nearly every day of the week to see how I am. Those sort of things you couldn't even imagine when I was a girl

About all I could say I was short of in my life is my dear husband. I still can't get over him going, I don't think you can do if you've been married like we were for forty-nine years. It would have been nice if we could have made it the fifty but it wasn't to be. I shan't complain about that though: they were very good years, we had a good life and lovely children who grew up to be very good to us, and we were very fortunate. It breaks my heart to hear of people who say they don't get on with their children, I think they must be very sad people.

Funny you know, I think the time when I miss him most is when I'm out shopping. I'll go in the Co-op or somewhere and I'll be looking at the meat, and I'm thinking to myself that a piece will make a nice stew for two. Then I suddenly remember that now it's only for one, and I get this sad feeling inside of me; I think about coming home and how Bert isn't going to be there. Silly things like that remind you of a person when you've lived all your life with them. You see something in a shop window perhaps, you think you must remember to tell your husband about it when you get back home: and then you think oh no.

Or the other thing where I miss him is the rheumatism. We both used to have it together: it makes me laugh to talk about it, I'd have it in my elbows and he'd have it in his hip. On the days when the weather was cold and damp we used to sit and talk about it: I'd tell him my arms were hurting like the very dickens, he'd say he was lucky because his wasn't all that bad that particular day. Then another time he'd start like drawing in his breath as though he'd got a sudden pain. I'd ask him what was the matter and he'd say it was his rheumatism giving him gyp. Very often if it was true I'd say it was peculiar because mine wasn't troubling me at all. And then there were days when we both had it together, as well as days when we neither of us had it. So it always gave us a lot to talk about, did our rheumatism: I was interested in his and he was interested in mine.

– A lot of this business you hear of nowadays between young people and old people, I think most of it is the old person's fault very often. You'll get the kids playing about round here outside, riding their bikes or kicking a football and the girls screaming and trying to get the boys to chase them and so on. It's no different from what it always was, I remember just that sort of thing from when I was a girl except possibly the boys weren't well off enough to afford to have a bike. And if you're an old person and you go out shouting and swearing at them and telling them to be quiet, like I'm sorry to say a lot of old people do, what are they going to do except shout and swear at you back? I've always found if you speak to young people politely you'll get much further with them than if you rave and call them names. I think people respond to you in the same way as you treat them; if you start straight off by making it clear to them you've no time for them, you can't be surprised if they make it clear they've no time for you.

All this vandalism you hear about and see the examples of in the corridors and up the stairways and everywhere: I think a lot of it could be stopped if you got the children themselves onto committees and tried to get them to take an interest in keeping their surroundings nice. It's all wrong to set the adults against the youngsters, it won't get anywhere at all in my opinion. They should have children on the residents' association committees, at least in my opinion they should. That's what my Bert was always very keen on, asking young people what their own opinion was and how was the right way to go about something. In my mind that's much more sensible than trying to dream up ways of controlling children. I think children will control themselves if you make it clear to them that you think they are grown up and responsible. But if you don't you've only yourself to blame for what you bring down on your head.

– I'm not a very travelled person so I don't expect my ideas are really much good to you. They say travel broadens the mind don't they; but well I have to admit the furthest I've ever been from here is one day about twelve years ago now when I went on a coach trip to Yarmouth for the day. We set off at seven o'clock in the morning and we came back at eleven at night. It was while Bert was still alive, but he couldn't go because he was bad with his rheumatism so I went on my own. I didn't like it one bit, and I've never wanted to go anywhere again. I'm perfectly happy here, I don't hold with a lot of rushing about. It's all go go go these days, and I don't think people are any the better for it. Why not just stay where you are and be thankful for what you've got, that's what I say.

CRAMNER

'Relax relax'

Royston Turner

– The first thing I would say of myself is that I am black. A handsome stoutish black man of fifty eh, who's been in this country for twenty-five years? He's married with three children, and has a quite good job with the electricity board as a maintenance engineer.

Saying as the first thing that I am black is natural: I live in a predominantly white society and being black is the first thing that people see about me when they meet me. It is just as it would be if you went to Jamaica: the first thing that would be said of you is that you were white and only secondly that you were a writer. It is an obvious description you see; people at work will refer to me and use that word without it being in any way racialist of anything of that sort. In the country I come from, similarly people refer to white men and women and there is nothing racial about that either. Altogether I think people get too uptight about this. There is a young man at work who works with me and he is black like I am; but he becomes very angry when white people mention it. He says he is a human being, what does it matter what colour he is? I think if you were to be going on like that all the time, you could never find any happiness in life. I've always said to my children they mustn't take offence from the words people use, they should practise at getting used to it because after all they live as I said in a white society. I think that is the right way to live: relax relax.

A pale blue shirt, royal blue slacks, red socks and moccasin shoes; a heavy silver chain bracelet on one wrist, a gold watch on the other, and a gold signet ring on each little finger. Soft-voiced and smiling,

with greying curly hair. His manner was always casual and friendly.
Because he liked it he said, sometimes he sat cross-legged on the floor.
Now and again he looked round with quiet pride at his sitting-room
whiteness: the walls, the carpet, the curtains, the leather upholstery of
the three-piece suite, everything was ivory or cream. Along one wall
there was a huge shelving fitment crammed with books.

– The reason I came to England as a young man was I wanted to get
an education. There was not really opportunity for someone of my
age to better himself that way in Jamaica, so I came over here. I had
no relatives or friends but I'd heard that it was possible to make
yourself a good living. I was only interested in money insofar as it
would buy me somewhere to live and give me enough to eat while I
studied at night school.

That was my intention. I look back now and I think how naïve I
was, because of course only the most menial jobs were available to
black people who had no formal education. As a result I worked as
a kitchen porter, as a station porter on the underground, in several
different factories as a warehouseman and goodness knows what else.
I worked long hours and became very tired; I was so busy keeping
body and soul together I had no opportunity even to think about
trying to become educated as well.

Then I had a lucky break. I went to work with a young man,
younger than I was, who was trying to set up in business as a self-
employed electrician. He was very good at the work and had all the
necessary examinations and qualifications. I learned a very great deal
from him, and I found to my surprise I seemed to have a facility for
electrics. He encouraged me to study, the working hours were not as
long as what I'd been doing, and although the pay was not particularly
high it did enable me then to start going to night school. I was able
in a year or two to get the basic qualifications for being an electrician,
and then I was able to get a job almost anywhere. Time went on, I
learned as much as I could and got as much experience of different
types of work as I could, and in the end I was able to apply for a job
with the electricity board. I thought that perhaps my colour would be
against me, but I'm happy to say it wasn't and I've been with the
board ever since.

The only difficulty of course was that when I'd had in mind coming
to England to be educated, it was not as what you might call a
technician. I had had more in mind literature and art and history and
things of that sort. I was naïve as I said to you, and it was several
years before I realized that that sort of education could only fit you

for a job as a teacher, which was not something I was at all interested in. Now I am old enough to know better. Now I have reached the age of wisdom when I know that if you have a skill then you can always earn your living.

So I have kept my education for my hobby; and just two years ago now I obtained my Bachelor of Arts degree with the Open University. It took me in all six years to do it but I am a little bit proud of myself about it. I intend to continue to study, but I am not so concerned now about getting further certificates, I do it just for the enjoyment.

Also of course my three children, two girls and a boy, they are now in their teens. So the time is coming near when my wife and I have to put their needs first. Two of them will I think be clever enough to go to university, so we cannot expect to have the financial responsibility for them taken off our hands for several years to come. I hope they will go forward as it were from the point I myself have reached educationally. I should be very proud indeed if my children were to become teachers, even though it's not something I would have liked for myself. Our daughter Rachel the eldest one, I think she shows signs of one day becoming a painter or designer. She is very interested in interior decoration; we have hopes she may be able to go to an art college. Our second daughter Ruth is of a different turn of mind: I think she will become a scientist of some kind. The youngest, our son Harrison, well he is very young and at the moment all he wants to be is a professional footballer. There is nothing wrong with that, but I would think he would have to be exceptionally good before there could be any reality in the idea. Football is not something which interests me very much so I am not the person to judge whether he has it in him; but when he reaches school-leaving age we will obviously talk the matter over with him and his school and see if we can perhaps get an informed opinion.

My two daughters I'm glad to say have not so far shown any interest in the idea of marriage as a career. They have boyfriends of course, and later if they wish to do so they will leave home and live on their own or with whoever they wish. I do not think these days it is essential or even necessary for young people to marry if they want to live together; society is much more tolerant about such things than it used to be, and I think this is very good. Although I am one of the fortunate ones who is happily married, I have seen too many others who have spent many unhappy years of being tied to a person who they no longer love and who no longer loves them.

– Things were very hard for my wife and me when we first got married, which is now almost exactly twenty years ago. We met at a club for black people in a town in Kent, which was where I was working at the time. She was a domestic worker in a hospital and we discovered that we'd both come from almost the same town in Jamaica. She was living then with her sister, but when we fell in love with each other we wanted to live on our own. It was difficult because we felt we should ask her sister to live with us after our marriage. But we were fortunate, not long afterwards she herself got married.

My wife had had even less schooling than I'd had in Jamaica. She was not as keen on becoming educated as I was, and she has made many sacrifices to enable me to continue with my studies and to help at the same time to bring up the children. We had little money, but I could say now that we are comfortable. But a lot of it is because my wife was always a prudent housekeeper and because she was ready to go out to work whenever extra money was needed. All the same I'm conscious that she has always put herself last.

For many years we lived in limited accommodation with hardly any room, especially as we had the children. We came to this flat three years ago and it is as you will know if you have been in any of the others here superbly large and very suitable for our needs. All I would like extra would be a little balcony outside the window there, where I could sit in the evenings in the summer and watch the traffic of London roaring along on the road below. I'm saying that not entirely as a joke – I really do like living in a big city, I'm not the sort of person who would want to live somewhere in the countryside where everything was very quiet and you never saw people or motorcars. London is a good city to live in, and we live now on one of its estates in one of its nicest parts. It is convenient for me for my work, there is a tube station just at the other side of the park and from there I can be at work within a quarter of an hour. Equally if we want to go up to the West End for shopping or to the cinema, that also takes only a quarter of an hour. The children have made many friends here, and we are very happy.

We don't take much part in the community life of the estate as such, perhaps because it seems to consist mostly of bingo and old-time dancing and that sort of thing which we are not very interested in. But as a family I think we are connected at many points with the community: as I've said the children have their friends, my wife goes along to help at one of the clubs for old people, and I go once a week on Friday nights to the pub for a drink and I have made a number of friends there.

Some of them are white, some of them are black, and to me there is no difference in how I behave towards them nor any in how they are towards me. Much of this feeling between black and white people is almost a convention: people are shy of mixing and because of that they very often put the blame on other people and say they are the ones who are being difficult. There is a lady who lives on this corridor just two doors along from here. She and her husband and their children have always been friends of ours, sometimes they come here into our home and at other times we go into theirs. At Christmas and birthdays for a drink, times of that sort. They are white people; but only a few weeks ago she came here and told me they had just got new neighbours on the other side of them who were a black family. She had come to ask me if I would go and see them and welcome them to this corridor, and asked me if I would please make sure to tell them she was a friendly person who they could approach at any time and talk to or ask a favour of. I found this absolutely incredible. I asked her why on earth she was asking me to do that, why she didn't go and knock on their door herself? She said she was shy, she thought they might take it the wrong way. It is astounding.

Once I was the same. I know when I first came to England I had not been here long when I met an Australian girl who asked me if I would go to a party with her. When she told me everyone who would be there would be white I didn't go. So that is the sort of thing that has to be struggled against and overcome. Each individual can only do it for themselves, but it would be of great help to good relationships between black and white if it could be practised. I am not pretending that all white people are friendly to blacks and vice versa, because it's obviously not so. You only have to see the things written on the walls of the lifts and corridors and staircases in this building, 'Blacks is shit' and things of that kind. It's not surprising that it makes some black people hostile to whites, but then I think this is understandable, and I often wonder how the people of Jamaica would react if large numbers of white people went to live there and worked: I don't mean as employers but as employees. I think many black people would take it as white people taking over their jobs.

In the balance the responsibility for good behaviour lies to my mind on the blacks in this country. Many people would say that we should not be subservient, but I don't regard it as being that. I think we can be independent and we can be proud, but we are strangers to this country in the first place and it is up to us to behave ourselves. I don't care what the provocation is by the National Front, but it upsets me deeply to see young black people rioting in the streets in response. However hard it is I think we must be above that.

It is easy I know for you and I to sit here talking in the comfort of my home and for us to agree that it is a big problem. That is not doing anything to solve it, but I think we would be deluding ourselves if we felt there was any single thing that we could do that would solve it. It is going to take many years, many generations. The only way tension between different races can lessen is if those races become less well defined in themselves. In other words mixed marriages, so that it is no longer of great importance what colour you are or what shade of what colour. I honestly do not see any other solution than a natural process of that sort occurring over a period of time.

It has been my pleasure to talk to you.

CRAMNER

'A cold cold wind'

Christine Brown

A slight dark-haired pale-faced young woman of twenty-four; slender, almost thin, and neatly dressed in a white turtle-necked jumper and an olive green skirt. Her complexion was fresh and clear and she used no make-up; her voice was bright and carefully modulated. She sat neatly arranged in one of the big armchairs, sipping at a mug of coffee and gently drawing on a cigarette. From time to time she curled up her fingers and examined her fingernails.

– When Brian said he'd introduce you to me, did he tell you anything about me? Oh well then in that case it's really up to me isn't it to say what I want about myself, but I wonder where to start? I suppose I'd better begin by saying who I am and where I come from, mmm? All right well I'm married and I have two small children, a little boy of four and a half and a baby girl of just over a year. My husband's away working as a diver on a North Sea oil rig. It's not so good familywise because he's away a lot and we don't like being separated; but it's very good financially, the money's fantastic. By the time he's thirty we'll be able to have our own house and everything.

I'm not a London girl, I come from Devon originally. That was a long time ago; I've lost my accent completely or I think I have, you'll be able to tell better than me. We've lived in this flat four years now, we were lucky because we got it when we got married. We went to the Housing Department and said had they got anywhere, and this was the first place they offered us: we thought we could go a long way before we found anything even as remotely good inside. It's very nice, very light and airy, and as you can see we've got it furnished very comfortably in the modern style. Nearly all our furniture comes from the Habitat shops: we like glass-topped tables like that one, black leather and chromium chairs and all the rest of it. I've never been one for the old-fashioned things.

The matching wallpaper and curtains, they're very swish aren't they? We can afford to buy more or less what we like really and nothing on HP, everything that you see is paid for. I wouldn't be surprised to be quite honest if we were the only people in the whole of Cramner who could truthfully say we owned outright every single thing that's in our home. I think you can very easily get into trouble if you don't keep a firm hand on the money. My husband and I have always been very particular about that sort of thing, we like to be able to say we don't owe a penny to anyone in the world.

I used to work before I got married, I was with one of the big travel agents. I quite liked it but I was glad to be able to give up when I got married. It was in the West End, and the thing I disliked most about it was the propositions that you used to get made to you. You'd be surprised at the sort of customers you got in a place like that. They were mostly wealthy people and they seemed to think money would buy anything. I think there must be an awful lot of lonely people in the world. It used to happen very regularly that a middle-aged or even an old man would come in and book a holiday for himself, perhaps a trip to the Bahamas or something of that sort, and then just because you were a young and quite good-looking girl he'd ask you if you'd like to go with him. I mean just like that, someone you'd never ever seen before in your life, and it was like he was buying a package holiday which included a girl. I thought that was very very distasteful. There were some of the girls there who weren't so fussy, they'd go off with anyone so long as it meant a free holiday for them, and they used to be quite proud of it. Some of them almost had a competition to see which one could get on the most expensive holiday; they weren't against offering themselves quite blatantly as companions.

The manager was horrible, he said we were there to provide a service for the customers. One day he got really annoyed with me because I'd been rude to some lord or other when I could see which way the conversation between us was going. The manager told me I could lose business for the company if I was going to be like that, and if I didn't want to go myself at least I could have passed him over to one of the girls who would. I told the manager that if that was the sort of business he was running, then I wasn't in the least bit interested; and I walked out more or less there and then.

I'd be very glad to talk to you whenever you like; once a week on a Wednesday afternoon would be fine, I'm not usually busy with anything else then. If you don't mind though I'd sooner you gave me a ring first just to check it's convenient. I do sometimes have friends or my sister here or something like that.

Today the children are out, they're over with the girl in the flat opposite. She likes to have them and I pay her for it, and I didn't think it would be all that good talking if they started to cry or anything.

The little boy stood in the middle of the room sucking the ear of his teddy bear and turning himself shyly from side to side. Down one cheek he had a long angry red mark. She gave him a bag of crisps and a packet of Jaffa cakes, kissed him on the top of his head and gently ushered him out of the room and shut the door behind him.

– He's a jolly little chap but it takes him a bit of time to get used to strangers. He'll be all right now for an hour or so watching 'Jackanory'. He had a nasty shock this morning, he fell over in the kitchen and hit himself on the washing machine. I didn't know whether I ought to take him to the doctor or not, but you don't want to be rushing round there all the time at every little thing do you.

What was I saying to you last week, oh yes I know about my job at the travel agents wasn't I? Men is something I've always had rather a lot of trouble with, I don't know if I've been particularly unfortunate or whether all men are just like that naturally. You can't get annoyed about it but it does make you a bit fed-up at times. But then there's the very plain girls who never have a man look at them in their lives; sometimes I feel quite sorry for them, I think I'm one of the fortunate ones because at least I've got reasonably good looks and so on.

Loneliness while my husband is away is something I find it's hard to cope with. I'm not the sort of person who likes to be on her own very much, and it can get very lonely sometimes. Now and again I must admit I have a little party with my friends in an evening; not many of us, perhaps seven or eight of the girls and their husbands from round about. We have a few drinks and a bit of a dance, all very respectable and I do find it gives me something to look forward to. I don't invite anyone from immediately round here; not anyone from this block at all to be truthful.

I don't know why it is but some of the women along this corridor particularly are very unfriendly. I even had one the other day banging on my front door there and shouting the most filthy things through the letter-box. It got so bad I was even contemplating ringing up the police and complaining about it to be honest. I don't know what was on her mind, perhaps she'd got some idea about her husband or something. Which is ridiculous – I hardly know the man, I've seen him about twice on the stairs that's about all. She's a very bedraggled, slutty sort of woman, he might have made some remark to her comparing her appearance with mine. I don't know, you've no way of telling with things like that have you? Anyway I don't see why I should be responsible for what her husband says to her about me. I used to be very quiet and shy when I was young, but if there's any more of that sort of thing from her I might well go along and give her a piece of my mind. I would have thought that what she was shouting was slander or libel, I never know which is which. It's not a nice thing to repeat but I'll be honest with you, one of the things she was shouting was 'Bloody whore'.

There's a club that I go to for young wives with young children twice a week. It's not on this estate, it's on another one over the other side of Tullbrook Road. A sort of luncheon club, it's nice to get away now and again. You take your own sandwiches and they give you coffee, then for an hour after that they've got people who look after your kids while you all sit round in a group and have a good old natter. I think it's a very nice idea, it gives you a break.

– I'm afraid I can't let Andrew come in to say hello to you today, he's been very naughty and I've had to give him a smack and put him to bed. What he did was he threw his ice-lolly stick in the toilet again. He's always doing it and it floats and it won't go down. I told him the next time it happened he'd have to be the one who put his hand in and got it out. Of course the little sod wouldn't do it would he so I had to push his hand in myself. And then what does he do, he bites me; he sunk his teeth into me right there where you can see the mark on my thumb. I really walloped him, I'm not having that kind of thing.

I meant to tell you last week when we were talking and I said that sometimes I had a little party, that I didn't want you to get the impression I was just a very frivolous sort of person without an idea in her head. I can quite often be serious too, I mean I do do a lot of reading. My favourite authors are people like that one what's he called Ronald Dahl? Another one I like is Doris Lessing, and I like quite a lot of Iris Murdoch's things too. I've often thought I wished I'd had a proper education myself, I'd like to be a writer. I've had a lot of experience of life, and I seem to be able to look at people and put myself into their character. I don't know whether I'll ever get round to it; who knows I might one day. I think on the whole women writers are best, they seem to understand more of what life's really about than men do. All in all I don't think I really like men very much at all, but that may be because I've had mostly unhappy experiences with them.

What I mean by that to be honest with you is my father was a horrible man. If you want to know truthfully, I'll have to say he interfered with me when I was a very little girl. I'm talking about when I was six or seven, and in the end he went to prison for it. People could say if they liked that he must have been a sick person to do that sort of thing I suppose, but it's left its mark on me for the whole of my life ever since. Even at the age I am now I still wake up in the night sometimes and have the feeling that he's in the room. I'll never have sex with a man in the dark, I just can't bear it: I start imagining it's my father.

My mother married again, and then what happens when I'm twelve I think it was, or thirteen? My stepfather starts it, doesn't he? Why didn't you tell me, why didn't you tell me? That's what my mother'd said after it happened with my father. So this time I told her: all the things he'd done to me, and all the horrible things he'd made me do to him, I told her everything. And what does she do? She gets a stick and lays into me and gives me a right lathering, and tells me I'm wicked and dirty and if I ever say so much as one word about it to anyone she'll kill me. After that I kept running away from home, I wandered all round the country for two years or more and in the end I finished up in a club in Soho. I was a hostess in a crummy out-of-hours drinking club, I don't think you can sink anywhere lower than that.

Then four years ago I got married to this bloke whose baby I was going to have, but it was only about six months and he pissed off with someone else. Once I'd got pregnant he didn't want to know really. I suppose I shouldn't have made him marry me. There were one or two other blokes but they weren't the marrying kind either. I'm not going to say what he does or who he is, but one of them had a bit of influence in one or two places and he was the one who set me up here. I don't have any illusions about it, I know it was to get me off his back; perhaps he was frightened his wife would find out about me. He comes round here now and again; not very often, maybe once in six weeks. He knows what I do for a living and I think so long as I'm not asking him for money he's happy to let it go on like that. Men are bastards, all of them: I've never met one who wasn't. I hate them all; they think you must like men to do what I do, but I don't and that's God's truth.

370

Now you know about me. I'm not crying, I never cry, and I don't feel sorry for myself. I've found a way of life and I'm going to follow it and make as much money as I can. I have the same dream that everyone on the game has, that one day I'll have saved up enough money to go away and start a new life free of it all. I do have a fair bit of money saved up, so maybe for me it's not such an unrealistic dream at all.

Anyway, so that's it.

When I went the next week I hadn't been able to phone first. There was no reply when I rang the bell at her door. I waited in the corridor for a while and then the woman from the flat opposite came out, going on her way to go shopping. There was no point in me waiting she said, the person I was waiting for wasn't coming back. Was something wrong, had something happened to her, had there been an accident? Yes in a way you could say that, the woman said: she'd been taken away by the police and the Social Services had been for her children and taken them into care. Or rather they'd taken one of them; the other one was in hospital, he'd been badly knocked about and there was a rumour he might even possibly die.

As I left the block with my last interview on Providence uncompleted, the late-afternoon June rain was teeming and swirling down the road outside the block. There was no one in sight anywhere, and there was a cold cold wind.

Acknowledgements

The idea for this book came from Tim Cook when he was head of Cambridge House in Camberwell. Not only did he suggest my doing it, but he also supported my application for a grant to finance it to the Monument Trust, whose correspondent Hugh de Quetteville helped a most prompt and generous response to a request for funds.

What I had originally envisaged as a project which would take eighteen months proved eventually to be for a variety of reasons one which in fact dragged on for five years. But at no time during that long period did either of the two sponsors lose patience or even with justification put pressure on me to complete the work I'd undertaken to do. Their quietly confident and continuing acceptance that I would in the fullness of time one day finish the book was an unfailing source of comfort: my hopes and intentions were never queried. No other employer or publisher could ever have been so tolerant.

The third person who had every reason to be exasperated at the delay but never was, or at least not so that it was ever apparent to me, was Colin Rochester who subsequently took over as head of Cambridge House when Tim Cook moved on to become director of Family Service Units. Among all his many other problems he found himself responsible for the completion of a book which he must often have thought seemed neither to exist nor ever to be in every sense more than a work of imagination. From time to time he did venture tentatively to inquire how it was coming along. Every writer I know hates to be asked that question, and will go to great lengths to avoid answering it, not least because any kind of positive statement seems like flagrant tempting of fate. I am no exception, and my response was usually churlishly uninformative. Despite that he was never anything other than patient and warmly encouraging.

I am most grateful to all three of these men: without their support I should have given up.

A second and larger group of people gave me more immediate and equally essential assistance, and I owe greater thanks to them than

I could ever adequately express. My wife Margery has been, as always, loving and encouraging throughout. Despite the inordinate length of time between my first discussing the idea and finally finishing the book my agent Anthony Sheil was continuously solicitous and inspiriting. Both Harold Harris and Tony Whittome of Hutchinson were patient and helpful friends, all and more than editors should be. Anne Clark typed the first half of the manuscript with careful efficiency; and Gene Broad typed endless drafts and rewritings of the second half swiftly and accurately and with unfailing willingness to go to endless trouble. Josephine Hugo took on the burden of reading and checking the cross-references in the manuscript. To anyone else it would surely have been time-consuming and wearisome, but she made light of it.

An enormous number of organizations, both statutory and voluntary, gave me unstinting assistance all the time I was working on Providence Estate. The GLC Housing Department allowed me to use temporary accommodation in several different places. The local police, albeit unofficially, were never anything other than helpful and cooperative. So too were the Social Services departments in the area, the Probation Service, the Inner London Education Authority, the Department of Health and Social Security, the local magistrates' bench, the Fire Service, and London Transport. Literally dozens of private individuals also helped me; many of them did so on condition they would not be named. It would be invidious to mention some but not others, so I will only say that I thank them all.

The people I talked to who lived or worked on the estate invited me into their homes, gave me tea and coffee and sometimes fed me; and they talked and allowed me to record our conversations. When I first arrived in the area as a total stranger I thought at the beginning that possibly I would never meet anyone who would be willing to talk to me for a book which I could only at that stage describe in very vague terms. I had no idea who I would meet and what sort of a picture would finally emerge. But a year later I had talked and made recordings with more than 200 people, and had over 340 hours of taped material. The people I met and got to know ranged in age from four to ninety-one; some had lived on Providence for more than twenty years, others were newcomers who when we first came into contact had only been there for a few days.

I hope the selection which has been presented will give some kind of picture of the estate, seen through the eyes and expressed in the words of a cross-section of the people who live there. 'Providence' is of course a fictitious name, as are the names of the people concerned; but nothing else has been altered. This is what was said, and I hope

Acknowledgements

it conveys too something of the peopled world that exists behind the outward appearance of anonymity and characterlessness of a modern housing estate.

Tony Parker
Westleton, Suffolk

Catherine Caufield
In The Rainforest £4.99

'If I had an award to give I would give it to this book. *In The Rainforest* is the epitome of detailed, on-the-ground, investigative journalism applied to a problem that encompasses corruption, greed, disaster, and murder for the sake of money and land. All this applies to the ecological rape of the tropical forests. There is so much in this book that I could continue praising. It should be required reading, cover to cover, for all those who control the social, economic and ecological destiny of tropical moist forests' *New Scientist*

'Caufield gives admirable vignettes of local experiences, a polished journalistic treatment. When she is describing her meetings and discussion with indigenous tribes of the Amazon, a pioneer farmer in Costa Rica or a logger in the Philippines, she is at her best. Her book is refreshingly free of jargon or irritating stylistic peculiarities.'
The Observer

Germaine Greer
The Madwoman's Underclothes
Essays 1968–85 £4.99

From sources as diverse as *Spare Rib*, *Forum*, the *Spectator* and the
New York Times, this collection represents a mosaic of essays, long
and short, some of which are appearing for the first time in print. The
subject matter is as various as John F. Kennedy and vaginal
deodorants, rape and artificial insemination, Willie Hamilton's Sex
Discrimination Bill and the death of Jimi Hendrix. And whether the
topic covered is the aftermath of Bangladesh, UN conferences in
International Women's Year or Mick Farren and the Pink Fairies or
cosmetic surgery, the implications and ideas she draws out of the
latter relate in scale to those that are aired around the former.
Explosive, angry and funny, they also reveal tenderness and sadness,
and what underlies all the essays is that Germaine Greer cares.

Marina Warner
Alone of All Her Sex £6.99

'Marina Warner begins with the gospels, noting the slight allusions to Mary, and the curious confusions between the two women of that name. She points out the falsities, fables and manifest fabrications that have shaped mariolatry. This intriguing and intelligent book is an attempt to explain the origins, growth, appeal and persistence of the Virgin's cult. The narrative is a rich, allusive tapestry set in a framework of theological commentary' *New Society*

'A dramatic, informative and entertaining book about the Virgin Mary. Her understanding of the relationship between art and ideas is exceptional: a substantial and provocative book' TLS

'A convincing challenge to a social model of femininity in which Western women are trapped . . . an exciting book and a very major contribution to feminist history' *Time Out*

All Pan Books are available at your local bookshop or newsagent, or can be ordered direct from the publisher. Indicate the number of copies required and fill in the form below.

Send to: Pan C. S. Dept
      Macmillan Distribution Ltd
      Houndmills Basingstoke RG21 2XS
or phone: 0256 29242, quoting title, author and Credit Card number.

Please enclose a remittance* to the value of the cover price plus £1.00 for the first book plus 50p per copy for each additional book ordered.

*Payment may be made in sterling by UK personal cheque, postal order, sterling draft or international money order, made payable to Pan Books Ltd.

Alternatively by Barclaycard/Access/Amex/Diners

Card No.

Expiry Date

Signature

Applicable only in the UK and BFPO addresses.

While every effort is made to keep prices low, it is sometimes necessary to increase prices at short notice. Pan Books reserve the right to show on covers and charge new retail prices which may differ from those advertised in the text or elsewhere.

NAME AND ADDRESS IN BLOCK LETTERS PLEASE

Name

Address

3/87